ARGOPREP
STUDY SMARTER, NOT HARDER

SHSAT
SPECIALIZED HIGH SCHOOL ADMISSIONS TEST

1000+MATH
PRACTICE QUESTIONS

BOOK 3

At ArgoPrep we beleive in providing smart learning solutions so that every student can succeed in life.

ARGOPREP
ARGOPREP.COM/SHSAT

TABLE OF CONTENTS

ARGOPREP
ARGOPREP.COM/SHSAT

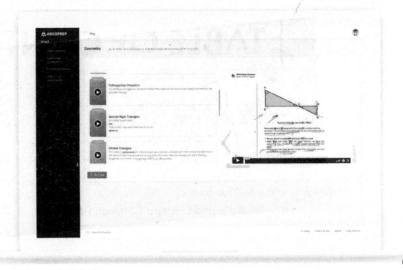

The most effective online test prep course for boosting your
SHSAT score

Over 550+ Practice Questions

30+ hours of video lectures from real teachers that cover everything you need to know for the exam!

15+ hours of detailed video explanations for all practice questions, breaking down each answer choice and modeling analytical thinking

Live chat support feature to answer any questions you may have.

Our SHSAT prep course isn't just about telling students what's on the test! It also provides students with...

• Real teachers and test prep coaches modeling thinking strategies that lead to success on the SHSAT and beyond.
• Strategies to break down any kind of question they might encounter.
• An organized approach to analyzing any written passage.

We pride ourselves on creating materials that are...

ENGAGING

so students are motivated to invest time in preparing for test day

RIGOROUS

so students are ready for even the most difficult questions

DIVERSE

so students see all the different ways the exam might challenge them

INSTRUCTIONS FOR STUDENTS

Visit our website at argoprep.com/shsat

Click on the JOIN FOR FREE button.

Enter date of birth and e-mail address.

Verify your email address by clicking on the verification link in your inbox.

Create a password.

Click on Book Video Explanations.

Select the workbook you are using.

Unlock this section by answering security questions.

Congratulations! You can now access video explanations to all the questions in the workbook.

Awesome news! A 20% discount has been automatically applied for access to our full online SHSAT test prep course.

INSTRUCTIONS FOR PARENTS

(Students under the age of 13 will need parental consent. As a parent, you can create an account for them by following the steps below!)

Visit our website at argoprep.com/shsat

Click on the JOIN FOR FREE button.

Choose Parent.

Enter your email address.

Verify your email address by clicking on the verification link in your inbox.

Create a password.

Add your child by clicking ADD CHILD in your profile menu.

Click Add Child.

Put child's date of birth.

Create Nickname and password for your child account.

Choose SHSAT Exam.

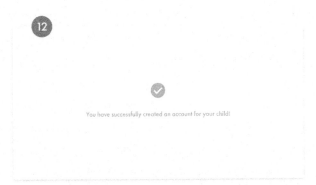

Your child account has been successfully created.

13

My Profile

Add Child

Logout

Log out and log in to child's account.

14

Video Lecture

Practice Questions

Official Handbook
Test Explanations

Book Video
Explanations

Looking f

Click on Book Video Explanations.

Select the workbook you are using.

16

Awesome! Let's have you unlock this book so you can access video explanations.

Unlock book

What is the last word on page 50?

Enter your answer here

Unlock this section by answering security questions.

17

Official Tests Explanations

Simplifying & Multiplying Algebraic Expressions

Simplifying & Multiplying Algebraic Expressions

Simplifying & Multiplying Algebraic Expressions

Congratulations! You can now access video explanations of all the questions in the workbook.

18

Discount

ArgoPrep offers a 20% discount to students who have one of our workbooks.

◯ Workbook Discount   20%

Congratulations! You have unlocked a 20% discount offer to our premium content.

Awesome news! A 20% discount has been automatically applied for access to our full online SHSAT test prep course.

SHSAT COMPREHENSIVE STUDY

ArgoPrep offers comprehensive resources for students studying for the Specialized High Schools Admissions Test (SHSAT). Check out our three other workbooks along with our online learning platform!

OTHER BOOKS BY ARGOPREP

Here are some other test prep workbooks by ArgoPrep you may be interested in. All of our workbooks come equipped with detailed video explanations to make your learning experience a breeze! Subscribe to our mailing list at www.argobrothers.com to receive custom updates about your education.

GRADE 2

GRADE 3

GRADE 4

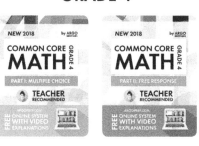

GRADE 5

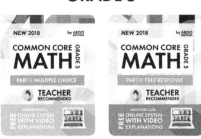

GRADE 6

GRADE 7

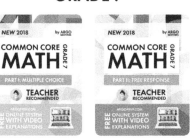

GRADE 4

GRADE 5

PRESCHOOL

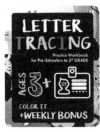

Arithmetic

ARGOPREP
ARGOPREP.COM/SHSAT

1. The set of possible values of n is $\{-2, 1, 4\}$. What is the set of possible values of m if $3m = n - 7$?

   A. $\{-27, -18, -9\}$
   B. $\{-9, -6, -3\}$
   C. $\{-6, -3, 0\}$
   D. $\{-3, -2, -1\}$

Difficulty: Medium

2. If $m + 1$ is an even integer, which one of the following must be an odd integer?

   E. $m - 1$
   F. $2m - 2$
   G. $2m + 1$
   H. $2m + 2$

Difficulty: Medium

3. If $3k$ is an even integer, which of the following **cannot** be an even integer?

   A. k C. $\dfrac{k}{2}$

   B. $k - 1$ D. $3k$

Difficulty: Medium

4. The product of 3 different positive integers is 8. What is the sum of these integers?

   E. 7
   F. 11
   G. 13
   H. 14

Difficulty: Medium

5. The least of 4 consecutive integers is m, and the greatest is n. What is the value of $\dfrac{m+n}{2}$ in terms of m?

   A. $m - \dfrac{3}{2}$ C. $2m$

   B. $m + \dfrac{3}{2}$ D. $3m + 1$

Difficulty: Hard

6.
$$\frac{10}{17} = 0.5882352941176470$$

In the infinitely repeating decimal above, five is the first digit in the repeating pattern. What is the 264th digit?

   E. 1   G. 5
   F. 4   H. 9

Difficulty: Hard

7. When n is divided by 5, the remainder is 3. What is the remainder when 3n is divided by 5?

   A. 1   C. 4
   B. 3   D. 9

Difficulty: Medium

8. The product of two positive even consecutive integers is 168. What is the sum of these integers?

   E. 17   G. 26
   F. 21   H. 32

Difficulty: Hard

9. The decimal 0.125 can be written as the fraction $\dfrac{n}{40}$. What is the value of n?

   A. 2
   B. 5
   C. 8
   D. 10

Difficulty: Medium

10. K is an element of the set $\{0.1, 0.2, 2.5, 3.0\}$. What is K, if $\dfrac{8.4K}{3.5}$ is an integer?

   E. 0.1   G. 2.5
   F. 0.2   H. 3.0

Difficulty: Hard

Video Explanations
at argoprep.com/shsat

11. If $M = 1.\overline{34}$, what is the value of M expressed as a fraction?

   A. $\dfrac{124}{90}$

   B. $\dfrac{133}{99}$

   C. $\dfrac{125}{90}$

   D. $\dfrac{135}{99}$

   Difficulty: Medium

12. How many positive integers are between $\dfrac{34}{5}$ and $\dfrac{98}{5}$?

   E. 8

   F. 10

   G. 13

   H. 14

   Difficulty: Medium

13. When n is divided by 3, the remainder is 1. What is the remainder when 2n is divided by 3?

   A. 1

   B. 2

   C. 3

   D. 4

   Difficulty: Medium

14. Johnny is now 18 years old. In 6 years, he will be three times as old as his sister. How old is his sister now?

   E. 1 year old

   F. 2 years old

   G. 4 years old

   H. 7 years old

   Difficulty: Hard

15. How many positive integers are between $\dfrac{3}{2}$ and $\dfrac{21}{4}$?

   A. 2

   B. 3

   C. 4

   D. 5

   Difficulty: Easy

16. Between which two consecutive positive integers is $\sqrt{4^2 + 5^2}$?

   E. 4 and 5

   F. 5 and 6

   G. 6 and 7

   H. 8 and 9

   Difficulty: Hard

17. The sum of two consecutive even integers is -10. What is the larger integer?

   Difficulty: Medium

18. The sum of two consecutive integers is 25. If you take two times the smaller integer and add it to 5 plus the larger integer, what is the total sum?

   Difficulty: Medium

19. The sum of two consecutive integers is 35. If you take three times the smaller integer, what is the number?

   51

   Difficulty: Medium

20. The sum of the numbers k, l, and m is 25. The ratio of k to l is 1:3 and m is 5 more than k. What is the value of l ?

   $l = 12$

   Difficulty: Hard

1. First, rewrite the equation $3m = n - 7$ to solve for m.
$$m = \frac{n - 7}{3}$$
Now, substitute each value of n to find the values of m:
$$m = \frac{-2 - 7}{3} = -\frac{9}{3} = -3$$
$$m = \frac{1 - 7}{3} = -\frac{6}{3} = -2$$
$$m = \frac{4 - 7}{3} = -\frac{3}{3} = -1$$
The set of possible values of m is $\{-3, -2, -1\}$.
The correct answer is D.

2. If $m + 1$ is even, then m is an odd integer. Then $m - 1$ is even as well as $2m$. Therefore, $2m - 2$ and $2m + 2$ are even integers. Since $2m$ is even, then $2m + 1$ is an odd integer.
The correct answer is G.

3. If $3k$ is an even integer, it implies that k is an even integer too. Therefore, the only integer that cannot be even is $k - 1$ because integers k, $\frac{k}{2}$, and $3k$ can be even.
The correct answer is B.

4. The list of possible factors of 8 includes 1, 2, 4, and 8.
The only 3 integers from the list above whose product is 8 are 1, 2, and 4. The sum of these integers is $1 + 2 + 4 = 7$.
The correct answer is E.

5. If the first consecutive integer is m, then the next consecutive integers are $m + 1$, $m + 2$, and $m + 3$. n is the greatest integer, therefore, $n = m + 3$. Substitute $m + 3$ for n and simplify:
$$\frac{m + n}{2} = \frac{m + (m + 3)}{2} = \frac{m + m + 3}{2} = \frac{2m + 3}{2} = m + \frac{3}{2}$$
The correct answer is B.

6. There are 16 digits in the repeating decimal (5882352941176470). To find the 264th digit, divide 264 by 16 and the result is 16 $R8$.
Since the remainder is 8, that means that the 264th digit is the same as the 8th digit, which is 9.
The correct answer is H.

7. If $\frac{n}{5}$ has a remainder of 3, then $3 \times \frac{n}{5}$ will have a remainder of $3 \times (3) = 9$. The number 5 goes into 9 once leaving us with a remainder of 4.

If you try the number $n = 8$ to check your answer, $\frac{8}{5} = 1$ $R3$.
Then $\frac{3 \times 8}{5} = 4$ $R4$.
So the remainder is 4.
The correct answer is C.

8. Suppose x is a smaller integer, and then the next even consecutive integer is $x + 2$. The product of these integers is $x(x + 2) = 168$.
Solve the equation for x:
$$x^2 + 2x - 168 = 0$$
Factor the equation above:
$$(x - 12)(x + 14) = 0$$
Therefore, $x = 12, -14$.
-14 is not a valid result because it is a negative number.
Therefore, the smaller integer is 12 and the larger integer is $12 + 2 = 14$. The sum is $12 + 14 = 26$.
The correct answer is G.

9. 0.125 can be considered as a remainder of the fraction $\frac{n}{40}$. Therefore, we can write an expression $\frac{n}{40} = 0.125$.
Solve for n:
$n = 0.125 \times 40 = 5$.
The correct answer is B.

10. First, simplify the fraction:
$$\frac{8.4K}{3.5} = \frac{84K}{35} = \frac{12K}{5}$$
$\frac{12K}{5}$ is an integer and K is an element of the set.
The only possible value of K from the set above is 2.5 because $\frac{12 \times 2.5}{5} = 6$.
The other elements of the set will not yield an integer when substituting them for K.
The correct answer is G.

11. First, we need to rewrite the equation to express it as a sum of an integer and decimal part.
$$M = 1.\overline{34} = 1 + 0.\overline{34}$$
Since $0.\overline{34}$ is a repeating decimal, we can rewrite the expression:
$$1 + \frac{34}{99} = \frac{99}{99} + \frac{34}{99} = \frac{133}{99}$$
The correct answer is B.

Video Explanations
at argoprep.com/shsat

12. First, convert each fraction into the decimal form.

$$\frac{34}{5} = 6.8 \text{ and } \frac{98}{5} = 19.6.$$

The first positive integer is 7 and the last positive integer is 19. Therefore, the list of positive integers between $\frac{34}{5}$ and $\frac{98}{5}$ is 7, 8, 9, 10, 11, 12, 13, 14, 15, 16, 17, 18, 19.

The number of positive integers between $\frac{34}{5}$ and $\frac{98}{5}$ is 13.

The correct answer is G.

---

13. The best way to approach this question is to use a hypothetical number. If n is divided by 3 and the remainder is 1, then a possible value for n can be 4. Plug in the value $n = 4$ for $2n$ divided by 3.

$$2(4) = \frac{8}{3} = 2 \text{ Remainder } 2$$

The remainder is 2.

The correct answer is B.

---

14. In 6 years, Johnny will be 24 years old. Since he will be three times as old as his sister, then his sister will be $\frac{24}{3} = 8$ years old in 6 years. Therefore, she is $8 - 6 = 2$ years old now.

The correct answer is F.

---

15. $\frac{3}{2}$ is equivalent to 1.5 and $\frac{21}{4}$ is equivalent to 5.25. The positive integers between 1.5 and 5.25 are 2, 3, 4 and 5. Therefore, we have a total of 4 integers.

The correct answer is C.

---

16. First, calculate the quantity under the square root sign.

$$\sqrt{4^2 + 5^2} = \sqrt{16 + 25} = \sqrt{41}$$

41 falls between the squares of 6 and 7, which are 36 and 49, respectively.

$$36 < 41 < 49$$
$$6^2 < 41 < 7^2$$
$$6 < \sqrt{41} < 7$$

The correct answer is C.

---

17. If we represent x as the smaller integer, the larger integer will be represented as $x + 2$. Since their sum is -10, we have the equation $x + (x + 2) = -10$. Find x:

$$2x + 2 = -10; 2x = -12; x = -6$$

The smaller integer is -6, and the larger integer is $-6 + 2 = $ **-4**.

---

18. If x is the smaller consecutive integer, then $x + 1$ is the larger consecutive integer. The sum of these two integers is 25 so we have the equation

$$x + (x + 1) = 25$$

Solve for x:

$$2x + 1 = 25; 2x = 24$$

$x = 12$ is the smaller integer.

Then the larger integer is $12 + 1 = 13$.

The next step is to find the sum of the new integers:

$$(2(12) + 5) + 13 = \textbf{42}.$$

---

19. If x is the smaller consecutive integer, then $x + 1$ is the larger consecutive integer. The sum of these two integers is 35 so we have the equation

$x + (x + 1) = 35$

Solve for x:

$x = 17$ is the smaller integer.

If we take three times the smaller integer, we get $17 \times 3 = 51$.

The correct answer is 51.

---

20. Since the ratio of k to l is 1:3, then $k = \frac{l}{3}$ or $l = 3k$.

m is 5 more than k can be written as $m = k + 5$.

The sum of the three numbers is $k + l + m = 25$.

Rewrite the sum of the three numbers in terms of k.

$$k + 3k + (5 + k) = 25$$

Solve for k:

$$5k + 5 = 25$$
$$5k = 20$$
$$k = 4$$

Solve for l:

$$l = 3k$$
$$l = 3 \times (4)$$
$$\textbf{l = 12}$$

1.
$$3 \times (257 - 239) + \frac{100}{(13-8)^2} =$$

   A. 52   **B.** 55   **C.** 58   **D.** 81

   Difficulty: Medium

2. Maria and her friends eat pizza for lunch. There are 6 pizzas with 10 slices each. If Maria and her 15 friends eat 3 slices each, how many slices are left over?

   E. 15   **F.** 12   **G.** 10   **H.** 7

   Difficulty: Medium

$16 \cdot 3 =$ $6 \cdot 10 = 60$

3. David has four bags of apples and two bags of mangoes. The first four bags contain 6 apples each and the bags with mangoes contain 3 mangoes each. If David and his friends ate 2 apples from each bag and 2 mangoes from each bag, what is the total number of fruits left over?

   A. 12   **B.** 16   **C.** 18   **D.** 20

   Difficulty: Medium

   $3 \cdot 2 = 6$ $6 \cdot 4 = 24$

4. Multiply 3 by thirteen. Take the result and add it to the difference between the number of days in December and 35. What is the final result?

   E. 29   **F.** 35   **G.** 37   **H.** 43

   Difficulty: Medium

   $13 \cdot 3 = 39$

5. Mark went to the bookstore. He bought 3 books for $6.00 each and two magazines for $3.50 each. He received a 25% discount on his purchase. If he handed the cashier $20, how much change did Mark get back?

   A. $1.25   **C.** $2.50
   B. $1.75   **D.** $3.00

   Difficulty: Medium

   25.00

6. There are 9 chocolates in each jar and there are 4 jars. Max took n chocolates from each jar and now there are 16 chocolates left over in the jars. How many pieces of chocolate did Max take from each jar?

   E. 2   **F.** 3   **G.** 5   **H.** 6

   Difficulty: Hard

   $36 - 16 = 20$

7. What is the value of $(m-n)(n+m)$ when $m=3$ and $n=4$?

   A. -7 **C.** 4
   B. -3 **D.** 7

   Difficulty: Medium

8. Divide 6 by the number of hours in two days and add to the number of days in February (non-leap year) divided by 4. Write you answer as a mixed fraction.

   E. $1\frac{7}{8}$ **G.** $7\frac{1}{8}$
   F. $3\frac{1}{4}$ **H.** $\frac{3}{8}$

   Difficulty: Hard

   $48 \div 6 = 8$

9. $25(1 + 0.2) - \frac{10}{0.5} + 0.25(25 - 5) =$

   $25 \cdot 1.2 = 30$ $0.25 \cdot 20 = 5$

   A. 5   **C.** 15
   B. 10   **D.** 25

   Difficulty: Medium

10. Evaluate the following expression

$$(7 + 2) \times (3^2 + 1) \times \frac{(9^2 - 75)}{2} =$$

   $9 \cdot 28 = 252$

   E. 108   **G.** 270
   F. 216   **H.** 540

   Difficulty: Medium

Video Explanations
at argoprep.com/shsat

$5^3 = 125$

11. Cube the sum of 2 and 3 and subtract the result from the squared difference of 305 and 294.

   A. −246   C. 4
   B. −4   D. 246

   Difficulty: Medium

12. Which of the following is equivalent to the expression

   $$b\,(a + b(a - b(b + a)))\ ?$$

   E. $-b^4 - ab^3 + ab^2 + ab$
   F. $-b^4 - ab^3 - ab^2 + ab$
   G. $b^4 + ab^3 - ab^2 + ab$
   H. $b^4 + ab^3 - ab^2 - ab$

   Difficulty: Hard

13. Evaluate the expression $-2x - 5(x - 3)(y + 4)$ if $x = 2$ and $y = -1$

   A. −19   B. 11   C. 6   D. 11

   Difficulty: Medium

14. A taxi company charges $2.50 for each ride plus an additional $0.70 for each half of a mile ridden. Estimate the total cost if a passenger had a 6.5 mile ride.

   E. $3.20   G. $7.55
   F. $4.55   H. $11.60

   Difficulty: Hard

15. There are 16 yellow marbles in the first can and 9 green marbles in the second can. Linda took 5 marbles from the first can and gave them to Steven. She also took n marbles from the second can and gave them to Jennifer. How many green marbles did Linda give to Jennifer if there are 16 marbles left in both cans?

   A. 2   B. 4   C. 7   D. 9

   Difficulty: Hard

16. Evaluate the following expression if $a = -2$ and $b = 4$

   $$a(a + b(a - b)) - b(b + a)$$

   E. −52
   F. 28
   G. 44
   H. 52

   Difficulty: Medium

17. Divide 12 by the sum of 2 and 4 and add the result to the sum of the number of weekdays in a week and the number of days in a weekend divided by 6. What is the final answer?

   Difficulty: Medium

18.

   $$(5 - 15) \div (3 - 8)$$

   If the parentheses are removed from the above expression, what will be the value of the new expression?

   Difficulty: Medium

19. John had $50 and withdrew $250 from his bank account. He bought 2 pairs of shoes for $29 each, 3 shirts for $18 each, and 4 T-shirts for $12 each. How much money does John have left?

   Difficulty: Easy

20. Solve:

   $$\frac{(1 + 9) \times (1 + 7^2) \times (4^2 + 2)}{2} =$$

   Difficulty: Medium

Video Explanations
at argoprep.com/shsat

1. Order of operations follows the rule "PEMDAS": Parentheses, Exponents, Multiplication and Division, Addition and Subtraction.

$$3(257 - 239) + \frac{100}{(13-8)^2} = 3(18) + \frac{100}{5^2} = 3(18) + \frac{100}{25}$$

$$= 54 + \frac{100}{25} = 54 + 4 = 58$$

The correct answer is B. C ✓

---

2. Rewrite the problem into a mathematical statement and solve using PEMDAS in order to find out how many slices were left over.

Pay attention to the fact that there are 16 people (Maria and her 15 friends).

$$6(10) - 16(3) = 60 - 48 = 12$$

Therefore, there are 12 pizza slices left over.

The correct answer is F.

---

3. Rewrite the problem above into a mathematical expression and solve using PEMDAS.

Total number of fruits that were in the bags: $(4 \times 6) + (2 \times 3)$

2 apples from each bag were eaten: $-(4 \times 2)$ 2 mangos from each bag were eaten: $-(2 \times 2)$ Therefore, the solution is:

$$4(6) + 2(3) - 4(2) - 2(2) =$$
$$24 + 6 - 8 - 4 =$$
$$30 - 8 - 4 = 18$$

The correct answer is C.

---

4. Translate the problem into a mathematical expression and use PEMDAS:

$$3(13) + (31 - 35) =$$
$$3(13) + (-4) =$$
$$39 + (-4) =$$
$$39 - 4 = 35$$

The correct answer is F.

---

5. According to the problem, we can write the following mathematical expression:

$$0.75[3(6.00) + 2(3.50)]$$

Solve the problem by applying PEMDAS:

$0.75[3(6.00) + 2(3.50)] = 0.75[18 + 7] = 0.75[25] = 18.75$

Mark spent $18.75 on his purchase.

He got $20 - \$18.75 = \$1.25$ back.

The correct answer is A.

---

6. Since Max took n chocolates from each jar, then the total number of chocolates that he took is $4n$.

Write an equation in order to solve the problem above:
$$4(9) - 4n = 16$$
Solve the resulting equation for n: $36 - 4n = 16$
$$-4n = -16 - 36$$
$-4n = -20$ multiply both parts of the equation by -1.
$$4n = 20$$
$$n = 5$$

Max took 5 chocolates from each jar.

The correct answer is G.

---

7. Substitute $m = 3$ and $n = 4$ into $(m - n)(n + m) = (3 - 4)(4 + 3)$

According to PEMDAS, perform the mathematical operations within the parentheses first, then proceed with multiplication.

$$(3 - 4)(4 + 3) = (-1)(7) = -7$$

The correct answer is A.

---

8. Rewrite the problem above into the mathematical expression and solve according to PEMDAS:

$$\frac{6}{48} + \frac{28}{4} = \frac{1}{8} + 7 = \frac{1 + 56}{8} = \frac{57}{8} = 7\frac{1}{8}$$

The correct answer is G.

---

9. Perform the required calculations:

$$25(1 + 0.2) - \frac{10}{0.5} + 0.25(25 - 5) =$$

$$25(1.2) - \frac{10}{0.5} + 0.25(20) =$$

$$30 - \frac{10}{0.5} + 5 = 30 - 20 + 5 = 15$$

The correct answer is C.

10.

$$(7 + 2) \times (3^2 + 1) \times \frac{(9^2 - 75)}{2} = (9) \times (10) \times \frac{6}{2}$$

$$(9) \times (10) \times \frac{6}{2} = \frac{540}{2}$$

$$\frac{540}{2} = 270.$$

The correct answer is G.

Video Explanations at argoprep.com/shsat

11. The problem written as a mathematical expression is $(305 − 294)^2 − (2 + 3)^3$

Solve the expression:
$$(305 − 294)^2 − (2 + 3)^3 =$$
$$11^2 − 5^3 =$$
$$121 − 125 = −4$$

The correct answer is B.

12.
$$b\,(a + b(a − b(b + a))) = b(a + b(a − b^2 − ab))$$
$$= b(a + ab − b^3 − ab^2) = ab + ab^2 − b^4 − ab^3$$

Rewrite the resulting expression from the highest degree to the lowest degree: $−b^4 − ab^3 + ab^2 + ab$.

The correct answer is E.

---

13. Substitute $x = 2$ and $y = −1$ into the expression:
$$−2(2) − 5(2 − 3)(−1 + 4)$$

Solve the resulting expression:
$$−2(2) − 5(2 − 3)(−1 + 4) =$$
$$−2(2) − 5(−1)(3) =$$
$$−4 + 15 = 11$$

The correct answer is D.

---

14. Suppose C is the total cost of a ride paid by the passenger and x is the number of half miles ridden. Then, the equation is $C(x) = 0.70x + 2.50$.

First, find x: $x = \dfrac{6.5}{0.5}$

Therefore, the cost of the ride is $C(6.5) = 0.70 \left(\dfrac{6.50}{0.5}\right) + 2.50$
$= 4.55 + 2.50 = \$11.60$

The correct answer is H.

---

15. Write an equation that models the situation described above:
$$(16 − 5) + (9 − n) = 16$$

Solve the equation for n: $11 + 9 − n = 16$
$$−n = 16 − 11 − 9$$
$$−n = −4$$
$$n = 4$$

Therefore, Linda gave 4 marbles to Jennifer.

The correct answer is B.

---

16. Substitute the values of a and b into the original expression and solve:
$$−2(−2 + 4(−2 − 4)) − 4(4 + (−2)) =$$
$$−2(−2 + 4(−6)) − 4(2) =$$
$$−2(−2 − 24) − 4(2) =$$
$$−2(−26) − 4(2) = 52 − 8 = 44$$

The correct answer is G.

---

17. Rewrite the problem as a mathematical expression.
$$\frac{12}{2 + 4} + \left(5 + \frac{2}{6}\right)$$

Follow PEMDAS:
$$\frac{12}{2 + 4} + \left(5 + \frac{2}{6}\right) = \frac{12}{6} + \left(\frac{32}{6}\right) = \frac{44}{6} = \frac{22}{3}$$

The final answer is $\dfrac{22}{3}$.

---

18. If the parentheses are removed, the expression above will change to $5 − 15 ÷ 3 − 8$.

The first mathematical operation that will be performed in this case is division: $5 − 5 − 8$.

Then the result is $5 − 5 − 8 = \mathbf{−8}$.

---

19. Write an expression that defines the problem above:
$$(50 + 250) − 2(29) − 3(18) − 4(12)$$

Solve the expression:
$$(50 + 250) − 2(29) − 3(18) − 4(12) =$$
$$300 − 2(29) − 3(18) − 4(12) =$$
$$300 − 58 − 54 − 48 = 140$$

20.
$$\frac{(1 + 9) \times (1 + 7^2) \times (4^2 + 2)}{2} =$$
$$\frac{(10) \times (50) \times (18)}{2} =$$
$$\frac{9{,}000}{2} = 4{,}500$$

The answer is **4,500**.

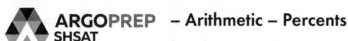
(handwritten work at top of page)
14,000   205
192
0.1
205)340   20   24)205
205
1350

1. What is the difference between 80% of 8 and 8% of 80?

   A. 0   **C.** 6.45
   B. 3   **D.** 64

   Difficulty: Medium

2. A is 25% of B, and B is 35% of 2,000. What is the value of A?

   E. 50   **G.** 250
   F. 175   **H.** 500

   Difficulty: Medium

3. A DVD collection had a price of $15.87 last week. This week the same DVD collection costs $14.39. What is the percent decrease in price?

   A. 3.58%
   B. 7.04%
   C. 9.33%
   D. 12.27%

   (handwritten) $\dfrac{15.87 - 14.39}{15.87}$

   Difficulty: Medium

4. The original cost of a dress that Nancy wants to buy is $84. How much did Nancy pay for the dress if she bought it with a 60% discount?

   E. $21.15
   F. $33.60
   G. $50.40
   H. $62.35

   Difficulty: Medium

5. Steven runs one mile in 9 minutes this year, while he was able to run one mile in 7.5 minutes last year. By what percent did his time decrease?

   A. 6%   **C.** 17%
   B. 11%   **D.** 20%

   Difficulty: Medium

6. James is currently training for a cycle race. In the first week of training, he cycled 205 miles. In the second week, he cycled 239 miles. What is the percent increase in distance that James was able to ride?

   E. 11.3%   **G.** 16.6%
   F. 14.2%   **H.** 18.4%

   Difficulty: Medium

7. A book normally costs $7.99. What is the percent decrease if the new price on sale is $4.79?

   A. 35.07%   **C.** 52.43%
   B. 40.05%   **D.** 66.81%

   Difficulty: Medium

8. It is expected that 750 people will attend the concert. In fact, 600 people attended. 600 is what percent of the expected number?

   E. 60%   **G.** 80%
   F. 74%   **H.** 86%

   Difficulty: Medium

9. After measuring the volume and mass of a substance, a chemist calculated the density as 1.87 g/mL. The correct value of the density for this substance is 1.75 g/mL. What is the percent error of the chemist's measurement?

   A. 5.76%   **C.** 6.86%
   B. 6.42%   **D.** 7.32%

   Difficulty: Hard

10. There are three integers, the second integer is 20% larger than the first integer, and the third integer is 25% larger than the second integer. What is the largest integer if the sum of the three integers is 37?

    E. 10   **F.** 12   **G.** 15   **H.** 18

    Difficulty: Hard

Video Explanations
at argoprep.com/shsat

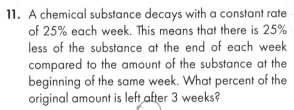

11. A chemical substance decays with a constant rate of 25% each week. This means that there is 25% less of the substance at the end of each week compared to the amount of the substance at the beginning of the same week. What percent of the original amount is left after 3 weeks?

   A. 75%   C. 42.2%
   B. 56.25%   D. 25%

   Difficulty: Hard

12. In 2012, a company's revenue was estimated at $2,464,753. In 2013, there was 7% drop in the company's revenue with a subsequent 15% increase in 2014. What was the company's revenue in 2014?

   E. $2,292,220.29
   F. $2,464,753
   G. $2,636,053.33
   H. $2,742,325.47

   Difficulty: Hard

13. Paul decided to increase an area of a garden with the current dimensions of 24×36 meters. If he plans to increase each dimension by 25%, what is the percent increase of the garden's area?

   A. 25%   C. 50%
   B. 32.50%   D. 56.25%

   Difficulty: Hard

14. In a bag of 35 marbles, 20% of the marbles are green. If you randomly pick a marble from the bag, what is the probability that the marble picked is NOT green?

   E. 0.20   G. 0.65
   F. 0.50   H. 0.80

   Difficulty: Hard

15. The regular price of a washing machine is $500. How much more money would Steven save by buying this washing machine at 10 percent off the regular price rather than buying it on sale at 5 percent off the regular price with an additional discount of 5 percent off the sale price?

   A. $1.00   B. $1.25   C. $5.50   D. $8.75

   Difficulty: Hard

16. A DVD store is going out of business and offers a final sale. The first week the store decreased the prices by 25%. The second week the store reduced the price 20% more. What is the sale price of a DVD if it was originally priced at $10?

   E. $8.50   F. $7.50   G. $6.00   H. $4.75

   Difficulty: Medium

17. Lisa completed 45 pages in her Italian workbook. This is 25% of the total number of pages in the workbook. How many pages are in the workbook?

   Difficulty: Medium

18. What is Christina's percent weight loss if she went from 120 pounds to 105 pounds?

   Difficulty: Medium

19. A family put a 16 x 52 foot garden on the end of their back yard. The garden covered 26% of their yard. What is the total area of their yard?

   Difficulty: Medium

20. A tank is partially filled with x liters of gasoline. If John adds 15 liters of gasoline to the tank, it would be 70% full. If John were to add 20 liters of gasoline to the tank, it would be 90% full. What is the value of x ?

   Difficulty: Hard

Video Explanations
at argoprep.com/shsat

23

1. 80% of 8 = 0.8 × 8 = 6.4
    8% of 80 = 0.08 × 80 = 6.4
    So the difference is 0.
    The correct answer is A.

2. First, find the value of B: 0.35 × 2,000 = 700
    Therefore, the value of A is 0.25 × 700 = 175
    The correct answer is F.

3. To find the percent decrease in price, we need to calculate the change in price, divide it by the original price, and multiply the result by 100%.
    Therefore, we have $\frac{15.87-14.39}{15.87} \times 100\% = \frac{1.48}{15.87} \times 100\%$
    $= 9.33\%$
    The correct answer is C.

4. Since Nancy bought the dress with 60% discount, she paid 40% of its original price.
    Therefore, Nancy paid 84 × 0.40 = $33.60.
    The correct answer is F.

5. The original time is 7.5 minutes and the amount of change is 7.5 − 9 = −1.5.
    Therefore, the percent change is $\frac{-1.5}{7.5} \times 100\% = 20\%$.
    Steven's time decreased by 20% compared to the previous year.
    The correct answer is D.

6. For this problem, percent increase can be calculated by using the following formula:
    $$\% \text{ Increase} = \frac{\text{New distance} - \text{Old distance}}{\text{Old distance}} \times 100\%$$
    Percentage increase will be $\frac{239-205}{205} \times 100\% = 16.6\%$
    The correct answer is G.

7. Percent decrease is calculated according to the formula
    $$\% \text{ decrease} = \frac{\text{Old price} - \text{New price}}{\text{Old price}} \times 100\%$$.
    In our case, the old price is $7.99, and the new price is 4.79.
    $$\% \text{ decrease} = \frac{7.99 - 4.79}{7.99} \times 100\% = 40.05\%$$
    The correct answer is B.

8. To find what percent of the expected number is 600, divide 600 by 750.
    $$\frac{600}{750} = 0.8$$
    So 600 is 80% of 750.
    The correct answer is G.

9. Percent error can be calculated by using the following formula:
    $$\% \text{ error} = \frac{\text{correct value} - \text{experimental value}}{\text{correct value}} \times 100\%$$
    Substitute the value into the formula and calculate % error.
    $$\% \text{ error} = \frac{1.75 - 1.87}{1.75} \times 100\% = \frac{-0.12}{1.75} \times 100\% = -6.86\%$$
    It can be written as 6.86% because % error is usually an absolute value.
    The correct answer is C.

10. Suppose a, b, and c are three numbers. From the problem given:
    $$b = 1.2a$$
    $$c = 1.25b = 1.25(1.2a) = 1.5a$$
    The sum of these three numbers:
    $$a + 1.2a + 1.5a = 37, \ 3.7a = 37$$
    $$a = \frac{37}{3.7} = 10$$
    Now, find the values of b and c.
    $$b = 1.2 \times 10 = 12$$
    $$c = 1.5 \times 10 = 15$$
    The integers are 10, 12, and 15.
    The correct answer is G.

11. Since 25% of the chemical substance decayed after the first week, there is 75% of the original amount left at the end of the first week. The amount of the substance after the second week: 75% of the amount that was left at the end of the previous week. Therefore, the amount at the end of the second week is 0.75 × 0.75 = 0.5625.
    The amount at the end of the third week:
    0.5625 × 0.75 = 0.422, or 42.2%.
    The correct answer is C.

Video Explanations
at argoprep.com/shsat

12. Since there was 7% drop in the company's revenue, then its value was $2,464,753 × 0.93 = $2,292,220.29 in 2013.

In 2014, the company's revenue was increased by 15% compared to 2013. Therefore, the company's revenue in 2014 was $2,292,220.29 × 1.15 = $2,636,053.33

The correct answer is G.

13. Calculate the area of the current garden: 24 × 36 = 864m².

The width of the garden is 24 meters and the length of the garden is 36 meters.

Increase each of the dimensions by 25% by multiplying each of them by 1.25.

Therefore, the new garden's width is 24 × 1.25 = 30 meters and the new length is 36 × 1.25 = 45 meters.

Calculate the area of the new garden: 30 × 45 = 1,350m².

The percent increase is $\frac{1,350-864}{864} \times 100\% = 56.25\%$.

The correct answer is D.

14. Since 20% of the marbles are green, then the probability of picking a green marble is 0.20. Therefore, the probability of randomly picking a marble other than green would be 1 − 0.20 = 0.80.

The correct answer is H.

15. If buying the washing machine at 10 percent off the regular price, Steven would pay 500 × 0.9 = $450.

If buying the washing machine at 5 percent off the regular price with an additional discount of 5 percent off the sale price, Steven would pay 500 × 0.95 × 0.95 = $451.25.

Steven would save $451.25 − $450 = $1.25.

The correct answer is B.

16. After the first week, the new price was $10 × 0.75 = $7.50. During the second week, the price dropped 20% from the final price of the first week. Therefore, the final price at the end of the second week was

$$\$7.50 \times 0.80 = \$6.00.$$

The correct answer is G.

17. Suppose n is a total number of pages in the Italian workbook. That means that 25% of n is 45. Now, set up a proportion to solve the problem for n:

$$\frac{25}{100} = \frac{45}{x}$$
$$25x = 4,500$$
$$x = \frac{4,500}{25} = \textbf{180 pages}$$

18. We usually calculate the rate of change with respect to the original value.

There is 120 − 105 = 15 pounds decrease so the percent weight loss is $\frac{15}{120} = 0.125$, which is equal to **12.5%**.

19. The total area of the garden is 16 × 52 = 832 which is 26% of the total area of the back yard.

Suppose x is the total area of the back yard. Then, 0.26x = 832. Solve for x:

$$x = \frac{832}{0.26} = \textbf{3200 ft}^2.$$

20. Suppose y is the total number of liters the tank can hold. Then, we can set up two equations:

$$\frac{x+15}{y} = 70\% \text{ and } \frac{x+20}{y} = 90\%$$

Solve each equation for y:

1) $\frac{x+15}{y} = \frac{70}{100}$; $\frac{x+15}{y} = \frac{7}{10}$
$$7y = 10(x+15)$$
$$y = \frac{10x+150}{7}$$

2) $\frac{x+20}{y} = \frac{9}{10}$
$$9y = 10(x+20)$$
$$y = \frac{10x+200}{9}$$

Set the two resulting equations equal to each other and solve for x:

$$\frac{10x+150}{7} = \frac{10x+200}{9}$$
$$7(10x+200) = 9(10x+150)$$
$$70x + 1400 = 90x + 1350$$
$$-20x = -50$$
$$x = \textbf{2.5 liters}.$$

Video Explanations
at argoprep.com/shsat

1. The sum of two prime integers is 32 and their difference is 6. What is the larger number?

   A. 9   C. 19
   B. 13   D. 23

   Difficulty: Hard

2. The product of two composite numbers is 96 and their quotient is 6. What is the smaller number?

   E. 4   G. 15
   F. 6   H. 24

   Difficulty: Hard

3. Which of the following numbers is prime?

   A. 1   C. 11
   B. 9   D. 35

   Difficulty: Easy

4. How many distinct prime factors are in the number 120?

   E. 2   G. 5
   F. 3   H. 7

   Difficulty: Easy

5. If z is a prime number, then what is 3z?

   A. odd
   B. a prime number
   C. even
   D. cannot be determined

   Difficulty: Medium

6. How many positive even factors of 64 are greater than 32 and less than 64?

   E. 5   G. 2
   F. 4   H. 0

   Difficulty: Medium

7. What is the greatest prime factor of 330?

   A. 5   C. 55
   B. 11   D. 165

   Difficulty: Medium

8. What is the sum of the two greatest prime factors of 190?

   E. 38   G. 21
   F. 24   H. 7

   Difficulty: Medium

9. Mike's phone password is a 4-digit number and all the digits in the password are prime numbers. The numbers are in ascending order and they start with the first prime number. What is the phone password?

   A. 1234   C. 2357
   B. 2346   D. 3579

   Difficulty: Medium

10. George's current age is a prime number and the age of his older sister, Julia, is also a prime number. The difference between their ages is also a prime number. If they are both between 16 and 25 years old, how old is Julia?

    E. 16 years old   G. 19 years old
    F. 17 years old   H. 23 years old

    Difficulty: Medium

11. Find the number from the following clues: this integer is between 20 and 30 and has two prime factors. The sum of the prime factors is 10.

    A. 21   C. 25
    B. 23   D. 27

    Difficulty: Hard

Video Explanations at argoprep.com/shsat

12. What is the product of the two largest prime factors of 120?

    E. 4   **F.** 6   **G.** 10   **H.** 15

                        Difficulty: Medium

13. What is the difference between the third and the second prime factors of 150?

    A. 3   **B.** 2   **C.** 1   **D.** 0

                        Difficulty: Medium

14. What is the sum of the smallest and largest prime factor of 264?

    E. 4   **G.** 13

    F. 5   **H.** 14

                        Difficulty: Medium

15. What is the quotient if the largest prime factor of 364 is divided by the smallest prime factor of 364?

    A. 1   **C.** 3.5

    B. 1.75   **D.** 6.5

                        Difficulty: Hard

16. How many distinct prime factors are in the number 75?

    E. 2   **F.** 3   **G.** 5   **H.** 7

                        Difficulty: Medium

17. What is the sum of the second prime factor of 55 and the second prime factor of 115?

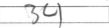

                        Difficulty: Medium

18. Anna is thinking about a number, which is a prime factor of 76. When you add the number to 5 the sum is 24. What number is Anna thinking about?

                        Difficulty: Hard

19. Nick is studying about prime and composite numbers and he needs to determine the number of distinct prime factors in the number 135. How many distinct prime factors are in the number 135?

                        Difficulty: Hard

20. What is the squared sum of the smallest and largest prime factor of 112?

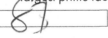

                        Difficulty: Hard

Answer Explanation

1. Suppose a and b are two prime numbers.

Since their sum is 32, $a + b = 32$. Their difference is 6, so $a - b = 6$.

Rewrite the second equation for a: $a = b + 6$

Substitute the resulting expression for a into the first equation and solve for a:

$$6 + b + b = 32$$
$$2b = 26$$
$$b = \frac{26}{2} = 13$$

Now, find a: $a + 13 = 32$. $a = 19$. The larger prime number is 19.

The correct answer is C.

2. Suppose m and n are two numbers. We can rewrite the problem into two equations:

$$mn = 96 \text{ and } \frac{m}{n} = 6$$

Rewrite the second equation for m: $m = 6n$. Substitute it into the first equation and solve for m:

$$n(6n) = 96,$$
$$6n^2 = 96$$
$$n^2 = 16$$
$$n = \pm 4$$

We are only interested in positive numbers so one of the two composite numbers is 4. Find the second number: $m = 6 \times 4 = 24$. The smaller number is 4.

The correct answer is E.

Video Explanations
at argoprep.com/shsat

3. A prime number is a whole number greater than one whose only factors are 1 and itself.

Students often think 1 is a prime number, so do not be tricked by the first answer choice. The only number that has the factors 1 and itself is answer choice C, 11.

The correct answer is C.

4. Find the prime factorization of 120 to determine the number of distinct prime factors.

What are two factors that multiply to 120? The numbers 10 and 12 multiply to 120, however, since they are not prime numbers, keep on factoring 10 and 12. The factors of 10 are 2 and 5, which are primes. The factors of 12 are 2 and 6 and the factors of 6 are 2 and 3, which are prime. So the prime factorization of 120 is $2 \times 2 \times 2 \times 3 \times 5$. The number of distinct prime factors is 3.

The correct answer is F.

5. In order to solve this question, pick a few prime numbers. If we use the prime number 2, then $3z$ gives us 6. If we use the prime number 3, then $3z$ gives us 9. As you can see, we cannot determine whether or not it is an even or odd number, and therefore the answer cannot be determined.

The correct answer is D.

6. The following pairs of numbers can be the factors of 64: 1 and 64, 2 and 32, 4 and 16, 8 and 8.

There are no factors that are greater 32 and less than 64.

The correct answer is H.

7. Perform prime factorization of 330: $330 = 2 \times 165 = 2 \times 3 \times 55 = 2 \times 3 \times 5 \times 11$.

The greatest prime factor from the primes listed above is 11.

The correct answer is B.

8. Prime factorization of 190 gives us $190 = 2 \times 95 = 2 \times 5 \times 19$.

The two greatest prime factors of 190 is 5 and 19 and their sum is 24.

The correct answer is F.

9. A prime number is a whole number greater than one whose only factors are 1 and itself.

The first four prime numbers are 2, 3, 5, and 7. Therefore, the phone password is 2357.

The correct answer is C.

10. List all the prime numbers between 16 and 25: 17, 19, 23.

The only difference between two of the numbers 17, 19, and 23 that results in a prime number, is $19 - 17 = 2$.

So George is 17 years old and Julia is **19 years old**.

The correct answer is G.

11. The only number between 20 and 30 with 2 different prime factors is 21. Its factors are 3 and 7, which are both prime and have a sum of 10.

The correct answer is A.

12. Find the prime factorization of 120.

$120 = 2 \times 60 = 2 \times 2 \times 30 = 2 \times 2 \times 2 \times 15 = 2 \times 2 \times 2 \times 3 \times 5$

Therefore, the two largest prime factors of 120 are 3 and 5 and their product is 15.

The correct answer is H.

13. Find the prime factorization of 150.

$150 = 2 \times 75 = 2 \times 3 \times 25 = 2 \times 3 \times 5 \times 5$

The third prime factor of 150 is 5 and the second prime factor of 150 is 3. Their difference is 2.

The correct answer is B.

14. Find the prime factorization of 264.

$$264 = 2 \times 132 = 2 \times 2 \times 66 = 2 \times 2 \times 2 \times 33$$
$$= 2 \times 2 \times 2 \times 3 \times 11$$

The first prime factor of 264 is 2 and the last prime factor of 264 is 11. Their sum is 13.

The correct answer is G.

15. Find the prime factorization of 364: $364 = 2 \times 182 = 2 \times 2 \times 91 = 2 \times 2 \times 7 \times 13$.

The largest prime factor of 364 is 13 and the smallest prime factor of 364 is 2.

The quotient is $\frac{13}{2} = 6.5$.

The correct answer is D.

16. Prime factorization of 75: $75 = 3 \times 25 = 3 \times 5 \times 5$

Therefore, the third factor is 5.

The correct answer is E.

Video Explanations
at argoprep.com/shsat

17. Find the prime factorization of 55: $55 = 5 \times 11$

Find the prime factorization of 115: $115 = 5 \times 23$

The second prime factor of 55 is 11 and the second prime factor of 115 is 23. Their sum is **34**.

18. Find the prime factorization of 76: $76 = 2 \times 38 = 2 \times 2 \times 19$.

The sum of one of the prime factors listed above and 5 is 24. Therefore, the only possible number that Anna was thinking about is 19 because $19 + 5 = $ **24**.

19. The prime factorization of 135 gives us the following: $135 = 3 \times 45 = 3 \times 3 \times 15 = 3 \times 3 \times 3 \times 5$. There are 4 prime factors in total, and **2** of them are distinct (3 and 5).

20. The prime factorization of 112 gives us the following: $112 = 2 \times 56 = 2 \times 2 \times 28 = 2 \times 2 \times 2 \times 14 = 2 \times 2 \times 2 \times 2 \times 7$.

The smallest prime factor is 2 and the largest prime factor is 7. Therefore, $(2 + 7)^2 = 9^2 = $ **81**.

▶ **Video Explanations**
at argoprep.com/shsat

1. What is the least common multiple of 13, 39, and 117?

A. 351 C. 117
B. 156 D. 78

Difficulty: Medium

2. What is the least common multiple of 2, 4x, 3y, 6xy, and 8y?

E. $48x^2y^2$
F. $48xy$
G. $24xy$
H. $18xy$

Difficulty: Medium

3. Julia has dance lessons every third day and cooking lessons every fourth day. If she had a dance lesson and a cooking lesson on April 5, when will be the next date on which she has both dance and cooking lessons?

A. April 8 C. April 15
B. April 12 D. April 17

Difficulty: Medium

4. Anna asked her friend Maria about the second smallest possible number that is divisible by both 3 and 11. What is the number?

E. 22 G. 42
F. 33 H. 66

Difficulty: Medium

5. Tommy is thinking about a number that is divisible by both 17 and 3. What is the smallest possible number that he could be thinking of?

A. 68 C. 42
B. 51 D. 34

Difficulty: Medium

6. What is the least common multiple of 3, 5a, 9b, 5ab, and 15b?

E. $45a^2b^2$
F. $45ab$
G. $15ab$
H. $9ab$

Difficulty: Medium

7. Pens come in a package of 6, while notebooks come in a package of 5. Jill wants to purchase the smallest number of pens and notebooks so that she will have exactly 1 pen per notebook. How many packages of pens and notebooks should Jill buy?

A. 3 packages of pens, 4 packages of notebooks.
B. 4 packages of pens, 4 packages of notebooks.
C. 5 packages of pens, 5 packages of notebooks.
D. 5 packages of pens, 6 packages of notebooks.

Difficulty: Medium

8. Two light bulbs are turned on at the same time. The first light bulb blinks every 6 seconds and the second light bulbs blinks every 4 seconds. In 60 seconds, how many times will they blink at the same time?

E. 0 times
F. 2 times
G. 3 times
H. 5 times

Difficulty: Medium

9. Martin cut two wires with lengths of 256 cm and 644 cm into equal pieces without any wire left over. Find the greatest possible length of the pieces.

A. 4 C. 64
B. 16 D. 92

Difficulty: Hard

Video Explanations
at argoprep.com/shsat

10. Megan has 12 apples, 15 oranges, and 9 pears. She wants to divide the number of fruits between the baskets with each basket having the same number of fruits in it. Without mixing the fruits, what is the greatest number of pieces of fruit Megan can put in each basket?

E. 2   F. 3   G. 5   H. 6

Difficulty: Medium

11. Jolly and Jane both have a piece of ribbon of the same length. Jolly cuts her piece of ribbon into equal lengths of 3 m, while Jane cuts her ribbons into equal lengths of 7 m. Find the shortest possible length of ribbon they had at the beginning if there was no remainder in both cases.

A. 9   C. 21
B. 14   D. 28

Difficulty: Medium

12. Tommy has a bag of 28 candy bars and Peter has a bag of 35 orange-flavored cookies. They want to divide up the candy bars and cookies into small packs so that each pack contains the same number candy bars and orange flavored cookies. If there is no remainder, what is the largest possible number of sweets in each bag?

E. 14   G. 7
F. 9   H. 5

Difficulty: Medium

13. A teacher wants to arrange 54 boys and 63 girls into rows. He wants each row to have the same number of students but each row will have either all boys or all girls. What is the greatest number of students that can be arranged in a row?

A. 3   C. 9
B. 7   D. 18

Difficulty: Hard

14. Josie is making party bags for her birthday. Balloons come in packs of five and whistles come in packs of four. What is the fewest amount of packs of balloons and whistles Josie must buy so there are no items left over?

E. 8   G. 20
F. 16   H. 40

Difficulty: Medium

15. Hand towels are sold in a pack of 12 and bath towels are sold in a pack of 16. Anna is a hotel manager and she needs to buy towels for the hotel. If she needs the same number of each towel, what is the smallest number of packs for each type of towel that she should buy?

A. 2 packs of hand towels and 2 packs of bath towels

B. 2 packs of hand towels and 3 packs of bath towels

C. 3 packs of hand towels and 4 packs of bath towels

D. 4 packs of hand towels and 3 packs of bath towels

Difficulty: Medium

16. Brandon prepares for a party and he puts food onto plates. The chocolate cake is cut into 12 pieces and pizza is cut into 18 pieces. If he wants to prepare identical plates without having any food left over, what is the greatest number of plates he can prepare?

E. 9   F. 6   G. 4   H. 2

Difficulty: Medium

17. Rick decides to buy candy bars and apples to share with his friends. Candy bars are sold in bags of 15 and apples are sold in packs of 5. What is the least number of packages of apples he needs to buy if he wants to have the same number of candy bars and apples to share with his friends?

Difficulty: Medium

18. A racing car completes one lap in 24 seconds. The other racing car completes the same lap in 18 seconds. If they start at the same time, after how many seconds will they be side by side again?

Difficulty: Medium

19. Ryan needs to ship 16 rock music CDs, 18 classic music CDs, and 28 pop music CDs. He can pack only one type of CD in each box and he must pack the same number of CDs in each box. What is the greatest number of CDs Ryan can pack in each box?

Difficulty: Hard

20. Mei decided to throw a birthday party and went to the store to buy party cups and plates. There are 4 plates in each package and 6 cups in each package. What is the least number of packages of each she needs to buy if she wants to have the same number of each for the party?

Difficulty: Medium

Answer Explanation

1. Since 39 and 117 are both multiples of 13, find the least common multiple of 39 and 117.
Multiples of 39: 39, 78, 117, 156...
Multiples of 117: 117, 234, 351, 468...
The least common multiple of 13, 39, and 117 is 117.
The correct answer is C.

2. The least common multiple for all the numbers in the list given is 24 because it is the smallest number that can be evenly divided by 6 and 8. For x and y, we don't have any exponents in the list, so the least common multiple for the entire list would be $24xy$.
The correct answer is G.

3. First, find LCM of 3 and 4. Multiples of 3: 3, 6, 9, 12, 15...
Multiples of 4: 4, 8, 12...
The least common multiple is 12.
Therefore, the next date on which she has both dance and cooking lessons is April 17.
The correct answer is D.

4. Find LCM of 3 and 11:
Multiples of 3: 3, 6, 9, 12, 15, 18, 21, 24, 27, 30, 33, 36, 39, 42, 45, 48, 51, 54, 57, 60, 63, 636...
Multiples of 11: 11, 22, 33, 44, 55, 66
The least common multiple of 3 and 11 is 33. The second smallest common multiple of 3 and 11 is 66.

Therefore, the possible number is 66.
The correct answer is H.

5. Find LCM of 17 and 3:
Multiples of 17: 17, 34, 51...
Multiples of 3: 3, 6, 9, 12, 15, 18, 21, 24, 27, 30, 33, 36, 39, 42, 45, 48, 51...
So the least common multiple of 17 and 3 is 51. The smallest possible number that Tommy could be thinking of is 51.
The correct answer is B.

6. The least common multiple for all the numbers in the list is 45 because it is the smallest number that can be evenly divided by 9 and 15. For a and b, we don't have any exponents in the list, so the least common multiple for the entire list would be $45ab$.
The correct answer is F.

7. List the multiples of 5 and the multiples of 6. Multiples of 5: 5, 10, 15, 20, 25, 30...
Multiples of 6: 6, 12, 18, 24, 30...
The least common multiple of 5 and 6 is 30.
Jill should buy 30 pens and 30 notebooks. Since pens come in a package of 6 and notebooks come in a package of 5, she should buy $\frac{30}{6} = 5$ packages of pens and $\frac{30}{5} = 6$ packages of notebooks.
The correct answer is D.

Video Explanations
at argoprep.com/shsat

8. First, list the multiples of 6 and multiples of 4. Multiples of 6: 6, 12, 18, 24, 30, 36, 42, 48, 54, 60.

Multiples of 4: 4, 8, 12, 16, 20, 24, 28, 32, 36, 40, 44, 48, 52, 56, 60.

The common multiples of 6 and 4 are 12, 24, 36, 48, and 60. So there are 5 common multiples of 6 and 4. Therefore, two bulbs will blink at the same time 5 times in 60 seconds.

The correct answer is H.

---

9. Factors of 256: 1, 2, 4, 8, 16, 32, 64, 128, 256.

Factors of 644: 1, 2, 4, 7, 14, 23, 28, 46, 92, 161, 322, 644.

The greatest common factor of 256 and 644 is 4.

Therefore, the greatest possible length of the wire pieces is 4 cm.

The correct answer is A.

---

10. To solve the problem you need to find the factors of 12, 15 and 9 and find their greatest common factor.

Factors of 12: 1, 2, 3, 4, 6, 12.

Factors of 15: 1, 3, 5, 15.

Factors of 9: 1, 3, 9.

The greatest common factor is 3.

Megan can put 3 pieces of fruit in each basket.

The correct answer is F.

---

11. Identify the multiples of 3: 3, 6, 9, 12, 15, 18, 21, 24...

Identify the multiples of 7: 7, 14, 21, 28... The least common multiple of 3 and 7 is 21.

So Jolly and Jane were given a ribbon with a length of at least 21 meters.

The correct answer is C.

---

12. Factors of 28: 1, 2, 4, 7, 14, 28.

Factors of 35: 1, 5, 7, 35.

The greatest common factor of 28 and 35 is 7.

The largest possible number of sweets in each bag is 7.

The correct answer is G.

---

13. To solve this problem, find the factors of 54 and 63. Factors of 54: 1, 2, 3, 6, 9, 18, 27, 54.

Factors of 63: 1, 3, 7, 9, 21, 63.

The greatest common factor for 54 and 63 is 9.

The greatest number of students that can be arranged in a row is 9.

The correct answer is C.

14. The question asks us what is the smallest number of packs of balloons and whistles Josie must buy, so there are no items left over.

List the multiples of 4: 4, 8, 12, 16, 20, 24

List the multiples of 5: 5, 10, 15, 20, 25

The least common multiple of 4 and 5 is 20, therefore Josie must buy 20 packs of balloons and whistles.

The correct answer is G.

---

15. Find LCM of 12 and 16 to solve this problem. Multiples of 12: 12, 24, 36, 48...

Multiples of 16: 16, 32, 48...

The least common multiple of 12 and 16 is 48.

Therefore, Anna needs to buy 4 packs of hand towels and 3 packs of bath towels.

The correct answer is D.

---

16. Find GCF:

Factors of 12: 1, 2, 3, 4, 6, 12. Factors of 18: 1, 2, 3, 6, 9, 18.

Greatest common factor of 12 and 18 is 6.

Therefore, Brandon has to prepare 6 food plates.

The correct answer is F.

---

17. Identify the multiples of 15: 15, 30, 45, 60...

Identify the multiples of 5: 5, 10, 15, 20... The least common multiple is 15.

Therefore, he needs to buy one package of candy bar and $\frac{15}{5}$ = **3 packages of apples**.

---

18. Multiples of 24: 24, 48, 72, 96... Multiples of 18: 18, 36, 54, 72...

The least common multiple of 24 and 18 is 72.

The two cars will be side by side again after **72 seconds**.

---

19. First, we need to list the factors for 16, 18, and 28 separately.

Factors of 16: 1, 2, 4, 8, 16.

Factors of 18: 1, 2, 6, 18.

Factors of 28: 1, 2, 4, 7, 14, 28. The greatest common factor is 2.

Ryan should pack 2 CDs in each box.

---

20. First, identify the lists of the multiples 4 and 6 separately. Multiples of 4: 4, 8, 12, 16, 20... Multiples of 6: 6, 12, 18, 24...

The least common multiple of 4 and 6 is 12.

Mei needs to buy 12 cups and 12 plates. Therefore, she should buy **3 packages of cups and 2 packages of plates** to have the same number of each for the party.

Video Explanations
at argoprep.com/shsat

33

1. Joanna bought a bottle of medicine, which holds 37 ml. How many spoonfuls will she get out of it if each spoon holds 6 ml?

   A. 4   C. 6
   B. 5   D. 9

   Difficulty: Easy

2. There are 25 friends planning to go to the football game in cars. Seven friends can fit in each car. How many cars are needed?

   E. 3   G. 5
   F. 4   H. 7

   Difficulty: Medium

3. Using the approximation 2.54 centimeters = 1 inch, how many centimeters are in 13 inches?

   A. 13 cm
   B. 25.4 cm
   C. 33.02 cm
   D. 35.76 cm

   Difficulty: Medium

4. Jessica bought 6 packs of candy for $2.39 each. What was the total cost of the purchase? Round the final answer to the nearest tenth.

   E. $2.39
   F. $7.2
   G. $14.3
   H. $14.4

   Difficulty: Medium

5. There were 10,746 fans at a local football game. Round the number of people to the nearest hundred.

   A. 10,700   C. 10,800
   B. 10,750   D. 11,000

   Difficulty: Medium

6. In a scaled diagram, 1 centimeter represents 50 meters. How many centimeters represent 15 meters?

   E. 0.03 cm   G. 1.3 cm
   F. 0.3 cm   H. 3.3 cm

   Difficulty: Medium

7. A lunch for 5 people costs $55.65. What is the cost of lunch per person?

   A. $27.83
   B. $18.55
   C. $11.13
   D. $9.28

   Difficulty: Medium

8. Each box can hold 27 books. How many boxes are needed to hold 90 books?

   E. 2
   F. 3
   G. 4
   H. 5

   Difficulty: Medium

9. A metal cone must have a length of 0.07 cm, with an allowable error of 1.5 percent. What is the greatest allowable length of the metal cone?

   A. 0.06895 cm
   B. 0.07 cm
   C. 0.0007 cm
   D. 0.07105 cm

   Difficulty: Hard

10. Jennifer needs 4 eggs to bake a pancake. How many pancakes can she bake if she has 17 eggs?

    E. 4   G. 2
    F. 3   H. 1

    Difficulty: Medium

Video Explanations
at argoprep.com/shsat

11. A football team has 11 players. What is the maximum number of teams that can be formed from 75 players?

A. 7
C. 5
B. 6
D. 3

Difficulty: Medium

12. There are 853 students in a high school. How many groups of 35 students can be made?

E. 25
G. 23
F. 24
H. 21

Difficulty: Medium

13. One lemon costs $0.89 and one apple costs $0.45. Nick bought 6 lemons and 7 apples. How much did Nick pay for his purchase?

A. $17.42
B. $8.93
C. $8.50
D. $8.49

Difficulty: Medium

14. After being on a diet, Mila lost 76 ounces of weight. How much did she lose in pounds if there are 16 ounces in one pound?

E. 5.20
G. 4.50
F. 4.75
H. 3.80

Difficulty: Medium

15. A group of 18 friends is going on a trip and they decided to hire a tour guide to explore a certain city. The cost of hiring a tour guide for a whole day is $265. If they decide to split the cost evenly, how much did each friend pay for the tour guide?

A. $13.50
C. $14.72
B. $14.35
D. $15.24

Difficulty: Medium

16.

$$5.47 + 1.12(2.50 - 1.78) - (0.89 - 1.43)$$

What is the value of the expression above? Round all calculations to the hundredths place.

E. 5.68
G. 6.82
F. 6.22
H. 8.60

Difficulty: Hard

17.

$$\frac{a}{b} = \frac{y}{x}$$

What is the value of b if $a = 3.2$, $y = 1.6$, and $x = 0.2$?

Difficulty: Hard

18. The height of a ball can be estimated by the following equation

$$h(t) = 8t^2 + 4t + 125$$

where t is time, in seconds, after the ball was thrown and $h(t)$ is the corresponding height, in meters. What is the height at $t = 2.3$ seconds?

Difficulty: Medium

19.

$$3a^2 - 2a + 7 - \frac{2}{4a^2}$$

If $a = 1.2$, what is the value of the expression above? Round your answer to the nearest hundredths place.

Difficulty: Hard

20. One row in a cinema can hold 55 people. If there are 325 people that came to watch the new film, what is the minimum number of rows needed for each person to have a seat?

Difficulty: Medium

1. Divide the total amount of medicine in the bottle, 37 ml, by the amount each spoon can hold, 6 ml to get the number of spoonfuls that Joanna can get from the bottle. $\frac{37}{6} = 6.1667$ There are a total of 6 spoonfuls that Joanna can get from the bottle.
   The correct answer is C.

2. Multiples of 7 are 7, 14, 21, 28...
   Therefore, there are 3 cars needed to take 21 friends and the fourth car to take 25 – 21 = 4 friends. The total number of cars needed is 4.
   The correct answer is F.

3. To find the number of centimeters in 13 inches, multiply the number of centimeters that corresponds to 1 inch by 13 inches. Therefore, $2.54 \times 13 = 33.02$.
   There are 33.02 centimeters in 13 inches.
   The correct answer is C.

4. To find the total cost, multiply the price of one pack of candy by the number of packs: $2.39 \times 6 = \$14.34 \approx \$14.3$.
   The correct answer is G.

5. To solve this problem, identify which digit represents hundreds. The number directly to the right of the hundreds place is the tens place, which has a 4 in it. The number 4 is less than 5, meaning the number in the hundreds place remains a 7 and is not rounded up. You are rounding the entire number down. So 10,746 rounded to the nearest hundred is 10,700.

6. Suppose x is the number of centimeters that represents 15 meters on a scaled diagram.
   $\frac{1}{50} = \frac{x}{15}$, $x = \frac{15 \times 1}{50} = 0.3$ cm .
   The correct answer is F.

7. To find the cost of lunch for one person, divide the total cost of the lunch by the number of people: $55.65 \div 5 = \$11.13$.
   The correct answer is C.

8. The total number of boxes needed to hold 90 books can be found by dividing the number of boxes by the number books that one box can hold. The number of boxes is $\frac{90}{27} = 3.3$ boxes. 3 boxes can hold a maximum $3 \times 27 = 81$ books so

the next 9 books can be put into the fourth box. Therefore, four boxes are needed.
The correct answer is G.

9. 1.5 percent = 0.015
   First, find the greatest possible error in cm:
   $0.07 \times 0.015 = 0.00105$ cm. The greatest allowable length will be equal to 0.07 plus error in cm, which equals 0.00105 cm. The greatest allowable length is
   $0.07 + 0.00105 = 0.07105$ cm.
   The correct answer is D.

10. To find the number of pancakes that Jennifer can bake, divide the number of eggs she has by the number of eggs needed to bake one pancake.
    $\frac{17}{4} = 4.25$ pancakes. Therefore, she has enough eggs for 4 pancakes.
    The correct answer is E.

11. The maximum number of teams can be found by dividing the total number of players by the number of players on one team.
    $\frac{75}{11} = 6.8$
    Therefore, the maximum number of football teams that can be formed from 75 players is 6.
    The correct answer is B.

12. The possible number of groups formed can be estimated by dividing the total number of students in high school by the number of students in one group.
    $\frac{853}{35} = 24.4$
    Therefore, the maximum possible number of groups for 35 students is 24.
    The correct answer is F.

13. Find the total cost of 6 lemons: $0.89 \times 6 = \$5.34$. Then find the total cost of 7 apples: $0.45 \times 7 = \$3.15$.
    The total cost that Nick paid for 6 lemons and 7 apples is $5.34 + \$3.15 = \$8.49$.
    The correct answer is D.

Video Explanations
at argoprep.com/shsat

ARGOPREP – Arithmetic – Rounding – Answer Explanation

14. Suppose x is the number of pounds that Mila lost. Since there are 16 ounces in one pound, we can set up the equation $16x = 76$.

Solve for x: $\frac{76}{16} = 4.75$ pounds.

The correct answer is F.

15. Since the total cost of hiring a tour guide is $265 and there are 18 friends, the price that each friend has to pay is

$$\frac{\$265}{18} = \$14.72 .$$

Each of the friends has to pay $14.72.

The correct answer is C.

16. Perform the necessary operations to solve the problem given using PEMDAS.
$$5.47 + 1.12(0.72) - (-0.54)$$
$$5.47 + 1.12(0.72) - (-0.54) = 5.47 + 0.81 + 0.54$$
$$5.47 + 0.81 + 0.54 = 6.82$$

The correct answer is G.

17. First, rewrite the equation given for b:
$$by = ax$$
$$b = \frac{ax}{y}$$

Now, substitute values of a, y, and x into the equation above in order to solve for b:
$$b = \frac{3.2 \times 0.2}{1.6} = \frac{0.64}{1.6} = 0.4$$

The answer is $b = 0.4$.

18. To find the height at $t = 2.3$, substitute 2.3 into the equation and calculate $h(2.3)$.
$$h(2.3) = 8(2.3)^2 + 4(2.3) + 125 = 8(5.29) + 9.2 + 125 =$$
$$42.32 + 9.2 + 125 = \textbf{176.52 meters}.$$

19. Substitute the value of a into the expression and solve it:
$$3(1.2)^2 - 2(1.2) + 7 - \frac{2}{4(1.2)^2} =$$
$$3(1.44) - 2.4 + 7 - \frac{2}{4(1.44)} =$$
$$4.32 - 2.4 + 7 - \frac{2}{5.76} =$$
$$4.32 - 2.4 + 7 - 0.35 = \textbf{8.57}$$

20. To find the minimum number of rows needed, divide the total number of people by the number of people that can sit in one row.

$$\text{So } \frac{325}{55} = 5.91 \text{ rows}.$$

Therefore, **6 rows** are needed for 325 people.

Video Explanations
at argoprep.com/shsat

1. What is the value of the following expression?

$$\frac{2}{3} + \frac{1}{6} - \frac{3}{4} + \frac{1}{12}$$

A. 0

C. $\frac{1}{6}$

B. $\frac{1}{12}$

D. $\frac{1}{4}$

Difficulty: Medium

2. If $\frac{a}{25} = 5b$, what is the value of b when $a = 1$?

E. $\frac{1}{5}$

G. $\frac{1}{50}$

F. $\frac{1}{25}$

H. $\frac{1}{125}$

Difficulty: Medium

3. Maria has a ribbon with a length of $4\frac{2}{7}$ m. If she wants to cut it into 5 equal pieces, what would be the length of a single piece?

A. $\frac{150}{7}$ m

C. $\frac{6}{7}$ m

B. $\frac{30}{7}$ m

D. $\frac{2}{7}$ m

Difficulty: Medium

4. On a number line, $AB = 3\frac{2}{3}$. The position of point B is $\frac{2}{5}$. What is the position of point A ?

E. $2\frac{13}{15}$

G. $4\frac{1}{15}$

F. $3\frac{1}{2}$

H. $4\frac{3}{8}$

Difficulty: Hard

5.

$$\frac{7}{12} = \frac{3x}{9}$$

In the equation above, what is the value of x?

A. $\frac{4}{7}$

C. $1\frac{3}{4}$

B. $\frac{4}{21}$

D. $5\frac{1}{4}$

Difficulty: Medium

6. Tommy ate $\frac{5}{12}$ of pizza, Johnny ate $\frac{1}{4}$ of the pizza, and Mike ate $\frac{1}{12}$ of the same pizza. How much of the pizza did they eat together?

E. $\frac{5}{12}$ F. $\frac{3}{4}$ G. $\frac{2}{3}$ H. $\frac{5}{6}$

Difficulty: Medium

7. On Tuesday, Emily spent $2\frac{2}{5}$ hours studying and on Friday she studied $1\frac{3}{5}$ hours more than on Tuesday. How many hours did she spend studying on Tuesday and Friday?

A. $2\frac{2}{5}$

C. 4

B. $3\frac{21}{25}$

D. $6\frac{2}{5}$

Difficulty: Hard

8. Jane bought $5\frac{3}{5}$ boxes of raspberries and $2\frac{1}{4}$ boxes of strawberries. How many more boxes of raspberries did Jane buy?

E. $2\frac{1}{4}$

G. $3\frac{7}{20}$

F. $2\frac{7}{20}$

H. $7\frac{17}{20}$

Difficulty: Medium

▶ **Video Explanations**
at argoprep.com/shsat

9. A zoo is open for $10\frac{1}{2}$ hours every day. There are two security guards on duty at a time and each shift is $3\frac{1}{2}$ hours. How many shifts are there per day?

   A. 1 shift   **C.** 3 shifts
   B. 2 shifts   **D.** 4 shifts

   Difficulty: Hard

10. Tina spends $\frac{5}{6}$ of an hour exercising every day. Today, she has already exercised for $\frac{3}{5}$ of an hour. How much more time should she spend exercising today in order to reach her daily goal?

    E. 5 minutes   **G.** 12 minutes
    F. 10 minutes   **H.** 14 minutes

    Difficulty: Hard

11. One week Jim went to his fitness club on Tuesday, Thursday, and Saturday. On Tuesday, he jogged on the treadmill for $\frac{2}{5}$ hour and stretched for $\frac{1}{4}$ hour. On Thursday, he lifted weights for $\frac{2}{3}$ hour and then stretched for $\frac{1}{5}$ hour. On Saturday, he rode his bike for $3\frac{2}{5}$ hours. How many hours did he spend stretching and riding his bike at his fitness club that week?

    A. $\frac{4}{5}$

    B. $2\frac{3}{5}$

    C. $3\frac{2}{5}$

    D. $3\frac{17}{20}$

    Difficulty: Hard

12. Jonathan worked on his math homework for $2\frac{2}{3}$ hours. He spent $\frac{3}{4}$ of this time practicing a new solving technique. How many hours did Jonathan spend practicing a new solving technique?

    E. $2\frac{1}{3}$ **G.** $1\frac{2}{3}$

    F. 2   **H.** $\frac{3}{4}$

    Difficulty: Hard

13. Joanna's daughter is $\frac{2}{3}$ of a year old and Julia's son is $\frac{1}{6}$ of a year younger than Joanna's daughter. How old is Julia's son?

    A. $\frac{1}{3}$ of a year   **C.** $\frac{3}{4}$ of a year

    B. $\frac{1}{2}$ of a year   **D.** $\frac{2}{5}$ of a year

    Difficulty: Hard

14. Connie needs $2\frac{1}{3}$ cups of sugar for baking one chocolate cake. What is the greatest number of cakes that can be baked from $6\frac{1}{2}$ cups of sugar?

    E. 1 cake   **G.** 3 cakes
    F. 2 cakes   **H.** 4 cakes

    Difficulty: Hard

15. What is the value of the expression below?

    $$2\frac{1}{2} - 1\frac{1}{2}\left(\frac{2}{3} + 1\frac{1}{2}\right)$$

    A. $-1\frac{1}{3}$ **C.** $2\frac{1}{4}$

    B. $-\frac{3}{4}$ **D.** $5\frac{3}{4}$

    Difficulty: Hard

Video Explanations
at argoprep.com/shsat

16. Two pizzas were cut into 6 pieces each. James ate $\frac{1}{3}$ of the chicken pizza and $\frac{2}{3}$ of the mushroom pizza. How many pieces of pizza did he eat altogether?

E. 2   G. 5
F. 4   H. 6

Difficulty: Medium

17. On Monday, Maria ran $3\frac{2}{3}$ of a mile in the morning and $2\frac{3}{4}$ of a mile in the evening. What was the total distance she ran on Monday?

 6.9

Difficulty: Medium

18. Kate evenly divided $6\frac{3}{4}$ liters of orange juice between 3 bottles. What amount of juice does each bottle contain?

Difficulty: Medium

19.

$$2\frac{3}{5} + \frac{2}{3}\left(\frac{5}{6} \div \frac{1}{3}\right) - 3\frac{4}{5}$$

Find the value of the expression above.

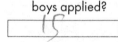

Difficulty: Hard

20. 60 students applied for the College Algebra class. Three-fourths of them were girls. What number of boys applied?

15

Difficulty: Medium

Answer Explanation

1. First, find a common denominator for all fractions. That would be the least possible number divisible by 3, 6, 4, and 12. The number is 12. For each fraction, divide the common denominator by the fraction's own denominator and multiply the corresponding numerator by the quotient.

Therefore, we have:

$$\frac{2}{3} + \frac{1}{6} - \frac{3}{4} + \frac{1}{12} = \frac{4(2)+2(1)-3(3)+1}{12} = \frac{8+2-9+1}{12} = \frac{2}{12}$$
$$= \frac{1}{6}$$

The correct answer is C.

2. Substitute $a = 1$ into the original equation and solve for b:

$$\frac{1}{25} = 5b, \quad b = \frac{1}{25} \div 5 = \frac{1}{25} \times \frac{1}{5} = \frac{1}{125}$$

The correct answer is H.

3. To find the length of a single piece of ribbon, divide the original length of the ribbon by the number of pieces.

First, convert $4\frac{2}{7}$ from a mixed number to an improper fraction.

$$4\frac{2}{7} = \frac{30}{7}$$

Divide by 5: $\frac{30}{7} \div 5 = \frac{30}{7} \times \frac{1}{5} = \frac{30}{35} = \frac{6}{7}$ m

The correct answer is C.

4. To find the position of the point A, add $\frac{2}{5}$ to $3\frac{2}{3}$.

$$3\frac{2}{3} + \frac{2}{5} = \frac{11}{3} + \frac{2}{5}$$

The common denominator for 3 and 5 is 15.

Therefore, $\frac{11}{3} + \frac{2}{5} = \frac{5(11)+3(2)}{15} = \frac{61}{15} = 4\frac{1}{15}$

The position of the point A is $4\frac{1}{15}$.

The correct answer is G.

5. First, solve the equation given for $3x$:

$$3x = \frac{7 \times 9}{12} = \frac{7 \times 3}{4} = \frac{21}{4}$$

Then, solve the resulting equation for x:

$$x = \frac{21}{4} \div 3 = \frac{21}{4} \times \frac{1}{3} = \frac{21 \times 1}{4 \times 3} = \frac{7}{4} = 1\frac{3}{4}$$

The correct answer is C.

Video Explanations
at argoprep.com/shsat

ARGOPREP SHSAT — Arithmetic – Fractions – Answer Explanation

6. To find the amount of pizza the three friends ate together, add the amount that each of them ate.

Therefore: $\frac{5}{12}+\frac{1}{4}+\frac{1}{12}$

The common denominator is 12 so we have

$$\frac{5}{12}+\frac{1}{4}+\frac{1}{12}=\frac{5+3(1)+1}{12}=\frac{9}{12}=\frac{3}{4}$$

They ate $\frac{3}{4}$ of the whole pizza.

The correct answer is F.

7. First, find the time Emily spent studying on Friday: $2\frac{2}{5}+1\frac{3}{5}$
Convert both mixed numbers to improper fractions and add them:

$$2\frac{2}{5}+1\frac{3}{5}=\frac{12}{5}+\frac{8}{5}=\frac{20}{5}=4\,\text{hours}$$

Emily spent 4 hours studying on Friday.

Now, find the total time she spent studying on Tuesday and Friday.

$$2\frac{2}{5}+4=\frac{12}{5}+4=\frac{12+20}{5}=\frac{32}{5}=6\frac{2}{5}\,\text{hours}$$

The correct answer is D.

8. Subtract $2\frac{1}{4}$ from $5\frac{3}{5}$ to find how many more boxes of raspberries Jane bought.

First, convert $2\frac{1}{4}$ and $5\frac{3}{5}$ to improper fractions.

$$2\frac{1}{4}=\frac{9}{4}$$
$$5\frac{3}{5}=\frac{28}{5}$$

Then, perform subtraction: $\frac{28}{5}-\frac{9}{4}$

The least common denominator of 5 and 4 is 20.

$$\frac{28}{5}-\frac{9}{4}=\frac{4(28)-5(9)}{20}=\frac{112-45}{20}=\frac{67}{20}=3\frac{7}{20}$$

Jane bought $3\frac{7}{20}$ more boxes of raspberries.

The correct answer is G.

9. Since a zoo is open for $10\frac{1}{2}$ hours every day and each shift is $3\frac{1}{2}$ hours, the number of shifts can be found by dividing the total number of hours by the number of hours in one shift.

Convert $10\frac{1}{2}$ and $3\frac{1}{2}$ to improper fractions.

$$10\frac{1}{2}=\frac{21}{2}\text{ and }3\frac{1}{2}=\frac{7}{2}$$

Then, $\frac{21}{2}\div\frac{7}{2}=\frac{21}{2}\times\frac{2}{7}$

Cancel 2 out and the result is $\frac{21}{7}=3$ shifts .
There are 3 shifts per day.

The correct answer is C.

10. Since she has already spent $\frac{3}{5}$ of an hour exercising today, she still needs to exercise for $\frac{5}{6}-\frac{3}{5}=\frac{25-18}{30}=\frac{7}{30}$ of an hour, which is equal to $\frac{7}{30}\times60$ minutes $=14$ min .

The correct answer is H.

11. The total time Jim spent stretching on two days is $\frac{1}{4}+\frac{1}{5}=\frac{5+4}{20}=\frac{9}{20}$ of an hour.

Convert the time he spent riding on his bike to an improper fraction:

$$3\frac{2}{5}=\frac{17}{5}$$

Add $\frac{17}{5}$ and $\frac{9}{20}$ together to find the total time he spent stretching and riding his bike that week:

$$\frac{17}{5}+\frac{9}{20}=\frac{4(17)+9}{20}=\frac{68+9}{20}=\frac{77}{20}=3\frac{17}{20}\,\text{hours.}$$

The correct answer is D.

12. To solve this problem, multiply the total time that Jonathan worked on his homework by the time that he spent practicing the new problem solving technique.

First, convert $2\frac{2}{3}$ to an improper fraction: $2\frac{2}{3}=\frac{8}{3}$.

$$\frac{8}{3}\times\frac{3}{4}=2\,\text{hours}$$

Jonathan spent 2 hours practicing the new solving technique.

The correct answer is F.

13. To find the age of the son, divide Joanna's daughter's age by $\frac{1}{6}$.

$$\frac{2}{3}-\frac{1}{6}=\frac{2(2)-1}{6}=\frac{3}{6}=\frac{1}{2}\text{ of a year.}$$

Julia's son age is $\frac{1}{2}$ of a year.

The correct answer is B.

Video Explanations
at argoprep.com/shsat

14. Divide the total amount of sugar by the amount of sugar needed to bake one cake.

To do that, convert each mixed number into an improper fraction.

$$6\frac{1}{2} = \frac{13}{2}$$

$$2\frac{1}{3} = \frac{7}{3}$$

Divide: $\frac{13}{2} \div \frac{7}{3} = \frac{13}{2} \times \frac{3}{7} = \frac{39}{14} = 2\frac{11}{14}$

Therefore, the least number of cakes that Connie can bake from $6\frac{1}{2}$ cups of sugar is 2.

The correct answer is F.

---

15. First, perform an operation within the parentheses:

$$\frac{2}{3} + 1\frac{1}{2} = \frac{2}{3} + \frac{3}{2} = \frac{4+9}{6} = \frac{13}{6}$$

Multiply the result of the previous step by $-1\frac{1}{2}$:

$$-1\frac{1}{2} \times \frac{13}{6} = -\frac{3}{2} \times \frac{13}{6} = -\frac{13}{4}$$

Then, the last step:

$$2\frac{1}{2} - \frac{13}{4} = \frac{5}{2} - \frac{13}{4} = \frac{10-13}{4} = -\frac{3}{4}$$

The correct answer is B.

---

16. Since each pizza was cut into 6 pieces, find the number of pieces of each pizza that he ate by multiplying 6 by the proportion of pizza that was eaten.

Number of pieces of chicken pizza that James ate: $6 \times \frac{1}{3} = 2$.

Number of pieces of mushroom pizza that James ate: $6 \times \frac{2}{3} = 4$.

Total number of pieces of pizza that was eaten is $2 + 4 = 6$.

The correct answer is H.

---

17. Add two values together to find the total distance that Maria ran on that day.

$$3\frac{2}{3} + 2\frac{3}{4} = \frac{11}{3} + \frac{11}{4} = \frac{44+33}{12} = \frac{77}{12} = 6\frac{5}{12}$$ of a mile.

Maria ran $6\frac{5}{12}$ of a mile on that day.

---

18. To find the amount that each bottle contains, divide the total amount of juice by the number of bottles:

$$6\frac{3}{4} \div 3 = \frac{27}{4} \times \frac{1}{3} = \frac{9}{4} = 2\frac{1}{4}$$ liters.

Each of the bottles contains $2\frac{1}{4}$ liters of orange juice.

19.

$$\frac{5}{6} \div \frac{1}{3} = \frac{5}{6} \times 3 = \frac{5}{2}$$

Multiply the result of the previous step by $\frac{2}{3}$:

$$\frac{2}{3} \times \frac{5}{2} = \frac{5}{3}$$

Add:

$$2\frac{3}{5} + \frac{5}{3} = \frac{13}{5} + \frac{5}{3} = \frac{3(13)+5(5)}{15} = \frac{39+25}{15} = \frac{64}{15}$$

Subtract:

$$\frac{64}{15} - 3\frac{4}{5} = \frac{64}{15} - \frac{19}{5} = \frac{64-3(19)}{15} = \frac{64-57}{15} = \frac{7}{15}$$

$$2\frac{3}{5} + \frac{2}{3}\left(\frac{5}{6} \div \frac{1}{3}\right) - 3\frac{4}{5} = \mathbf{\frac{7}{15}}$$

---

20. Since $\frac{3}{4}$ of the applicants were girls, then the proportion of boys is $4 - \frac{3}{4} = \frac{1}{4}$.

The number of boys that applied was: $\frac{1}{4} \times 60 = 15$.

There were **15** boys that applied for the College Algebra class.

▶ **Video Explanations**
at argoprep.com/shsat

1. Peter has 0.75 liters of orange juice and Karen has 1.25 liters of orange juice. If they sold a fifth of what they have together, what is the amount of juice left over?

   A. 0.80
   B. 0.90
   C. 1.49
   D. 1.60

   Difficulty: Medium

2. In a zoo, a baby gorilla weighs 2.60 kg. If its weight increases at a rate of 4 kg/month, what will its weight be after 2 years?

   E. 91.6 kg
   F. 93.7 kg
   G. 98.6 kg
   H. 100.15 kg

   Difficulty: Medium

3. Emily buys 3.5 meters of fabric A, which costs $6.20/meter and 2 meters of fabric B, which costs $5.50/meter. How much does she have to pay for the two fabrics?

   A. $32.7   C. $49.7
   B. $40.5   D. $64.8

   Difficulty: Medium

4. A pizza is divided between 3 people: Michelle, Steven, and David. If Michelle ate $\frac{1}{4}$ of the pizza, Steven ate two times the amount that Michelle ate, and David ate $\frac{2}{3}$ the amount Michelle ate, how much pizza was left over? Write the final answer as a decimal rounded to the nearest hundredth.

   E. 0.05   G. 0.13
   F. 0.08   H. 0.17

   Difficulty: Medium

5. What is the value of the following expression rounded to the nearest hundredth?

   $$\frac{3}{2}\left(\frac{1}{2}+\frac{2}{3}\right)-\frac{2}{5}\left(\frac{2}{3}-\frac{1}{3}\right)$$

   A. 0.97
   B. 1.62
   C. 1.93
   D. 2.78

   Difficulty: Medium

6. Twelve cookies were split between four students. Michael ate $\frac{1}{4}$ of the cookies, Steven ate $\frac{1}{3}$ of the cookies and Joann ate $\frac{1}{4}$ of the cookies. How many cookies did the fourth student eat?

   E. 1   F. 2   G. 3   H. 4

   Difficulty: Medium

7. The chicken bought by Angel is 2.5 times as heavy as the chicken bought by Charles. If the chicken bought by Charles has a mass of 1.8 kg, what is the mass of the chicken bought by Angel?

   A. 3.7
   B. 4.5
   C. 4.7
   D. 6.8

   Difficulty: Medium

8. Laura bought 10.2 kg of spices. She poured the spices equally into 6 bottles. There was 0.9 kg of spices left over. What was the mass of the spices in one bottle?

   E. 1.55 kg   G. 3.80 kg
   F. 2.46 kg   H. 4.20 kg

   Difficulty: Medium

Video Explanations
at argoprep.com/shsat

9. A box contains 10 tins of powdered milk. There is 0.45 kg of powdered milk in each tin. What is the total mass of powdered milk in four boxes?

A. 10   C. 15
B. 12   D. 18

Difficulty: Medium

10. What is the value of the following expression? Round your answer to the nearest thousandth.

$$2(1+0.2)-0.25 \times \frac{1}{2}$$

E. 1.893   G. 3.800
F. 2.275   H. 4.290

Difficulty: Medium

11. Karen goes to school every morning. It takes her 0.25 hours to walk from her house to the bus station. When she gets to the station, she sits down for 10 minutes waiting for the bus. It takes her 0.3 hours to get to the school by bus. How many minutes does it take for Karen to go from her house to the school?

A. 20 minutes   C. 43 minutes
B. 38 minutes   D. 50 minutes

Difficulty: Hard

12. A manufacturing company produced 20,000 transistors in 2009. In 2010, the production decreased by $\frac{1}{8}$. In 2011, the production increased by $\frac{1}{4}$ of the production amount in 2010. How many transistors did the company produce in 2011?

E. 21,875   G. 28,900
F. 23,780   H. 30,600

Difficulty: Hard

13. What is the value of the expression?

$$2\left(1+\frac{1}{5}\right)+1.5(1+3(1-0.7))-0.25$$

A. 2   B. 5   C. 9   D. 11

Difficulty: Medium

14. A certain box contains 24 pencils. If $\frac{1}{6}$ of the pencils were given to students in a classroom and $\frac{3}{8}$ of the pencils given to teachers, how many pencils remain in the box?

E. 8   F. 10   G. 11   H. 14

Difficulty: Medium

15. What is the value of the expression below?

$$\frac{\frac{2}{5}+\frac{3}{4}\left(\frac{1}{2}+0.3\right)}{\frac{1}{2}(2-1.5)}$$

A. 2   B. 3   C. 4   D. 5

Difficulty: Hard

16. John and Lauren are counting the months until they get a vacation from their jobs. John has to wait $\frac{3}{4}$ of the year and Lauren has to wait $\frac{1}{3}$ of the year. How many months longer does John have to wait than Lauren?

E. 3   F. 5   G. 7   H. 9

Difficulty: Easy

17. A classroom has 32 students. Half of them are boys. $\frac{1}{4}$ of the boys and $\frac{3}{8}$ of the girls take Spanish classes. How many students take Spanish class?

Difficulty: Medium

Video Explanations
at argoprep.com/shsat

44

18. What is the value of the following expression?

$$\frac{\frac{5}{3}+\frac{3}{4}\left(\frac{1}{5}+\frac{1}{3}\right)}{0.2\left(8-\frac{1}{2}\right)+\frac{3}{4}}$$

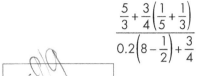

Difficulty: Hard

19. There are 60 people at the Chemical and Petroleum Engineering Conference. Out of 60 people, $\frac{1}{3}$ are chemical engineers and $\frac{2}{3}$ are petroleum engineers. $\frac{3}{4}$ of chemical engineers are women and $\frac{1}{2}$ of petroleum engineers are women. How many women are there in the conference?

A. 15   C. 25
B. 18   D. 35

Difficulty: Hard

20. According to a survey, it was determined that $\frac{1}{3}$ of the population surveyed is allergic to canned food, $\frac{3}{5}$ of the population surveyed is allergic to pets, and 30 people are allergic to antibiotics. If the number of people allergic to antibiotics represents $\frac{1}{5}$ of the total number of people surveyed, what is the number of people allergic to pets?

Difficulty: Hard

Answer Explanation

1. First, find the total amount of juice that both Peter and Karen have.

$$0.75 + 1.25 = 2 \text{ liters}$$

They sold $\frac{1}{5}$ of the total amount of juice $= \frac{2}{5} = 0.4$ liters. The amount of juice left $= 2 - 0.4 = 1.6$ liters.

The correct answer is D

2. There are 24 months in 2 years so the weight of the gorilla baby will be $4\frac{\text{kg}}{\text{month}} \times 24$ months $= 96$ kg more than the original weight.

Therefore, the weight of the gorilla baby after 2 years $=$ $2.60 + 96.0 = 98.6$ kg

The correct answer is G

3. Find the amount of money she spent for each fabric:
Fabric A: $3.50 \times 6.20 = \$21.7$
Fabric B: $2 \times 5.50 = \$11$

Find the total amount of money that she has to pay:
$$\$21.7 + \$11.0 = \$32.7$$

The correct answer is A

4. First, find the amount of pizza that was eaten by each of the three friends.

Michelle: $\frac{1}{4}$

Steven: $2 \times \frac{1}{4} = \frac{1}{2}$

David: $\frac{2}{3} \times \frac{1}{4} = \frac{1}{6}$

Add:
$$\frac{1}{4}+\frac{1}{2}+\frac{1}{6} = \frac{3+6+2}{12} = \frac{11}{12}$$

Amount of pizza that is left over:
$$1 - \frac{11}{12} = \frac{1}{12} \approx 0.083$$

The correct answer is F.

 Video Explanations
at argoprep.com/shsat

5. First, perform the operations inside the parentheses and then proceed with multiplication and subtraction.

$$\frac{3}{2}\left(\frac{1}{2}+\frac{2}{3}\right)-\frac{2}{5}\left(\frac{2}{3}-\frac{1}{3}\right)$$

$$\frac{3}{2}\left(\frac{7}{6}\right)-\frac{2}{5}\left(\frac{1}{3}\right)=\frac{21}{12}-\frac{2}{15}=\frac{97}{60}=1.62$$

The correct answer is B

---

6. Michael ate $\frac{1}{4}\times12=3$ cookies.

Steven ate $\frac{1}{3}\times12=4$ cookies.

Joann ate 3 cookies. Therefore, the fourth student ate $12-3-3-4=2$ cookies.

The correct answer is F.

---

7. If the mass of the chicken bought by Charles is 1.8 kg, then the mass of the chicken bought by Angel: $2.5\times1.8=4.5$ kg

The correct answer is B

---

8. First, find the mass of the spices poured into 6 bottles: $10.2-0.9=9.3$ kg.

The mass of the spices in each bottle is $\frac{9.3}{6}=1.55$ kg .

The correct answer is E.

---

9. 1 box of milk = 10 tins

1 tin = 0.45 kg powdered milk

Mass of a box of powdered milk = 10 tins × 0.45 kg = 4.5 kg
4 boxes of powdered milk = 4 × 4.5 kg = 18 kg

The correct answer is D

---

10. Solve the parentheses and then the product of decimals and fractions:

$$2(1.2)-0.25\times\frac{1}{2}=2.400-0.125=2.275$$

The correct answer is F

---

11. Calculate the time it takes to go from the house to the bus station:

$$0.25\,\text{hr}\times60\frac{\text{min}}{\text{hr}}=15\,\text{min}$$

Time of waiting for the bus: 10 minutes

Time of bus ride: $0.3\times60\frac{\text{min}}{\text{hr}}=18$ minutes

Total amount of time: $15+10+18=43$ minutes

The correct answer is C.

---

12. In 2010, the production decreased by $\frac{1}{8}$ of the original production.

$$\frac{20,000}{8}=2,500$$

Production in 2010 = 20,000 − 2,500 = 17,500 transistors.

In 2011, the production increased by $\frac{1}{3}$ of the production in 2010.

$$\frac{17,500}{4}=4,375$$

Production in 2011 = 4,375 + 17,500 = 21,875 transistors.

The correct answer is E.

13.

$$2\left(\frac{6}{5}\right)+1.5(1+3(0.3))-0.25$$

$$\frac{12}{5}+1.5(1.9)-0.25$$

$$2.40+2.85-0.25=5$$

The correct answer is B.

---

14. Calculate the number of pencils the students and teachers received.

Students: $\frac{1}{6}\times24=4$

Teachers: $\frac{3}{8}\times24=9$

The number of pencils that is left in the box is $24-9-4=11$ pencils.

The correct answer is G.

15.

$$\frac{\frac{2}{5}+\frac{3}{4}(0.5+0.3)}{\frac{1}{2}(0.5)}$$

$$\frac{\frac{2}{5}+\frac{3}{4}\times\frac{8}{10}}{\frac{1}{2}\times\frac{1}{2}}=\frac{\frac{2}{5}+\frac{24}{40}}{\frac{1}{4}}=\frac{\frac{2}{5}+\frac{3}{5}}{\frac{1}{4}}=\frac{1}{\frac{1}{4}}=4$$

The correct answer is C.

▶ **Video Explanations** at argoprep.com/shsat

16. 1 year = 12 months

Find the number of months John and Lauren have to wait:

$\frac{3}{4} \times 12 = 9$ – John

$\frac{1}{3} \times 12 = 4$ – Lauren

Then 9 − 4 = 5 months

The correct answer is F.

---

17. Number of boys and girls in the classroom:

$$\frac{1}{2} \times 32 = 16 \text{ boys and } \frac{1}{2} \times 32 = 16 \text{ girls}$$

Number of students taking Spanish Class:

$$\text{Boys} = \frac{1}{4} \times 16 = 4$$

$$\text{Girls} = \frac{3}{8} \times 16 = 6$$

Therefore, there are 4 + 6 = **10 students** in the Spanish class.

---

18. Work out the numerator and denominator separately. Be sure to perform all operations according to PEMDAS rule.

$$\frac{\frac{5}{3}+\frac{3}{4}\left(\frac{1}{5}+\frac{1}{3}\right)}{0.2\left(8-\frac{1}{2}\right)+\frac{3}{4}} = \frac{\frac{5}{3}+\frac{3}{20}+\frac{1}{4}}{\frac{1}{5}\left(\frac{15}{2}\right)+\frac{3}{4}} = \frac{\frac{31}{15}}{\frac{9}{4}} = \frac{124}{135} = \mathbf{0.919}$$

---

19. The number of chemical engineers: $\frac{1}{3} \times 60 = 20$ individuals.

The number of chemical engineers: $\frac{2}{3} \times 60 = 40$ individuals.

Number of women (chemical engineers): $\frac{3}{4} \times 20 = 15$

Number of women (petroleum engineers): $\frac{1}{2} \times 40 = 20$

Total number of women = 15 + 20 = 35

The correct answer is D.

---

20. Suppose x is the number of persons surveyed. Since we know the fraction and number of people allergic to antibiotics, find the total number of people surveyed.

$$\frac{1}{5} x = 30; \ x = 150$$

Total number of people surveyed = 150

The number of people allergic to pets: $\frac{3}{5} \times 150 = \mathbf{90}$.

Video Explanations
at argoprep.com/shsat

1. Josh is thinking of an even number that is greater than 11 but is less than 17 and can be evenly divided by 3. What is the number?

   A. 12   C. 15
   B. 14   D. 16

   Difficulty: Easy

2. A rectangular garden has the dimensions of 15 × 38 meters. What is the perimeter of the garden?

   E. 53 m   G. 76 m
   F. 106 m   H. 570 m²

   Difficulty: Medium

3. There are 15 green marbles, 7 yellow marbles, and 8 white marbles in a bag. If Kelly took 4 marbles out of the bag, how many marbles are left?

   A. 23   C. 26
   B. 25   D. 28

   Difficulty: Medium

4. Nina had 8 apples and she gave $\frac{3}{4}$ of the apples to her brother, John. How many apples did John get?

   E. 4   G. 6
   F. 5   H. 7

   Difficulty: Medium

5. There are 3 apple trees, 6 mango trees, and 13 papaya trees in the garden. How many more papaya trees than apple and mango trees are there in the garden?

   A. 10
   B. 7
   C. 5
   D. 4

   Difficulty: Medium

6. Steven and George went hiking. On the first day of their hike, they walked $10\frac{2}{3}$ miles and on the second day, they walked 15% more than on the first day. What was the total distance they walked during the two days of the hiking trip?

   E. $10\frac{2}{3}$ G. $15\frac{3}{4}$
   F. $12\frac{4}{15}$ H. $22\frac{14}{15}$

   Difficulty: Hard

7. Julia's average test score for 5 exams is 75. What should the sixth test score be in order for Julia to get a 78 as a final average score for the class?

   A. 75   C. 87
   B. 78   D. 93

   Difficulty: Medium

8. Mr. Johnson bought two pairs of shoes for $32.49 each and 3 shirts for $10.95 each. If he gives $100 to the cashier, how much money did he receive back?

   E. $2.17
   F. $13.12
   G. $17.85
   H. $34.66

   Difficulty: Medium

9. There are 12 students currently enrolled in an after-school program. If there are 4 new students enrolling in the program every week, in how many weeks will there be 28 students in the class?

   A. 2   C. 4
   B. 3   D. 5

   Difficulty: Easy

Video Explanations
at argoprep.com/shsat

10. Mark has 58 books in his collection. He gave 4 books to John, 7 books to Emily, and 9 books to Jane. How many books are left in Mark's collection?

   E. 47
   F. 45
   G. 42
   H. 38

   Difficulty: Easy

11. How many hours are in 1 week 3 days and 4 hours?

   A. 244 hours
   B. 168 hours
   C. 142 hours
   D. 96 hours

   Difficulty: Medium

12. The sum of two consecutive integers is 35 and their difference is 1. What is the smaller number?

   E. 21   G. 17
   F. 18   H. 15

   Difficulty: Hard

13. Kelly has 14 cups of sugar and wants to bake cakes. She needs $3\frac{3}{5}$ cups of sugar to bake one cake. What is the maximum number of cakes she can bake using 14 cups of sugar?

   A. 1   C. 3
   B. 2   D. 4

   Difficulty: Hard

14. Add 5 to the largest prime factor of 72 and then subtract the number by 13. What is the result?

   E. −8   G. 0
   F. −5   H. 2

   Difficulty: Easy

15. One bottle contains 350 milliliters of orange juice. How many liters of orange juice are there in 24 of these bottles?

   A. 9.5   C. 6.8
   B. 8.4   D. 5.2

   Difficulty: Medium

16. Tom's hourly salary is $8.25 for regular working hours and $9.50 for each overtime hour. If his regular workweek has 40 hours and he worked 45 hours during that week, how much did he get paid?

   E. $330   G. $377.50
   F. $380   H. $421.25

   Difficulty: Medium

17. Mr. Anderson saves $945 from his income every month. How much will he save in 15 months?

   Difficulty: Easy

18. There are 80 visitors in a local restaurant. There are only two menu options today: chicken or fish. If 20% of the visitors ordered chicken, how many visitors ordered fish?

   Difficulty: Medium

19. If 1 mile has 5280 feet and Emily's house is 2.3 miles away from the school, what is the distance to the school in feet?

   Difficulty: Medium

20. Two-fifth of a math class of 40 students are girls. If 9 boys and 1 girl were dropped from the class, what percentage of the class would be boys?

   Difficulty: Hard

Video Explanations
at argoprep.com/shsat

49

1. The even numbers between 11 and 17 are: 12, 14, and 16. Only 12 can be evenly divided by 3. Therefore, the possible number is 12.

   The correct answer is A.

2. We are given that the length of the garden is 38 meters and the width of the garden is 15 meters. To find the perimeter, add the values of length and width together and multiply the result by 2. Perimeter= 2(38 + 15) = 106 meters.

   The correct answer is F.

3. First, find the total number of marbles in the bag: 15 + 7 + 8 = 30 marbles.

   If Kelly took 4 marbles out of the bag, there were 30 – 4 = 26 marbles left.

   The correct answer is C.

4. Multiply the total number of apples by $\frac{3}{4}$: $8 \times \frac{3}{4} = 6$ apples .
   Therefore, Nina gave 6 apples to John.

   The correct answer is G.

5. The total number of mango and apple trees: 6 + 3 = 9.

   So there are 13 – 9 = 4 more papaya trees than apple and mango trees.

   The correct answer is D.

6. Convert $10\frac{2}{3}$ to an improper fraction: $10\frac{2}{3} = \frac{32}{3}$
   On the second day, they walked 15% more than on the first day, which is: $\frac{32}{3} \times 0.15 = \frac{4.8}{3} = 1.6$ miles .

   Convert 1.6 miles to the improper fraction to make your calculations easier: $1.6 = 1\frac{6}{10} = 1\frac{3}{5} = \frac{8}{5}$.

   Now, find the distance they walked on the second day:
   $\frac{8}{5} + \frac{32}{3} = \frac{3(8) + 5(32)}{15} = \frac{24 + 160}{15} = \frac{184}{15} = 12\frac{4}{5}$ miles

   Then, find the total distance:
   $\frac{32}{3} + \frac{184}{15} = \frac{5(32) + 184}{15} = \frac{160 + 184}{15} = \frac{344}{15} = 22\frac{14}{15}$ miles

   The correct answer is H.

7. Suppose x is the sixth test score. Then, $\frac{5(75) + x}{6} = 78$
   Rewrite the equation above in order to solve for x.
   $$5(75) + x = 468$$
   $$375 + x = 468$$
   $$x = 468 - 375 = 93$$
   Julia needs to get a score of 93 on the last test in order to get a 78 as a final average score for the class.

   The correct answer is D.

8. The total cost of two pairs of shoes is: $32.49 × 2 = $64.98. The total cost of 3 shirts is: $10.95 × 3 = $32.85.

   The total cost that Mr. Johnson paid for his purchase is: $64.98 + $32.85 = $97.83.

   Therefore, he will receive $100 – $97.83 = $2.17 back.

   The correct answer is E.

9. First find the difference between the final and initial number of students: 28 – 12 = 16.

   Suppose n is the number of weeks. Therefore, $4n = 16$;
   $n = \frac{16}{4} = 4$.

   So 4 weeks are needed to get 28 students in the program.

   The correct answer is C.

10. First, find the total number of books that Mark gave to his friends: 4 + 7 + 9 = 20 books.

    He had 58 books before giving the books to his friends. Therefore, the number of books that are left in his collection is 58 – 20 = 38 books.

    The correct answer is H.

11. One day has 24 hours. Therefore, there are 7 × 24 = 168 hours in a week. Three days is equal to 3 x 24 = 72 hours.

    So the total number of hours in 1 week 3 days and 4 hours is 168 + 72 + 4 = 244 hours.

    The correct answer is A.

Video Explanations at argoprep.com/shsat

12. Suppose x is a smaller number and y is a larger number. Then,
$$x + y = 35$$
$$x - y = -1$$
Solve the second equation for x:
$$x = y - 1$$
Substitute the expression for x into the first equation and solve it for x
$$y - 1 + y = 35$$
$$2y = 36$$
$$y = 18$$
Find x: $x = 18 - 1 = 17$.
Therefore, the smaller number is 17.
The correct answer is G.

13. Since one cake requires $3\frac{3}{5}$ cups of sugar and Kelly has 14 cups of sugar, then the number of cakes that she can bake is:
$$14 \div 3\frac{3}{5} = 14 \div \frac{18}{5} = 14 \times \frac{5}{18} = \frac{7 \times 5}{9} = \frac{35}{9} = 3\frac{8}{9}$$
Therefore, the maximum number of cakes that Kelly can bake using 14 cups of sugar is 3.
The correct answer is C.

14. First, find the prime factorization of 72: $72 = 2 \times 36 = 2 \times 2 \times 18 = 2 \times 2 \times 2 \times 9 = 2 \times 2 \times 2 \times 3 \times 3$. Therefore, the largest prime factor of 72 is 3. Then, we have:
$$5 + 3 - 13 = -5$$
The result of adding 5 to the largest prime factor of 72, and then subtracting 13 is -5.
The correct answer is F.

15. We need to multiply the amount of orange juice in one bottle by the number of bottles.
Before that, convert milliliters to liters: 350 milliliters = 0.350 liters. Therefore, we have: $0.350 \times 24 = 8.4$ liters of orange juice.
The correct answer is B.

16. Calculate Tom's earnings for 40 regular hours: $\$8.25 \times 40 = \$330$. Then, his earning for 5 overtime hours is $\$9.50 \times 5 = \$47.50$.
Therefore, his total earnings for 45 hours of work is: $\$330 + \$47.50 = \$377.50$.
The correct answer is G.

17. Mr. Anderson saves \$945 every month. To calculate how much he saves in 15 months, multiply $\$945 \times 15 = \mathbf{\$14,175}$.

18. If 20% of the visitors ordered chicken, then 80% of the visitors ordered fish.
Find the number of visitors who ordered fish: $0.8 \times 80 = 64$.
So 64 visitors ordered fish.

19. To find the distance from Emily's house to the school in feet, multiply the number of feet in 1 mile by the actual distance in miles.
Therefore, we have: $5280 \times 2.3 = \mathbf{12,144\ feet}$.

20. First calculate how many boys and girls are currently in the math class. The number of girls is $\frac{2}{5} \times 40 = 16$. Therefore, the number of boys is $40 - 16 = 24$.
The new class size after 10 students dropped from the class is 30. The new number of boys is $24 - 9 = 15$. Therefore, the percentage of boys is $\frac{15}{30} = 0.5 = \mathbf{50\%}$.

Video Explanations
at argoprep.com/shsat

1. Express this number in standard form:

$$1.5446 \times 10^6$$

A. 15,446,000   C. 154,460
B. 1,544,600   D. 15446

Difficulty: Medium

2. Express the following number in scientific notation.

264,010,000

E. 0.26401×10^9 G. 26.401×10^9
F. 2.6401×10^8 H. 2.6401×10^9

Difficulty: Medium

3. Use scientific notation to find the answer to the following problem:

$$4.2356 \times 10^{-15} \cdot 3.4 \times 10^{-12}$$

A. 14.40104×10^{-27}
B. 1.4×10^{-27}
C. 1.4×10^{-26}
D. 14.4×10^{-25}

Difficulty: Hard

4. Use scientific notation to find the answer to the following problem:

$$264.5 + 13.264 + 8.575$$

E. 286.3   G. 286.339
F. 286.34   H. 287

Difficulty: Medium

5. After performing calculations, round your answer to the correct number of significant figures.

$$2.354 \times 10^4 \cdot 3.45 \times 10^{-2}$$

A. 81.21   C. 8.12×10^2
B. 8.1213×10^2 D. 8×10^3

Difficulty: Hard

6. Use scientific notation to find the answer to the following problem:

$$\frac{5.387 \times 10^7}{3.543 \times 10^{-2}}$$

E. 1.520×10^5 G. 1.5205×10^9
F. 1.521×10^8 H. 1.520×10^9

Difficulty: Hard

7. Use scientific notation to find the answer to the following problem:

$$10.363 - 6.45 + 3.2645$$

A. 7.20   C. 7.178
B. 7.18   D. 7.0

Difficulty: Medium

8. Ron works on his math homework and he deals converts numbers from standard form into scientific notation form. How can he write 0.00000000538 in scientific notation?

E. 53.8×10^{-9} G. 5.38×10^{-9}
F. 5.38×10^{-10} H. 0.538×10^{-11}

Difficulty: Medium

9. Emily wants to write 6.235×10^9 in scientific notation. How many zeros should that number have in scientific notation if she performs the conversion correctly?

A. 9   B. 7   C. 6   D. 5

Difficulty: Medium

10. Write the following number in scientific notation:

$$-647$$

E. -6.47×10^2 G. 6.47
F. -6.47×10^3 H. 6.47×10^2

Difficulty: Medium

Video Explanations
at argoprep.com/shsat

11.

$$c = \lambda v$$

The equation above represents the wave equation, which describes the speed of light, c, in terms of wavelength, λ, and frequency, v, where $c = 3 \times 10^8$ m/sec. What is the frequency of the wave if the wavelength is 9.85×10^{-9} m?

A. 3×10^{15} **C.** 3×10^{16}
B. 3.01×10^{15} **D.** 3.046×10^{16}

Difficulty: Hard

12. The speed of light is 3×10^8 m/sec and the distance from the Sun to Earth is 1.496×10^{11} m. How many seconds does it take for sunlight to reach Earth? Write your answer in scientific notation.

E. 485   **G.** 500
F. 498.7   **H.** 505.3

Difficulty: Hard

13. In a biotechnological laboratory, there are approximately 1.2×10^3 bacteria in a Petri dish that were grown. If the total number of bacteria in a lake is approximately 13×10^{28}, how many times greater is the population of bacteria in the lake than the number of bacteria in the Petri dish?

A. 11×10^{31} **C.** 10.8×10^{24}
B. 11×10^{25} **D.** 11×10^{23}

Difficulty: Hard

14. A piece of paper is 5.5×10^{-4} inches thick. If Jennifer has 35 such pieces, how thick is the whole stack? Write your answer in standard form.

E. 0.01925   **G.** 192.5×10^{-4}
F. 0.019   **H.** 0.020

Difficulty: Hard

15. The mass of Earth is 5.9×10^{24} kg and the mass of moon is 7.3×10^{22} kg. What is the combined mass of Earth and the moon?

A. 597.3×10^{22} **C.** 597.3×10^{22}
B. 6.0×10^{24} **D.** 6.0×10^{25}

Difficulty: Hard

16. Compute the value of the following expression:

$$6.7 \times 10^{-8} - 2.3 \times 10^{-9}$$

E. 6.5×10^{-9} **G.** 6.47×10^{-7}
F. 6.5×10^{-8} **H.** 6.5×10^{-7}

Difficulty: Medium

17. Compute the value of the following expression:

$$5.34 \times 10^4 + 3.87 \times 10^3$$

Difficulty: Medium

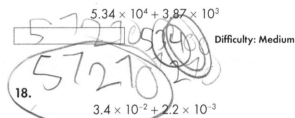

18.

$$3.4 \times 10^{-2} + 2.2 \times 10^{-3}$$

What is the value of the expression above? Write your answer in scientific notation.

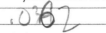

Difficulty: Medium

19. Express the following number in scientific notation:

$$224,056,000$$

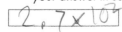

Difficulty: Medium

20. If there are about 2.9×10^4 microbes on a hand of a child and 5.6×10^6 microbes on a hand of an adult, how many more microbes are there on a hand of an adult than on a hand of a child? Write your answer in scientific notation.

Difficulty: Hard

1. There are six powers of ten in 1.5446×10^6. Therefore, we need to move the decimal place 6 places to the right.

   So 1.5446×10^6 in standard form is $1,544,600$.

   The correct answer is B.

2. To convert the number from standard form to scientific notation, move the decimal to the left until you reach the point between the first two numbers. Count how many places you moved the decimal point to the left and that would be the power of 10. Therefore, $264,010,000$ written in scientific notation equals to
$$2.6401 \times 10^8.$$
   The correct answer is F.

3. When multiplying numbers with different numbers of significant digits, round the result to the same number of significant digits as the least-accurate number. Keep the base the same and add the exponents. Therefore, we have:

   $4.2356 \times 10^{-15} \cdot 3.4 \times 10^{-12} = 14.40104 \times 10^{-27} = 1.4 \times 10^{-26}$

   The correct answer is C.

4. When adding numbers with different numbers of significant digits, round the answer to the same decimal place as the least-accurate number.

   The first number, 264.5, is only accurate to the tenths place. All other numbers are more accurate because they have a greater number of significant digits. So we will need to round the final answer to the tenths place.

   Therefore, we have:
$$264.5 + 13.264 + 8.575 = 286.339 \approx 286.3$$
   The correct answer is E.

5. When multiplying numbers with different numbers of significant digits, round the result to the same number of significant digits as the least-accurate number.

   Keep the base the same and add the exponents.

   In our case, the least-accurate number is 3.45 and it has 3 significant figures. Therefore, we will need to round our answer to 3 significant digits too.
$$2.354 \times 10^4 \cdot 3.45 \times 10^{-2} = 8.1213 \times 10^2 \approx 8.12 \times 10^2$$
   The correct answer is C.

6. When dividing numbers with different numbers of significant digits, round the result to the same number of significant digits as the least-accurate number.

   Keep the base the same and subtract the exponents.

   In our case, however, both numbers have 4 significant digits

so we will round the final answer to 4 significant digits as well.
$$\frac{5.387 \times 10^7}{3.543 \times 10^{-2}} \approx 1.520 \times 10^9$$
The correct answer is H.

7. When adding or subtracting numbers with different numbers of significant digits, round the answer to the same decimal place as the least-accurate number. In our case, the least-accurate number is 6.45 because it is accurate only to the hundreds place. Therefore, we will round the final answer to the same number of decimal places as 6.45.
$$10.363 - 6.45 + 3.2645 = 7.1775 \approx 7.18$$
   The correct answer is B.

8. To write 0.00000000538 in scientific notation, Ron needs to move the decimal to the right until he gets a number that is at least equal to 1 but less than 10. In his case, Ron needs to move the decimal 9 places to the right and he will get the following:
$$0.00000000538 = 5.38 \times 10^{-9}$$
   The correct answer is G.

9. To write the number 6.235×10^9 in scientific notation, move the decimal point 9 places to the right.
$$6.235 \times 10^9 = 6,235,000,000$$
   As seen above, the number of zeros is 6.

   The correct answer is C.

10. Move the decimal point to the left until you get a number at least equal to 1 but less than 10 and multiply the resulting number by 10 to the power which corresponds to the number of times you moved the decimal point. So -647 would be equal to -6.47×10^2.

    The correct answer is E.

11. In our case, $c = 3 \times 10^8$ m/sec and $\lambda = 9.85 \times 10^{-9}$. Rewrite the formula to solve for v:
$$v = \frac{c}{\lambda} = \frac{3 \times 10^8 \text{ m/sec}}{9,85 \times 10^{-9}}$$
    When dividing the numbers with different numbers of significant digits, round the result to the same number of significant digits as the least-accurate number. In our case, the least-accurate number is 3 and it has one significant digit. Therefore, our answer should be rounded to one significant digit too.
$$\frac{3 \times 10^8 \text{ m/sec}}{9,85 \times 10^{-9} \text{ m}} \approx 3.05 \times 10^{16} = 3 \times 10^{16}$$
    The correct answer is C.

Video Explanations at argoprep.com/shsat

– Arithmetic – Scientific Notation – Answer Explanation

12. Divide the distance by the speed of light to find the time needed for sunlight to reach Earth.

When dividing the numbers with different numbers of significant digits, round the result to the same number of significant digits as the least-accurate number. In our case, the least-accurate number is 3 and it has one significant digit. Therefore, our answer should be rounded to one significant digit too.

$$\frac{1.496\times10^{11} \text{ m}}{3\times10^{8} \text{ m}} = 498.7 \text{ seconds} \approx 500 \text{ seconds}$$

The correct answer is G.

13. Divide the total number of bacteria in the oceans by the number of bacteria in the Petri dish.

When dividing the numbers with different numbers of significant digits, round the result to the same number of significant digits as the least-accurate number. In our case, both numbers have 2 significant digits.

$$\frac{13\times10^{28}}{1.2\times10^{3}} = 10.83\times10^{25} \approx 11\times10^{25}$$

Therefore, the population of the bacteria in the oceans is approximately 11×10^{25} greater than the number of bacteria in our Petri dish.

The correct answer is B.

14. Since the thickness of one piece of paper is 5.5×10^{-4} inches and Jennifer has 35 same pieces of paper, multiply both numbers to find how thick the whole stack is.

$$5.5 \times 10^{-4} \times 35 = 192.5 \times 10^{-4} \text{ inches.}$$

Convert that number to standard form. To do that, move the decimal point 4 places to the left.

$$192.5 \times 10^{-4} = 0.01925 \text{ inches.}$$

Round to the same decimal place as the least-accurate number. 0.01925 is rounded to 0.019.

The correct answer is F.

15. First, write each number with the same exponent.

$$5.9 \times 10^{24} = 590 \times 10^{22} \text{ kg.}$$

Add two masses together.

When adding or subtracting the numbers with different numbers of significant digits, round the answer to the same decimal place as the least-accurate number.

$$590 \times 10^{22} + 7.3 \times 10^{22} = 597.3 \times 10^{22} = 5.973 \times 10^{24} =$$
$$6.0 \times 10^{24} \text{ kg.}$$

The correct answer is B.

16. The first step is to make sure that each number has the same power of 10.

We have $2.3 \times 10^{-9} = 0.23 \times 10^{-8}$

When adding or subtracting the numbers with different numbers of significant digits, round the answer to the same decimal place as the least-accurate number. The final answer should be rounded to the nearest tenth.

Then perform subtraction:

$$6.7 \times 10^{-8} - 0.23 \times 10^{-8} = 6.47 \times 10^{-8} \approx 6.5 \times 10^{-8}$$

The correct answer is F.

17. The first step is to make sure that each number has the same power of 10.

We have $3.87 \times 10^{3} = 0.387 \times 10^{4}$

When adding or subtracting the numbers with different numbers of significant digits, round the answer to the same decimal place as the least-accurate number. The final answer should be rounded to the nearest hundredth.

Then perform addition:

$$\mathbf{5.34 \times 10^{4} + 0.387 \times 10^{4} = 5.727 \times 10^{4} \approx 5.73 \times 10^{4}}$$

18. One way to approach this problem is to first convert the two numbers from scientific notation into standard form.

$3.4 \times 10^{-2} = 0.034$

$2.2 \times 10^{-3} = 0.0022$

Add the two numbers. $0.034 + 0.0022 = 0.0362$. Convert the number back into scientific notation.

$$\mathbf{3.62 \times 10^{-2}}$$

19. Move the decimal to the left and place it between the first two numbers. Count how many places you moved the decimal point to the left and that is the power of 10.

Therefore, we have:

$$\mathbf{224056000 = 2.24056 \times 10^{8}}$$

20. Subtract the number of microbes on the child's hand from the number of microbes on the adult's hand.

The first step is to make sure that each number has the same power of 10.

We have $2.9 \times 10^{4} = 0.029 \times 10^{6}$.

When subtracting the numbers with different numbers of significant digits, round the answer to the same decimal place as the least-accurate number. The final result should be rounded to the nearest tenth.

$$5.6 \times 10^{6} - 0.029 \times 10^{6} = 5.571 \times 10^{6} \approx 5.6 \times 10^{6}$$

There are **5.6×10^{6} more microbes** on the adult's hand than on the child's hand.

Video Explanations
at argoprep.com/shsat

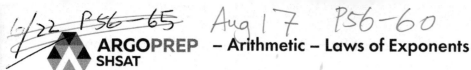

ARGOPREP – Arithmetic – Laws of Exponents
SHSAT

1.

$$\frac{(a^2)^3 a^4 b^3}{a^3 (b^3)^5}$$

What is the value of the expression above?

A. $\dfrac{a^7}{b^{12}}$ **C.** $\dfrac{a^6}{b^{12}}$

B. $\dfrac{a^{12}}{b^7}$ **D.** $a^6 b^5$

Difficulty: Medium

2. Simplify the following expression:

$$(3a^4 b^2)(2a^{-1} b^3)^2$$

E. $6a^{-8}b^{12}$ **G.** $12a^2 b^8$
F. $6a^5 b^7$ **H.** $12a^3 b^5$

Difficulty: Medium

3.

$$\frac{(5x^{-2}y^3 z^2)^{-2}}{(xz^{-4})^0}$$

Simplify the expression above.

A. $\dfrac{25x^4}{y^6 z^4}$ **C.** $\dfrac{x^4 y^6 z^4}{25}$

B. $\dfrac{x^4}{25y^6 z^4}$ **D.** $25x^4 y^6 z^4$

Difficulty: Medium

4.

$$\frac{3xy^4}{x^5} \cdot \frac{2x^3 y}{3y^2}$$

Simplify the expression above.

E. $\dfrac{y^3}{2x^2}$ **G.** $\dfrac{2y^3}{x^2}$

F. $\dfrac{2x^2}{y^3}$ **H.** $\dfrac{2x^3}{y^2}$

Difficulty: Medium

5.

$$\left(\frac{a^{-2} b^5}{c^{-3}}\right)^{-4}$$

What is the value of the expression above?

A. $\dfrac{1}{a^8 b^{20} c^{12}}$ **C.** $\dfrac{b^{20} c^{12}}{a^8}$

B. $\dfrac{a^8}{b^{20} c^{12}}$ **D.** $a^8 b^{20} c^{12}$

Difficulty: Hard

6.

$$(-3x^2 z^6)^{-3}(5x^4 y^7)$$

What is the value of the expression above?

E. $-\dfrac{5y^7}{27x^2 z^{18}}$ **G.** $-15x^{10}y^7 z^{18}$

F. $-\dfrac{27x^2 z^{18}}{5y^7}$ **H.** $-\dfrac{15y^7}{x^2 z^{18}}$

Difficulty: Medium

7. Simplify the following expression:

$$\frac{4u^9 v^{-5} \cdot u^{-2} v^{-3}}{(-v^3)^{-2}}$$

A. $\dfrac{4u^7}{v^2}$ **C.** $4u^9$

B. $\dfrac{v^2}{4u^7}$ **D.** $4v^3$

Difficulty: Hard

8. Simplify the following expression:

$$-\left(\frac{a^{-2} b^6}{2a^{-1} \cdot ab^5}\right)^0$$

E. -1 **G.** $-\dfrac{b}{2a^2}$

F. 0 **H.** $-\dfrac{1}{2}$

Difficulty: Medium

Video Explanations
at argoprep.com/shsat

56

9.

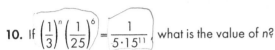

$$((x^{-4}y^{-2})^{-3} \cdot (-x^3y^0))^{-2}$$

Find the value of the expression above.

A. $\dfrac{1}{x^{30}y^{12}}$ C. $x^{30}y^{12}$

B. $\dfrac{1}{x^{17}y^8}$ D. $x^{17}y^8$

Difficulty: Hard

10. If $\left(\dfrac{1}{3}\right)^n \left(\dfrac{1}{25}\right)^6 = \dfrac{1}{5 \cdot 15^{11}}$, what is the value of n?

E. 3   F. 7   G. 9   H. 11

Difficulty: Hard

11. What is the value of $\dfrac{16^{\frac{7}{2}}}{16^{\frac{3}{2}}}$?

A. 4   B. 16   C. 64   D. 256

Difficulty: Hard

12. What is the value of the expression below?

$$\dfrac{(-3)^2}{(2^3 + 3^2)}$$

E. $-\dfrac{9}{17}$ G. 2

F. $\dfrac{9}{17}$ H. $\dfrac{17}{9}$

Difficulty: Medium

13. What is the value of the expression $125^{\frac{1}{3}}$?

A. 25   C. 5

B. 15   D. $\dfrac{1}{5}$

Difficulty: Medium

14. Simplify the following expression:

$$\dfrac{25a^4b^3}{45a^5b^7}$$

E. $\dfrac{9}{5ab^4}$ G. $\dfrac{5ab^4}{9}$

F. $\dfrac{5}{9ab^4}$ H. $\dfrac{9ab^4}{5}$

Difficulty: Medium

15.

$$(a^2 - 2b + 3b^3)^2$$

What is the value of the expression above if $a = 2$ and $b = -1$?

A. 1   C. 25

B. 9   D. 81

Difficulty: Medium

16. Solve the equation below.

$$\left(\dfrac{3x^2}{y^3}\right)^{-2}$$

E. $\dfrac{y^6}{9x^4}$ G. $\dfrac{y^6}{3}$

F. $\dfrac{9x^4}{y^6}$ H. $\dfrac{y^5}{3x^4}$

Difficulty: Medium

17. What is the result if you rewrite 2.25×10^3 so the exponent is 4, but the value of the expression remains the same?

Difficulty: Medium

18. Simplify the following expression:

$$\dfrac{32m^2n^3}{-2mn^2}$$

Difficulty: Medium

19. Simplify $27^{\frac{2}{3}}$.

9

Difficulty: Hard

20. Simplify the following equation:

$$(2a^3b^2c^6)^3$$

Difficulty: Medium

Answer Explanation

1. There are three laws of exponents that need to be used to solve this question.

First law: Multiply the powers when raising a base with a power to another power.

Second law: Keep the base the same when multiplying the same bases. Third law: If you have the same base and you are dividing, simply subtract the exponents.

Therefore, we have:

$$\frac{(a^2)^3\,a^4b^3}{a^3(b^3)^5} = \frac{a^6a^4b^3}{a^3b^{15}} = \frac{a^{10}b^3}{a^3b^{15}} = a^7b^{-12} = \frac{a^7}{b^{12}}$$

The correct answer is A.

2. There are three laws of exponents that need to be used to solve this question. First law: Multiply the powers when raising a base with a power to another power.

Second law: Keep the base the same when multiplying the same bases. Third law: If you have the same base and you are dividing, simply subtract the exponents.

Therefore, we have:

$$(3a^4b^2)(2a^{-1}b^3)^2$$
$$(2a^{-1}b^3)^2 = 2^2 \cdot a^{-1(2)} \cdot b^{3(2)} = 4a^{-2}b^6$$
$$(3a^4b^2)(2a^{-1}b^3)^2 = (3a^4b^2)(4a^{-2}b^6) = 3 \cdot 4a^{4+(-2)}b^{2+6}$$
$$= 12a^2b^8$$

The correct answer is G.

3. There are three laws of exponents that need to be used to solve this question. First law: Multiply the powers when raising a base with a power to another power.

Second law: Keep the base the same when multiplying the same bases. Third law: Keep the base the same and subtract the denominator exponent from the numerator exponent when dividing like bases.

First, solve the numerator and the denominator separately:

$$(5x^{-2}y^3z^2)^{-2} = 5^{-2}x^{-2(-2)}y^{3(-2)}z^{2(-2)} = \frac{1}{25}x^4y^{-6}z^{-4}$$

$$= \frac{x^4y^{-6}z^{-4}}{25} = \frac{x^4}{25y^6z^4}$$

Anything raised to zero power is 1.

$$(xz^{-4})^0 = 1$$

$$\frac{(5x^{-2}y^3z^2)^{-2}}{(xz^{-4})^0} = \frac{\frac{x^4}{25y^6z^4}}{1} = \frac{x^4}{25y^6z^4}$$

The correct answer is B.

4. There are three laws of exponents that need to be used to solve this question. First law: Multiply the powers when raising a base with a power to another power.

Second law: Keep the base the same when multiplying the same bases. Third law: Keep the base the same and subtract the denominator exponent from the numerator exponent when dividing like bases.

$$\frac{3xy^4}{x^3} \cdot \frac{2x^5y}{3y^7} = \frac{3y^4}{x^2} \cdot \frac{2x^5}{3y^6} = \frac{y^4}{x^2} \cdot \frac{2x^5}{y^6} = y^{4-6}2x^{5-2} = y^{-2}2x^3 = \frac{2x^3}{y^2}$$

The correct answer is H.

5. There are three laws of exponents that need to be used to solve this question. First law: Multiply the powers when raising a base with a power to another power.

Second law: Keep the base the same when multiplying the same bases. Third law: Keep the base the same and subtract the denominator exponent from the numerator exponent when dividing like bases.

Note, that $a^{-1} = \frac{1}{a}$

$$\left(\frac{a^{-2}b^5}{c^{-3}}\right)^{-4} = \frac{(a^{-2})^{-4}(b^5)^{-4}}{(c^{-3})^{-4}} = \frac{a^8b^{-20}}{c^{12}} = \frac{a^8}{b^{20}c^{12}}$$

The correct answer is B.

6. There are three laws of exponents that need to be used to solve this question. First law: Multiply the powers when raising a base with a power to another power.

Second law: Keep the base the same when multiplying the same bases. Third law: Keep the base the same and subtract the denominator exponent from the numerator exponent when dividing like bases.

Video Explanations
at argoprep.com/shsat

Note, that $a^{-1} = \dfrac{1}{a}$

$(-3x^2z^6)^{-3}(5x^4y^7) = -\dfrac{1}{27x^6z^{18}} \cdot (5x^4y^7) = -\dfrac{5y^7}{27x^2z^{18}}$

The correct answer is E.

---

7. There are three laws of exponents that need to be used to solve this question. First law: Multiply the powers when raising a base with a power to another power.

    Second law: Keep the base the same when multiplying the same bases. Third law: Keep the base the same and subtract the denominator exponent from the numerator exponent when dividing like bases.

    Note, that $a^{-1} = \dfrac{1}{a}$

    $\dfrac{4u^9v^{-5} \cdot u^{-2}v^{-3}}{(-v^3)^{-2}} = \dfrac{4u^7}{\frac{v^8}{v^6}} = \dfrac{4u^7}{v^2}$

    The correct answer is A.

---

8. Since anything raised to zero power is 1, then $\left(\dfrac{a^{-2}b^6}{2a^{-1} \cdot ab^5}\right)^0 = 1$

    So $-\left(\dfrac{a^{-2}b^6}{2a^{-1} \cdot ab^5}\right)^0 = -1$

    The correct answer is E.

---

9. There are three laws of exponents that need to be used to solve this question. First law: Multiply the powers when raising a base with a power to another power.

    Second law: Keep the base the same when multiplying the same bases. Third law: Keep the base the same and subtract the denominator exponent from the numerator exponent when dividing like bases.

    Note, that $a^{-1} = \dfrac{1}{a}$

    $(x^{-4}y^{-2})^{-3} = x^{12}y^6$
    $((x^{-4}y^{-2})^{-3} \cdot -x^3y^0)^{-2} = (x^{12}y^6 \cdot (-x^3y^0))^{-2} = (-x^{15}y^6)^{-2}$
    $= \dfrac{1}{(-x^{15}y^6)^2} = \dfrac{1}{x^{30}y^{12}}$

    The correct answer is A.

---

10. There are three laws of exponents that need to be used to solve this question. First law: Multiply the powers when raising a base with a power to another power.

    Second law: Keep the base the same when multiplying the same bases. Third law: Keep the base the same and subtract the denominator exponent from the numerator exponent when dividing like bases

---

$\left(\dfrac{1}{3}\right)^n\left(\dfrac{1}{25}\right)^6 = \dfrac{1}{5 \cdot 15^{11}}$

$\dfrac{1^n}{3^n}\dfrac{1^6}{25^6} = \dfrac{1}{3^n}\dfrac{1}{25^6} = \dfrac{1}{3^n25^6} = \dfrac{1}{3^n(5^2)^6} = \dfrac{1}{3^n5^{12}}$

$\dfrac{1}{5 \cdot 15^{11}} = \dfrac{1}{5 \cdot (3 \cdot 5)^{11}} = \dfrac{1}{5 \cdot 3^{11} \cdot 5^{11}} = \dfrac{1}{3^{11}(5 \cdot 5^{11})} = \dfrac{1}{3^{11} \cdot 5^{12}}$

$\dfrac{1}{3^n5^{12}} = \dfrac{1}{3^{11} \cdot 5^{12}}$

$n = 11$

The correct answer is H.

---

11. Rewrite the expression in order to simplify it:

    $\dfrac{16^{\frac{7}{2}}}{16^{\frac{3}{2}}} = \dfrac{\sqrt{16^7}}{\sqrt{16^3}} = \sqrt{\dfrac{16^7}{16^3}} = \sqrt{16^7 - 16^3} = \sqrt{16^{7-3}} = \sqrt{16^4} = 16^{\frac{4}{2}}$
    $= 16^2 = 256$

    The correct answer is D.

---

12. There are three laws of exponents that need to be used to solve this question. First law: Multiply the powers when raising a base with a power to another power.

    Second law: Keep the base the same when multiplying the same bases. Third law: Keep the base the same and subtract the denominator exponent from the numerator exponent when dividing like bases.

    $\dfrac{(-3)^2}{(2^3 + 3^2)} = \dfrac{9}{(8+9)} = \dfrac{9}{17}$

    The correct answer is F.

---

13. Rewrite the expression in order to solve it:

    $125^{\frac{1}{3}} = \sqrt[3]{125} = 5$

    The correct answer is C.

---

14. There are three laws of exponents that need to be used to solve this question. First law: Multiply the powers when raising a base with a power to another power.

    Second law: Keep the base the same when multiplying the same bases. Third law: Keep the base the same and subtract the denominator exponent from the numerator exponent when dividing like bases.

    $\dfrac{25a^4b^3}{45a^5b^7} = \dfrac{5}{9ab^4}$

    The correct answer is F.

Video Explanations
at argoprep.com/shsat

15. Substitute the value of a and b into the original expression and solve it.

$(a^2 - 2b + 3b^3)^2 = (2^2 - 2(-1) + 3(-1)^3)^2 = (4 + 2 - 3)^2 = 3^2$
$= 9$

The correct answer is B.

---

16. There are three laws of exponents that need to be used to solve this question. First law: Multiply the powers when raising a base with a power to another power.

Second law: Keep the base the same when multiplying the same bases. Third law: Keep the base the same and subtract the denominator exponent from the numerator exponent when dividing like bases.

Since $a^{-1} = \dfrac{1}{a}$, then $\left(\dfrac{3x^2}{y^3}\right)^{-2} = \left(\dfrac{y^3}{3x^2}\right)^2$

$$\left(\dfrac{y^3}{3x^2}\right)^2 = \dfrac{y^6}{9x^4}$$

The correct answer is E.

17. You need to move the decimal point 1 place to the left to get the number with 4 as the exponent.

Therefore, $2.25 \times 10^3 = \mathbf{0.225 \times 10^4}$

---

18. There are three laws of exponents that need to be used to solve this question. First law: Multiply the powers when raising a base with a power to another power.

Second law: Keep the base the same when multiplying the same bases. Third law: Keep the base the same and subtract the denominator exponent from the numerator exponent when dividing like bases.

$$\dfrac{32m^2n^3}{-2mn^2} = \mathbf{-16mn}$$

---

19. Rewrite the expression:

$$27^{\frac{2}{3}} = \sqrt[3]{27^2} = \sqrt[3]{(3^3)^2}$$

$\sqrt[3]{(3^3)^2}$ is equal to $\sqrt[3]{(3^2)^3}$

So $\sqrt[3]{(3^3)^2} = \sqrt[3]{(3^2)^3} = 3^2 = \mathbf{9}$

---

20. To solve the problem multiply the powers when raising a base with a power to another power.

$$(2a^3b^2c^6)^3 = \mathbf{8a^9b^6c^{18}}.$$

Video Explanations
at argoprep.com/shsat

1. What is the value of this expression?
$$\sqrt{49x^6y^3}$$
A. $49x^3y$
B. $7x^6y^2$
C. $7x^3y\sqrt{y}$
D. $49x^3y\sqrt{y}$

Difficulty: Medium

2. What is the value of this expression?
$$\frac{\sqrt{16x^6y^4}}{2}$$
E. $2x^2y^2$
F. $8x^3y$
G. $2x^3y^3$
H. $2x^3y^2$

Difficulty: Medium

3.
$$\sqrt{8x^3}\cdot\sqrt{2x^5}$$
What is the value of the expression above?
A. $16x^4$
B. $4x^4$
C. $2x^8$
D. $4x^8$

Difficulty: Medium

4. What is the value of the expression $\frac{\sqrt{x^2}}{\sqrt{x^6}}$?
E. x^4
F. $\frac{1}{x^4}$
G. $\frac{1}{x^2}$
H. $\frac{1}{\sqrt{x}}$

Difficulty: Medium

5.
$$\sqrt{a^3+b^2+1}$$
What is the value of the expression above if $a = 2$ and $b = 4$?
A. 5   B. 4   C. 3   D. 6

Difficulty: Medium

6. What is the value of the following expression?
$$\frac{\sqrt{x^4}\cdot\sqrt{x^3}}{\sqrt{x^3}}$$
E. x^2
F. x^3
G. x^4
H. x

Difficulty: Hard

7. What is value of the following expression?
$$\sqrt{x^9y}\cdot\sqrt{32xy}$$
A. $32x^3y^4$
B. $4x^{10}y^{10}$
C. $4\sqrt{2}x^5y^2$
D. $4\sqrt{2}x^3y^5$

Difficulty: Hard

8. Solve the equation below:
$$\frac{\sqrt{9x^9}}{\sqrt{81x^7}}$$
E. $9x^2$
F. x^2
G. $\frac{x}{3}$
H. $\frac{x}{9}$

Difficulty: Medium

9. What is the value of expression below?
$$\sqrt{x^2y^8}\sqrt{y^6x^4}$$
A. x^2y^5
B. $x^2y^5\sqrt{y}$
C. x^3y^2
D. $\sqrt{xy^2}$

Difficulty: Hard

10. What is $\sqrt{256}$?
E. 25
F. 12
G. 21
H. 16

Difficulty: Medium

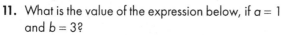

11. What is the value of the expression below, if $a = 1$ and $b = 3$?

$$\frac{\sqrt{a^2 + 3b^2} - a}{\sqrt{a^3} + b}$$

$\frac{27}{4}$

   A. 4   C. $\frac{3\sqrt{3}}{2}$

   B. $3\sqrt{3}$ D. 3

   Difficulty: Hard

12. If $\sqrt{x^5} \cdot \sqrt{x^n} = \sqrt{x^{15}}$, what is the value of n?

   E. 10   F. 5   G. 15   H. 2

   Difficulty: Hard

$5\sqrt{34}$

13. Evaluate $\frac{2\sqrt{34} + 3\sqrt{34}}{\sqrt{17}}$.

   A. $2\sqrt{17}$ C. $\sqrt{17}$

   B. $5\sqrt{34}$ D. $5\sqrt{2}$

   Difficulty: Hard

14. What is the value of the expression $\frac{4\sqrt{3}}{2} \times \frac{3\sqrt{6}}{\sqrt{2}}$?

   E. 9   G. 12

   F. 18   H. $3\sqrt{6}$

   Difficulty: Hard

15. What is the value of the following expression:

$$\frac{\sqrt{x^4y^3 + x^2y}}{\sqrt{x^2y}}$$

   A. x^3y^3 C. $x^4 + 1$

   B. $\sqrt{x^2y^2 + 1}$ D. $x^2\sqrt{y}$

   Difficulty: Hard

16. What is the value of the expression $\frac{\sqrt{8} \times \sqrt{5} + 2\sqrt{40}}{\sqrt{10} + \sqrt{10}}$?

   E. 3
   F. 20
   G. $2\sqrt{5}$
   H. 8

   Difficulty: Hard

17. Evaluate $\frac{\sqrt{12}}{\sqrt{3}}$.

   [   ]

   Difficulty: Medium

18.

$$\sqrt{\frac{a^2}{b^3} + 2}$$

   What is the value of the expression above, if $a = 4$ and $b = 2$?

   [   ]

   Difficulty: Medium

19. Simplify the following expression:

$$\sqrt{\frac{8\sqrt{6} + \sqrt{6}}{\sqrt{3} \times \sqrt{2}}}$$

   [   ]

   Difficulty: Hard

20. Evaluate $\sqrt{12} \times 2\sqrt{3}$.

   [   ]

   Difficulty: Medium

Video Explanations at argoprep.com/shsat

1. Find the largest perfect square for each factor and take its square root (which allows you to bring the square roots outside the radical).

Note that $\sqrt{x^2} = x$

Therefore, we have:

$$\sqrt{49x^6y^3} = \sqrt{(7)^2(x^3)^2(y)^2y} = 7x^3y\sqrt{y}$$

The correct answer is C.

2. First, find the value of the denominator. For this, find the largest perfect square for each factor and use its square root.

Therefore, we have:

$$\sqrt{16x^6y^4} = \sqrt{(4)^2(x^3)^2(y^2)^2} = 4x^3y^2$$

Then, divide by 2:

$$\frac{4x^3y^2}{2} = 2x^3y^2$$

The correct answer is H.

3. First, multiply the radicands:

$$\sqrt{8x^3} \cdot \sqrt{2x^5} = \sqrt{8x^3 \cdot 2x^5} = \sqrt{16x^3x^5}$$

Keep the base the same and add the powers. Therefore, we have:

$$\sqrt{16x^3x^5} = \sqrt{16x^{3+5}} = \sqrt{16x^8}$$

Then, find the largest perfect square for each factor and find its square root. Note that $\sqrt{x^2} = x$.

Therefore, we have:

$$\sqrt{16x^8} = \sqrt{(4)^2(x^4)^2} = 4x^4$$

The correct answer is B.

4. First, divide the radicands:

$$\frac{\sqrt{x^2}}{\sqrt{x^6}} = \sqrt{\frac{x^2}{x^6}}$$

Then keep the base the same and subtract the denominator exponent from the numerator exponent when dividing like bases.

$$\sqrt{\frac{x^2}{x^6}} = \sqrt{\frac{1}{x^{6-2}}} = \sqrt{\frac{1}{x^4}}$$

Find the largest perfect square for each factor and take its square root.

$$\sqrt{\frac{1}{x^4}} = \sqrt{\frac{1}{(x^2)^2}} = \frac{1}{x^2}$$

The correct answer is G.

5. Substitute the values of a and b into the original expression and find its square root:

$$\sqrt{a^3 + b^2 + 1} = \sqrt{2^3 + 4^2 + 1} = \sqrt{8 + 16 + 1} = \sqrt{25} = \sqrt{5 \times 5} = \sqrt{5^2} = 5$$

The correct answer is A.

6. First, multiply the radicands in the numerator together and add the powers:

$$\sqrt{x^4} \cdot \sqrt{x^3} = \sqrt{x^4 \cdot x^3} = \sqrt{x^{4+3}} = \sqrt{x^7}$$

Therefore, we have:

$$\frac{\sqrt{x^7}}{\sqrt{x^3}}$$

Second, divide the radicands and subtract the powers:

$$\frac{\sqrt{x^7}}{\sqrt{x^3}} = \sqrt{\frac{x^7}{x^3}} = \sqrt{x^{7-3}} = \sqrt{x^4}$$

Then, find the square root:

$$\sqrt{x^4} = \sqrt{(x^2)^2} = x^2$$

The correct answer is E.

7. First, multiply the radicands together. Then keep the base the same and add the powers:

$$\sqrt{x^9y} \times \sqrt{32xy^3} = \sqrt{32x^{9+1}y^{1+3}} = \sqrt{32x^{10}y^4}$$

Find the largest perfect square for each factor and find its square root. Therefore, we have:

$$\sqrt{32x^{10}y^4} = \sqrt{(16 \times 2)(x^5)^2(y^2)^2} = x^5y^2\sqrt{(4)^2 \times 2} = 4\sqrt{2}x^5y^2$$

The correct answer is C.

8. First, divide the radicands.

$$\frac{\sqrt{9x^9}}{\sqrt{81x^7}} = \sqrt{\frac{9x^9}{81x^7}}$$

Second, divide numerator and denominator by $\sqrt{9}$ and subtract the powers.

Therefore, we have:

$$\sqrt{\frac{9x^9}{81x^7}} = \sqrt{\frac{x^9}{9x^7}} = \sqrt{\frac{x^{9-7}}{9}} = \sqrt{\frac{x^2}{9}}$$

Then, take its square root:

$$\sqrt{\frac{x^2}{9}} = \sqrt{\frac{x^2}{3^2}} = \frac{x}{3}$$

The correct answer is G.

Video Explanations
at argoprep.com/shsat

9. First, take the inner square root. For that, find the largest perfect square for each factor and take its square root.

Therefore, we have:

$$\sqrt{y^6 x^4} = \sqrt{(y^3)^2 (x^2)^2} = y^3 x^2$$

We have:

$$\sqrt{x^2 y^8} \sqrt{y^6 x^4} = \sqrt{x^2 y^8 y^3 x^2}$$

Keep the same bases and add the powers. Therefore, we have:

$$\sqrt{x^2 y^8 y^3 x^2} = \sqrt{x^{2+2} y^{8+3}} = \sqrt{x^4 y^{11}} = \sqrt{(x^2)^2 (y^5)^2 y} = x^2 y^5 \sqrt{y}$$

The correct answer is B.

---

10. Rewrite the expression:

$$\sqrt{256} = \sqrt{4 \times 64}$$
$$4 = 2^2 \text{ and } 64 = 8^2$$
$$\sqrt{256} = \sqrt{4 \times 64} = \sqrt{2^2 \times 8^2} = 2 \times 8 = 16$$

The correct answer is H.

---

11. First, solve the numerator and the denominator separately. Substitute the values of a and b into the original expression. For the numerator, we have:

$$\sqrt{a^2 + 3b^2 - a} = \sqrt{1^2 + 3 \times (3)^2 - 1} = \sqrt{1 + 3 \times 9 - 1} = \sqrt{3 \times 9} = 3\sqrt{3}$$

For the denominator, we have:

$$\sqrt{a^3 + b} = \sqrt{1^3 + 3} = \sqrt{1 + 3} = \sqrt{4} = \sqrt{2 \times 2} = 2$$

Then, divide the numerator by the denominator. Therefore, we have:

$$\frac{\sqrt{a^2 + 3b^2 - a}}{\sqrt{a^3 + b}} = \frac{3\sqrt{3}}{2}$$

The correct answer is C.

---

12. First, multiply the radicands. Then keep the base the same and add the powers.

$$\sqrt{x^5} \times \sqrt{x^n} = \sqrt{x^5 x^n} = \sqrt{x^{5+n}}$$

We have:

$$\sqrt{x^{5+n}} = \sqrt{x^{15}}$$
$$x^{5+n} = x^{15}$$

The base is the same, so the powers are equal. Therefore, we have:

$$5 + n = 15$$
$$\text{So } n = 15 - 5 = 10$$

The correct answer is E.

---

13. First, add the numbers with the same radicands in the numerator:

$$2\sqrt{34} + 3\sqrt{34} = 5\sqrt{34}$$

Then, rewrite $\sqrt{34}$ as $\sqrt{17 \times 2}$ and divide by $\sqrt{17}$

$$\frac{5\sqrt{34}}{\sqrt{17}} = \frac{5\sqrt{17 \times 2}}{\sqrt{17}} = \frac{5\sqrt{17}\sqrt{2}}{\sqrt{17}} = 5\sqrt{2}$$

The correct answer is D.

---

14. First, rewrite this expression as

$$\frac{4\sqrt{3} \times 3\sqrt{6}}{2\sqrt{2}}$$

Then multiply the radicands in the numerator and divide by the denominator.

Therefore, we have:

$$\frac{4\sqrt{3} \times 3\sqrt{6}}{2\sqrt{2}} = \frac{12\sqrt{3 \times 6}}{2\sqrt{2}} = \frac{6\sqrt{18}}{\sqrt{2}} = 6\sqrt{\frac{18}{2}} = 6\sqrt{9} = 6\sqrt{3^2} = 6 \times 3 = 18$$

The correct answer is F.

---

15. Factor out the common terms in the numerator:

$$\frac{\sqrt{x^4 y^3 + x^2 y}}{\sqrt{x^2 y}} = \sqrt{\frac{x^2 y \left(x^2 y^2 + 1 \right)}{x^2 y}}$$

The denominator cancels out with the top left portion of the numerator. You are left with square root of $\sqrt{x^2 y^2 + 1}$.

The correct answer is B.

---

16. First, multiply the radicands together and then add the same radicands in the numerator and the denominator.

$$\frac{\sqrt{8} \times \sqrt{5} + 2\sqrt{40}}{\sqrt{10} + \sqrt{10}} = \frac{\sqrt{8 \times 5} + 2\sqrt{40}}{2\sqrt{10}} = \frac{\sqrt{40} + 2\sqrt{40}}{2\sqrt{10}} = \frac{3\sqrt{40}}{2\sqrt{10}}$$

Then, divide the radicands and take the square root:

$$\frac{3\sqrt{40}}{2\sqrt{10}} = \frac{3}{2}\sqrt{\frac{40}{10}} = \frac{3}{2}\sqrt{4} = \frac{3}{2}\sqrt{2^2} = \frac{3}{2} \times 2 = 3$$

The correct answer is E.

Video Explanations
at argoprep.com/shsat

17. First, divide the radicands under the same radical:

$$\frac{\sqrt{12}}{\sqrt{3}} = \sqrt{\frac{12}{3}}$$

Then, divide 12 by 3 and take its square root. Therefore, we have:

$$\sqrt{\frac{12}{3}} = \sqrt{4} = \sqrt{2^2} = 2$$

---

18. Substitute the values of a and b into the original expression and take its square root:

$$\sqrt{\frac{a^2}{b^3} + 2} = \sqrt{\frac{4^2}{2^3} + 2} = \sqrt{\frac{16}{8} + 2} = \sqrt{2 + 2} = \sqrt{4} = \sqrt{2^2} = 2$$

---

19. First, add the same radicands in the numerator and multiply the radicands together in the denominator:

$$\frac{8\sqrt{6} + \sqrt{6}}{\sqrt{3} \times \sqrt{2}} = \frac{9\sqrt{6}}{\sqrt{3 \times 2}} = \frac{9\sqrt{6}}{\sqrt{6}} = 9$$

Then, take the square root of the result:

$$\sqrt{9} = 3$$

---

20. First, multiply the radicands under one radical and then solve the resulting expression.

$$\sqrt{12} \times 2\sqrt{3} = 2\sqrt{12 \times 3} = 2\sqrt{36} = 2\sqrt{6^2} = 2 \times 6 = 12$$

Video Explanations
at argoprep.com/shsat

1. What is the value of the following expression?

$$|-12+5|$$

A. 17   C. 7
B. −7   D. −17

Difficulty: Medium

2. What is the value of the following expression?

$$\frac{|-10|+2}{|-2|+4}$$

E. 2   G. −8
F. 4   H. −4

Difficulty: Medium

3. Find the value of the following expression.

$$\frac{9}{|-3|}\times|-5|$$

A. −15   C. 10
B. 15   D. −9

Difficulty: Medium

4. What is the value of the expression below?

$$-8+-5|$$

E. 13
F. −13
G. −3
H. 3

Difficulty: Medium

5. What is the solution of $x = 5$?

A. $x = 5$
B. $x = -5$
C. $x = -5$ or $x = 5$
D. no solution

Difficulty: Medium

6. What is the solution of the following expression?

$$2x = 8$$

E. $x = 4$ G. $x = -4$
F. $x = -1$ H. $x = 4$ or $x = -4$

Difficulty: Hard⁺

7. What is the value of the following expression?

$$\frac{|2\cdot|-5|+4\cdot|-3||}{2}$$

A. 10   C. 8
B. 11   D. −6

Difficulty: Medium

8.
$$2a - 3b^2$$

What is the value of the expression above if $a = 1$ and $b = 2$?

E. −10   G. 10
F. 12   H. 3

Difficulty: Medium

9. What is the value of the following expression?

$$\frac{|-8+4|}{2}\times\frac{5}{|-6+1|}$$

A. 4   C. 2
B. −5   D. 8

Difficulty: Medium

10.
$$5a^3 - 9b^2$$

What is the value of the expression above, if $a = 1$ and $b = -1$?

E. 6   G. −4
F. −6   H. 4

Difficulty: Medium

Video Explanations
at argoprep.com/shsat

11. What is the solution of $|2x + 4| = 8$?

   A. $x = 3$
   B. $x = -6$ or $x = 2$
   C. $x = 6$
   D. $x = 2$ or $x = -2$

Difficulty: Hard

12. What is the solution of $x - 2 = -3$?

   E. No solution
   F. $x = -1$
   G. $x = -1$ or $x = 5$
   H. $x = 5$

Difficulty: Medium

13. What is the value of the expression below?

$$|-7| + 4 + -12 + 4 \times |-2|$$

   A. 12   **C.** 10
   B. -4   **D.** 15

Difficulty: Medium

14.

$$\frac{||2a^2 + 4| + 8|}{|2b| - 5}$$

What is the value of the expression above, if $a = 2$, and $b = -5$?

   E. 2   **G.** -1
   F. 4   **H.** 7

Difficulty: Medium

15. What is the solution of $\frac{|x + 3|}{2} = 4$?

   A. $x = -11$
   B. $x = 5$
   C. $x = -11$ or $x = 5$
   D. $x = 8$

Difficulty: Medium

16. What is the value of $x < 3$?

   E. $x < 3$
   F. $x > -3$
   G. $x < 3$
   H. $-3 < x < 3$

Difficulty: Medium

17. What is the value of a, if $5 - a = 4$?

Difficulty: Medium

18. What is the value of x, if $x = \frac{|-16 + 4|}{|8 - 2|} \cdot |-2|$?

Difficulty: Medium

19. What is the solution of $x - 2 < 5$?

Difficulty: Medium

20. What is the value of the expression below, if $a = 2$ and $b = 2$?

$$\frac{|2b - 5a| \times |b - a^2|}{|b^2| \times |a^2 + b|}$$

Difficulty: Medium

Video Explanations
at argoprep.com/shsat

67

1. First, add two numbers. Therefore, we have:
$$-12 + 5 = -7$$
Then, take its absolute value. Note that $-1 = 1$. We have:
$$-7 = 7$$
The correct answer is C.

2. First, find the absolute value of the numbers in numerator and the denominator. Note that $-1 = 1$.
Therefore, we have:
$$-10 = 10$$
And
$$-2 = 2$$
Second, add the numbers in the numerator and the denominator and then divide the numerator by the denominator. We have:
$$\frac{|-10| + 2}{|-2| + 4} = \frac{10 + 2}{2 + 4} = \frac{12}{6} = 2$$
The correct answer is E.

3. First, find the absolute value of the numbers. Note that $-1 = 1$
Therefore, we have:
$$-3 = 3$$
And
$$-5 = 5$$
Then, multiply the numerator by 5 and divide the result by the denominator:
$$\frac{9}{|-3|} \times |-5| = \frac{9 \times 5}{3} = \frac{45}{3} = 15$$
The correct answer is B.

4. First, find the inner absolute value. Note that $-1 = 1$. Therefore, we have:
$$-5 = 5$$
Then, add two numbers and take the absolute value of the result.
$$-8 + -5 = -8 + 5 = -3 = 3$$
The correct answer is H.

5. There is a law of absolute value that needs to be used to solve the problem.
For any real number x, the absolute value is defined as
$$|x| = \begin{cases} -x, & \text{if } x < 0 \\ x, & \text{if } x \geq 0 \end{cases}$$
So $x = 5$ or $x = -5$

The correct answer is C.

6. There is law of absolute value that needs to be used to solve the problem.
For any real number x, the absolute value is defined as
$$|x| = \begin{cases} -x, & \text{if } x < 0 \\ x, & \text{if } x \geq 0 \end{cases}$$
Therefore, we have:
$2x = 8$
$2x = -8$
From the first equation we have:
$$x = \frac{8}{2} = 4$$
From the second:
$$x = \frac{-8}{2} = -4$$
The correct answer is H.

7. First, find the absolute value of the numbers inside the absolute value symbol. Note that $-1 = 1$.
Therefore, we have:
$$-5 = 5$$
And
$$-3 = 3$$
Second, multiply the numbers in the numerator, then add it and take its absolute value.
Therefore, we have:
$$\frac{|2 \times |-5| + 4 \times |-3||}{2} = \frac{|2 \times 5 + 4 \times 3|}{2} = \frac{|10 + 12|}{2} = \frac{|22|}{2} = 11$$
The correct answer is B.

8. First, substitute the value of a and b into the original expression:
$2a - 3b^2 = 2 \times 1 - 3 \times 2^2 = 2 - 3 \times 4 = 2 - 12 = -10$
Then, take the absolute value. Note that $-1 = 1$. Therefore, we have:
$$-10 = 10$$
The correct answer is G.

9. First, add the numbers:
$$-8 + 4 = -4$$
And
$$-6 + 1 = -5$$
Second, take its absolute value. Note that $-1 = 1$. Therefore, we have:

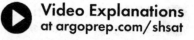
Video Explanations
at argoprep.com/shsat

$$-4 = 4$$

And

$$-5 = 5$$

Then, divide the numerators by denominator and multiply it:

$$\frac{4}{5} \times \frac{5}{5} = 2 \times 1 = 2$$

The correct answer is C.

10. First, substitute the values of a and b into the original expression:
$5\ a^3 - 9\ b^3 | = 5 \times 1^3 - 9 \times (-1)^2 =$
$5 \times 1 - 9 \times 1 = 5 - 9 = -4$
Then, take its absolute value. Note that $-1 = 1$. We have:
The correct answer is H.

11. There is the law of absolute value that needs to be used to solve the problem given.
For any real number x, the absolute value is defined as

$$|x| = \begin{cases} -x, & \text{if } x < 0 \\ x, & \text{if } x \geq 0 \end{cases}$$

Therefore, we have:

$$2x + 4 = 8$$

Or

$$2x + 4 = -8$$

From the first equality we have:

$$2x = 8 - 4$$
$$2x = 4$$
$$x = \frac{4}{2} = 2$$

From the second we have:

$$2x = -8 - 4$$
$$2x = -12$$
$$x = \frac{-12}{2} = -6$$

The correct answer is B.

12. There is law of absolute value that needs to be used to solve the problem.
The absolute value of a real number x is the non-negative value of x without regard to its sign.
In this case, the absolute value is equal to a negative number, so there are no solutions.
The correct answer is E.

13. First, take the absolute value of the numbers inside. Note that

$-1 = 1$ and $1 = 1$.
Therefore, we have:

$$-7 = 7$$

And

$$-2 = 2$$

Second, substitute it into the expression and add the numbers. We have:
$|-7 + 4 + -12 + 4 \times -2| = 7 + 4 + -12 + 4 \times 2 = 11 + -4$
Then, take its absolute value. We have:

$$11 + -4 = 11 + 4 = 15$$

The correct answer is D.

14. First, substitute the value of a and b into the original expression:

$$\frac{||2a^2 + 4| + 8|}{|2b| - 5} = \frac{||2 \times 2^2 + 4| + 8|}{|2 \times (-5)| - 5} = \frac{||8 + 4| + 8|}{|-10| - 5} = \frac{||12| + 8|}{|-10| - 5}$$

Second, find the absolute values inside. Note that $-1 = 1$. Therefore, we have:

$$12 = 12$$

And

$$-10 = 10$$

Then, substitute it into equation, add the numbers and take its absolute value.
We have:

$$\frac{||12| + 8|}{|-10| - 5} = \frac{|12 + 8|}{10 - 5} = \frac{|20|}{5} = \frac{20}{5} = 4$$

The correct answer is F.

15. First, multiply the left and right sides by 2: Therefore, we have:

$$\frac{|x + 3|}{2} \times 2 = 4 \times 2$$
$$x + 3 = 8$$

There is the law of the absolute value that needs to be used to solve the problem.
For any real number x, the absolute value is defined as

$$|x| = \begin{cases} -x, & \text{if } x < 0 \\ x, & \text{if } x \geq 0 \end{cases}$$

We have:

$$x + 3 = 8$$
$$x + 3 = -8$$

From the first equation we have:

$$x = 8 - 3 = 5$$

From the second equation we have:

$$x = -8 - 3 = -11$$

The correct answer is C.

Video Explanations
at argoprep.com/shsat

16. There is the law of absolute value that needs to be used to solve the problem.

For any real number x, the absolute value is defined as

$$|x| = \begin{cases} -x, & \text{if } x < 0 \\ x, & \text{if } x \geq 0 \end{cases}$$

$$-3 < x < 3.$$

The correct answer is H.

---

17. There is the law of absolute value that needs to be used to solve the problem.

For any real number x, the absolute value is defined as

$$|x| = \begin{cases} -x, & \text{if } x < 0 \\ x, & \text{if } x \geq 0 \end{cases}$$

We have:

$$5 - a = 4$$
$$a = 5 - 4 = 1$$

Or

$$5 - a = -4$$
$$a = 5 + 4 = 9$$

---

18. First, add the numbers in the numerator and subtract the denominator. We have:

$$x = \frac{|-16 + 4|}{|8 - 2|} \times |-2| = \frac{|-12|}{|6|} \times |-2|$$

Then, take the absolute value of these numbers. Note that $-1 = 1$ and $1 = 1$. Therefore, we have:

$$-12 = 12, \ 6 = 6, \ -2 = 2$$

We have:

$$x = \frac{|-12|}{|6|} \times |-2| = \frac{12}{6} \times 2 = 2 \times 2 = 4$$

---

19. The law of absolute value needs to be used to solve the problem.

For any real number x, the absolute value is defined as

$$|x| = \begin{cases} -x, & \text{if } x < 0 \\ x, & \text{if } x \geq 0 \end{cases}$$

Therefore, we have:

$$-5 < x - 2 < 5$$

Then, add 2:

$$-5 + 2 < x < 5 + 2$$
$$-3 < x < 7$$

20. First, substitute the values of a and b into the original expression:

$$\frac{|2b - 5a| \times |b - a^2|}{|b^2| \times |a^2 + b|} = \frac{|2 \times 2 - 5 \times 2| \times |2 - 2^2|}{|2^2| \times |2^2 + 2|} = \frac{|4 - 10| \times |2 - 4|}{4 \times |4 + 2|} = \frac{|-6| \times |-2|}{4 \times |6|}$$

Then, take the absolute value. Note that $-1 = 1$ and $1 = 1$. Therefore, we have:

$$-6 = 6, \ -2 = 2, \ 6 = 6$$

We have:

$$\frac{|2b - 5a| \times |b - a^2|}{|b^2| \times |a^2 + b|} = \frac{|-6| \times |-2|}{4 \times |6|} = \frac{6 \times 2}{4 \times 6} = \frac{2}{4} = \frac{1}{2}$$

Video Explanations
at argoprep.com/shsat

1. What number divides into 345 evenly?

   A. 2
   B. 7
   C. 9
   D. 5

   Difficulty: Medium

2. What number divides into 234 evenly?

   E. 5
   F. 4
   G. 9
   H. 7

   Difficulty: Medium

3. What number divides into 122 evenly?

   A. 5
   B. 4
   C. 2
   D. 3

   Difficulty: Medium

4. What number divides into 133 evenly?

   E. 7
   F. 3
   G. 5
   H. 2

   Difficulty: Medium

5. What number divides into 102 evenly?

   A. 9
   B. 4
   C. 3
   D. 7

   Difficulty: Medium

6. Which of the following numbers is evenly divisible by 5?

   E. 155
   F. 271
   G. 43
   H. 91

   Difficulty: Medium

7. Which of the following numbers is evenly divisible by 2?

   A. 122
   B. 85
   C. 63
   D. 39

   Difficulty: Medium

8. Which of the following numbers is evenly divisible by 4?

   E. 225
   F. 121
   G. 112
   H. 109

   Difficulty: Medium

9. Which of the following numbers is evenly divisible by 9?

   A. 95
   B. 82
   C. 63
   D. 31

   Difficulty: Medium

10. Which of the following numbers is evenly divisible by 10?

    E. 143
    F. 120
    G. 105
    H. 67

    Difficulty: Easy

Video Explanations
at argoprep.com/shsat

11. What number divides into 4,105 evenly?

    A. 3
    B. 2
    C. 5
    D. 10

    Difficulty: Hard

12. What number divides into 31,816 evenly?

    E. 8
    F. 5
    G. 9
    H. 10

    Difficulty: Hard

13. Which of the following numbers is evenly divisible by 11?

    A. 132
    B. 144
    C. 100
    D. 108

    Difficulty: Medium

14. Which of the following numbers is evenly divisible by 9?

    E. 51,682
    F. 35,937
    G. 45,896
    H. 28,579

    Difficulty: Hard

15. Which of the following numbers is evenly divisible by 4?

    A. 6116
    B. 3003
    C. 5789
    D. 7542

    Difficulty: Hard

16. Ann made 33 chocolate desserts. She arranged the desserts on platters, with the same number of dessert on each platter. How many desserts could Ann have put on each platter?

    E. 5
    F. 6
    G. 4
    H. 3

    Difficulty: Medium

17. Is the expression below evenly divisible by 5?

    4589 – 1256

    Difficulty: Hard

18. Is the expression below evenly divisible by 9?

    7523 – 5579

    Difficulty: Hard

19. Is the expression below evenly divisible by 10?

    546 – 322
    ─────────
        3

    Difficulty: Hard

20. Is the number 412 evenly divisible by 3 or 4?

    Difficulty: Easy

Video Explanations
at argoprep.com/shsat

1. There are laws that need to be used to solve the problem given. First law: If after doubling the last digit of the number and subtracting it from the number made by the other digits, if that result is divisible by 7, then the original number is also divisible by 7.

   Second law: If the sum of the digits of a number is divisible by 9, the original number is divisible by 9.

   Third law: If the last digit of a number is 0 or 5, the original number is divisible by 5.

   Fourth law: If the last digit is: 0, 2, 4, 6, 8, this number is divisible by 2.

   The last digit of the number 345 is 5:

   $$\frac{345}{5} = 69$$

   The correct answer is D.

2. There are laws that need to be used to solve the problem given.

   First law: If the last digit of a number is 0 or 5, the original number is divisible by 5.

   Second law: If the sum of the digits of a number is divisible by 9, the number is divisible by 9.

   Third law: If after doubling the last digit of the number and subtracting it from the number made by the other digits, if that result is divisible by 7, then the original number is also divisible by 7.

   Fourth law: If the last two digits of number are divisible by 4, the original number is divisible by 4.

   The sum of the digits of number 234 is $2 + 3 + 4 = 9$.

   $$\frac{9}{9} = 1$$

   The number 234 is divisible by 9.

   The correct answer is G.

3. There are laws that need to be used to solve the problem given. First law: If the last digit of a number is 0 or 5, the number is divisible by 5.

   Second law: If the last digit is even (0, 2, 4, 6, 8), the number is divisible by 2.

   Third law: If the sum of the digits of a number is divisible by 3, the number is divisible by 3.

   Fourth law: If the last two digits of a number are divisible by 4, the number is divisible by 4.

   The last digit of the number 122 is 2, so the number is divisible by 2.

   The correct answer is C.

4. There are laws that need to be used to solve the problem given.

   First law: If the last digit of a number is 0 or 5, the number is divisible by 5.

   Second law: If the last digit is: 0, 2, 4, 6 or 8 then the number is divisible by 2.

   Third law: If the sum of the digits of a number is divisible by 3, that number is divisible by 3.

   Fourth law: If after doubling the last digit of the number and subtracting it from the number made by the other digits, if that result is divisible by 7, then the original number is also divisible by 7.

   First, double the last digit of the number 133:

   $$3 \times 2 = 6$$

   Then, subtract :

   $$13 - 6 = 7$$

   Check if this number divisible by 7

   $$\frac{7}{7} = 1$$

   The number 133 is divisible by 7.

   The correct answer is E.

5. There are laws that need to be used to solve the problem given.

   First law: If the sum of the digits of the number is divisible by 3, this number is divisible by 3.

   Second law: If the last two digits of the number are divisible by 4, this number is divisible by 4.

   Third law: If after doubling the last digit of the number and subtracting it from the number made by the other digits, if that result is divisible by 7, then the original number is also divisible by 7.

   Fourth law: If the sum of the digits of a number is divisible by 9, the original number is divisible by 9.

   The sum of the digits of the number 102 is:

   $$1 + 0 + 2 = 3$$

   Check if this number divisible by 3:

   $$\frac{3}{3} = 1$$

   The number 102 is divisible by 3.

   The correct answer is C.

6. The law is that the number is divisible by five when the last digit is 0 or 5.

   There is only one option that has the last digit that is 5. It's the number 155.

   The correct answer is E.

7. The number is divisible by 2 when the last digit is:

   0, 2, 4, 6, or 8.

   In our case, the only option is number 122 (the last digit is 2).

   The correct answer is A.

Video Explanations
at argoprep.com/shsat

8. The number is divisible by 4 when the last two digits of the number are divisible by 4.

The only option that has the last two digits that are divisible by 4 is 112:

$$\frac{112}{4} = 28$$

The correct answer is G.

9. The number is divisible by 9 when the sum of the digits of the number is divisible by 9.

The only option is 63, because

$$6 + 3 = 9$$

Check whether this number is divisible by 9:

$$\frac{9}{9} = 1$$

The correct answer is C.

10. A number is divisible by 10 when the number ends in 0.

From those options, there is one number that ends in 0. It's 120.

The correct answer is F.

11. There are laws that need to be used to solve the problem given.

First law: If the last digit is 0, 2, 4, 6, 8, then the number is divisible by 2.

Second law: If the sum of the digits of a number is divisible by 3, the number is divisible by 3.

Third law: If the last digit of a number is 0 or 5, the number is divisible by 5.

Fourth law: If the number ends in 0, this number is divisible by 10.

The number 4105 ends in 5, so it's divisible by 5.

The correct answer is A.

12. There are laws that need to be used to solve the problem given.

First law: If the sum of the digits of a number is divisible by 9, the number is divisible by 9.

Second law: If the sum of the digits of a number is divisible by 3 , this number is divisible by 3.

Third law: If the number ends in 0, this number is divisible by 10.

Fourth law: If the last three digits are divisible by 8, this number is divisible by 8.

The last three digits of the number 31,816 is divisible by 8:

$$\frac{816}{8} = 102$$

This number is divisible by 8.

The correct answer is E.

13. A law states that a number is divisible by 11 if the last digit can be subtracted from the other digits and the result is divisible by 11.

From these options, it's number 132:

$$13 - 2 = 11$$

Check if this number divisible by 11:

$$\frac{11}{11} = 1$$

This number is divisible by 11.

The correct answer is A.

14. A number is divisible by 9 if the sum of its digits is divisible by 9. Check each option by adding digits. First, check number 51,682:

$$5 + 1 + 6 + 8 + 2 = 22$$

Then check whether this number is divisible by 9:

$$\frac{22}{9} = 2\frac{4}{9}$$

This number isn't divisible by 9. Check the next number.

$$3 + 5 + 9 + 3 + 7 = 27$$

Then, check whether this number is divisible by 9.

$$\frac{27}{9} = 3$$

The number 35,937 is divisible by 9.

The correct answer is F.

15. A number is divisible by 4 if the last two digits are divisible by 4. In our case, the number is 6116. The last two digits are 16:

$$\frac{16}{4} = 4$$

The correct answer is A.

16. A number is divisible by 6 if it is divisible by both 2 and 3. A number is divisible by 5 if its last digit is a 0 or 5.

A number is divisible by 4 if the last two digits are divisible by 4. A number is divisible by 3 if the sum of the digits is divisible by 3.

First try the "divisible by 5" rule on 33. The last digit is not a 0 or 5. The rule says that 33 is not divisible by 5.

Next try the "divisible by 6" rules on 33. The rule says that 33 is not divisible by 6.

Then, try the "divisible by 4" rule on 33. The rule says that 33 is not divisible by 4. Finally, try the "divisible by 3" rule on 33. We have:

$$3 + 3 = 6; \quad \frac{6}{3} = 2$$

The rule says that 33 is divisible by 3.

 **Video Explanations**
at argoprep.com/shsat

Ann could have put 3 chocolate desserts on each platter.
The correct answer is H.

17. A number is divisible by 5 if its last digit is a 0 or 5. First, subtract the numbers:
$$4589 - 1256 = 3333$$
The last digit is 3.
The rule says that this expression isn't divisible by 5.

18. A number is divisible by 9 if the sum of its digits is divisible by 9. First, subtract these numbers:
$$7523 - 5579 = 1944$$
Then, check if the sum of digits is divisible by 5.
$$1 + 9 + 4 + 4 = 18;$$
$$\frac{18}{9} = 2 .$$
The expression is divisible by 9.

19. A number is divisible by 10, if its last digit is a 0.
First, subtract the numbers in the numerator and then divide by the denominator:
$$\frac{546 - 322}{3} = \frac{224}{2} = 112$$
The last digit is 2.
The rule says that this expression isn't divisible by 10.

20. A number is divisible by 4 if the last two digits are divisible by 4. A number is divisible by 3 if the sum of the digits is divisible by 3.
First, try the "divisible by 3" rule on 412. The sum of the digit is
$$4 + 1 + 2 = 7; \; \frac{7}{3} = 3\frac{4}{3}$$
The number 412 isn't divisible by 3. Then, try the "divisible by 4" rule on 412. The last two digits are 12.
We have:
$$\frac{12}{4} = 3$$
The number 412 is divisible by 4.

ARGOPREP SHSAT – Arithmetic – Challenge Questions

1. Simplify the following expression:
$$\frac{3m^3}{7n^5} \div \frac{3m^8}{21\ln^5}$$

A. $\frac{3m^5 n}{7}$ C. $21m^3 n$

B. $\frac{3}{m^5}$ D. $21mn^3$

Difficulty: Medium

2. $(x-2y)^2 + 3(y-x)$

What is the value of the expression above if $x=-2$ and $y=3$?

E. −79   G. 65
F. −49   H. 79

Difficulty: Medium

3. What is the sum of the two largest prime factors of 88?

A. 4   B. 13   C. 22   D. 24

Difficulty: Medium

4. Calculate the value of the following expression:
$$2\sqrt{72} - 3\sqrt{8} + 2\sqrt{32}$$

E. 2   G. $7\sqrt{2}$
F. $\sqrt{2}$ H. $14\sqrt{2}$

Difficulty: Medium

5. Tommy has $32.50 and he wants to buy 2 pens for $1.25 each and 3 notebooks for $2.45 each. How much money will Tommy have after his purchase?

A. $19.85   C. $22.65
B. $21.40   D. $23.85

Difficulty: Medium

6. Express the following number in scientific notation:

52,010,000

E. 5.201×10^{-7}
F. 0.5201×10^8
G. 5.201×10^7
H. 52.01×10^6

Difficulty: Medium

7. Perform the indicated operations to find the value of the expression below:
$$\frac{2}{9} - \frac{1}{3}\left(1\frac{1}{3} + 2\frac{1}{4}\right)$$

A. $-1\frac{1}{35}$ C. $\frac{1}{3}$

B. $-\frac{35}{36}$ D. $\frac{2}{9}$

Difficulty: Medium

8. Maria bought a pack of candies. She ate 10 candies and 75% of the original amount of candies were left over. How many candies were initially in the pack?

E. 15
F. 24
G. 40
H. 55

Difficulty: Hard

9. Calculate the value of the following expression. Round the final answer to the nearest tenth.

$$3.2(1.05 + 0.8) - 2.1$$

A. 5.92
B. 4.6
C. 3.9
D. 3.8

Difficulty: Medium

 Video Explanations at argoprep.com/shsat

76

10.

$$\frac{3x^2y^5z^3}{5y^2z} \cdot \frac{z}{15xy^6}$$

(handwritten: $\frac{xz^3}{25y^3}$)

Simplify the expression above.

E. $\dfrac{5x^3y}{z}$

G. $\dfrac{xz^3}{25y^3}$ *(circled)*

F. $\dfrac{z^3}{15xy}$

H. $\dfrac{x^3z^2}{y^3}$

Difficulty: Medium

11. When 7 times a number is increased by 5, the result is 54. Find the number.

A. 2
B. 7 *(circled)*
C. 5
D. 12

Difficulty: Medium

12. Find the least common multiple of 5 and 7.

E. 35 *(circled)*
F. 12
G. 25
H. 49

Difficulty: Medium

13. Anna is working out a problem involving the fraction $\dfrac{3}{4}$. She needs to enter this into a calculator. What decimal will she enter into the calculator?

A. 0.4
B. 3.25
C. 0.5
D. 0.75 *(circled)*

Difficulty: Medium

14. What is the value of the expression below if $a = 2$ and $b = 1$?

$$\frac{|b^2 - 5a|}{\left\lvert |a^3 + 3| - 8 \right\rvert}$$

E. 3
F. 6
G. 1
H. −8

Difficulty: Medium

15. Which one of the following numbers is evenly divisible by 5?

A. 134
B. 445 *(circled)*
C. 89
D. 76

Difficulty: Medium

16. Which of the following numbers is prime?

E. 8
F. 6
G. 13 *(circled)*
H. 10

Difficulty: Medium

17. There were 3,555 spectators in the theatre, of which 1,980 were men. Of the remaining spectators, there were 2 times as many children as women. How many children were there?

A. 525
B. 780
C. 1000
D. 1050 *(circled)*

Difficulty: Hard

18. Kate bought a box of apples. If five apples represent 20% of the total apples in the box, how many apples are in the box?

E. 15
F. 25 *(circled)*
G. 40
H. 17

Difficulty: Medium

Video Explanations
at argoprep.com/shsat

19.

$$\frac{\sqrt{a^2 - 4b^2 + 1}}{\sqrt{a^3 + b}}$$

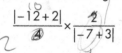

What is the value of the expression above, if $a = 2$ and $b = 1$?

A. 4
C. $\frac{1}{3}$
B. $3\sqrt{2}$
D. 5

Difficulty: Hard

20. Rita has $41.50 and she wants to buy 3 pens for $1.75 each and 3 books for $10.15 each. How much money will Rita have after her purchase?

E. $5.80
F. $22.30
G. $19.65
H. $17.80

30.45
$+ 5.25$
35.70

Difficulty: Medium

21. What is the value of the following expression?

$$\frac{|-12+2|}{4} \times \frac{2}{|-7+3|}$$

A. 1
B. −1.5
C. 1.25
D. 3

Difficulty: Hard

22. Express the following number in scientific notation:

0.0000243

E. 2.43×10^{-5}
F. 0.243×10^5
G. 0.243×10^{-5}
H. 24.3×10^6

Difficulty: Medium

23. Calculate the value of the following expression. Round the final answer to the nearest hundredth.

$$1.7(3.45 - 0.7) + 5.7$$

A. 10.38
C. 10.375
B. 6.4
D. 11.04

Difficulty: Medium

24. When 8 times a number is decreased by 2 and then divided by 2, the result is 35. Find the number.

E. 2
F. 9
G. 7
H. −1

Difficulty: Hard

25. Find the least common multiple of 9 and 3.

A. 27   B. 3   C. 12   D. 9

Difficulty: Easy

26. Alex works as a house painter and earns $17.09 per hour. If he worked 5 hours yesterday, how much money did he earn?

E. $85.45
F. $70.76
G. $65.98
H. $34.5

Difficulty: Medium

27. Which of the following numbers is evenly divisible by 3?

A. 445
B. 720
C. 89
D. 91

Difficulty: Medium

Video Explanations
at argoprep.com/shsat

28. Inna went to the hardware store and bought 4 identical wooden boards. When Inna placed all the boards end-to-end, they formed a line that was 7 meters long. How long was each board?

E. 28 m   G. 3.04 m
F. 5.76 m   H. 1.75 m

Difficulty: Medium

29. The city park is $5\frac{3}{4}$ miles from Roland Elementary School. The cinema is $2\frac{1}{8}$ miles from the same school. How much farther from the school is the park than the cinema?

A. 4   C. $2\frac{1}{4}$

B. $3\frac{1}{2}$ D. $3\frac{5}{8}$

Difficulty: Medium

30. Perform the indicated operations to find the value of the expression below:

$$\left(2\frac{1}{3} - 1\frac{1}{5}\right) \times \frac{1}{2} \div \left(\frac{5}{2} + \frac{1}{2}\right)$$

E. $1\frac{1}{90}$ G. $2\frac{2}{5}$

F. $\frac{2}{9}$ H. $\frac{17}{90}$

Difficulty: Hard

31. What is the solution of $6x - 2 = 10$?

A. $x = 5$

B. $x = 2$ or $x = -\frac{4}{3}$

C. $x = -1$ or $x = 2$

D. $x = 4$

Difficulty: Hard

32. If $\dfrac{\sqrt{x^3} \cdot \sqrt{x^n}}{\sqrt{x^5}} = \sqrt{x^7}$, what is the value of n?

E. 4   (F.) 9   G. 11   H. 8

Difficulty: Hard

33. Mrs. Don had $7,000 in her savings account. Each year she earns 20% interest on the account. If she leaves her money in the account for three years, how much money will she have at the end of the third year?

Difficulty: Hard

34. What is the value of the expression below?

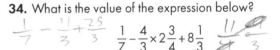

$$\frac{1}{7} - \frac{4}{3} \times 2\frac{3}{4} + 8\frac{1}{3}$$

Difficulty: Medium

35. Rewrite the following expression in scientific notation.

$$\frac{0.0065}{0.01} \times 0.004$$

Difficulty: Hard

36. What is the difference between the two smallest distinct prime factors of 70?

Difficulty: Hard

37. Jane ate $\frac{4}{6}$ of a pizza pie. David ate $\frac{1}{3}$ of the pizza pie. What fraction of the pizza pie did Jane and David eat together?

Difficulty: Medium

38. The sum of three consecutive integers is 822. What is the largest integer?

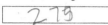

Difficulty: Medium

39. 46% of 95 is what number? Round your answer to the nearest tenth.

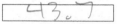

Difficulty: Medium

40. Calculate the value of the following expression. Round the final answer to the nearest tenth.

$$\frac{4.5(7.8-3.4)+2.2}{5.12-3.12}$$

Difficulty: Hard

Answer Explanation

1. The laws you need to follow when solving problems with exponents: First law: Multiply the powers when raising a base with a power to another power. Second law: Keep the base the same when multiplying the same bases. Third law: Keep the base the same and subtract the denominator exponent from the numerator exponent when dividing like bases.

Therefore, we have:

$$\frac{3m^3}{7n^5} \div \frac{3m^8}{2\ln^5} = \frac{3m^3}{7n^5} \cdot \frac{2\ln^5}{3m^8}$$

After canceling like terms, we have the following:

$$\frac{3m^3}{7n^5} \cdot \frac{2\ln^5}{3m^8} = \frac{3}{m^5}$$

The correct answer is B.

2. Substitute the values of x and y into the original equation and perform operations in order that satisfy the PEMDAS rule.

We have:

$$(-2 - 2(3))^2 + 3(3 - (-2)) = (-2 - 2(3))^2 + 3(3 + 2)$$
$$= (-2 - 6)^2 + 3(5) = (-8)^2 + 15 = 64 + 15 = 79$$

The correct answer is H.

3. Prime factorization of 88 gives us $88 = 2 \times 44 = 2 \times 2 \times 22 = 2 \times 2 \times 2 \times 11$.

Two largest prime factors of 86 are 2 and 11. Therefore, their sum is 13.

The correct answer is B.

4. Rewrite the expression so we have the same radicand under each of the radicals.

$$2\sqrt{72} - 3\sqrt{8} + 2\sqrt{32} = 2\sqrt{36 \times 2} - 3\sqrt{4 \times 2} + 2\sqrt{16 \times 2}$$

Since we have perfect squares under each of the radicals, we can find their square roots..

$$2\sqrt{36 \times 2} - 3\sqrt{4 \times 2} + 2\sqrt{16 \times 2} = 12\sqrt{2} - 6\sqrt{2} + 8\sqrt{2} = 14\sqrt{2}$$

The correct answer is H.

5. Tommy will pay $1.25 × 2 = $2.50 for 2 pens and $2.45 × 3 = $7.35 for 3 notebooks. The total price is $2.50 + $7.35 = $9.85. Therefore, Tommy will have $32.50 − $9.85 = $22.65 after his purchase.

The correct answer is C.

6. To convert the number from standard form to scientific notation move the decimal point to the left until you reach the point where the resulting number is at least 1 but less than 10.

In 52,010,000 you need to move the decimal point 7 places to the left and you will get 5.201×10^7.

The correct answer is G.

7. First, convert each mixed number to an improper fraction.

$$1\frac{1}{3} = \frac{4}{3}$$
$$2\frac{1}{4} = \frac{9}{4}$$

Then perform the calculations according to the PEMDAS rule.

$$\frac{2}{9} - \frac{1}{3}\left(\frac{4}{3} + \frac{9}{4}\right) = \frac{2}{9} - \frac{1}{3}\left(\frac{4(4) + 9(3)}{12}\right) = \frac{2}{9} - \frac{1}{3}\left(\frac{16 + 27}{12}\right)$$
$$= \frac{2}{9} - \frac{1}{3}\left(\frac{43}{12}\right) = \frac{2}{9} - \frac{43}{36} = \frac{8 - 43}{36} = -\frac{35}{36}$$

The correct answer is B.

8. Since there are 75% of the candies left over, then 25% of the whole pack of candies corresponds to 10 candies.

We can set up the proportion. Suppose n is the total number of candies in a pack. Then we have:

 **Video Explanations** at argoprep.com/shsat

$$\frac{10}{25\%} = \frac{n}{100\%}$$

Solve for n:

$$25n = 1000$$

$$n = \frac{1000}{25} = 40$$

The original number of candies in a pack is 40.

The correct answer is G.

---

9. Solve the expression given by following the PEMDAS rule.

$$3.2(1.05 + 0.8) - 2.1 = 3.2(1.85) - 2.1 = 3.82$$

3.82 rounded to the nearest tenth is 3.8.

The correct answer is D.

---

10. Before you start solving this problem, make sure you follow the laws of exponents:

Keep the base the same when multiplying the same bases.

Keep the base the same and subtract the denominator exponent from the numerator exponent when dividing like bases.

We have:

$$\frac{3x^2y^5z^3}{5y^2z} \cdot \frac{z}{15xy^6} = \frac{3x^2y^3z^2}{5} \cdot \frac{z}{15xy^6} = \frac{x^2y^3z^2}{5} \cdot \frac{z}{5xy^6} = \frac{x^{2-1}z^{2+1}}{25y^{6-3}} = \frac{xz^3}{25y^3}$$

The correct answer is G.

---

11. Letting x stand for the number gives the equation

$$7x + 5 = 54$$

Then, subtract 5 from each side:

$$7x + 5 - 5 = 54 - 5$$

$$7x = 49$$

$$x = \frac{49}{7} = 7$$

The number is 7.

The correct answer is B.

---

12. These numbers have no common prime factors, so they are coprime. Therefore, their least common multiple is their product, 35.

The correct answer is E.

---

13. Multiply both the numerator and the denominator by 25 to get 100 in the denominator:

$$\frac{3}{4} = \frac{3 \times 25}{4 \times 25} = \frac{75}{100} = 0.75$$

The correct answer is D.

---

14. First, substitute the value of a and b into the original expression:

$$\frac{|b^2 - 5a|}{||a^3 + 3| - 8|} = \frac{|1^2 - 5 \times 2|}{||2^3 + 3| - 8|} = \frac{|1 - 10|}{||8 + 3| - 8|} = \frac{|-9|}{||11| - 8|}$$

Then, take an inner absolute value. Note that $-1 = 1$ and $1 = 1$ Therefore, we have:

$$-9 = 9$$

And

$$11 = 11$$

Then, substitute it into the equation, add the numbers and take the absolute value.

We have:

$$\frac{|-9|}{||11| - 8|} = \frac{9}{|11 - 8|} = \frac{9}{3} = 3$$

The correct answer is E.

---

15. The law is that a number is divisible by five when the last digit is 0 or 5.

From the options given, the only number that has 5 as a last digit is 445.

The correct answer is B.

---

16. A prime number has EXACTLY 2 factors - 1 and itself. The number "1" is not prime because it only has ONE factor.

When the number can be divided evenly by numbers other than 1 or itself, it is a composite number.

Check each option:

8 can be divided evenly by 1, 2, 4, and 8 so it is a composite number. 6 can be divided evenly by 1, 2, 3, and 6 so it is a composite number. 13 can be divided evenly by only 1 and 13 so it is a prime number.

The correct answer is G.

---

17. First, find the number of women and children:

$$3555 - 1980 = 1575$$

Then find the number of women:

$$1575 \div 3 = 525$$

Finally, find the number of children:

$$525 \times 2 = 1050$$

The correct answer is D.

---

18. Since there are 80% of the apples left over, then 20% of the whole pack of apples corresponds to 5 apples.

We can set up the proportion. Suppose n is a total number of apples in a pack. Then we have:

Video Explanations
at argoprep.com/shsat

$$\frac{5}{20\%} = \frac{n}{100\%}$$

Solve for n:

$$40n = 1000$$
$$n = \frac{500}{20} = 25$$

The original number of apples in a pack is 25.

The correct answer is F.

19. First, solve the numerator and the denominator separately. Substitute the value of a and b into the original expression. For the numerator, we have:

$$\sqrt{a^2 - 4b^2 + 1} = \sqrt{2^2 - 4 \times 1^2 + 1} = \sqrt{4 - 4 + 1} = \sqrt{1} = 1$$

For the denominator, we have:

$$\sqrt{a^3 + b} = \sqrt{2^3 + 1} = \sqrt{8 + 1} = \sqrt{9} = 3$$

Then, divide the numerator by the denominator. Therefore, we have:

$$\frac{\sqrt{a^2 - 4b^2 + 1}}{\sqrt{a^3 + b}} = \frac{1}{3}$$

The correct answer is C.

20. Rita will pay $1.75 \times 3 = $5.25 for 3 pens and $10.15 \times 3 = $30.45

for 3 books. The total price is $5.25 + $30.45 = $35.7. Therefore, Rita will have $41.50 − $35.70 = $5.80 after her purchase.

The correct answer is E.

21. First, add the numbers inside the absolute value symbols:

$$-12 + 2 = -10$$

And

$$-7 + 3 = -4$$

Then, take their absolute values. Note that $-1 = 1$. Therefore, we have:

$$-10 = 10$$

And

$$-4 = 4$$

Then, divide the numerators by the denominators and multiply them:

$$\frac{10}{4} \times \frac{2}{4} = \frac{20}{16} = \frac{5}{4} = 1.25$$

The correct answer is C.

22. To convert a number from standard form to scientific notation, move the decimal point to the left until you reach the point where the resulting number is at least 1 but less than 10.

For the number 0.0000243, you need to move the decimal point 5 places to the right and you will get 2.43×10^{-5}.

The correct answer is E.

23. Solve the expression given by following the PEMDAS rule.

$$1.7(3.45 - 0.7) + 5.7 = 1.7(2.75) + 5.7 = 10.375$$

10.375 rounded to the nearest hundredth is 10.38.

The correct answer is A.

24. Letting x stand for the number gives the equation

$$\frac{8x - 2}{2} = 35$$

Multiply each side by 2 and then, add 2 to each side :

$$\frac{8x - 2}{2} \times 2 = 35 \times 2$$
$$8x - 2 = 70$$
$$8x = 72$$
$$x = \frac{72}{8} = 9$$

The number is 9.

The correct answer is F.

25. The first few multiples of 9 are $9, 18 \ldots$ and the first few multiples of 3 are $3, 6, 9, 12 \ldots$ The smallest number to appear in both sequences is 9, so it is the LCM of 9 and 3.

The correct answer is D.

26. If Alex earns $17.09 per hour for 5 hours he would earn $5 \times $17.09 = $85.45

The correct answer is E.

27. A number is divisible by 3 if the sum of its digits is divisible by 3. Check each option.
First, try number 445:

$$4 + 4 + 5 = 13; \frac{13}{3} = 4\frac{1}{3}$$

This number isn't divisible by 3. Try the next one:

$$7 + 2 + 0 = 9; \frac{9}{3} = 3$$

This number is divisible by 3.

The correct answer is B.

Video Explanations
at argoprep.com/shsat

28. To solve this problem, divide 7 by 4.

Multiply the numerator and the denominator by 25:

$$\frac{7}{4} = \frac{7 \times 25}{4 \times 25} = \frac{175}{100} = 1.75$$

The correct answer is H.

---

29. First, find common denominator.

The common denominator is 8. $5\frac{3}{4} = 5\frac{3 \times 2}{4 \times 2} = 5\frac{6}{8}$.

$$5\frac{6}{8} - 2\frac{1}{8} = 3\frac{5}{8}$$

The park is $3\frac{5}{8}$ miles farther.

The correct answer is D.

---

30. First, convert each mixed number to an improper fraction.

$$2\frac{1}{3} = \frac{7}{3}$$
$$1\frac{1}{5} = \frac{6}{5}$$

Then perform the calculations according to the PEMDAS rule.

$$\left(2\frac{1}{3} - 1\frac{1}{5}\right) \times \frac{1}{2} \div \left(\frac{5}{2} + \frac{1}{2}\right) = \left(\frac{7}{3} - \frac{6}{5}\right) \times \frac{1}{2} \div 3$$

$$= \frac{(7(5) - 6(3))}{15} \times \frac{1}{2} \div 3 = \frac{35 - 18}{15} \times \frac{1}{2} \div 3 = \frac{17}{15 \times 2} \div 3$$

$$= \frac{17}{30} \div 3 = \frac{17}{90}$$

The correct answer is H.

---

31. There is a law of absolute value that needs to be used to solve the problem given:

For any real number x, the absolute value is defined as

$$|x| = \begin{cases} -x, \text{ if } x < 0 \\ x, \text{ if } x \geq 0 \end{cases}$$

Therefore, we have:

$$6x - 2 = 10$$

Or

$$6x - 2 = -10$$

From the first equation we have:

$$6x = 10 + 2$$
$$6x = 12$$
$$x = \frac{12}{6} = 2$$

From the second equation we have:

$$6x = -10 + 2$$

$$6x = -8$$
$$x = \frac{-8}{6} = -\frac{4}{3}$$

The correct answer is B.

---

32. First, multiply and then divide the radicands together. Then keep the base the same and add the powers:

$$\frac{\sqrt{x^3} \times \sqrt{x^n}}{\sqrt{x^5}} = \sqrt{\frac{x^3 x^n}{x^5}} = \sqrt{x^{3+n-5}} = \sqrt{x^{n-2}}$$

We have:

$$\sqrt{x^{n-2}} = \sqrt{x^7}$$
$$x^{n-2} = x^7$$

The base is the same, so the powers are equals. Therefore, we have:

$$n - 2 = 7$$
$$n = 7 + 2 = 9$$

The correct answer is F.

---

33. $A = P \times (1 + i)^t$, where A = total amount, P = principle (starting amount), i = interest rate (as a decimal) and t = time.

$$A = 7000 \times (1 + 0.2)^3$$
$$A = 7000 \times (1.2)^3$$
$$A = 7000 \times 1.728$$
$$A = 12096$$

The amount Mrs. Don will have is **$12,096**.

---

34. First, convert each mixed number to an improper fraction:

$$2\frac{3}{4} = \frac{11}{4}$$
$$8\frac{1}{3} = \frac{25}{3}$$

Then, perform the multiplication operation:

$$\frac{4}{3} \times 2\frac{3}{4} = \frac{4}{3} \times \frac{11}{4} = \frac{11}{3}$$

Therefore, we have:

$$\frac{1}{7} - \frac{4}{3} \times 2\frac{3}{4} + 8\frac{1}{3} = \frac{1}{7} - \frac{11}{3} + \frac{25}{3} = \frac{1 \times 3 - 11 \times 7 + 25 \times 7}{21} = \frac{101}{21}$$

$$= 4\frac{17}{21}$$

35. First, find the value of this expression:

$$\frac{0.0065}{0.01} \times 0.004 = 0.0026$$

To convert the number from standard form to scientific notation move the decimal point to the right until you reach the point where the resulting number is at least 1 but less than 10.

For 0.0026, you need to move the decimal point 3 places to the right and you will get **2.6×10^{-3}**.

---

36. Prime factorization of 86 gives us $70 = 10 \times 7 = 2 \times 5 \times 7$. Two smallest prime factors of 70 are 2 and 5. Therefore, their difference is **3**.

---

37. First, find the common denominator. The common denominator is 6.

Therefore, we have:

$$\frac{4}{6} + \frac{1}{3} = \frac{4}{6} + \frac{1 \times 2}{6} = \frac{4+2}{6} = 1$$

They ate **one pizza**.

---

38. Let the smallest integer equal x, $x + 1$ is the next consecutive integer and the largest consecutive integer is $x + 2$.

Therefore, we have:

$$x + x + 1 + x + 2 = 822$$
$$3x + 3 = 822$$
$$3x = 819$$
$$x = \frac{819}{3} = 273$$

The largest integer is $273 + 2 = $ **275**.

39. First, make a proportion:

$$\frac{x}{95} = \frac{46}{100}$$

Then, solve for x:
We have:

$$x = \frac{95 \times 46}{100} = \mathbf{43.7}$$

---

40. Solve the expression given by following the PEMDAS rule:

$$\frac{4.5(7.8 - 3.4) + 2.2}{5.12 - 3.12} = \frac{4.5 \times 4.4 + 2.2}{2} = \frac{22}{2} = 11$$

The answer is **11**.

Video Explanations
at argoprep.com/shsat

Algebra

1. Simplify the following expression:

$$2a - 3b - 4a + 2b$$

A. $-2a - b$ **C.** $2a + 4b$
B. $a + b$ **D.** $-a - 4b$

Difficulty: Easy

2. Simplify the following expression:

$$3(a - b) + 4a + 6b$$

E. $2a + b$ **G.** $7a + 3b$
F. $6a - 4$ **H.** $3a - 7b$

Difficulty: Medium

3. Simplify the expression below:

$$4(x - 2) + 5(x + 1) - 8$$

A. $x - 2$ **C.** $7x + 2$
B. $9x - 11$ **D.** $3x - 5$

Difficulty: Medium

4. Simplify the following expression:

$$x^2 + 4y^2 + 2 + 3x^2 + y^2 - 7$$

E. $6x^2 + 3y^2$ **G.** $4x^2 - y^2$
F. $2x^2 - y^2 - 7$ **H.** $4x^2 + 5y^2 - 5$

Difficulty: Easy

5. Simplify the algebraic expression below:

$$4(a + 7) + 3(a - 5)$$

A. $a - 12$ **C.** $7a - 3$
B. $2a + 7$ **D.** $7a + 13$

Difficulty: Medium

6. Simplify the expression below:

$$\frac{a - 4b + 7a + 4b}{a - 2b + 5a}$$

E. $2a - b$ **G.** $\dfrac{a}{a + 5b}$
F. $\dfrac{4a}{3a - b}$ **H.** $7a - 4b$

Difficulty: Medium

7. Simplify the following expression:

$$\frac{a + 2b}{3a - b - 2a + 3b} + a + b$$

A. $a + b + 1$ **C.** $a + b$
B. $3a + 2b$ **D.** $a - b$

Difficulty: Medium

8. If $a = -1$ and $b = 2$, what is the value of the following expression?

$$3ab - b + 4a + 2b - ab$$

E. 3 **G.** -6
F. 2 **H.** -2

Difficulty: Medium

9. Simplify the following expression:

$$2b + \frac{1}{2}a\left(b - \frac{2}{3}\right) + 4ab$$

A. $4a - 5b + \dfrac{3}{2}ab$ **C.** $3a + 5b - ab$
B. $-\dfrac{1}{3}a + 2b + \dfrac{9}{2}ab$ **D.** $\dfrac{1}{2}a - ab$

Difficulty: Hard

Video Explanations
at argoprep.com/shsat

10. Simplify the following expression:

$$\frac{2(a^2 - b^2)}{a - b} + 3a - b$$

- E. $5a + b$
- G. $a^2 - 2b + a$
- F. $-3a - b$
- H. $\frac{a^2}{b^2} + 2b - a$

Difficulty: Hard

11. Simplify the following expression:

$$x^3 + xy - 5x^2 - 3x^3 + 5xy + 2x^2$$

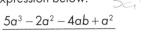

- A. $8x^3 - 7xy$
- C. $4x^3 - 6x^2 - 5xy$
- B. $3x^3 + 4x^2 - 5$
- D. $-2x^3 - 3x^2 + 6xy$

Difficulty: Medium

12. Simplify the following expression:

$$5(x - 1) + y(x + 4) - xy + 2(y - xy)$$

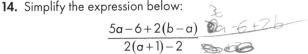

- E. $4x - 3y + xy - 9$
- G. $5x + 6y - 2xy - 5$
- F. $x + 5xy$
- H. $4x + 4x - 2xy + 1$

Difficulty: Hard

13. Simplify the expression below:

$$\frac{5a^3 - 2a^2 - 4ab + a^2}{a}$$

- A. $3a^3 - 2a^2 + 2ab$
- C. $5a^2 - a - 4b$
- B. $\frac{5a^3 - ab + a^2}{a}$
- D. $3a^3 + 4a - 2b$

Difficulty: Medium

14. Simplify the expression below:

$$\frac{5a - 6 + 2(b - a)}{2(a + 1) - 2}$$

- E. $5a + 2b - 1$
- G. $a - 6b$
- F. $\frac{3a + 2b - 6}{2a}$
- H. $\frac{6a - b}{4a}$

Difficulty: Hard

15. If $x = 3$ and $y = -1$, what is the value of the following expression?

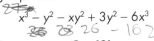
$$x^3 - y^2 - xy^2 + 3y^2 - 6x^3$$

- A. -35
- C. 121
- B. -136
- D. 4

Difficulty: Hard

16. Simplify the expression below:

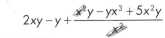
$$\frac{1}{2}b - \frac{3}{4}a - 3\left(\frac{1}{6}b + a\right)$$

- E. $\frac{-15a}{4}$
- G. $a + b$
- F. $3a - \frac{1}{2}b$
- H. $\frac{3}{4}a - \frac{3}{2}b$

Difficulty: Hard

17. Simplify the following expression:

$$(a^3 + b^2)b + 3(b^3 + ab^2) - ab^2$$

Difficulty: Medium

18. Simplify the following expression:

$$2xy - y + \frac{x^2y - yx^3 + 5x^2y}{x^2}$$

Difficulty: Hard

19. If $x = 1$ and $y = 1$, what is the value of the following expression?

$$x^2y^2 - xy + 12xy^2 + 7x^2y^2 - 6xy$$

Difficulty: Medium

20. Simplify the following expression:

$$\frac{(a^3 + 3)b^3 - a^3(b^3 - 2)}{a^2b + b^2a + 4a^2b}$$

Difficulty: Hard

1. Rewrite the expression to get like terms placed together and perform the necessary operations:

$$2a - 3b - 4a + 2b = 2a - 4a - 3b + 2b = -2a - b$$

The correct answer is A.

2. First, use the distributive property to get rid of the parentheses and then rewrite the expression to get like terms placed together and add or subtract the like terms:

$$3(a - b) + 4a + 6b = 3a - 3b + 4a + 6b = 3a + 4a - 3b + 6b = 7a + 3b$$

The correct answer is G.

3. First, use the distributive property to get rid of the parentheses:

$$4(x - 2) + 5(x + 1) - 8 = 4x - 8 + 5x + 5 - 8$$

Then rewrite the expression to get like terms placed together and add or subtract them:

$$4x - 8 + 5x + 5 - 8 = 4x + 5x - 8 - 8 + 5 = 9x - 11$$

The correct answer is B.

4. Rewrite the expression to get like terms placed together and add or subtract them:

$$x^2 + 4y^2 + 2 + 3x^2 + y^2 - 7 = x^2 + 3x^2 + 4y^2 + y^2 + 2 - 7$$
$$= 4x^2 + 5y^2 - 5$$

The correct answer is H.

5. First, use the distributive property to get rid of the parentheses:

$$4(a + 7) + 3(a - 5) = 4a + 4 \times 7 + 3a - 3 \times 5 = 4a + 28 + 3a - 15$$

Then rewrite the expression to get like terms placed together and add or subtract them:

$$4a + 28 + 3a - 15 = 4a + 3a + 28 - 15 = 7a + 13$$

The correct answer is D.

6. Simplify the numerator and the denominator separately.

First, rewrite the expression to get like terms placed together and add or subtract them.

Therefore, in the numerator, we have:

$$a - 4b + 7a + 4b = a + 7a + 4b - 4b = 8a$$

In the denominator, we have:

$$a - 2b + 5a = a + 5a - 2b = 6a - 2b$$

Then divide the numerator by the denominator and simplify the result:

$$\frac{8a}{6a - 2b} = \frac{8a}{2(3a - b)} = \frac{4a}{3a - b}$$

The correct answer is F.

7. First, simplify the fraction. Rewrite the expression to get like terms placed together and add or subtract them:

$$\frac{a + 2b}{3a - b - 2a + 3b} = \frac{a + 2b}{3a - 2b - b + 3b} = \frac{a + 2b}{a + 2b} = 1$$

We have:

$$\frac{a + 2b}{3a - b - 2a + 3b} + a + b = 1 + a + b$$

The correct answer is A.

8. First, rewrite the expression to get like terms placed together and add or subtract them:

$$3ab - b + 4a + 2b - ab = 3ab - ab - b + 2b + 4a = 2ab + b + 4a$$

Then substitute the value of a and b into the simplified expression:

$$2ab + b + 4a = 2(-1)2 + 2 + 4(-1) = -4 + 2 - 4 = -6$$

The correct answer is G.

9. First, use the distributive property to get rid of the parenthesis:

$$2b + \frac{1}{2}a\left(b - \frac{2}{3}\right) + 4ab = 2b + \frac{1}{2}ab - \frac{1}{2} \times \frac{2}{3}a + 4ab$$

$$= 2b + \frac{1}{2}ab - \frac{1}{3}a + 4ab$$

Then rewrite the expression to get like terms placed together and add or subtract them.

We have:

$$2b + \frac{1}{2}ab - \frac{1}{3}a + 4ab = 2b - \frac{1}{3}a + \frac{1}{2}ab + 4ab$$

$$= 2b - \frac{1}{3}a + \left(\frac{1 + 4(2)}{2}\right)ab = -\frac{1}{3}a + 2b + \frac{9}{2}ab$$

The correct answer is B.

10. First, simplify the fraction. Note that $a^2 - b^2 = (a - b)(a + b)$. Therefore, we have:

$$\frac{2(a^2 - b^2)}{a - b} = \frac{2(a + b)(a - b)}{a - b} = 2(a + b) = 2a + 2b$$

We have:

$$\frac{2(a^2 - b^2)}{a - b} + 3a - b = 2a + 2b + 3a - b$$

Rewrite the expression to get like terms placed together and add or subtract them:

$$2a + 2b + 3a - b = 2a + 3a + 2b - b = 5a + b$$

The correct answer is E.

 **Video Explanations**
at argoprep.com/shsat

11. Rewrite the expression to get like terms placed together and add or subtract them:

$$x^3 + xy - 5x^2 - 3x^3 + 5xy + 2x^2$$
$$= x^3 - 3x^3 - 5x^2 + 2x^2 + xy + 5xy$$
$$= -2x^3 - 3x^2 + 6xy$$

The correct answer is D.

12. First, use the distributive property to get rid of the parentheses:

$$5(x - 1) + y(x + 4) - xy + 2(y - xy)$$
$$= 5x - 5 + xy + 4y - xy + 2y - 2xy$$

Then, rewrite the expression to get like terms placed together and add or subtract them:

$$5x - 5 + xy + 4y - xy + 2y - 2xy = 5x + 4y + 2y + xy - xy$$
$$- 2xy - 5 = 5x + 6y - 2xy - 5$$

The correct answer is G.

13. First, rewrite the expression to get like terms placed together and add or subtract them and divide the result by a.

$$\frac{5a^3 - 2a^2 - 4ab + a^2}{a} = \frac{5a^3 - 2a^2 + a^2 - 4ab}{a} = \frac{5a^3 - a^2 - 4ab}{a}$$
$$= 5a^2 - a - 4b$$

The correct answer is C.

14. Simplify the numerator and the denominator separately using the distributive property to get rid of the parentheses. Rewrite the expression to get like terms placed together and add or subtract them.

In the numerator, we have:
$$5a - 6 + 2(b - a) = 5a - 6 + 2b - 2a = 5a - 2a + 2b - 6$$
$$= 3a + 2b - 6$$

In the denominator, we have:
$$2(a + 1) - 2 = 2a + 2 - 2 = 2a$$

Therefore, we have:
$$\frac{5a - 6 + 2(b - a)}{2(a + 1) - 2} = \frac{3a + 2b - 6}{2a}$$

The correct answer is F.

15. First, rewrite the expression to get like terms placed together and add or subtract them.

$$x^3 - y^2 - xy^2 + 3y^2 - 6x^3 = x^3 - 6x^3 - y^2 + 3y^2 - xy^2$$
$$= -5x^3 + 2y^2 - xy^2$$

Then substitute the value of x and y in this expression:
$$-5x^3 + 2y^2 - xy^2 = -5 \times 3^3 + 2 \times (-1)^2 - 3 \times (-1)^2 =$$
$$-135 + 2 - 3 = -136$$

The correct answer is B.

16. First, use the distributive property to get rid of the parentheses, then rewrite the expression to get like terms placed together and add or subtract them:

$$\frac{1}{2}b - \frac{3}{4}a - 3\left(\frac{1}{6}b + a\right) = \frac{1}{2}b - \frac{3}{4}a - 3 \times \frac{1}{6}b - 3a$$
$$= \frac{1}{2}b - \frac{3}{4}a - \frac{1}{2}b - 3a = \frac{1}{2}b - \frac{1}{2}b - \frac{3}{4}a - 3a$$
$$= -\frac{3}{4}a - 3a = \left(\frac{-3a - 3(4)a}{4}\right) = \frac{-3a - 12a}{4} = \frac{-15}{4}a$$

The correct answer is A.

17. First, use the distributive property to get rid of the parentheses:
$$(a^3 + b^2)b + 3(b^3 + ab^2) - ab^2 = b^3 + a^3 b + 3ab^2 + 3b^3 - ab^2$$
Then rewrite the expression to get like terms placed together and add or subtract them:
$$b^3 + a^3 b + 3ab^2 + 3b^3 - ab^2 = a^3 b + b^3 + 3b^3 + 3ab^2 - ab^2$$
$$= \mathbf{a^3 b + 4b^3 + 2ab^2}.$$

18. First, simplify the fraction. To do this, rewrite the expression to get like terms placed together and add or subtract them:
$$\frac{x^2y - yx^3 + 5x^2y}{x^2} = \frac{x^2y + 5x^2y - yx^3}{x^2} = \frac{6x^2y - yx^3}{x^2}$$

The expression is being divided by x^2. Apply the laws of exponents (when you divide by the same base, you subtract the exponents). We have:
$$\frac{6x^2y - yx^3}{x^2} = 6y - yx$$

Therefore, we have:
$$2xy - y + \frac{x^2y - yx^3 + 5x^2y}{x^2} = 2xy - y + 6y - yx$$
$$= 2xy - yx + 5y = \mathbf{xy + 5y}.$$

19. First, rewrite the expression to get like terms placed together and add or subtract them:
$$x^2y^2 - xy + 12xy^2 + 7x^2y^2 - 6xy = x^2y^2 + 7x^2y^2 + 12xy^2 - xy$$
$$- 6xy = 8x^2y^2 + 12xy^2 - 7xy$$

Both x and y are 1. The number 1 is easy to work with since 1 raised to any exponent is still 1 and 1 times any number is that number.
$$8x^2y^2 + 12xy^2 - 7xy = 8(1)(1) + 12(1)(1) - 7(1)(1)$$
$$= 8 + 12 - 7 = \mathbf{13}.$$

20. Use the distributive property to get rid of the parentheses and rewrite the expression to get like terms placed together and add or subtract them:
$$\frac{(a^3 + 3)b^3 - a^3(b^2 - 2)}{a^2b + b^2a + 4a^2b} = \frac{a^3b^3 - a^3b^3 + 3b^3 + 2a^3}{a^2b + b^2a + 4a^2b}$$
$$\frac{3b^3 + 2a^3}{5a^2b + b^2a} = \frac{\mathbf{3b^3 + 2a^3}}{\mathbf{ab(5a + b)}}$$

1. Multiply the following expressions:
$$(x - 1)(x + 2)$$

   A. $x^2 - 3x + 2$ **C.** $x^2 + x - 2$
   B. $2x^2 + x - 2$ **D.** $x^2 - x - 1$

   Difficulty: Easy

2. Multiply the following expressions:
$$(a + b)(a^2 + b - a)$$

   E. $a^3 - a^2 + b^2 + ba^2$ **G.** $a^3 - 3a^2 + b^3$
   F. $2a^3 - 3b^2 + ab$ **H.** $3a^3 + 2a^2 - ab$

   Difficulty: Easy

3. Multiply the expression below:
$$\frac{x}{x - 2} \cdot \frac{(x - 2)(x + 4)}{2x}$$

   A. $x + 4$ **C.** $x - 2$
   B. $\dfrac{x + 4}{2}$ **D.** $\dfrac{x - 2}{x}$

   Difficulty: Medium

4. Perform the operation indicated below:
$$2(a - b) \div (a^2 - b^2)$$

   E. $\dfrac{a + b}{b}$ **G.** $2a - b$
   F. $a^3 - 2b^2$ **H.** $\dfrac{2}{a + b}$

   Difficulty: Medium

5. Multiply the expressions below:
$$2ab \cdot (3a - b)(a + b)$$

   A. $4a^3b^2 - 3ab$
   B. $6a^2b^2 - 6ab^3 - 3a^3b$
   C. $6a^3b + 4a^2b^2 - 2ab^3$
   D. $3ab^2 - 4ab^3$

   Difficulty: Medium

6. Multiply the following expressions:
$$\frac{(a - 2)(a + 4)}{a} \cdot \frac{4a}{(a - 1)(a - 2)}$$

   E. $\dfrac{a + 4}{a}$ **G.** $\dfrac{a - 2}{a + 4}$
   F. $\dfrac{4a + 16}{a - 1}$ **H.** $a + 4$

   Difficulty: Medium

7. Multiply the following expressions:
$$\frac{(a - b)^2}{a + b} \cdot \frac{1}{a - b}$$

   A. $\dfrac{a - b}{a + b}$ **C.** $a - b$
   B. $\dfrac{(a - b)^2}{a}$ **D.** $a + b$

   Difficulty: Medium

8. Multiply the expressions below:
$$\frac{x(x - 2)}{x + 2} \cdot \frac{x + 2}{x - 2}$$

   E. $x(x - 3)$
   F. x
   G. $\dfrac{x}{x + 2}$
   H. $(x - 2)(x + 2)$

   Difficulty: Medium

9. If $x = 1$ and $y = 2$, what is the value of the following expression?
$$(x - 4) \cdot \frac{y + 1}{x + y}$$

   A. 3   **C.** 4
   B. 1   **D.** -3

   Difficulty: Medium

Video Explanations
at argoprep.com/shsat

10. What is the value of the following expression?

$$\frac{(x+2)(x-3)}{(x-5)(x-2)} \div \frac{x+2}{x-5}$$

E. $\dfrac{x+2}{x-7}$　　　G. $\dfrac{x-3}{x-7}$

F. $\dfrac{x-3}{x-5}$　　　H. $\dfrac{(x+2)^2}{x-7}$

Difficulty: Medium

11. Multiply the following expression:

$$(x^3 + y^2)(y^2 + 2xy + x^3)$$

A. $x^3 - y^3 + x^6$
B. $y^6 + x^3 + y^3 - 4xy$
C. $x^6 + y^4 + 2x^3y^2 + 2x^4y + 2xy^3$
D. $2x^6 + 6x^3y^2 - 5xy^3$

Difficulty: Hard

12. Expand the following:

$$(x^3 + xy) \cdot (x + y)$$

E. $x^3 + xy + 1$　　　G. $x^4 + x^3y + x^2y + xy^2$
F. $x^3y^3 + 2xy + y^3$　　H. $x^4 + xy^3 + xy$

Difficulty: Hard

13. Multiply the following expression:

$$\frac{(a-8)}{(a+7)(a-8)} \times \frac{a-3}{(a-6)(a+4)} \div \frac{a-8}{(a-6)(a+4)}$$

A. $a - 8$

B. $\dfrac{1}{a+7}$

C. $\dfrac{a-8}{a+4}$

D. $\dfrac{a-3}{a+7}$

Difficulty: Hard

14. Multiply the expression below:

$$\frac{a^3 - 8}{(a-2)^2} \times (a-2)$$

E. $a^3 - 8$　　　G. $a + 2$
F. $a^2 + 2a + 4$　　H. $a^2 - 3a + 1$

Difficulty: Hard⁺

15. If $a = 2$ and $b = -3$, what is the value of the following expression?

$$\frac{a+b}{7a+3b} \cdot \frac{2a-b}{b^2}$$

A. 6　　　C. $-\dfrac{7}{45}$

B. $\dfrac{17}{18}$　　D. -1

Difficulty: Hard

16. Multiply the expressions below:

$$\frac{(x^2 + xy^2)}{xy} \times \frac{(x-2y^2)}{(x+y)}$$

E. $x^3 + 2xy - y^4$　　G. $x^3 - y^3$
F. $\dfrac{x^2 - y}{2xy}$　　H. $\dfrac{x^2 - xy^2 - 2y^4}{xy + y^2}$

Difficulty: Hard⁺

17. What is the value of the following expression, if $a = 1$ and $b = 2$?

$$\frac{(a+2)}{(a-7)(b+5)} \times \frac{b+3}{(b-6)(a+2)}$$

Difficulty: Hard

18.

$$\frac{(x+4)(x-5)}{(x-8)(x+2)} \times \frac{x+2}{x-5} \times \frac{x-8}{x+4}$$

Multiply the expressions above.

Difficulty: Hard

19. Multiply the expression below:

$$\frac{(x-1)^3}{(x+2)(x-3)} \times \frac{(x+2)^2}{(x-1)^2}$$

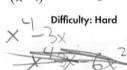

Difficulty: Hard

20. What is the value of *n* if:

$$\frac{(x+3)(x-4)}{(x-5)(x+6)} \div \frac{x-4}{x+6} = \frac{x-n}{x-5}$$

Difficulty: Hard⁺

Answer Explanation

1. Use the distributive property to get rid of the parentheses and combine like terms:

$$(x-1)(x+2) = x \cdot x + 2x - x - 2 = x^2 + x - 2$$

The correct answer is C.

_____

2. First, use the distributive property to get rid of the parentheses and then rewrite the equations to combine like terms:

$$(a+b)(a^2+b-a) = a \cdot a^2 + ab - a^2 + ba^2 + b^2 - ab$$
$$= a^3 - a^2 + ba^2 + b^2 + ab - ab$$
$$= a^3 - a^2 + ba^2 + b^2$$

The correct answer is E.

_____

3. Cancel out the like factors. In this case, they are *x* and *x* − 2. Therefore, we have:

$$\frac{x}{x-2} \cdot \frac{(x-2)(x+4)}{2x} = \frac{x+4}{2}$$

The correct answer is B.

_____

4. Rewrite this expression as:

$$\frac{2(a-b)}{a^2-b^2}$$

Note that $a^2 - b^2 = (a-b)(a+b)$

Therefore, we have:

$$\frac{2(a-b)}{a^2-b^2} = \frac{2(a-b)}{(a-b)(a+b)} = \frac{2}{a+b}$$

The correct answer is H.

_____

5. Use the distributive property to get rid of the parentheses and combine like terms:

$$2ab \cdot (3a-b)(a+b) = 2ab \cdot (3a \cdot a + 3a \cdot b - b \cdot a - b \cdot b)$$
$$= 2ab(3a^2 + 3ab - ab - b^2) = 2ab(3a^2 + 2ab - b^2)$$
$$= 2ab \cdot 3a^2 + 2ab \cdot 2ab - 2ab \cdot b^2$$
$$= 6a^3b + 4a^2b^2 - 2ab^3$$

The correct answer is C.

6. First, cancel out like factors.
Therefore, we have:

$$\frac{(a-2)(a+4)}{a} \cdot \frac{4a}{(a-1)(a-2)} = \frac{a+4}{1} \cdot \frac{4}{a-1}$$

Then multiply:

$$\frac{a+4}{1} \cdot \frac{4}{a-1} = \frac{4(a+4)}{a-1} = \frac{4a+16}{a-1}$$

The correct answer is F.

_____

7. First, rewrite the expressions to cancel out like factors. Note that $a^2 = a \cdot a$.

Therefore, we have:

$$\frac{(a-b)^2}{a+b} \cdot \frac{1}{a-b} = \frac{(a-b)(a+b)}{a+b} \cdot \frac{1}{a-b} = \frac{a-b}{a+b}$$

The correct answer is A.

_____

8. Cancel out like factors and you will get the following:

$$\frac{x(x-2)}{x+2} \cdot \frac{x+2}{x-2} = x \cdot \frac{x-2}{x+2} \cdot \frac{x+2}{x-2} = x$$

The correct answer is F.

_____

9. Substitute the values of *x* and *y* into the original expression:

$$(x-4) \cdot \frac{y+1}{x+y} = (1-4) \cdot \frac{2+1}{1+2} = (-3) \cdot \frac{3}{3} = -3$$

The correct answer is D.

_____

10. First, rewrite this expression:

$$\frac{(x+2)(x-3)}{(x-5)(x-7)} \div \frac{x+2}{x-5} = \frac{(x+2)(x-3)}{(x-5)(x-7)} \cdot \frac{x-5}{x+2}$$

Cancel out like factors.
We have:

$$\frac{(x+2)(x-3)}{(x-5)(x-7)} \cdot \frac{x-5}{x+2} = \frac{x-3}{x-7}$$

The correct answer is G.

Video Explanations
at argoprep.com/shsat

11. First, use the distributive property to get rid of the parentheses:

$$(x^3 + y^2)(y^2 + 2xy + x^3)$$
$$= x \cdot y^2 + 2xy \cdot x^3 + x^3 \cdot x^3 + y^2 \cdot y^2 + y^2 \cdot 2xy + y^2 \cdot x^3$$

Combine like terms. Keep the base the same and add the powers.

Therefore, we have:

$$x^3 y^2 + 2xy \cdot x^3 + x^3 \cdot x^3 + y^2 \cdot y^2 + y^2 \cdot 2xy + y^2 \cdot x^3$$
$$= x^3 y^2 + x^3 y^2 + 2x^4 y + x^6 + y^4 + 2xy^3$$
$$= 2x^3 y^2 + 2x^4 y + x^6 + y^4 + 2xy^3$$

The correct answer is C.

---

12. First, use the distributive property to get rid of the parentheses:

$$(x^3 + xy) \cdot (x + y) = x^3 \cdot x + x^3 y + xy \cdot x + xy \cdot y$$

Combine like terms. Keep the base the same and add the powers:

$$x^3 \cdot x + x^3 y + xy \cdot x + xy \cdot y = x^{3+1} + x^3 y + yx^{1+1} + xy^{1+1}$$
$$= x^4 + x^3 y + x^2 y + xy^2$$

The correct answer is G.

---

13. First, multiply the first two fractions and cancel out like factors.
Therefore, we have:

$$\frac{(a-8)}{(a+7)(a-3)} \times \frac{a-3}{(a-6)(a+4)} = \frac{a-8}{(a+7)(a-6)(a+4)}$$

Rewrite the expressions:

$$\frac{(a-8)}{(a+7)(a-6)(a+4)} \div \frac{a-8}{(a-6)(a+4)}$$
$$= \frac{(a-8)}{(a+7)(a-6)(a+4)} \times \frac{(a-6)(a+4)}{a-8} = \frac{1}{a+7}$$

The correct answer is B.

---

14. Use the formula for the difference of cubes:

$$a^3 - b^3 = (a - b)(a^2 + ab + b^2)$$

Note that $a^2 = a \cdot a$ and $8 = 2^3$.

Therefore, we have:

$$\frac{a^3 - 8}{(a-2)^2} \times (a-2) = \frac{(a-2)(a^2 + 2a + 4)}{(a-2)(a-2)} \times (a-2)$$
$$= \frac{a-2}{a-2} \times \frac{a-2}{a-2} \times (a^2 + 2a + 4) = a^2 + 2a + 4$$

The correct answer is F.

---

15. Substitute the value of a and b into the original expression:

$$\frac{a+b}{7a+3b} \cdot \frac{2a-b}{b^2} = \frac{2-3}{7 \cdot 2 + 3 \cdot (-3)} \cdot \frac{2 \cdot 2 - (-3)}{(-3)^2} = \frac{-1}{5} \cdot \frac{7}{9} = -\frac{7}{45}$$

The correct answer is C.

---

16. First, rewrite the product of the expressions:

$$\frac{(x^2 + xy^2)}{xy} \times \frac{(x - 2y^2)}{(x+y)} = \frac{(x^2 + xy^2) \times (x - 2y^2)}{xy(x+y)}$$

Then use the distributive property to get rid of the parentheses:

$$\frac{(x^2 + xy^2) \times (x - 2y^2)}{xy(x+y)} = \frac{x^2 \cdot x - 2y^2 \cdot x^2 + xy^2 \cdot x - 2y^2 \cdot xy^2}{xy(x+y)}$$

Combine like terms. Keep the base the same and add the powers. We have:

$$\frac{x^2 \cdot x - 2y^2 \cdot x^2 + xy^2 \cdot x - 2y^2 \cdot xy^2}{xy(x+y)} = \frac{x^3 - x^2 y^2 - 2xy^4}{xy(x+y)}$$
$$= \frac{x(x^2 - xy^2 - 2y^4)}{xy(x+y)} = \frac{x^2 - xy^2 - 2y^4}{yx + y^2}$$

The correct answer is H.

---

17. First, cancel out like factors to avoid unnecessary calculations. Notice we have an $(a + 2)$ in the numerator and denominator so we can cancel those terms. Next, substitute your given values of a and b and solve to get the answer.

$$\frac{(a+2)}{(a-7)(b+5)} \times \frac{b+3}{(b-6)(a+2)} = \frac{(2)+3}{((1)-7)((2)+5)((2)-6)} = \frac{5}{168}$$

---

18. First, rewrite the expressions:

$$\frac{(x+4)(x-5)}{(x-8)(x+2)} \times \frac{x+2}{x-5} \times \frac{x-8}{x+4} = \frac{x+4}{x+4} \times \frac{x-5}{x-5} \times \frac{x+2}{x+2} \times \frac{x-8}{x-8}$$

Therefore, we have:

$$\frac{(x+4)(x-5)}{(x-8)(x+2)} \times \frac{x+2}{x-5} \times \frac{x-8}{x+4} = 1 \times 1 \times 1 \times 1 = \mathbf{1}$$

---

19. First, cancel out like factors. Keep the base the same and add or subtract the powers.

Therefore, we have:

$$\frac{(x-1)^3}{(x+2)(x-3)} \times \frac{(x+2)^2}{(x-1)^2} = \frac{(x-1)^{3-2}}{x-3} \times (x+2)^{2-1} = \frac{(x-1)(x+2)}{x-3}$$

Then use the distributive property to get rid of the parentheses and combine the like terms:

$$\frac{(x-1) \times (x+2)}{x-3} = \frac{x \cdot x + 2x - x - 2}{x-3} = \frac{\mathbf{x^2 + x - 2}}{\mathbf{x-3}}$$

---

20. First, rewrite the expressions:

$$\frac{(x+3)(x-4)}{(x-5)(x+6)} \div \frac{x-4}{x+6} = \frac{(x+3)(x-4)}{(x-5)(x+6)} \times \frac{x+6}{x-4}$$

Then cancel out like factors. We have:

$$\frac{(x+3)(x-4)}{(x-5)(x+6)} \times \frac{x+6}{x-4} = \frac{x+3}{x-5} = \frac{x-n}{x-5}$$

The denominators are the same, so set the numerators equal to each other:

$$x + 3 = x - n; -n = 3; \mathbf{n = -3}$$

▶ Video Explanations
at argoprep.com/shsat

1.

$$\frac{12}{7} = \frac{n}{14}$$

In the equation above, what is the value of n?

- **A.** 2
- **B.** 7
- **C.** 24
- **D.** 168

Difficulty: Easy

2. Aiden bought 11 books. He decided to present 2 books to each of his friends and still have one book left. Find the number of friends who received books.

- **E.** 4
- **F.** 2
- **G.** 8
- **H.** 5

Difficulty: Easy

3. Logan has x tickets for an evening event. Liam has 5 more tickets than Logan. There are 17 tickets in total. How many tickets does Liam have?

- **A.** 5
- **B.** 6
- **C.** 11
- **D.** 17

Difficulty: Easy

4. $2(3x + 4) = 12$

In the equation above, what is the value of x?

- **E.** 4
- **F.** $\frac{2}{3}$
- **G.** 6
- **H.** $1\frac{1}{3}$

Difficulty: Medium

5. Alice and Lucas earned $36 in total. If Alice earned $12, how much money did Lucas earn?

- **A.** $36
- **B.** $24
- **C.** $15
- **D.** $12

Difficulty: Easy

6. The perimeter of a triangle is 36 cm. If one side is 12 cm and the second is 10 cm, find the length of the third side.

- **E.** 14 cm
- **F.** 18 cm
- **G.** 20 cm
- **H.** 22 cm

Difficulty: Easy

7. Solve the following equation for x:

$$5(x - 2) = 3(x + 2)$$

- **A.** 4
- **B.** 8
- **C.** 9
- **D.** 12

Difficulty: Medium

8. Michael read x books on his summer holiday. William read half as many books as Michael. If they read 15 books in total, how many books did Michael read?

- **E.** 6
- **F.** 8
- **G.** 10
- **H.** 11

Difficulty: Medium

9. There were 24 toys on a shelf in a certain store. One-eighth of the toys were removed from the shelf due to the product being defective. After the defective units were removed, $\frac{1}{7}$ of the remaining toys were sold later that day. How many toys remained on the shelf at the end of the day?

- **A.** 3
- **B.** 12
- **C.** 18
- **D.** 21

Difficulty: Medium

Video Explanations
at argoprep.com/shsat

10. Solve the following equation for x:

$$\frac{1}{4}x - 4 = 13$$

E. 28   G. 68
F. 35   H. 70

Difficulty: Medium

11. Mark has x butterflies in his collection. Anna has 6 more than Mark and the same as Sophia. If Sophia has 8 butterflies, how many butterflies does Mark have?

A. 1   C. 4
B. 2   D. 7

Difficulty: Medium

12. Carter has 2 pens less than Emily. Olivia has three times as many pens as Carter. If they have 17 pens in total, how many pens does Olivia have?

E. 5   G. 9
F. 6   H. 11

Difficulty: Hard

13.

$$\frac{3x - 10}{3} = \frac{x}{6}$$

In the equation above, what is the value of x?

A. 3   C. 7
B. 4   D. 11

Difficulty: Medium

14. Ella's garden contains roses, tulips and violets. There are twice as many roses as violets. There are 8 less violets than tulips. If there are 28 flowers in Ella's garden, how many violets are there?

E. 5   G. 13
F. 8   H. 20

Difficulty: Hard

15. Oliver spends $190 to buy a suit and a pair of shoes. The price of the pair of shoes was $30 less than the price of the suit. What was the price of the suit?

A. $78   C. $110
B. $90   D. $200

Difficulty: Medium

16. Andrew read a 215-page book in a week. He read 80 pages during the first four days. The last three days he read in total the same number of pages each day to complete the book. How many pages did Andrew read on one of the last three days?

E. 34   G. 70
F. 45   H. 100

Difficulty: Medium

17. There are 72 fruits in a basket: oranges, apples and pears. How many apples are in the basket if the ratio of oranges to apples to pears is 4:3:2?

Difficulty: Medium

18. What is the value of x in the expression below?

$$\frac{2}{x-4} = \frac{1-x}{(x+5)(x-4)}$$

Difficulty: Hard

19. There are black and red cars in a parking lot. The ratio of black cars to red cars is 3:4. How many black cars are in the parking lot if the number of red cars is 8?

Difficulty: Hard

20. There are x candies in a box. Chloe ate $\frac{1}{8}$ of the candies. Jason ate 6 more than Chloe. How many candies were in the box?

Difficulty: Medium

1. Cross multiply to get rid of the fractions:
$$7n = 12 \cdot 14$$
Divide both sides by 7:
$$n = 12 \cdot 2 = 24$$
The correct answer is C.

2. Let x be the number of friends that received books.

Aiden gave 2 books to each of his x friends, which is equal to $2x$. He also had one book left over.

Aiden had a total of $2x + 1$ books.

Since he had a total of 11 books, we have:
$$2x + 1 = 11$$
From the equation, find x. Subtract 1 from each side.

Therefore, we have:
$$2x + 1 - 1 = 11 - 1$$
$$2x = 10$$
Then divide both sides by 2:
$$x = 5$$
The correct answer is H.

3. Logan has x tickets, so Liam has $x + 5$ tickets. If there are 17 tickets in total, we have:
$$x + x + 5 = 17$$
Find x:
$$2x + 5 = 17$$
Subtract 5 from each side:
$$2x + 5 - 5 = 17 - 5$$
$$2x = 12$$
$$x = 6$$
Liam has $6 + 5 = 11$ tickets.
The correct answer is C.

4. First, divide both sides by 2:
$$\frac{2(3x+4)}{2} = \frac{12}{2}$$
$$3x + 4 = 6$$
Then subtract 4 from each side.

Therefore, we have:
$$3x + 4 - 4 = 6 - 4$$
$$3x = 2$$
$$x = \frac{2}{3}$$
The correct answer is F.

5. Let x be the amount that Lucas earned.

Write an equation:
$$12 + x = 36$$
$$x = 36 - 12 = 24$$
The correct answer is B.

6. The perimeter of a triangle is the sum of all sides.

Let x be the length of the third side.

Therefore, we have:
$$12 + 10 + x = 36$$
$$22 + x = 36$$
$$x = 36 - 22 = 14$$
The correct answer is E.

7. First, use the distributive property to get rid of the parentheses:

Therefore, we have:
$$5x - 5 \cdot 2 = 3x + 3 \cdot 2$$
$$5x - 10 = 3x + 6$$
Rewrite as
$$5x - 3x = 6 + 10$$
$$2x = 16$$
$$x = 8$$
The correct answer is B.

8. If Michael read x books, William read $\frac{x}{2}$ books. In total, they read 15 books, so we can write an equation:
$$x + \frac{x}{2} = 15$$
Multiply both sides by 2 to get rid of 2 in the denominator.

Therefore, we have:
$$2x + x = 2 \times 15$$
$$3x = 30$$
Then divide both sides by 3:
$$x = \frac{30}{3} = 10$$
The correct answer is G.

9. If $\frac{1}{8}$ of the toys were defective, we can multiply $\frac{1}{8} \times 24 = 3$. 3 toys were defective so we now have 21 toys left on the shelf. If $\frac{1}{7}$ of the remaining toys were sold, we can set up the following:

Video Explanations
at argoprep.com/shsat

$$21 \times \frac{1}{7} = 3$$

3 of the 21 toys were sold, so only 18 toys remain on the shelf.
The correct answer is C.

---

10. First, add 4 to both sides:

$$\frac{1}{4}x - 4 + 4 = 13 + 4$$

$$\frac{1}{4}x = 17$$

Then multiply both sides by 4:

$$\frac{1}{4} \times 4x = 17 \times 4$$

$$x = 68$$

The correct answer is G.

---

11. If Mark has x butterflies, then Anna has $x + 6$ butterflies.
If Anna and Sophia both have the same number of butterflies, we have:

$$x + 6 = 8$$
$$x = 8 - 6 = 2$$

The correct answer is B.

---

12. If Emily has x pens, then Carter has $x - 2$ and Olivia has $3(x - 2)$ pens.
Write an equation:

$$x + x - 2 + 3(x - 2) = 17$$

Use the distributive property and combine like terms to solve for x:

$$x + x - 2 + 3x - 6 = 17$$
$$2x + 3x = 17 + 6 + 2$$
$$5x = 25$$
$$x = 5$$

The number of pens that Carter has is $5 - 2 = 3$
Olivia has $3 \times 3 = 9$ pens.
The correct answer is G.

---

13. First, cross multiply to get rid of the fractions:
$$3x = 6(3x - 10)$$
Then divide both sides by 3:
$$x = 2(3x - 10)$$
$$x = 6x - 20$$
Rewrite the equation and solve for x:
$$6x - x = 20$$

$$5x = 20$$
$$x = \frac{20}{5} = 4$$

The correct answer is B.

---

14. Let x be the number of tulips.
Then, there are $x - 8$ violets and $2(x - 8)$ roses.
Write an equation:

$$2(x - 8) + x + x - 8 = 28$$

Get rid of the parentheses:

$$2x - 16 + x + x - 8 = 28$$

We have:

$$4x = 28 + 24 = 52$$
$$x = 13$$

There are $13 - 8 = 5$ violets.
The correct answer is E.

---

15. Let x be the price of a suit. The price of shoes is $x - 30$.
Write an equation:

$$x + x - 30 = 190$$
$$2x = 190 + 30 = 220$$

Then divide by 2.
Therefore, we have:

$$x = \$110$$

The correct answer is C.

---

16. Let x be the number of pages Andrew should read.
If Andrew read 80 pages, he still has $215 - 80 = 135$ pages to read and he has 3 days to finish the book.
Therefore, we can write an equation:

$$3x = 135$$

Then divide both sides by 3:

$$x = 45$$

The correct answer is F.

---

17. Let $4x$ be the number of oranges, $3x$ be the number of apples, and $2x$ be the number of pears.
In total there are 2 fruits, so we have:

$$4x + 3x + 2x = 72$$
$$9x = 72$$
$$x = 8$$

There are $3 \times 8 =$ **24 apples**.

Video Explanations
at argoprep.com/shsat

18. First, multiply both sides by $(x+5)(x-4)$.
Therefore, we have:

$$(x+5)(x-4)\times\frac{2}{x-4}=(x+5)(x-4)\times\frac{1-x}{(x+5)(x-4)}$$

Cancel out like factors and we have:

$$2(x+5)=1-x$$
$$2x+10=1-x$$

Rewrite as

$$2x+x=1-10$$
$$3x=-9$$
$$\mathbf{x=-3}$$

19. Let x be the number of black cars.
Make a proportion:

$$\frac{3}{4}=\frac{x}{8}$$

Cross multiply to get rid of fractions:

$$4x=3\times 8$$

Then divide both sides by 4:

$$x=\frac{24}{4}=6$$

There are 6 black cars.

20. Let x represent be the number of candies.
Chloe ate $\frac{1}{8}x$ and Jason ate $\frac{1}{8}x+6$.
Write an equation:

$$\frac{1}{8}x+\frac{1}{8}x+6=x$$

Multiply both sides by 8:

$$x+x+48=8x$$

Rewrite the equation and solve for x:

$$8x-2x=48$$
$$6x=48$$

Then divide both sides by 6:

$$x=8$$

There are 8 candies in the box.

Video Explanations
at argoprep.com/shsat

1. When $-3x + 5y = 14$, what is y in terms of x?

   A. $y = -\frac{3}{5}x + \frac{5}{14}$ C. $y = -\frac{3}{5}x + \frac{14}{5}$

   B. $y = \frac{3}{5}x + \frac{5}{14}$ D. $y = \frac{3}{5}x + \frac{14}{5}$

   Difficulty: Easy

2. The admission fee at a local zoo is $3.00 for children and $5.50 for adults. On a certain day, 1,800 people entered the zoo and $7,900 was collected. How many children visited the zoo?

   E. 500   G. 800
   F. 650   H. 1000

   Difficulty: Hard

3. The sum of two consecutive even integers is 14 and their quotient is $\frac{3}{4}$. What is the larger number?

   A. 5   C. 8
   B. 6   D. 10

   Difficulty: Hard

4. The sum of a 2-digit number is 12. The tens digit is 3 times less than the unit digit. Find the number.

   E. 39   G. 57
   F. 48   H. 93

   Difficulty: Medium

5. In a class of 30 students, the number of males is 5 less than 4 times the number of females. How many males are there in the class?

   A. 7   C. 19
   B. 12   D. 23

   Difficulty: Hard

6. Adriana bought 2 packs of apples and 1 pack of lemons. The price of the pack of lemons is 2 less than 3 times the price of the pack of apples. If she paid $15.50 in total, what is the price of 1 pack of apples?

   E. $2.75
   F. $3.50
   G. $7.00
   H. $8.50

   Difficulty: Hard

7. Two pens and three pencils cost a total of $6. Five pens and two pencils cost a total of $9.5. What is the price of one pen?

   A. $1.00
   B. $1.50
   C. $2.50
   D. $3.00

   Difficulty: Medium

8. Three DVDs and five CDs cost $25. Two CDs and two DVDs cost $16. What is the price of one DVD?

   E. $7.50
   F. $5.75
   G. $3.25
   H. $0.50

   Difficulty: Hard

9. A chemist wants to make 4 liters of 40% acid solution by mixing together a 55% acid solution and a 30% acid solution. How much of a 55% acid solution should the chemist use?

   A. 3.2 liters
   B. 1.8 liters
   C. 1.6 liters
   D. 0.5 liters

   Difficulty: Hard⁺

Video Explanations
at argoprep.com/shsat

101

(handwritten:) $-5x+y=8$ $x-2y=3$ $-3x-6y=9$

10.

(handwritten:) $-11y=7$

$$3x - 5y = -2$$
$$-4x + 3y = 5$$

What is the solution to the system of equations above?

E. $\left(-1\frac{8}{11}, -\frac{7}{11}\right)$ **G.** $\left(-1\frac{22}{33}, \frac{7}{11}\right)$

F. $\left(-\frac{33}{57}, -\frac{7}{11}\right)$ **H.** $\left(\frac{33}{57}, \frac{7}{11}\right)$

Difficulty: Medium

11. A first number minus twice a second number is 5. Twice the first number minus the second number is 22. What are the numbers?

A. 5 and 9   **C.** 12 and 8
B. 7 and 11   **D.** 13 and 4

Difficulty: Hard

12. What is the solution to the system of equations below?

(handwritten:) $3x-y=-3$

$$x - 2y = 4$$
$$2x + y = -7$$

(handwritten:) $5x=-10$

E. $(-2, -3)$ **G.** $(10, -3)$
F. $(2, -3)$ **H.** $(10, 3)$

Difficulty: Medium

13. Maria bought 7 erasers and 2 magazines. She spent a total of $17. If the price of one magazine is 5 times the price of one eraser, how much did she pay for the 7 erasers?

A. $0.70   **C.** $7.00
B. $1.00   **D.** $7.90

Difficulty: Hard

14. The first number is one-fourth of the second number and the sum of the first and second number is 10. What is the first number?

E. -8 **G.** 2
F. -2 **H.** 8

Difficulty: Hard

15. The sum of two numbers is 13 and their difference is -23. What is the smaller number?

A. -5 **C.** 5
B. 3   **D.** 13

Difficulty: Medium

16. 5 years ago, John was 3 times as old as Arnold. In 8 years, John will be 2 times as old as Arnold. Which of the following systems of equations can be used to solve this problem?

E. $\begin{cases} x - 5 = 3(y - 5) \\ x + 8 = 2(y + 8) \end{cases}$ **G.** $\begin{cases} x + 5 = 3(y - 5) \\ x - 8 = 2(y + 8) \end{cases}$

F. $\begin{cases} x + 5 = 3(y + 5) \\ x - 8 = 2(y - 8) \end{cases}$ **H.** $\begin{cases} x - 5 = 3(y + 5) \\ x + 8 = 2(y - 8) \end{cases}$

Difficulty: Hard

(handwritten:) $-3x=18$

17.

$$-2y = 6$$
$$-3x + 2y = 12$$

What is the solution (x, y) to the system of equations above?

Difficulty: Medium

(handwritten:) $x=6y-5$

18.

$$x = 2y - 5$$
$$y = 3x$$

What is the value of x for the system of equations above?

Difficulty: Medium

Video Explanations
at argoprep.com/shsat

$3x + 8y = 19$
$x - 2y = 5$

19. $\begin{cases} 2x - 5y = 12 \\ -x + 3y = -7 \end{cases}$

If (x, y) is a solution of the system above, what is the value of $-2y + 3x$?

7

Difficulty: Hard

20. If $x = -1$, what is the value of the following function?

$$y = \frac{4}{3x} + \frac{2}{x^2} + \frac{1}{x}$$

$-1/3$ -3

Difficulty: Hard

Answer Explanation

1. Add $3x$ to both sides of the equation to isolate y on the left side:
$$-3x + 5y + 3x = 14 + 3x$$
$$5y = 14 + 3x$$
Rewrite the equation:
$$5y = 3x + 14$$
Divide both sides by 5 to solve for y:
$$\frac{5y}{5} = \frac{3x + 14}{5}$$
$$y = \frac{3x + 14}{5} = \frac{3}{5}x + \frac{14}{5}$$
The correct answer is D.

---

2. Suppose n is the number of children who entered the zoo and m is the number of adults. Then $m + n = 1800$.

The question states the zoo made \$7,900 that day so you can create the following equation:
$$5.5m + 3n = 7900$$
Solve the first equation for n and substitute the result into the second equation:
$$n = 1800 - m$$
$$5.5m + 3(1800 - m) = 7900$$
$$5.5m + 5400 - 3m = 7900$$
$$2.5m = 2500$$
$$m = 1000$$
Find n:
$$n = 1800 - 1000 = 800$$
Therefore, 1000 adults and 800 children visited the zoo.
The correct answer is G.

---

3. Suppose a is the smaller number and b is the larger number. Therefore, we have:
$$a + b = 14$$
$$\frac{a}{b} = \frac{3}{4}$$

Solve the first equation for a and substitute the result into the second equation. Then solve it for b.
$$a = 14 - b$$
$$\frac{14 - b}{b} = \frac{3}{4}$$
Cross multiply:
$$3b = 4(14 - b)$$
$$3b = 56 - 4b$$
Add $4b$ to both sides to get rid of $4b$ on the right side:
$$3b + 4b = 56 - 4b + 4b$$
$$7b = 56$$
$$b = 8$$
Find a:
$$a = 14 - b = 14 - 8 = 6$$
The larger number is 8.
The correct answer is C.

---

4. Suppose x is a unit digit and y is a tens digit. Then we have:
$$x + y = 12$$
$$y = \frac{x}{3}$$
Solve the second equation for x and substitute the result into the first equation. Then solve it for y.
$$x = 3y$$
$$3y + y = 12$$
$$4y = 12$$
$$y = 3$$
Then $x = 3 \times 3 = 9$.
Therefore, the number is 39.
The correct answer is E.

▶ **Video Explanations**
at argoprep.com/shsat

5. Let $x =$ the number of males and $y =$ the number of females.
    Then:
    $$x + y = 30$$
    $$x = 4y - 5$$
    Substitute the second equation into the first one and solve for y.
    $$4y - 5 + y = 30$$
    $$5y = 35$$
    $$y = 7$$
    There are 7 females in the class.
    Find the number of males:
    $$x = 4 \times 7 - 5 = 28 - 5 = 23$$
    There are 23 males in the class.
    The correct answer is D.

6. Let a be the price of 1 pack of apples and b be the price of 1 pack of lemons.
    Then, we have:
    $$2a + b = \$15.50$$
    $$b = 3a - 2$$
    Substitute the second equation into the first one and solve for a:
    $$2a + 3a - 2 = 15.50$$
    $$5a - 2 = 15.50$$
    $$5a = 15.50 + 2 = 17.50$$
    $$a = 3.5$$
    Therefore, the price of 1 pack of apples is $3.50
    The correct answer is F.

7. Let $x =$ cost of one pen.
    Let $y =$ cost of one pencil.
    Therefore, we can write two equations:
    $$2x + 3y = 6$$
    $$5x + 2y = 9.5$$
    Rewrite the first equation for x and substitute the result into the second equation. Then solve for y.
    $$x = \frac{6 - 3y}{2}$$
    $$5\left(\frac{6 - 3y}{2}\right) + 2y = 9.5$$
    Distribute to remove the parentheses:
    $$\frac{30 - 15y}{2} + 2y = 9.5$$
    Multiply each term by 2 to get rid of the denominator:
    $$30 - 15y + 4y = 19$$
    $$-11y = -11$$

$$y = 1$$
Substitute the result into the equation for x and find x:
$$x = \frac{6 - 3 \cdot 1}{2} = \frac{3}{2} = 1.5$$
Therefore, the price of one pen is $1.50
The correct answer is B.

8. Suppose m is the price of one DVD and n is the price of one CD. Then set up two equations:
    $$3m + 5n = 25$$
    $$2m + 2n = 16$$
    Multiply the first equation by 2 and the second equation by 3.
    $$6m + 10n = 50$$
    $$6m + 6n = 48$$
    Substitute the second equation into the first equation and solve the resulting equation for n:
    $$4n = 2$$
    $$n = \frac{2}{4} = 0.50$$
    Substitute the value of n into the first equation and find m:
    $$3m + 5 \times 0.50 = 25$$
    $$3m + 2.50 = 25$$
    $$3m = 22.50$$
    $$m = \frac{22.50}{3} = 7.50$$
    Therefore, the price of one DVD is $7.50.
    The correct answer is E.

9. Let $x =$ amount of a 55% acid solution and $y =$ amount of a 30% acid solution.
    We can set up two equations:
    $$x + y = 4$$
    $$0.55x + 0.30y = 0.40 \times 4 = 1.6$$
    Solve the first equation for x and substitute the result into the second equation. Then solve for y.
    $$x = 4 - y$$
    $$0.55(4 - y) + 0.30y = 1.6$$
    $$2.2 - 0.55y + 0.30y = 1.6$$
    $$-0.25y = -0.6$$
    $$y = 2.4$$
    Calculate the value of x: $x = 4 - 2.4 = 1.6$ liters.
    Therefore, the chemist should use 1.6 liters of 55% acid solution.
    The correct answer is C.

Video Explanations at argoprep.com/shsat

10. Multiply the first equation by 4 and the second equation by 3. Then add the two equations together.

$$12x - 20y = -8$$
$$-12x + 9y = 15$$

After adding the two equations, we get the following:

$$-11y = 7$$
$$y = -\frac{7}{11}$$

Substitute the value of y into the first original equation and solve for x:

$$3x - 5\left(-\frac{7}{11}\right) = -2$$
$$3x + \frac{35}{11} = -2$$

Multiply all terms by 11 to get rid of the denominator:

$$33x + 35 = -22$$
$$33x = -57$$
$$x = -\frac{57}{33} = -1\frac{8}{11}$$

The correct answer is E.

---

11. Let x be the first number and y be the second number. Then we have:

$$x - 2y = 5$$
$$2x - y = 22$$

Multiply the first equation by 2:

$$2x - 4y = 10$$

Subtract the second equation from the first equation that was multiplied by 2:

$$-3y = -12$$
$$y = 4$$

Find the first number by substituting the value of y into the first equation and solving it for x:

$$x - 2 \times 4 = 5$$
$$x = 5 + 8 = 13$$

Therefore, the numbers are 13 and 4.

The correct answer is D.

---

12. Multiply the first equation by 2:

$$2x - 4y = 8$$

Subtract the second equation from the resulting equation:

$$-5y = 15$$
$$y = -3$$

Substitute the value of y into the first equation and find x:

$$x - 2(-3) = 4$$

$$x + 6 = 4$$
$$x = 4 - 6 = -2$$

The solution is $(-2, -3)$.

The correct answer is E.

---

13. Suppose x is the price of 1 eraser and y is the price of 1 magazine. Then we have:

$$7x + 2y = 17$$
$$y = 5x$$

Substitute the second equation into the first equation and solve for x:

$$7x + 2(5x) = 17$$
$$17x = 17$$
$$x = 1$$

The price of 1 eraser is $1. Therefore, Maria paid $7 for 7 erasers.

The correct answer is C.

---

14. Let a be the first number and let b be the second number. Then $a = \frac{b}{4}$, or $b = 4a$. The second equation is $a + b = 10$. Substitute $b = 4a$ into the second equation and solve for a: $a + 4a = 10$, $a = 2$.

The first number is 2.

The correct answer is G.

---

15. Let a be the first number and b be the second number, then $a + b = 13$ and $a - b = -23$.

Subtract the second equation from the first equation and the result is:

$$2b = 36$$
$$b = 18$$

Substitute the value of b into the first equation and find a:

$$a + 18 = 13$$
$$a = 13 - 18 = -5$$

The smaller number is -5.

The correct answer is A.

---

16. Suppose x is John's age and y is Arnold's age now. The first equation that can be used to model the relationship between their ages 5 years ago is $x - 5 = 3(y - 5)$. The second equation that can be used to model the relationship between their ages in 8 years is $x + 8 = 2(y - 8)$.

The correct answer is E.

Video Explanations
at argoprep.com/shsat

17. Divide both sides of the first equation by − 2 to solve for y:

$$-\frac{2y}{-2} = \frac{6}{-2}$$

$$y = -3$$

Substitute the value of y into the second equation and solve for x:

$$-3x + 2(-3) = 12$$

$$-3x - 6 = 12$$

$$-3x = 18$$

$$x = -6$$

The solution is (− 6, − 3).

---

18. We want to find the value of x. We know both equations have the same value of x and y so we can solve this question by substituting one of the equations into the other one.

The second equation is $y = 3x$.

Substitute the "$3x$" for y in the first equation. Our first equation is $x = 2y - 5$. Substituting $3x$ for y in the first equation results in

$$x = 2(3x) - 5$$

Solve for x.

$$x = 6x - 5$$

$$-5x = -5$$

$$x = 1$$

Therefore, the value of x is equal to **1**.

19. Subtract $3y$ from both sides of the bottom equation and you get $-x = -7 - 3y$, $x = 7 + 3y$.

Substitute the result into the top equation and solve for x:

$$2(7 + 3y) - 5y = 12.$$

$$14 + 6y - 5y = 12$$

Combine like terms:

$$y + 14 = 12.$$

Subtract 14 from both sides and you get $y = -2$.

Substitute the value of y into the equation for x and find x:

$$x = 7 + 3(-2) = 7 - 6 = 1$$

$x = 1$ and $y = -2$, then $-2y + 3x = -2(-2) + 3(1) = 4 + 3 = 7$.

The answer is 7.

---

20. Substitute $x = -1$ into the function and calculate its value:

$$y = \frac{4}{3(-1)} + \frac{2}{(-1)^2} + \frac{1}{-1} = -\frac{4}{3} + 2 - 1$$

The common denominator is 3, therefore, we have:

$$y = -\frac{4}{3} + 2 - 1 = \frac{-4 + 3(2) - 3(1)}{3} = \frac{-4 + 6 - 3}{3} = -\frac{1}{3}$$

The answer is $y = -\frac{1}{3}$.

Video Explanations
at argoprep.com/shsat

1. What are the solutions for $4x^2 + 9x - 9 = 0$?

   A. $x = -3, \dfrac{3}{4}$ C. $x = 4, -1$

   B. $x = -1, 4$ D. $x = 3, -\dfrac{3}{4}$

   Difficulty: Medium

2. If $g(x) = 2x^2 + x - 8$, what is $g(-4)$ equal to?

   E. -4 G. 20
   F. 4 H. 22

   Difficulty: Hard

3.
$$f(x) = -8 + ax^2$$

   For the function f defined above, a is a constant and $f(-2) = 0$. What is the value of $f(1)$?

   A. -10 C. 0
   B. -6 D. 4

   Difficulty: Hard

4.
$$f(x) = x^2 + 2$$
$$g(x) = x - 3$$

   What is the value of $f(g(-1))$?

   E. 18 G. 6
   F. 11 H. 3

   Difficulty: Medium

5. Given the function of one variable, evaluate the function $f(x) = 2^{2x}$ for $f(-1)$.

   A. 4 C. $-\dfrac{1}{4}$

   B. $\dfrac{1}{4}$ D. -4

   Difficulty: Hard⁺

6. $\dfrac{3}{4}x^2 + \dfrac{5}{4}x - 3 = 0$

   What is one of the solutions for x in the equation above?

   E. -3 G. $\dfrac{3}{4}$

   F. $-\dfrac{4}{3}$ H. 3

   Difficulty: Hard

7. If $f(x) = 3x^2 - 2x + 5$, what is $f(-2)$ equal to?

   A. -11 C. 13
   B. -3 D. 21

   Difficulty: Medium

8. A local taxi charges a base rate of $5 plus an additional $1.20 for each mile of the ride. Write an equation for the function that models the total cost of the ride.

   E. $y = 1.20x$ G. $y = 5x$
   F. $y = 1.20x + 5$ H. $y = 5x + 1.20$

   Difficulty: Easy

9. Which of the following is a solution of the function $f(x) = x^2 - 25$?

   A. -5 C. 0
   B. -1 D. 25

   Difficulty: Medium

10. Simplify the following equation of the function:
$$y = (2^x)(2)^7$$

   E. $y = 2^{x-7}$

   F. $y = 2^{x+7}$

   G. $y = 2^{\frac{x}{7}}$

   H. $y = 2^{7x}$

   Difficulty: Medium

Video Explanations
at argoprep.com/shsat

11. What is the slope of the line that passes through the points $(-5, 0)$ and $(2, 4)$?

A. 0   C. 1

B. $\frac{4}{7}$ D. $\frac{7}{4}$

Difficulty: Medium

12. What is the domain of the following function?

$$f(x) = \sqrt{3x - 15}$$

E. $x \le -5$ G. $x \le 5$

F. $x \ge -3$ H. $x \ge 5$

Difficulty: Hard

13. Calculate the value of the following quadratic function if $x = -2$:

$$f(x) = -3x^2 - 4x + 12$$

-12 +8 +12

A. -8 C. 16

B. 8   D. 32

Difficulty: Easy

14. If $f(x) = 3x^2 - 2$ and $g(x) = -2x^2 + 3x$, what is the value of $f(x) + g(x)$?

E. $5x^2 - 3x - 2$ G. $x^2 + 3x - 2$

F. $5x^2 + 3x - 2$ H. $x^2 + 3x + 2$

Difficulty: Medium

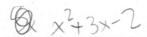 $x^2 + 3x - 2$

15. For the function $g(x) = -5x - 3$, calculate the value of $g(-3)$.

15

A. -18 C. 12

B. -12 D. 15

Difficulty: Easy

16. For the function $f(x) = 12x - 36$, $f(3) = 0$. How many units will the function change if $x = 0$?

E. 3   G. 24

F. 12   H. 36

Difficulty: Hard⁺

17.

$$f(x) = 3x + 5$$
$$g(x) = 2 - f(x)$$

The functions f and g are defined above. What is the value of $g(0)$?

Difficulty: Hard

18. Calculate $h(-1)$ for the following function:

$$h(x) = x^3 - \frac{3}{x^2} + 12$$

9

Difficulty: Hard

19. What is the domain of the following function?

$$f(x) = \frac{3}{x - 3}$$

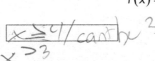
$x > 3$

Difficulty: Hard

20. Find the domain of the following function:

$$g(x) = \frac{5}{(x - 4)^2}$$

$x^2 - 16$

Difficulty: Hard

Video Explanations
at argoprep.com/shsat

1. The equation of the function can be factored into $(x+3)$ $(4x-3)=0$.
Set each factor equal to zero to find the solutions. $x+3=0$, so $x=-3$ and $4x-3=0$, $x=\dfrac{3}{4}$.
The correct answer is A.

2. Substitute $x=-4$ into the equation of the function and calculate the result:
$$g(-4)=2(-4)^2+(-4)-8$$
$$g(-4)=32-4-8$$
$$g(-4)=20$$
The correct answer is G.

3. First we need to find the value of a:
$$-12+a\times(-2)^2=0$$
$$-8+4a=0$$
$$4a=8$$
$$a=2$$
Now we can find the value of $f(1)$
$$f(1)=-8+2(1^2)=-8+2=-6$$
The correct answer is B.

4. First, input the value -1 for the function $g(x)$.
$$g(x)=(-1)-3=-4$$
Input the value of -4 into $f(x)$.
$$f(-4)=(-4)^2+2=18$$
The correct answer is E.

5. Substitute $x=-1$ into the equation of the function and evaluate its value.
$$f(-1)=2^{2(-1)}=2^{-2}$$
Since $a^{-1}=\dfrac{1}{a}$, then $f(-1)=2^{-2}=\dfrac{1}{2^2}=\dfrac{1}{4}$
The correct answer is B.

6. Multiply the equation of the function by 4 to get rid of 4 in the denominators:
$$\frac{3\times4}{4}x^2+\frac{5\times4}{4}x-3\times4=0$$
$$3x^2+5x-12=0$$
Factor the equation and you get $(x+3)\left(x-\dfrac{4}{3}\right)$

7. Set each factor equal to zero:
$$x+3=0; x-\frac{4}{3}=0$$
The solutions are $x=-3,\dfrac{4}{3}$
The correct answer is E.

7. Substitute $x=-2$ into the equation of the function and calculate the result:
$$f(-2)=3(-2)^2-2(-2)+5=3(4)+4+5=12+4+5$$
$$=21$$
The correct answer is D.

8. Let $x=$ the number of miles and $y=$ the total cost of the ride. Since the taxi charges \$1.20 for each mile, the cost paid for the number of miles ridden is 1.20x. The base rate is \$5 so the function that models the total cost of the ride is $y=1.20x+5$.
The correct answer is F.

9. Set the function equal to zero:
$$x^2-25=0$$
Factor the equation of the function:
$$(x-5)(x+5)=0$$
Which gives us
$$x=5 \text{ and } x=-5$$
Substitute the values of x to verify your solution:
$$5^2-25=25-25=0$$
$$(-5)^2-25=25-25=0$$
The solutions are 5 and -5.
The correct answer is A.

10. Since both terms in the function have the same base, keep it the same and add the exponents in order to simplify the function. Therefore, we have:
$$y=(2^x)(2)^7=2^{x+7}$$
The correct answer is F.

11. The slope the line can be calculated by using the following formula:
$$m=\frac{y_2-y_1}{x_2-x_1}$$
In our case, $y_1=0$, $y_2=4$, $x_1=-5$, and $x_2=2$.

Video Explanations
at argoprep.com/shsat

Substitute those values into the formula and find the slope of the line:

$$m = \frac{4-0}{2-(-5)} = \frac{4}{2+5} = \frac{4}{7}$$

The slope of the line is $\frac{4}{7}$.

The correct answer is B.

---

12. Since the square root of a negative number does not give us a real number, then the domain of the radical expression must always be ≥ 0.

Therefore, we have:

$$3x - 15 \geq 0$$

Add 15 to both sides:

$$3x - 15 + 15 \geq 0 + 15$$
$$3x \geq 15$$

Divide both sides by 3:

$$x \geq 5$$

The domain of the function $f(x) = \sqrt{3x-15}$ is $x \geq 5$.

The correct answer is H.

---

13. Substitute $x = -2$ into the equation of the function and calculate the value of $f(x)$.

$$f(-2) = -3(-2)^2 - 4(-2) + 12 = -3(4) + 8 + 12 = -12 + 8 + 12 = 8$$

Therefore, $f(-2) = 8$.

The correct answer is B.

---

14. To find the value of $f(x) + g(x)$, add the two functions together and combine like terms:

$$f(x) + g(x) = 3x^2 - 2 + (-2x^2 + 3x) = 3x^2 - 2 - 2x^2 + 3x = x^2 + 3x - 2$$

The correct answer is G.

---

15. Substitute -3 for x into the equation of the function to calculate the value of $f(-3)$:

$$g(-3) = -5(-3) - 3 = 15 - 3 = 12$$

The correct answer is C.

16. To find out how many units the function will change if $x = 0$, calculate the value of $f(3) - f(0)$.

$$f(3) - f(0) = 0 - (12(0) - 36) = 0 - (0 - 36) = 0 - (-36)$$
$$= 0 + 36 = 36$$

Therefore, the function will change its value by 36 units.

The correct answer is H.

---

17. As seen earlier, you need to substitute the function f into the function g and then substitute $x = 0$ to calculate the value of $g(0)$.

$$g(x) = 2 - (3x + 5) = 2 - 3x - 5 = -3x - 3$$
$$g(0) = -3(0) - 3 = 0 - 3 = -3$$

Therefore, $g(0) = -3$.

---

18. Substitute $x = -1$ into the equation of the original function and calculate the value of $h(-1)$.

$$h(-1) = (-1)^3 - \frac{3}{(-1)^2} + 12 = -1 - 3 + 12 = 8$$

The answer is $h(-1) = 8$.

---

19. For the function above, the denominator cannot equal zero. Therefore, we have:

$$x - 3 \neq 0$$

Add 3 to both sides:

$$x - 3 + 3 \neq 0 + 3$$
$$x \neq 3$$

Therefore, the domain is $x \in R: x \neq 3$.

---

20. For the function above, the domain is all real numbers except the values of x that make the denominator equal to zero.

Therefore, we have:

$$(x - 4)^2 \neq 0$$

Take the square root from both sides and you get the following:

$$x - 4 \neq 0$$

Add 4 to both sides:

$$x - 4 + 4 \neq 0 + 4$$
$$x \neq 4$$

Therefore, the domain is $x \in R: x \neq 4$.

Video Explanations
at argoprep.com/shsat

ARGOPREP SHSAT – Algebra – Word Problems

1. The ratio of apples to oranges in Maria's basket was 1:4. There were 8 apples. How many fruits were in the basket?

   A. 32   C. 40
   B. 36   D. 44

   Difficulty: Easy

2. Hunter has x CDs. Hunter has 3 more CDs than Evan. They both have 13 discs in total. How many CDs does Evan have?

   E. 5   G. 8
   F. 7   H. 11

   Difficulty: Easy

3. Victoria sold $\frac{2}{5}$ of her dresses and then bought 3 more dresses. Now she has 9 dresses. How many dresses did she have before she started selling them?

   A. 12   C. 7
   B. 10   D. 5

   Difficulty: Medium

4. Zoey had $70 to spend on 5 movie tickets. After buying them, she had $35. How much did each ticket cost?

   E. $12   G. $7
   F. $10   H. $3

   Difficulty: Medium

5. Ellie wants to order a new hat over the internet. Each hat costs $9.20 and shipping for the entire order is $4.40. Ellie can spend no more than $46. How many hats can Ellie order without exceeding her budget?

   A. 12   C. 6
   B. 8   D. 4

   Difficulty: Medium

6. Violet takes 4 hours to clean a room. Hailey takes 6 hours to finish the same job working alone. How many hours will it take to clean the room if both of them work together?

   E. 2.4   G. 5
   F. 4.7   H. 5.4

   Difficulty: Hard⁺

7. There are 340 books in a school library. One-fifth of all the books are hard covered and the rest of the books are paperbacks. What is the ratio of books that are hard covered to paperbacks?

   A. 2:3   C. 1:3
   B. 1:4   D. 4:1

   Difficulty: Medium

8. The ratio of Sophia's earnings to Cameron's earnings is 7:5. If Cameron earned $235, how much money did Sophia earn?

   E. $420   G. $329
   F. $390   H. $220

   Difficulty: Medium

9. Leo made 14 paper boxes. Blake made at least 7 more than Leo. What is the minimum number of paper boxes that Blake made?

   A. 21   C. 5
   B. 7   D. 3

   Difficulty: Easy

10. Caroline and Stella can cook a dinner in 1.3 hours working together. It would take Stella 3 hours to cook a dinner if she worked alone. How long would it take Caroline to cook a dinner alone?

   E. 4.7   G. 2.3
   F. 3.3   H. 1.7

   Difficulty: Hard⁺

Video Explanations at argoprep.com/shsat

111

$6x - 3 =$

11. Jason has 3 less notebooks than Chloe. Natalie has four times as many notebooks as Chloe. If they have 21 notebooks in total, how many notebooks does Natalie have?

A. 4   C. 8
B. 6   D. 16

Difficulty: Medium

12. Tyler is three times older than his daughter Melanie. The difference between Tyler's age and twice Melanie's age is 12. How old is Tyler?

E. 26   G. 36
F. 32   H. 42

Difficulty: Hard

13. Jenny's ratio of jeans to pants is 3:2 and 5 times the number of pants is 7 more than the number of jeans. How many jeans does Jenny have?

A. 3   C. 12
B. 8   D. 15

Difficulty: Hard

14. A taxi charges $3.20 plus $0.35 per kilometer for any trip in a town. Emma paid $14 for the taxi, how far did she travel?

E. 17 km   G. 30.86 km
F. 21 km   H. 41.40 km

Difficulty: Medium

15. Cooper ate 10 pancakes, which is at least 3 pancakes less than Jack. What is the minimum number of pancakes that Jack ate?

A. 20   C. 13
B. 15   D. 10

Difficulty: Medium

16. Nathan sold $\frac{1}{3}$ of his stamps and then bought 9 more. Now he has 27 stamps. How many stamps did he begin with?

E. 27   G. 19
F. 22   H. 10

Difficulty: Hard

17. Maria is saving $470 for a new camera. She currently has $256. If she saves $70 per week, how long will it take her to save at least $500 to cover taxes and extras?

Difficulty: Hard

18. Michael has 5 more candies than Isabelle. Colton has three times as many candies as Isabelle. In total, they have 30 candies. How many candies does Michael have?

Difficulty: Hard

19. The ratio of mugs to glasses is 4:5. The number of glasses is 3 more than the number of mugs. What is the number of mugs?

Difficulty: Hard

20. Jessica purchases three dolls and two balls for $50. If two dolls and one ball cost $42, how much does one doll cost?

Difficulty: Hard

Video Explanations
at argoprep.com/shsat

1. Let x = the number of oranges in Maria's basket.
Set up a proportion and solve for x:
$$\frac{1}{4}=\frac{8}{n}$$
Then cross multiply:
$$n = 4 \times 8 = 32$$
The total number of fruits is $32 + 8 = 40$
The correct answer is C.

2. Hunter has x CDs, so Evan has $x-3$ CDs. If in total there are 13 CDs, we have:
$$x + x - 3 = 13$$
Find x from this equation. Therefore, we have:
$$2x - 3 = 13$$
Add 3 to each side:
$$2x - 3 + 3 = 13 + 3$$
$$2x = 16$$
$$x = 8$$
Hunter has 8 CDs and Evan has 5.
The correct answer is E.

3. Let x = the number of dresses that Victoria had at the beginning.
Write an equation:
$$x - \frac{2}{5}x + 3 = 9$$
Multiply both sides by 5 to get rid of the denominator:
$$5x - 2x + 15 = 45$$
$$3x = 30$$
$$x = 10$$
The correct answer is B.

4. First, find the amount she spends on tickets:
$$70 - 35 = \$35$$
Then find the price of 1 ticket:
$$\frac{\$35}{5} = \$7$$
The correct answer is G.

5. Let x = the number of hats that Ellie can order without exceeding her budget.
Write an inequality to model the problem above:
$$9.20x + 4.40 \le 46$$
$$9.20x \le 41.6$$
$$x \le 4.52$$

It is not possible to order 4.52 hats so, Ella can order 4 hats without exceeding her budget.
The correct answer is D.

6. Let x = the time of cleaning the room if they work together.
If Violet can do the cleaning in 4 hours, then in one hour she can do $\frac{1}{4}$ of the job.
If Hailey can do the same cleaning in 6 hours, then in one hour she can do $\frac{1}{6}$ of the job.
Write an equation:
$$\frac{1}{4}x + \frac{1}{6}x = 1$$
Multiply by 24 to get rid of the denominator:
$$24 \times \frac{1}{4}x + 24 \times \frac{1}{6}x = 1 \times 24$$
$$6x + 4x = 24$$
$$10x = 24$$
$$x = 2.4$$
Therefore, it will take 2.4 hours if Violet and Hailey work together.
The correct answer is E.

7. First, find the number of books that are hard covered:
$$\frac{340}{5} = 68$$
Then find the number of books that are paperbacks:
$$340 - 68 = 272$$
Finally, find the ratio:
$$\frac{272}{68} = \frac{4}{1}$$
The ratio of books that are hard covered to paperbacks is 4:1.
The correct answer is D.

8. Let x = the amount of money that Sophia earned.
Then:
$$\frac{7}{5} = \frac{x}{235}$$
Then cross multiply:
$$5x = 1645$$
Divide by 5:
$$x = 329$$
Sophia earned $329.
The correct answer is G.

Video Explanations at argoprep.com/shsat

113

9. Let x be the number of paper boxes that Blake made.

Write an equation:
$$x - 7 \geq 14$$

Add 7 to both sides:
$$x - 7 + 7 \geq 14 + 7$$
$$x \geq 21$$

Blake made at least 21 paper boxes.

The correct answer is A.

---

10. Let t = time required for Caroline to cook a dinner alone.

Let the cooked dinner = 1. Then:
$$\frac{1.3}{3} + \frac{1.3}{t} = 1$$

Multiply the equation by $3t$ to get rid of the denominators:
$$1.3t + 3.9 = 3t$$
$$1.7t = 3.9$$
$$t = 2.3$$

The correct answer is G.

---

11. Say Chloe has x notebooks. Then Jason has $x - 3$ notebooks and Natalie has $4x$ notebooks. Write an equation:
$$x + 4x + x - 3 = 21$$
$$6x = 24$$
$$x = 4$$

Natalie has $4 \times 4 = 16$ notebooks.

The correct answer is D.

---

12. Let x = Melanie's age. Then $3x$ = Tyler's age.

Write an equation:
$$3x - 2x = 12$$
$$x = 12$$

Melanie is 12 years old. Tyler is 36 years old.

The correct answer is G.

---

13. Let x = the number of jeans, y = the number of pants.

Set up the proportion and write an equation:
$$\frac{3}{2} = \frac{x}{y}$$
$$5y = x + 7$$

Solve the second equation for x and substitute the result into the first equation. Then solve it for y:
$$x = 5y - 7$$
$$\frac{3}{2} = \frac{5y - 7}{y}$$

Then cross multiply:
$$3y = 2(5y - 7)$$
$$3y = 10y - 14$$
$$7y = 14$$
$$y = 2$$

Substitute the result into the equation for x and find x:
$$x = 5 \times 2 - 7 = 3$$

The correct answer is A.

---

14. Let x = the number of kilometers.

Then:
$$3.20 + 0.35x = 14$$
$$0.35x = 10.8$$
$$x = 30.86$$

The length of Emma's ride was 30.86 km.

The correct answer is G.

---

15. Let x be the number of pancakes that Jack ate.

Write an inequality:
$$x - 10 \geq 3$$
$$x \geq 3 + 10$$
$$x \geq 13$$

Jack ate at least 13 pancakes.

The correct answer is C.

---

16. Let x = the number of stamps Ethan began with.

Write an equation:
$$x - \frac{1}{3}x + 9 = 27$$

Multiply by 3 to get rid of the denominator:
$$3x - x + 27 = 81$$
$$2x = 54$$
$$x = 27$$

The correct answer is E.

---

17. Let x be the number of weeks Maria needs to save at least $500.

Write an equation:
$$256 + 70x \geq 500$$
$$70x \geq 244$$
$$x \geq 3.386$$

Maria should wait 4 weeks to save at least $500.

Video Explanations
at argoprep.com/shsat

18. Say Isabelle has x candies. Then Michael has $x + 5$ candies and Colton has $3x$ candies.

    Write an equation and solve it for x:
    $$x + x + 5 + 3x = 30$$
    $$5x = 25$$
    $$x = 5$$

    Michael has $5 + 5 = 10$ sweets.

---

19. Let $x =$ the number of mugs, $y =$ the number of glasses.

    Set up a proportion to write an equation:
    $$\frac{4}{5} = \frac{x}{y}$$
    $$y = x + 3$$

    Solve the second equation for x and substitute the result into the first equation. Then solve it for y:
    $$x = y - 3$$
    $$\frac{4}{5} = \frac{y - 3}{y}$$

    Then cross multiply:
    $$4y = 5(y - 3)$$
    $$4y = 5y - 15$$
    $$y = 15$$

    Substitute the result into the equation for x and find x:
    $$x = 15 - 3 = 12$$

    The number of mugs is 12.

---

20. Let $x =$ the price of a doll and $y =$ the price of a ball.

    Then we have:
    $$3x + 2y = 50$$
    $$2x + y = 42$$

    Solve the second equation for y and substitute the result into the first equation. Then solve it for x:
    $$3x + 2(42 - 2x) = 50$$
    $$3x + 84 - 4x = 50$$
    $$-x = -34$$
    $$x = 34$$

    1 doll costs $34.

Video Explanations
at argoprep.com/shsat

1. Andrew bought 5 boxes of chocolate as a birthday present for his friend. The number of chocolates in each box was 18, 19, 21, 22 and 20 respectively. What was the average number of chocolates in the 5 boxes?

   A. 12   **B.** 15   **C.** 18   **D.** 20

   Difficulty: Easy

2. Liam has 4 books. The number of pages in the first book is 420, and the second book has 70 pages more than the third book. The third and fourth book have 150 pages each. What is the average number of pages for the four books?

   E. 420   **G.** 315
   F. 390   **H.** 235

   Difficulty: Medium

3. Jacob measured the temperature outside for seven consecutive days. The results were 23°C, 26°C, 27°C, 25°C, 27°C, 30°C, 31°C. What was the average temperature for the data above?

   A. 23   **B.** 25   **C.** 27   **D.** 31

   Difficulty: Easy

4. David walked 3 hours on Monday, 5 hours on Tuesday and 4 hours during each of the next 3 days. What was the average number of hours David walked?

   E. 4   **G.** 10
   F. 7   **H.** 13

   Difficulty: Easy

5. Isabella, Emma, Anna and Zoey collect hats. Isabella has 4 hats, Emma has 7 hats and Anna has 5 hats. If the average number of hats is 5, how many hats does Zoey have?

   A. 8   **C.** 5
   B. 7   **D.** 4

   Difficulty: Medium

6. When a number y is added to the data set 5, 6, 12, 25, 33, the new mean is 15 . What is the value of y?

   E. 6   **F.** 9   **G.** 11   **H.** 15

   Difficulty: Medium

7. Michael and Julie sold handcrafted goods over a period of three days. Michael earned $720 and Julie earned $750. What was their average earnings per day during those three days?

   A. $670   **C.** $490
   B. $590   **D.** $420

   Difficulty: Easy

8. Sam visited the zoo for four consecutive days. On the first day, he saw 5 animals. On the second day, he saw 3 more animals than on the third day. On the fourth day he saw 6 animals. If the average number of animals Sam saw is 6, how many animals did Sam see on the second day? How many animals did Sam see on the third day?

   E. 8,5   **F.** 5,2   **G.** 8,4   **H.** 6,3

   Difficulty: Medium

9. There are 4 baskets with fruit on a table. There are 5 fruits in the first basket, and twice more fruits in the second basket than in the first basket. In the third basket there are 8 fruits and, in the fourth basket there is 1 less fruit than in the second basket. What is the average number of fruits in the four baskets?

   A. 4   **B.** 7   **C.** 8   **D.** 11

   Difficulty: Easy

10. The mean weight of a group of seven classmates is 53 kg. The weights of six of the classmates are 50 kg, 53 kg, 51 kg, 52 kg, 54 kg and 57 kg. What is the weight of the last classmate?

    E. 52 kg   **G.** 54 kg
    F. 53 kg   **H.** 55 kg

    Difficulty: Medium

Video Explanations
at argoprep.com/shsat

11. The average of six numbers is 32. If one of the numbers is excluded, the average gets reduced by 4. What is the excluded number?

    A. 28   **B.** 30   **C.** 52   **D.** 67

    Difficulty: Hard

12. Joey receives the following scores on his science tests: 81, 92, 78, 96. What score does he need on the next test in order to have an average of 88 on his science tests?

    E. 87   **F.** 93   **G.** 96   **H.** 100

    Difficulty: Medium

13. Lily earned $13 on Monday, 5 more dollars on Tuesday and x dollars on Wednesday. If the average amount of money Lily earned per day is $14, how much money did Lily earn on Wednesday?

    A. $11   **B.** $12   **C.** $13   **D.** $15

    Difficulty: Medium

14. Ava earned $30 per day for 3 days and $20 per day during the next 2 days. What was Ava's average earnings per day during those 5 days?

    E. $35   **G.** $26
    F. $31   **H.** $20

    Difficulty: Medium

15. Alec was on the computer for an average of 7 hours for the last three days. Dylan was on the computer for 4 hours on the first day, 6 hours on the second day and x hours on the third day. If Dylan's average number of hours is 2 less than Alec's, how many hours did Dylan use the computer on the third day?

    A. 6 hours   **C.** 4 hours
    B. 5 hours   **D.** 3 hours

    Difficulty: Medium

16. Logan's average score on the first 6 tests was 90. On the next 4 tests his average score was 87. What was his average score on all 10 tests?

    E. 92
    F. 90.5
    G. 88.8
    H. 87

    Difficulty: Hard

17. Kevin measured the height of 7 trees in his garden. The average height of the first four trees is 100 inches. The average height of the next two trees is 96 inches and the height of the seventh tree is 115 inches. What is the average height of Kevin's trees?

    Difficulty: Medium

18. Aiden drove for 5 hours with a speed of 65 miles per hour and for 3 hours with a speed of 80 miles per hour. What was his average speed for the whole journey? Round your answer to the nearest whole number.

    Difficulty: Medium

19. The average salary of 5 employees at ArgoPrep is $2,000/week. If four employees receive $1,600, $1,850, $2,300 and $2,150 per week, what is the salary per week of the 5th employee?

    Difficulty: Medium

20. A bus drove 1 hour at a speed of 65 km per hour and 2 hours at a speed of 70 km per hour. What was the average speed of the bus during the entire duration? Round your answer to the nearest tenths place.

    Difficulty: Medium

1. To find the average number of chocolates, add all the numbers together and then divide by the number of boxes.
   Therefore, we have:
   $$\frac{18+19+21+22+20}{5} = \frac{100}{5} = 20$$
   The correct answer is D.

2. There are 150 pages in the third book, so there are $150 + 70 = 220$ pages in the second book. Use that information to calculate the average number of pages.
   $$\frac{420+220+150+150}{4} = 235$$
   The correct answer is H.

3. To find the average temperature, add the numbers and then divide by the number of days.
   Therefore, we have:
   $$\frac{23+26+27+25+27+30+31}{7} = 27$$
   The correct answer is C.

4. During the next 3 days, David walked in total $4 \times 3 = 12$ hours. Use that information to calculate the average number of hours:
   $$\frac{3+5+12}{3} = 4$$
   The correct answer is E.

5. Let x be the number of hats that Zoey has. Then, the formula for the average number of hats is
   $$\frac{4+7+5+x}{4} = 5$$
   Cross multiply and solve for x:
   $$16 + x = 20$$
   $$x = 20 - 16 = 4$$
   The correct answer is D.

6. Using the average formula, plug in the information we are given.
   $$\text{Average} = \frac{\text{Sum of Numbers}}{\text{Number of Numbers}}$$
   $$\frac{5+6+12+25+33+y}{6} = 15$$
   Solve for y.
   $$\frac{81+y}{6} = 15$$

Multiply both sides by 6.
$$81 + y = 90$$
$$y = 9$$
The correct answer is F.

7. The question asks for their average earnings per day for the period of three days.
   Therefore, we have:
   $$\frac{720+750}{3} = \$490$$
   The correct answer is C.

8. Let x represent the number of animals Sam saw on the third day. The question states on the second day he saw 3 more animals than the third day, so we can represent that as $x + 3$. The average number of animals is 6, so we can set up the following:
   $$\frac{5+x+3+x+6}{4} = 6$$
   Cross multiply and solve for x:
   $$14 + 2x = 24$$
   $$2x = 10$$
   $$x = 5$$
   On the second day, Sam saw 8 animals and on the third day he saw 5 animals.
   The correct answer is E.

9. If there are 5 fruits in the first basket, then the second basket has 10 fruits. In the fourth basket, there are $10 - 1 = 9$ fruits. Use that information to calculate the average number of fruits:
   $$\frac{5+10+8+9}{4} = 8$$
   The correct answer is C.

10. Let x represent the weight of the last classmate. Use the average formula and plug in the known numbers. Then solve for x.
    $$\frac{50+53+51+52+54+57+x}{7} = 53$$
    $$371 = x + 317$$
    $$x = 54 \text{ kg}$$
    The correct answer is G.

11. If the average of six numbers is 32, we can use our average formula to figure out the sum.
    $$\frac{\text{SUM}}{6} = 32$$

Video Explanations
at argoprep.com/shsat

SUM = 192

We are now excluding one number, so the total number of numbers we are working with is $(6 - 1) = 5$ and the average is reduced by 4 so $(32 - 4) = 28$. Plug in your new numbers to the average formula.

$$\frac{SUM}{5} = 28$$

$$SUM = 140$$

Subtract the two sums to find the excluded number.

$$192 - 140 = 52$$

The correct answer is C.

---

12. Let x represent Joey's next test score. Plug in your known numbers to the average formula.

$$\frac{81 + 92 + 78 + 96 + x}{5} = 88$$

Solve for x.

$$347 + x = 440$$

$$x = 93$$

The correct answer is F.

---

13. First, find how much money Lily earned on Tuesday: $13 + 5 = \$18$. If the average amount of money Lily earned per day is $14, we have:

$$\frac{13 + 18 + x}{3} = 14$$

Cross multiply and solve for x:

$$31 + x = 14, x = 11$$

On Wednesday Lily earned $11.

The correct answer is A.

---

14. Ava earned $30 per day for 3 days and $20 per day for 2 days, so she earned $90 for 3 days and $40 for the next 2 days. Use that information to calculate the average of the last 5 days.

$$\frac{90 + 40}{5} = \$26$$

The correct answer is G.

---

15. If Alec's average is 7 hours, then Dylan's average is $7 - 2 = 5$ hours. Therefore, the formula for Dylan's average number of hours using the computer is

$$\frac{4 + 6 + x}{3} = 5$$

Cross multiply and solve for x:

$$10 + x = 15$$

$$x = 15 - 10 = 5$$

The correct answer is B.

---

16. Logan's average score on the first 6 tests was 90 and on the next 4 tests his average score was 87. Therefore, the sum of the score of 6 tests is $6 \times 90 = 540$ and the sum of the scores of 4 tests is $4 \times 87 = 348$. Since we know the sum of the 6 tests and 4 tests, we can calculate the average for the 10 tests by plugging in the information to our average formula.

$$\frac{540 + 348}{10} = 88.8$$

The correct answer is G.

---

17. In total, the sum of the heights of the first four trees is $4 \times 100 = 400$ inches and the total height of the next two trees is $2 \times 96 = 192$ inches. Use that information to calculate the average height of Kevin's trees.

$$\frac{400 + 192 + 115}{7} = 101$$

The average height of Kevin's trees is 101 inches.

---

18. The average speed is the ratio of the total distance to the total time. Total distance $= (65 \times 5) + (80 \times 3) = 565$ m.
We have:

$$\frac{565}{5 + 3} = 70.625 \approx 71 \text{ m/hr}.$$

The average speed was 71 miles per hour.

---

19. Let x represent the salary per week for the 5th employee. Plug in your known numbers to the average formula.

$$\frac{1,600 + 1,850 + 2,300 + 2,150 + x}{5} = 2,000$$

Solve for x.

$$x + 7,900 = 10,000$$

$$x = 2,100$$

The fifth employee receives **$2,100** per week.

---

20. The average speed is the ratio of the total distance to the total time.
Total distance $= 65 + (2 \times 70) = 205$ km.
We have:

$$\frac{205}{1 + 2} = 68.3 \text{ km/hr}.$$

The average speed of the bus was 68.3 km per hour.

Video Explanations
at argoprep.com/shsat

$$\frac{25}{\times 6}$$
$$\frac{}{1500}$$

1. A 24-foot ribbon is to be cut into three pieces with a ratio of 1:2:3. What will be the length of the longest piece?

   A. 2 feet   **C.** 12 feet
   B. 8 feet   **D.** 14 feet

   Difficulty: Easy

2. The perimeter of a triangle is 90 centimeters and the ratio of its sides is 3:5:7. What is the length of the smallest side?

   E. 15 cm   **G.** 30 cm
   F. 18 cm   **H.** 45 cm

   Difficulty: Easy

3. What is the value of x in the proportion below?

   $$\frac{21}{x+5} = \frac{15}{x+3}$$

   A. 2   **C.** 9
   B. 5   **D.** 17

   Difficulty: Easy

4. The angles of a triangle are related to each other in the ratio of 1:2:6. What is the value, in degrees, of the largest angle?

   E. 20   **G.** 90
   F. 60   **H.** 120

   Difficulty: Medium

5. Two wheels are connected by a belt. The first has a radius of 25 cm and the second has a radius of 75 cm. If the first wheel made 300 turns, how many turns did the second wheel make?

   A. 400   **C.** 900
   B. 600   **D.** 1200

   Difficulty: Medium

6. Calculate the value of y from the proportion below:

   $$\frac{4y+3}{2} = \frac{2y+6}{3}$$

   E. 0.512   **G.** 1.087
   F. 0.375   **H.** 2.375

   Difficulty: Medium

7. The ratio of a football team's wins to loses is 3:2. How many wins are expected if the team lost 30 games?

   A. 40   **C.** 90
   B. 45   **D.** 100

   Difficulty: Medium

   3000

8. An office assistant types 50 words in 2 minutes. How many words will she type in 1.5 hours?

   E. 510   **G.** 1500
   F. 870   **H.** 2250

   Difficulty: Medium

9. The sides of a quadrilateral are related to each other with a ratio of 1:3:5:7. What is the value of the longest side if the perimeter is 160 cm?

   A. 50 cm   **C.** 90 cm
   B. 70 cm   **D.** 100 cm

   Difficulty: Medium

10. The width and the length of a rectangle are related in the ratio of 3:5 respectively. What is the width if the perimeter is 80 cm?

    E. 5 cm   **G.** 15 cm
    F. 10 cm   **H.** 20 cm

    Difficulty: Medium

Video Explanations
at argoprep.com/shsat

11. Knowing that the slope is a function's rate of change, what is the rate of change of the function that passes through the point $(-3, 4)$ and the origin?

   A. $-\dfrac{4}{3}$ C. $\dfrac{3}{4}$

   B. $-\dfrac{3}{4}$ D. $\dfrac{4}{3}$

Difficulty: Hard

12. What is the possible value of x that satisfies the given proportion?

$$\frac{x-5}{8} = \frac{2}{x-5}$$

   E. 3   G. 9
   F. 8   H. 10

Difficulty: Medium

13. The two figures below are similar. What is the value of x that satisfies the proportion presented in the figures?

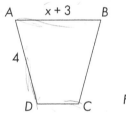

   A. 1   C. 7
   B. 4   D. 9

Difficulty: Hard

14. What is the possible value of x that satisfies the given proportion?

$$\frac{x+4}{6} = \frac{3}{x+1}$$

   E. 2   G. 12
   F. 8   H. 15

Difficulty: Medium

15. The two figures below are similar. What is the value of x that satisfies the proportion presented on the figures?

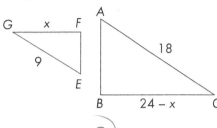

   A. 3   C. 8
   B. 5   D. 12

Difficulty: Hard

16. The perimeter of the triangle is 54. What are the values of X and Y respectively?

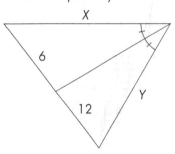

   E. 10, 15   G. 14, 28
   F. 12, 24   H. 16, 30

Difficulty: Hard

17. Four machines complete a production cycle in 10 days. How many days will it take to complete the production cycle if the number of machines was doubled?

   A. 3   C. 8
   B. 5   D. 12

Difficulty: Easy

▶ **Video Explanations**
at argoprep.com/shsat

18. A is proportional to B and C. If B = 2 and C = 5, then A = 30. What is the value of A, if B = 7 and C = 4?

E. 20   G. 90
F. 84   H. 98

Difficulty: Hard

20. M is proportional to L and P. If L = 12 and P = 20, then M = 960.

What is the value of M when L = 3 and P = 4?

E. 36   G. 92
F. 48   H. 98

Difficulty: Hard

19. On a farm, there are 300 chickens that eat a full truck of corn in 20 days. If the owner of the farm buys 100 more chickens, how many days will be needed to eat the same amount of food?

A. 8   C. 15
B. 10   D. 20

Difficulty: Hard

Answer Explanation

1. Let x be the length of the shortest piece.
   Since the total length is 24 feet, then the equation is
   $$1x + 2x + 3x = 24$$
   Combine like terms and solve for x:
   $$6x = 24$$
   $$x = \frac{24}{6} = 4$$
   Find the length of the longest piece:
   $$3 \times 4 = 12$$
   The length of the longest piece is 12 feet.
   The correct answer is C.

2. Let x be the length of the portion of the triangle's perimeter.
   Since the total perimeter is 90 cm then the equation is
   $$3x + 5x + 7x = 90$$
   Combine like terms and solve for x:
   $$15x = 90$$
   $$x = \frac{90}{15} = 6$$
   The smallest side is $3x = 3 \times 6 = 18$ cm.
   The correct answer is F.

3. Cross multiply and then solve for x:
   $$21(x + 3) = 15(x + 5)$$

Divide both sides by 3:
$$7(x + 3) = 5(x + 5)$$
Apply the distributive property to the parentheses:
$$7x + 21 = 5x + 25$$
$$7x - 5x = 25 - 21$$
$$2x = 4$$
$$x = \frac{4}{2} = 2$$
The correct answer is A.

4. The sum of the inner angles of a triangle must be 180°
   Therefore, we have:
   $$1x + 2x + 6x = 180$$
   Solve for x:
   $$9x = 180°$$
   $$x = 20°$$
   The largest angle is $6x = 6 \times 20° = 120°$
   The correct answer is H.

5. Suppose x is the number of turns that were made by the second wheel.
   Set up a proportion to solve the problem given:
   $$\frac{25}{300} = \frac{75}{x}$$

Video Explanations
at argoprep.com/shsat

Cross multiply and solve for x:

$$25x = 300 \times 75 = 22500$$
$$x = 900$$

The correct answer is C.

---

6. Cross multiply and solve for y:

$$3(4y + 3) = 2(2y + 6)$$

Apply the distributive property:

$$12y + 9 = 4y + 12$$
$$12y - 4y = 12 - 9$$
$$8y = 3$$
$$y = 0.375$$

The correct answer is F.

---

7. Set up the proportion to solve the problem given.

$$\frac{3}{2} = \frac{x}{30}$$

Then cross multiply and solve for x:

$$2x = 90$$
$$x = \frac{90}{2}$$
$$x = 45$$

The correct answer is B.

---

8. Set up the proportion to solve the problem given. Then cross multiply and solve for x:

$$\frac{50 \, \text{words}}{2 \, \text{min}} = \frac{x}{90 \, \text{min}}$$
$$2x = 4500$$
$$x = \frac{4500}{2}$$
$$x = 2250$$

The correct answer is H

---

9. Since the ratio of the sides is 1:3:5:7, then we can set up the equation:

$$x + 3x + 5x + 7x = 160$$
$$16x = 160$$

Solve for x:

$$x = \frac{160}{16}$$
$$x = 10$$

Therefore, the longer side = $7x = 7 \times 10 = 70$ cm.

The correct answer is B.

---

10. Since the ratio of the width to the length is 3:5, then we can set up the equation:

$$3x + 3x + 5x + 5x = 80$$

Combine like terms and solve for x:

$$16x = 80, \ x = 5$$

The width is $3x = 3 \times 5 = 15$ cm.

The correct answer is G.

---

11. Since the rate of change of a function is its slope, calculate the slope value.

The formula of the slope of the function is $m = \frac{y_2 - y_1}{x_2 - x_1}$

Substitute the values into the formula and calculate m:

$$m = \frac{0 - 4}{0 - (-3)} = -\frac{4}{3}$$

The correct answer is A.

---

12. Cross multiply:

$$(x - 5)(x - 5) = 16$$
$$x^2 - 10x + 25 = 16$$
$$x^2 - 10x + 9 = 0$$

Factor and solve for x:

$$(x - 9)(x - 1) = 0$$
$$x = 9 \text{ or } x = 1$$

The correct answer is G.

---

13. Proportion equation: $\frac{4}{3} = \frac{x + 3}{x + 2}$

Cross multiply:

$$4(x + 2) = 3(x + 3)$$

Apply distributive property:

$$4x + 8 = 3x + 9, \ 4x - 3x = 9 - 8$$

Solve for x:

$$x = 1$$

The correct answer is A.

---

14. Cross multiply:

$$(x + 4)(x + 1) = 18$$
$$x^2 + 5x + 4 = 18$$
$$x^2 + 5x - 14 = 0$$

Factor and solve for x:

$$(x + 7)(x - 2) = 0$$
$$x = -7 \text{ or } x = 2$$

The correct answer is E.

▶ Video Explanations
at argoprep.com/shsat

15. Proportion equation: $\dfrac{x}{24-x} = \dfrac{9}{18}$

Cross multiply and combine like terms:

$$\frac{x}{24-x} = \frac{1}{2}$$
$$2x = 24 - x$$

Solve for x:

$$3x = 24$$
$$x = 8$$

The correct answer is C.

---

16. Proportion equation: $\dfrac{X}{6} = \dfrac{Y}{12}$

$$12X = 6Y$$
$$12X - 6Y = 0$$

Divide both sides by 6:

$$2X - Y = 0$$

Perimeter equation:

$$X + Y + 18 = 54$$
$$X + Y = 36$$

System of equations:

$$X + Y = 36$$
$$2X - Y = 0$$

Multiply the first equation by 2 and subtract the second equation from the first equation and you get the following:

$$3Y = 72$$
$$Y = 24$$

Substitute the value of y into the first equation of the system and find the value of x:

$$X + 24 = 36$$
$$X = 36 - 24 = 12$$

Plug in the value of X into the first equation to get the value of Y.

$$12 + Y = 36$$
$$Y = 24$$

Therefore, $X = 12$ and $Y = 24$.

The correct answer is F.

17.

N° of machines	N° of days
4	10
8	X
2	X

Inverse proportion: more machines, less days.

18. Inverse proportion equation: $\dfrac{8}{4} = \dfrac{10}{x}$

Solve for x:

$$8x = 40$$
$$x = 5$$

The correct answer is B.

---

18. Direct proportion:

$$A = kBC$$

Substitute $A = 30$, $B = 2$ and $C = 5$ to find the value of the constant of proportionality k:

$$30 = k \times 2 \times 5$$
$$30 = 10k$$
$$k = 3$$

Find the value of A, when $B = 7$ and $C = 4$.

$$A = 3 \times 7 \times 4$$
$$A = 84$$

The correct answer is F.

19.

N° of chicken	N° of days the food lasts
300	20
400	X

Inverse proportion: more chickens, the amount of food decreases faster.

Inverse proportion equation: $\dfrac{x}{300} = \dfrac{20}{400}$

Solve for x:

$$400x = 6000$$
$$x = 15$$

The correct answer is C.

---

20. We can set up a direct proportion:

$M = kLP$ where k is a constant of proportionality.

Substitute $M = 960$, $L = 12$, and $P = 20$ to find the value of the constant of proportionality k:

$$960 = k \times 12 \times 20$$
$$960 = 240k$$
$$k = 4$$

Find the value of M when $L = 3$ and $P = 4$:

$$M = 4 \times 3 \times 4$$
$$M = 48$$

The correct answer is F.

Video Explanations
at argoprep.com/shsat

1. What is the value of x, if $x + 4 < 5$?
   A. $x < 1$ C. $x < 3$
   B. $x > 1$ D. $x < 9$
   Difficulty: Easy

2. Ryan had $33 and he went to the grocery store. He bought some apples and bananas for $25. He wants to spend the rest of his money on chocolate bars, which cost $2 each. What is the maximum number of chocolate bars that he can buy?
   E. 2   G. 6
   F. 4   H. 8
   Difficulty: Medium

3. What is the solution to the following compound inequality $-5 < \frac{x}{2} < 3$?
   A. $-5 < x < 6$ C. $-6 < x < 10$
   B. $-10 < x < -6$ D. $-10 < x < 6$
   Difficulty: Medium

4. What is the value of x, if $1 - x \leq 4$?
   E. $x \geq -3$
   F. $x \geq -1$
   G. $x \geq 1$
   H. $x \leq 1$
   Difficulty: Medium

5. Caleb has at least 2 more pens than Nathan. Which of the following inequalities gives the relationship between Caleb's number of pens (x) and Nathan's number of pens (y)?
   A. $x + y \geq 2$
   B. $x - y \geq 2$
   C. $2 - x \leq y$
   D. $2 - y \leq x$
   Difficulty: Medium

6. Levi earns $15 per hour working in a shop. He needs at least $300 for a bike. What is the minimum number of hours he needs to work to buy the bike?
   E. 13   G. 18
   F. 15   H. 20
   Difficulty: Easy

7. What is the value of x, if $x > 2(x + 1)$?
   A. $x < 2$ C. $x < -2$
   B. $x < 3$ D. $x > 4$
   Difficulty: Medium

8. Nora made 35 fruit cakes. Helga made at least 10 more than Nora. Which answer choice could be the number of cakes made by Helga?
   E. 16   G. 25
   F. 21   H. 83
   Difficulty: Medium

9. What is the value of x in the expression below?
   $$6x > 4(x - 2)$$
   A. $x > -8$ C. $x > 2$
   B. $x > -4$ D. $x > 10$
   Difficulty: Medium

10. What is the value of x, if $\frac{x + 5}{2} \leq 3$?
    E. $x \leq 1$
    F. $x \leq 2$
    G. $x \leq 3$
    H. $x \geq 6$
    Difficulty: Medium

▶ **Video Explanations**
at argoprep.com/shsat

95   6.9

11. Lily is renting an office space for a conference which charges a $45 flat fee and $4.30 for each person invited to the conference. Lily has a budget of $90. How many people can Lily invite to the conference without exceeding her budget?

- **A.** 15
- **B.** 12
- **C.** 10
- **D.** 7

Difficulty: Hard

12. What is the solution of $-3 \leq \dfrac{x-3}{2} \leq 5$?

- **E.** $2 \leq x \leq 10$
- **F.** $-6 \leq x \leq 10$
- **G.** $-3 \leq x \leq 13$
- **H.** $9 \leq x \leq 13$

Difficulty: Medium

13. Aaron's book of 430 pages has at least 50 pages less than Adam's book. What is the minimum number of pages in Adam's book?

- **A.** 350
- **B.** 390
- **C.** 420
- **D.** 480

Difficulty: Medium

14. What is the value of x from the expression below?

$$\frac{1}{x-1} \leq \frac{1}{2x+5}$$

- **E.** $x \leq 6$
- **F.** $x \geq 4$
- **G.** $x \geq -1$
- **H.** $x \leq -6$

Difficulty: Hard

15. Brayden is saving $600 for a new stereo system. Currently he has $320. If he saves $50 per week, how long until he saves at least $720 to cover taxes and extras?

- **A.** 1 week
- **B.** 3 weeks
- **C.** 5 weeks
- **D.** 8 weeks

Difficulty: Medium

16. Mark rented a bike for a fixed charge of $3.25 plus $1.8 per hour. How many hours can he use the bike without spending more than $15?

6.5   11.75

Difficulty: Medium

17. What are the solutions for $3x + 2 \leq y \leq 7 - 2x$ when $y = 1$?

$5x$ $3x + 2 \leq 7$

$-1/3, 3$

Difficulty: Hard

18. Tina wants to order cups over the internet. Each cup costs $8.75 and shipping for the entire order is $5.30. Tina can spend no more than $50 for the purchase. How many cups can Tina order without exceeding her $50 limit?

5   44.7

Difficulty: Hard

19. What is the solution for $4y - 12 < x + z < y - 2$ when $y = 2$ and $z = 2$?

$-4 < x + 2 < C$

< 6 400

Difficulty: Hard

385

20. Violet plans to take a trip that costs $450. Currently she has $135. If she saves $20 per week, how many weeks does she need to save at least $520 to cover taxes and extras?

20

Difficulty: Hard

Video Explanations at argoprep.com/shsat

1. Subtract 4 from each side.

We have:

$$x + 4 - 4 < 5 - 4$$
$$x < 1$$

The correct answer is A.

---

2. Let x be the number of chocolate bars he can buy.

Write an equation:

$$25 + 2x \leq 33$$
$$2x \leq 8$$
$$x \leq 4$$

Ryan can buy a maximum of 4 chocolate bars.

The correct answer is F.

---

3. Multiply each term by 2 to eliminate the fraction, and isolate x:

$$-5(2) < x < 3(2)$$
$$-10 < x < 6$$

Therefore, x must be between -10 and 6.

The correct answer is D.

---

4. Rewrite this expression as

$$-x \leq 4 - 1$$
$$-x \leq 3$$

Then divide by -1 and change the sign:

$$x \geq -3$$

REMEMBER: Whenever you multiply or divide an inequality by a negative number, you must flip the inequality sign.

The correct answer is E.

---

5. Caleb has at least 2 pens more than Nathan, which can be written as

$$x \geq y + 2$$

Rewrite this inequality to match the answer options:

$$x - y \geq 2$$

The correct answer is B.

---

6. Let h be the number of hours he should work to reach his goal.

Write an inequality:

$$15h \geq 300$$

Divide both sides by 15:

$$h \geq 20$$

Levi should work at least 20 hours to buy the bike.

The correct answer is H.

---

7. First, get rid of the parentheses:

$$x > 2x + 2$$

Rewrite as:

$$2x - x < -2$$
$$x < -2$$

The correct answer is C.

---

8. Let x be the number of cakes Helga made.

Write an inequality:

$$p - 35 \geq 10$$
$$p \geq 35 + 10$$
$$p \geq 45$$

Helga made at least 45 fruit cakes.

As you can see, answer choices E, F and G have numbers that are less than, 45. Helga made at least 45 fruit cakes so answer choice H is a possibility, 83 fruit cakes.

The correct answer is H.

---

9. Get rid of the parentheses and combine like terms:

$$6x > 4x - 8$$
$$2x > -8$$
$$x > -4$$

The correct answer is B.

---

10. First, multiply each side by 2.

Therefore, we have:

$$\frac{x+5}{2} \times 2 \leq 3 \times 2$$
$$x + 5 \leq 6$$

Then subtract 5 from both sides:

$$x + 5 - 5 \leq 6 - 5$$
$$x \leq 1$$

The correct answer is E.

---

11. Let p be the number of people invited to the conference.

Write an equation:

$$45 + 4.30p \leq 90$$
$$4.30p \leq 45$$
$$p \leq 10.4$$

Lily can invite 10 people to the conference without exceeding her limit.

The correct answer is C.

▶ **Video Explanations**
at argoprep.com/shsat

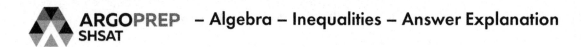

12. Multiply each term by 2 to eliminate the fraction and isolate x:
$$-6 \leq x-3 \leq 10$$
Then add 3 to each term:
$$-3 \leq x \leq 13$$
The correct answer is G.

13. Let x represent the number of pages in Adam's book.
Write the inequality:
$$p-50 \geq 430$$
$$p \geq 430+50$$
$$p \geq 480$$
Adam's book has at least 480 pages.
The correct answer is D.

14. Cross multiply to get rid of fractions:
$$2x+5 \leq x-1$$
Rewrite as
$$2x-x \leq -1-5$$
$$x \leq -6$$
The correct answer is H.

15. Let x represent the number of weeks Brayden must wait to save at least $720.
Write the inequality:
$$320+50x \geq 720$$
$$50x \geq 400$$
$$x \geq 8$$
Brayden must wait 8 weeks to save at least $720.
The correct answer is D.

16. Let h represent the number of hours he can use the bike without spending more than $15.
Write the inequality:
$$3.25+1.8h \leq 15$$
$$1.8h \leq 11.75$$
$$h \leq 6.5$$
He can use the bike **6 hours** without spending more than $15.

17. Separate the compound inequality into two pieces:
$$3x+2 \leq y \ \text{and} \ y \leq 7-2x$$
Substitute $y = 1$ into each inequality and solve for x:
$$3x+2 \leq 1$$
$$3x \leq -1$$

$$x \leq -\frac{1}{3}$$
$$1 \leq 7-2x$$
$$-6 \leq -2x$$
$$x \leq 3$$
We have:
$$x \leq -\frac{1}{3} \ \textbf{and} \ x \leq 3$$

18. Let x represent the number of cups Tina can order without exceeding her limit.
Write the inequality:
$$8.75x+5.30 \leq 50$$
$$8.75x \leq 44.7$$
$$x \leq 5.1$$
Tina can order **5 cups** without exceeding her limit.

19. Substitute $y = 2$ and $z = 2$ into each inequality and solve for x:
$$4(2)-12 < x+2 < 2-2$$
$$-4 < x+2 < 0$$
$$-4-2 < x < 0-2$$
$$-6 < x < -2.$$
$$\mathbf{-6 < x < -2.}$$

20. Let x represent the number of weeks Violet should wait to save at least $520.
Write the inequality:
$$135+20x \geq 520$$
$$20x \geq 385$$
$$x \geq 19.25$$
Therefore, Violet should wait **20 weeks** to save at least $520.

▶ **Video Explanations**
at argoprep.com/shsat

1. If $a{-}b = \dfrac{a+b}{b}$, what is the value of $4{-}1$?
   A. 1
   C. 5
   B. 3
   D. 7
   Difficulty: Easy

2. If $a \sim b = 3a - b$, what is the value of $2(5 \sim 2)$?
   E. 12
   G. 32
   F. 26
   H. 36
   Difficulty: Medium

3. If $(\Delta x) = x - 2$, when x is odd, and $(\Delta x) = 2(x-1)$, when x is even, what is the value of $((\Delta 7)+(\Delta 2))$?
   A. 5
   C. 10
   B. 7
   D. 12
   Difficulty: Medium

4. If $a \sim b = \dfrac{6a-4b}{2}$, what is the value of $1 \sim 1$?
   E. 6
   G. 2
   F. 4
   H. 1
   Difficulty: Medium

5. If $a\square b = \dfrac{a+2b}{a-b}$, what is the value of $\dfrac{3\square 2}{2}$?
   A. $\dfrac{7}{2}$
   C. 4
   B. $\dfrac{3}{2}$
   D. 7
   Difficulty: Medium

6. If $a\#b\#c = a+b-2c$, what is the value of $4\#2\#1$?
   E. 4
   G. 8
   F. 6
   H. 10
   Difficulty: Medium

7. If $(\bigcirc x) = x - 1$, when x is odd, and $(\bigcirc x) = 2x+1$, when x is even, what is the value of $\dfrac{(\bigcirc 4)-(\bigcirc 1)}{3}$?
   A. 9
   C. 5
   B. 7
   D. 3
   Difficulty: Medium

8. If $'x = 4x - 1$, what is the value of $('('2))$?
   E. 12
   G. 20
   F. 18
   H. 27
   Difficulty: Hard

9. If $\emptyset b = \dfrac{4-2b}{b}$, what is the value of $\emptyset 2 - \emptyset 1$?
   A. 1
   C. -2
   B. 0
   D. -4
   Difficulty: Hard

10. If $a \bowtie b = \dfrac{2a}{b}$, what is the value of $5 \bowtie 2$?
    E. 1
    G. 7
    F. 5
    H. 12
    Difficulty: Medium

Video Explanations at argoprep.com/shsat

129

11. If $\rightleftharpoons x = 2x$, what is the value of $(\rightleftharpoons (\rightleftharpoons (\rightleftharpoons 3)))$?

   A. 6   C. 24
   B. 12   D. 48

   Difficulty: Hard

12. If $x \heartsuit y \heartsuit z = 2x - 3y + z$, what is the value of $1 \heartsuit 2 \heartsuit 3$?

   E. 0   G. 3
   F. −1   H. 4

   Difficulty: Hard

13. If $(\triangle x) = \frac{x}{2} + 1$, what is the value of $(\triangle(\triangle 6))$?

   A. 1   C. 5
   B. 3   D. 7

   Difficulty: Hard

14. If $a \Box b \Box c = 2a(b - 1)(c + 3)$, what is the value $2 \Box 2 \Box 4 - 1 \Box 3 \Box 2$?

   E. 8   G. 5
   F. 6   H. −1

   Difficulty: Hard

15. If $a \diamond b \diamond c = \frac{2c - b}{2a}$, what is the value of $\frac{3 \diamond 3 \diamond 3}{1 \diamond 1 \diamond 1}$?

   A. $\frac{3}{2}$

   B. 3

   C. 0

   D. 1

   Difficulty: Hard⁺

16. If $a \top b \top c = 2a - 5b + 3c$, what is the value of $\frac{3 \top 1 \top 1}{6}$?

   E. 4
   F. 2
   G. $\frac{2}{3}$
   H. $\frac{1}{3}$

   Difficulty: Hard

17. If $(\diamondsuit x) = \frac{x}{3}$, what is the value of $(\diamondsuit(\diamondsuit(\diamondsuit 27)))$?

   Difficulty: Hard

18. If $a \llbracket b \llbracket c = (4a - b)^c$, what is the value of $\frac{3 \llbracket 3 \llbracket 3 - 2 \llbracket 2 \llbracket 2}{1 \llbracket 1 \llbracket 1}$?

   Difficulty: Hard⁺

19. If $x \theta y = \frac{2x}{y}$ and $2 \theta 1 = k \theta 6$, what is the value of k?

   Difficulty: Hard⁺

20. If $x \otimes y = \frac{3x - y}{y}$ and $1 \otimes 2 = k \otimes 8$, what is the value of k?

   Difficulty: Hard⁺

Video Explanations
at argoprep.com/shsat

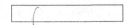

1. Plug in $a = 4$, $b = 1$:

Therefore, we have:

$$4 \neg 1 = \frac{4+1}{1} = 5$$

The correct answer is C.

2. First, plug in $a = 5$, $b = 2$:

$$5 \backsim 2 = 3 \times 5 - 2 = 15 - 2 = 13$$

Then multiply by 2.

Therefore, we have:

$$2(5 \backsim 2) = 2 \times 13 = 26$$

The correct answer is F.

3. First, find the value of $(\Delta 7)$. This number is odd so we have:

$$(\Delta 7) = 7 - 2 = 5$$

Then find the value of $(\Delta 2)$. This number is even so we have:

$$(\Delta 2) = 2(2 - 1) = 2$$

Therefore, we have:

$$((\Delta 7) + (\Delta 2)) = 5 + 2 = 7$$

The correct answer is B.

4. Substitute the value $a = 1$, $b = 1$ into the expression:

$$1 \backsim 1 = \frac{6 \times 1 - 4 \times 1}{2} = 1$$

The correct answer is H.

5. First, plug in $a = 3$ and $b = 2$:

$$3 \square 2 = \frac{3 + 2 \times 2}{3 - 2} = 7$$

Then divide by 2.

Therefore, we have:

$$\frac{3 \square 2}{2} = \frac{7}{2}$$

The correct answer is A.

6. Substitute the values $a = 4$, $b = 2$ and $c = 1$ into the expression:

$$4 \# 2 \# 1 = 4 + 2 - 2 \times 1 = 4$$

The correct answer is E.

7. First find the value of $(\bigcirc 4)$. This number is even so we have:

$$(\bigcirc 4) = 2 \times 4 + 1 = 9$$

Then find the value of $(\bigcirc 1)$. This number is odd so we have:

$$(\bigcirc 1) = 1 - 1 = 0$$

Therefore, we have:

$$\frac{(\bigcirc 4) - (\bigcirc 1)}{3} = \frac{9 - 0}{3} = 3$$

The correct answer is D.

8. First, find the value of $('2)$:

$$('2) = 4 \times 2 - 1 = 7$$

Then find the value of $('7)$:

$$('7) = 4 \times 7 - 1 = 27$$

The correct answer is H.

9. First, find the value of $\not{0} 2$:

$$\not{0} 2 = \frac{4 - 2 \times 2}{2} = 0$$

Then find the value of $\not{0} 1$:

$$\not{0} 1 = \frac{4 - 2 \times 1}{1} = 2$$

Therefore, we have:

$$\not{0} 2 - \not{0} 1 = 0 - 2 = -2$$

The correct answer is C.

10. Substitute the values of $a = 5$, $b = 2$ into the expression:

$$5 \bowtie 2 = \frac{2 \times 5}{2} = 5$$

The correct answer is F.

11. First, find the value of $(= 3)$:

$$(= 3) = 2 \times 3 = 6$$

Then find the value of $(= 6)$:

$$(= 6) = 2 \times 6 = 12$$

Finally, find the value of $(= 12)$:

$$(= 12) = 2 \times 12 = 24$$

The correct answer is C.

12. Substitute the values of $x = 1$, $y = 2$ and $z = 3$:

$$1 \heartsuit 2 \heartsuit 3 = 2 \times 1 - 3 \times 2 + 3 = -1$$

The correct answer is F.

13. First, find the value of $(\triangle 6)$:

$$(\triangle 6) = \frac{6}{2} + 1 = 4$$

Then find the value of $(\triangle 4)$:

$$(\triangle 4) = \frac{4}{2} + 1 = 3$$

The correct answer is B.

---

14. First, find the value of $2 \int 2 \int 4$.

Substitute the values $a = 2$, $b = 2$, $c = 4$ into the expression:

$$2 \int 2 \int 4 = 2 \times 1 \times (2-1) \times (4+3) = 4 \times 7 = 28$$

Then find the value of $1 \int 3 \int 2$.

Substitute the values of $a = 1$, $b = 3$ and $c = 2$ into the expression:

$$1 \int 3 \int 2 = 2 \times 1 \times (3-1)(2+3) = 4 \times 5 = 20$$

Therefore, we have:

$$2 \int 2 \int 4 - 1 \int 3 \int 2 = 28 - 20 = 8$$

The correct answer is E.

---

15. First, find the value of $3 \diamondsuit 3 \diamondsuit 3$.

Substitute the values $a = 3$, $b = 3$ and $c = 3$:

$$3 \diamondsuit 3 \diamondsuit 3 = \frac{2 \times 3 - 3}{2 \times 3} = \frac{1}{2}$$

Then find the value of $1 \diamondsuit 1 \diamondsuit 1$:

Substitute the values $a = 1$, $b = 1$ and $c = 1$:

$$1 \diamondsuit 1 \diamondsuit 1 = \frac{2 \times 1 - 1}{2 \times 1} = \frac{1}{2}$$

Therefore, we have:

$$\frac{3 \diamondsuit 3 \diamondsuit 3}{1 \diamondsuit 1 \diamondsuit 1} = \frac{1 \times 2}{2 \times 1} = 1$$

The correct answer is D.

---

16. First, find the value of $3 \top 1 \top 1$.

Substitute the values of $a = 3$, $b = 1$ and $c = 1$:

$$3 \top 1 \top 1 = 2 \times 3 - 5 \times 1 + 3 \times 1 = 4$$

Then divide by 6:

Therefore, we have:

$$\frac{3 \top 1 \top 1}{6} = \frac{4}{6} = \frac{2}{3}$$

The correct answer is G.

---

17. First, find the value of $(\diamondsuit 27)$:

$$(\diamondsuit 27) = \frac{27}{3} = 9$$

Then find the value of $(\diamondsuit 9)$:

$$(\diamondsuit 9) = \frac{9}{3} = 3$$

Finally, find the value $(\diamondsuit 3)$:

$$(\diamondsuit 3) = \frac{3}{3} = 1$$

So $(\diamondsuit(\diamondsuit(\diamondsuit 27))) = 1$.

---

18. First, find the value of $3 \llbracket 3 \llbracket 3$:

$$3 \llbracket 3 \llbracket 3 = (4 \times 3 - 3)^3 = 9^3 = 729$$

Then find the value of $2 \llbracket 2 \llbracket 2$:

$$2 \llbracket 2 \llbracket 2 = (4 \times 2 - 2)^2 = 36$$

Finally, find the value of $1 \llbracket 1 \llbracket 1$:

$$1 \llbracket 1 \llbracket 1 = (4 \times 1 - 1)^1 = 3$$

Therefore, we have:

$$\frac{3 \llbracket 3 \llbracket 3 - 2 \llbracket 2 \llbracket 2}{1 \llbracket 1 \llbracket 1} = \frac{729 - 36}{3} = \textbf{231}$$

---

19. First, plug in $x = 2$ and $y = 1$.

Therefore, we have:

$$\frac{2x}{y} = \frac{2 \times 2}{1} = \frac{4}{1}$$

Then, plug in $x = k$ and $y = 6$,

We have:

$$\frac{2x}{y} = \frac{2k}{6} = \frac{k}{3}$$

$$\frac{4}{1} = \frac{k}{3}$$

Then cross multiply and solve for k:

$$\boldsymbol{k = 12}$$

---

20. First, plug in $x = 1$ and $y = 2$.

Therefore, we have:

$$\frac{3x - y}{y} = \frac{3 \times 1 - 2}{2} = \frac{3 - 2}{2} = \frac{1}{2}$$

Then plug in $x = k$ and $y = 8$,

We have:

$$\frac{3x - y}{y} = \frac{3k - 8}{8}$$

$$\frac{3k - 8}{8} = \frac{1}{2}$$

Then cross multiply and solve for k:

$$2(3k - 8) = 8$$

$$6k - 16 = 8$$

$$6k = 8 + 16 = 24$$

$$k = \frac{24}{6} = \textbf{4}$$

Video Explanations
at argoprep.com/shsat

1. Simplify the following expression:

$$4a - 3b - 16a + b$$

   A. $a + 4b$
   B. $-a - b$
   C. $12a + 4b$
   D. $-12a - 2b$

   Difficulty: Easy

2.

$$4(x - 3) = 12$$

   In the equation above, what is the value of x?

   E. 8
   F. 6
   G. 4
   H. 1

   Difficulty: Medium

3. If $a \, D \, b = 3(a - 3b)$, what is the value of $8 \, D \, 5$?

   A. 12
   B. 3
   C. 0
   D. -21

   Difficulty: Medium

4. Mia has 3 bags. The number of toys in each bag is 6, 8 and x. What is the number of toys in the third bag if the average number of toys in the three bags is 6?

   E. 3
   F. 4
   G. 6
   H. 8

   Difficulty: Medium

5. If $f(x) = \dfrac{8x - 2}{2x}$, what is $f(1)$ equal to?

   A. 3
   B. 5
   C. 6
   D. 8

   Difficulty: Medium

6. In a zoo of 40 animals, the number of giraffes is 4 more than 3 times the number of zebras. How many giraffes are there in the zoo?

   E. 15
   F. 17
   G. 24
   H. 31

   Difficulty: Medium

7. Multiply the following expressions:

$$\frac{(4a - b)}{2} \cdot \frac{3}{4a - b}$$

   A. $\dfrac{12 - b}{a}$
   B. $\dfrac{(4a - b)^2}{b}$
   C. $\dfrac{4a - b}{2a}$
   D. $12a - 3b$

   Difficulty: Medium

8. If $(\lll x) = 2x - 5$, when x is odd, and $(\lll x) = 3x - 7$, when x is even, what is the value of $((\lll 3) - (\lll 1))$?

   E. 10
   F. 8
   G. 4
   H. 0

   Difficulty: Hard

9. What is the value of the following expression, if $a = 1$ and $b = 3$?

$$\frac{a - b}{a + b} \cdot \frac{2a + 2b}{a}$$

   A. -4
   B. 1
   C. $-\dfrac{9}{2}$
   D. 0

   Difficulty: Medium

10. What is the value of the following expression, if
$a = 1$ and $b = -2$?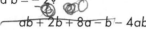
$$ab + 2b + 8a - b - 4ab$$

   E. -1 **G.** 9
   F. 3   **H.** 12

Difficulty: Easy

11. Simplify the algebraic expression below:
$$2(a - 1) + 3(2a + 1)$$

   A. $a - 11$ **C.** $a - 1$
   B. $8a + 1$ **D.** $a + 8$

Difficulty: Medium

12.
$$f(x) = x^3 - 2x$$
$$g(x) = 3x$$

What is the value of $f(g(1))$?

   E. 21   **G.** 12
   F. 18   **H.** 9

Difficulty: Medium

13.
$$\frac{x - 5}{4} = \frac{4x}{6}$$

In the equation above, what is the value of x?

   A. 12   **C.** 5
   B. 8   **D.** -15

Difficulty: Medium

14. What is the solution of the following compound
inequality?

$$-1 < \frac{x}{3} < 8$$

   E. $-8 < x < 24$ **G.** $0 < x < 8$
   F. $-3 < x < 24$ **H.** $-1 < x < 8$

Difficulty: Medium

15. Colton earns \$340 every month plus \$15 for each
new customer. Write an equation for the function
that models Colton's total earnings.

   A. $y = 15x$ **C.** $y = 15x + 340$
   B. $y = 340x + 15$ **D.** $y = 340x$

Difficulty: Easy

16. Erik bought x chocolates. Mark bought 2 more
chocolates than Erik. In total they bought 10 chocolates. How many chocolates did Mark buy?

   E. 18   **G.** 6
   F. 10   **H.** 4

Difficulty: Medium

17. Steven, John, Michael, George, and Jason drew
pictures. Steven drew 2 paintings, John drew 4
paintings, Michael drew 2 paintings, George
drew 4 paintings, and Jason drew 3 paintings.
Find the average number of paintings of those 5
friends.

   A. 6   **C.** 3
   B. 5   **D.** 2

Difficulty: Easy

Video Explanations
at argoprep.com/shsat

18. If ▯ $b = \dfrac{b-4}{2b}$, what is the value of ▯ 2 + ▯ 1?

E. − 4   G. 1

F. − 2   H. 6

Difficulty: Medium

19. Nolan bought 3 tickets for a movie and 4 tickets for a musical performance. The price of the performance ticket is 3 dollars less than 2 times the price of the movie ticket. If he paid $23.50, what is the price of one movie ticket?

A. $5.20   C. $3.50

B. $4.70   D. $3.23

Difficulty: Hard

20. Simplify the following expression:

$2x^3 + 3xy - x^2 + 2x^3 - 4xy + 2x^2$

E. $4x^3 + x^2 - xy$ G. $x^3 - 5xy$

F. $x^3 + x^2 - 1$ H. $2x^3 - 6x^2 - 2xy$

Difficulty: Easy

21.

$x - 2y = 10$
$2x + 3y = 5$

What is the solution to the system of equations above?

A. $\left(\dfrac{5}{7}, -\dfrac{3}{7}\right)$ C. $\left(5\dfrac{5}{7}, 7\dfrac{2}{7}\right)$

B. $\left(5\dfrac{5}{7}, -\dfrac{15}{7}\right)$ D. $\left(-3\dfrac{2}{7}, -1\dfrac{1}{7}\right)$

Difficulty: Hard

22. What is the value of x, if x − 2 > 4(x − 8)?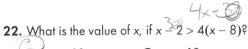

E. $x < 10$ G. $x > 10$

F. $x < 6$ H. $x > -2$

Difficulty: Medium

23. A first number plus twice a second number is 4. Twice the first number minus the second number is 12. What are these numbers?

A. 3 and − 1   C. $5\dfrac{3}{5}$ and $-\dfrac{4}{5}$

B. 4 and 5   D. 1 and 12

Difficulty: Hard

24. Simplify the expression below: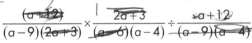

$$\dfrac{(a-12)}{(a-9)(2a+3)} \times \dfrac{2a+3}{(a-6)(a-4)} \div \dfrac{a+12}{(a-9)(a-4)}$$

E. $a - 9$ G. $\dfrac{1}{a-6}$

F. $\dfrac{1}{a+12}$ H. $\dfrac{a+12}{a-4}$

Difficulty: Medium

25. Given the function of two variables, evaluate the function $f(x,y) = \dfrac{x^3 - 4}{y - x}$ for $f(2, 1)$.

A. 3   C. − 1

B. 1   D. − 4

Difficulty: Medium

26. At a party, there are two kinds of drinks: juice and cola. The ratio of the number of juice drinks to the number of cola drinks is 1:2. How many cola drinks are at the party if the number of juice drinks is 12?

E. 6   G. 20

F. 12   H. 24

Difficulty: Medium

▶ **Video Explanations**
at argoprep.com/shsat

27. Maria bought 1 cup of coffee that costs $3. What is the cost of 2 cups of coffee?

A. $12   C. $4

B. $6   D. $2

Difficulty: Easy

28. Multiply the following expressions:

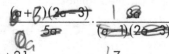

$$\frac{(a+7)(2a-3)}{5a} \cdot \frac{5a}{(a-1)(2a-3)}$$

E. $\frac{3a+21}{5a-5}$ G. $\frac{7}{a+4}$

F. $\frac{a-2}{2}$ H. $a+7$

Difficulty: Medium

29. If $\triangleleft x = x - 5$, what is the value of $(\triangleleft(\triangleleft(\triangleleft 7)))$?

A. -21 C. 1

B. -8 D. 3

Difficulty: Hard

30. Anna went to the store with $23. She bought 5 notebooks and 2 pens for $18. She spent the rest of her money on paper clips, which costs $0.75 each. What was the maximum number of paper clips that she was able to buy?

E. 3   G. 12

F. 6   H. 18

Difficulty: Medium

31. There are 15 cherries on 3 cakes. How many cherries will be on 5 cakes?

A. 100   C. 75

B. 80   D. 25

Difficulty: Easy

32. At the grocery store, 3 tomatoes cost $6. What is the price of 7 tomatoes?

E. $14   G. $10

F. $12   H. $7

Difficulty: Easy

$10.5 \rightarrow 11.4 \rightarrow 12.85$

33. Katia and David ordered fruit pie for $6.40, salad for $4.10, and 2 coffees for $0.70 each. The tax is $0.95. How much money should they get back if they hand the cashier $15.00?

2.15

Difficulty: Easy

34. Lily bought 2 books about cooking, 1 book about nature, and 4 books about flowers. Each book cost $5.90. How much did Lily spend on the books?

41.3

Difficulty: Easy

35. Carter earns $12 per hour working in a grocery store. He needs at least $150 for a new suit. How many hours should he work to buy the new suit?

13

Difficulty: Medium

36. Mila bought 2 boxes of chocolate sweets and 3 boxes of mint sweets. Each box of chocolate sweets contained 8 candies, and each box of mint sweets contained 12 candies. How many more mint sweets than chocolate did Mila buy?

Difficulty: Easy

Video Explanations
at argoprep.com/shsat

37. Simplify the following expression:

$$3(x + 2) - y(x - 6) + 4xy - 2(2y + xy)$$

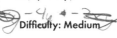
Difficulty: Medium

38. In a store, three hats and four scarves cost a total of $56.50. Four hats and two scarves cost a total of $67. What is the price of one hat?

Difficulty: Hard

39. $f(x) = x^2 - x^4 + 2a$

For the function f defined above, a is a constant and $f(4) = 0$. What is the value of $f(-1)$?

Difficulty: Hard

40. Kevin drove the car for 4 hours at a speed of 80 miles per hour and then for 5 hours at the speed of 75 miles per hour. What was his average speed during the whole ride?

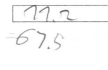
Difficulty: Hard

Answer Explanation

1. Rewrite the expression and combine like terms:
$$4a - 3b - 16a + b = 4a - 16a - 3b + b = -12a - 2b$$
The correct answer is D.

2. First, divide both sides by 4:
$$\frac{4(x-3)}{4} = \frac{12}{4}$$
$$x - 3 = 3$$
Then add 3 to each side.
Therefore, we have:
$$x - 3 + 3 = 3 + 3$$
$$x = 6$$
The correct answer is F.

3. Plug in $a = 8$, $b = 5$:
Therefore, we have:
$$8 \, D \, 5 = 3(8 - 15) = -21$$
The correct answer is D.

4. Write down the average formula and enter the known numbers. Therefore, we have:
$$Average = \frac{Sum\ of\ Numbers}{Number\ of\ Numbers}$$
$$6 = \frac{6+8+x}{3}$$
The correct answer is F.

5. Substitute $x = -2$ into the equation of the function and calculate the result:
$$f(x) = \frac{8 \times 1 - 2}{2 \times 1} = 3$$
The correct answer is A.

6. Let x = the number of giraffes and y = the number of zebras. Then:
$$x + y = 40$$
$$x = 3y + 4$$
Substitute the second equation into the first one and solve for y.
$$3y + 4 + y = 40$$
$$4y = 36$$
$$y = 9$$
There are 9 zebras in the zoo.
Find the number of giraffes:
$$x = 3 \times 9 + 4 = 27 + 4 = 31$$
There are 31 giraffes in the zoo.
The correct answer is H.

7. Rewrite the expressions and cancel like factors. Note that $a^2 = a \cdot a$.
Therefore, we have:
$$\frac{(4a-b)^2}{6a} \cdot \frac{3}{4a-b} = \frac{(4a-b)(4a-b)}{6a} \cdot \frac{3}{4a-b} = \frac{3(4a-b)}{6a}$$
$$\frac{4a-b}{2a}$$
The correct answer is C.

Video Explanations
at argoprep.com/shsat

8. First, find the value of ($\ll$ 3). This number is odd so we have:

$$(\ll 3) = 2 \times 3 - 5 = 1$$

Then find the value of ($\ll$ 1). This number is odd so we have:

$$(\ll 1) = 2 \times 1 - 5 = -3$$

Therefore, we have:

$$((\ll 3) - (\ll 1)) = 1 - (-3) = 4$$

The correct answer is G.

---

9. Substitute the values of a and b into the original expression:

$$\frac{a-b}{a+b} \cdot \frac{2a+2b}{a} = \frac{1-3}{1+3} \cdot \frac{2 \times 1 + 2 \times 3}{1} = \frac{-2}{4} \cdot \frac{8}{1} = -4$$

The correct answer is A.

---

10. Rewrite the expression and combine like terms:

$$ab + 2b + 8a - b - 4ab = ab - 4ab - b + 2b + 8a$$
$$= -3ab + b + 8a$$

Then substitute the values of a and b into the expression.

$$-3ab + b + 8a = (-3) \times (-2) \times 1 - 2 + 8 \times 1 = 6 - 2 + 8$$
$$= 12$$

The correct answer is H.

---

11. First, use the distributive property to get rid of the parentheses:

$$2(a - 1) + 3(2a + 1) = 2a - 2 + 6a + 3$$

Rewrite the expression and combine like terms:

$$2a - 2 + 6a + 3 = 2a + 6a - 2 + 3 = 8a + 1$$

The correct answer is B.

---

12. First, find the equation of $f(g(x))$:

$$f(g(x)) = (3x)^3 - 2(3x) = 27x^3 - 6x$$

Substitute $x = 1$ into the equation of $f(g(x))$:

$$f(g(1)) = 27(1^3) - 6 = 21$$

The correct answer is E.

---

13. First, cross multiply to get rid of any fractions:

$$3(x - 5) = 4x$$
$$3x - 15 = 4x$$

Rewrite the equation and solve for x:

$$4x - 3x = -15$$
$$x = -15$$

The correct answer is D.

---

14. Multiply each term by 3 to eliminate the fraction, and isolate x:

$$-1(3) < x < 8(3)$$
$$-3 < x < 24$$

Therefore, x must be between -3 and 24.

The correct answer is F.

---

15. Let x = the number of new customers and y = Colton's earnings. Since Colton earns $15 for each new customer, his earnings for the number of new clients is $15x$. The base earning is $340 so the function that models the total earnings is $y = 15x + 340$.

The correct answer is C.

---

16. Let x represent the number of chocolates that Erik bought. The number of chocolates that Mark bought is $x + 2$.

Write an equation and solve it for x:

$$x + x + 2 = 10$$
$$2x = 8$$
$$x = 4$$

Since Mark bought $x + 2$ chocolates, $(4) + 2 = 6$ chocolates. Mark bought 6 chocolates.

The correct answer is G.

---

17. To find the average score, add the number of paintings that each of the people drew and then divide by the number of people. Therefore, we have:

$$\frac{2 + 4 + 2 + 4 + 3}{5} = 3$$

The correct answer is C.

---

18. First, find the value of ⊓ 2:

$$⊓\, 2 = \frac{2-4}{2 \times 2} = \frac{-2}{4} = -\frac{1}{2}$$

Then find the value of ⊓ 1:

$$⊓\, 1 = \frac{1-4}{2 \times 1} = -\frac{3}{2}$$

Therefore, we have:

$$⊓\, 2 - ⊓\, 1 = -\frac{1}{2} - \frac{3}{2} = -2$$

The correct answer is F.

Video Explanations
at argoprep.com/shsat

19. Let x be the price of 1 movie ticket and y be the price of 1 performance ticket.

Then we have:
$$3x + 4y = \$23.50$$
$$y = 2x - 3$$

Substitute the second equation into the first equation and solve for x:
$$3x + 4(2x - 3) = 23.50$$
$$3x + 8x - 12 = 23.50$$
$$11x = 35.5$$
$$x = 3.23$$

Therefore, the price of 1 movie ticket is $3.23.

The correct answer is D.

---

20. Rewrite with like terms together and combine like terms:
$$2x^3 + 3xy - x^2 + 2x^3 - 4xy + 2x^2$$
$$= 2x^3 + 2x^3 - x^2 + 2x^2 + 3xy - 4xy$$
$$= 4x^3 + x^2 - xy$$

The correct answer is E.

---

21. Multiply the first equation by 2 and subtract the two equations to get rid of the variable x.
$$2x - 4y = 20$$
$$2x + 3y = 5$$

After subtracting the two equations, we get the following:
$$-7y = 15$$
$$y = -\frac{15}{7}$$

Substitute the value of y into the first original equation and solve for x.
$$x - 2\left(-\frac{15}{7}\right) = 10$$
$$x + \frac{30}{7} = 10$$

Subtract $\frac{30}{7}$ on both sides.
$$x = 10 - \frac{30}{7}$$
$$x = \frac{40}{7}$$

The correct answer is B.

---

22. First, get rid of the parentheses:
$$x - 2 > 4x - 32$$

Rewrite the inequality and combine like terms:
$$4x - x < 32 - 2$$

$$3x < 30$$
$$x < 10$$
The correct answer is E.

---

23. Let x be the first number and y be the second number.

Then we have:
$$x + 2y = 4$$
$$2x - y = 12$$

Multiply the first equation by 2:
$$2x + 4y = 8$$

Subtract the second equation from the first equation that is multiplied by 2:
$$5y = -4$$
$$y = -\frac{4}{5}$$

Find the first number by substituting the value of y into the first equation and solving it for x:
$$x + 2\times\left(-\frac{4}{5}\right) = 4$$

Multiply each term by 5:
$$5x - 8 = 20$$
$$x = \frac{28}{5} = 5\frac{3}{5}$$

Therefore, the numbers are $5\frac{3}{5}$ and $-\frac{4}{5}$.
The correct answer is C.

---

24. First, multiply the first two fractions and cancel out like factors. Therefore, we have:
$$\frac{(a+12)}{(a-9)(2a+3)}\times\frac{2a+3}{(a-6)(a-4)} = \frac{a+12}{(a-9)(a-6)(a-4)}$$

Then rewrite the division operation as a multiplication operation:
$$\frac{a+12}{(a-9)(a-6)(a-4)} \div \frac{a+12}{(a-9)(a-4)}$$
$$= \frac{a+12}{(a-9)(a-6)(a-4)}\times\frac{(a-9)(a-4)}{a+12} = \frac{1}{a-6}$$

The correct answer is G.

---

25. Substitute $x = 2$ and $y = 1$ into the equation of the function and evaluate its value.
$$f(2,1) = \frac{2^3 - 4}{1 - 2} = \frac{4}{-1} = -4$$

The correct answer is D.

Video Explanations
at argoprep.com/shsat

139

26. Let x represent the number of cola drinks.
Use the proportion:
$$\frac{1}{2} = \frac{12}{x}$$
Cross multiply to get rid of fractions:
$$x = 2 \times 12 = 24$$
The correct answer is H.

27. Let n = the price of 2 cups of coffee.
Set up a proportion:
$$\frac{1}{3} = \frac{2}{n}$$
Then cross multiply and solve for n:
$$n = \$6$$
The correct answer is B.

28. First, cancel out like factors.
Therefore, we have:
$$\frac{(a+7)(2a-3)}{5a} \cdot \frac{3a}{(a-1)(2a-3)} = \frac{a+7}{5} \cdot \frac{3}{a-1}$$
Then multiply:
$$\frac{a+7}{5} \cdot \frac{3}{a-1} = \frac{3(a+7)}{5(a-1)} = \frac{3a+21}{5a-5}$$
The correct answer is E.

29. First, find the value of $(\triangleleft 7)$:
$$(\triangleleft 7) = 7 - 5 = 2$$
Then find the value of $(\triangleleft 2)$:
$$(\triangleleft 2) = 2 - 5 = -3$$
Finally, find the value of $(\triangleleft(-3))$:
$$(\triangleleft(-3)) = -3 - 5 = -8$$
The correct answer is B.

30. Let x represent the number of paper clips that she bought.
Write an inequality:
$$18 + 0.75x \leq 23$$
$$0.75x \leq 5$$
$$x \leq 6.67$$
Anna can buy a maximum of 6 paper clips.
The correct answer is F.

31. Let x = the number of cherries on a cake.
Set up a proportion:
$$\frac{3}{15} = \frac{5}{x}$$
Then cross multiply and solve for x:
$$3x = 75$$
$$x = 25$$
The correct answer is D.

32. Set up the expression: tomatoes – cost
$$3 - \$6$$
$$1 - x$$
If 3 tomatoes cost $6, then 1 tomato costs $\frac{6}{3} = \$2$.
7 tomatoes cost $7 \times 2 = \$14$.
The correct answer is E.

33. Find the cost of the food.
$$\$6.40 + \$4.10 + \$0.70 + \$0.70 = \$11.90$$
Find the total cost, including tax.
$$\$11.90 + \$0.95 = \$12.85$$
Find how much money they should receive back?
$$\$15.00 - \$12.85 = \mathbf{\$2.15}$$

34. Find the total number of books.
$$2 + 1 + 4 = 7$$
Find the total cost of the books.
$$\$5.90 \times 7 = \mathbf{\$41.3}$$

35. Let h represent the number of hours he should work to be able to buy the new suit.
Write an inequality:
$$12h \geq 150$$
$$h \geq 12.5$$
Carter should work at least **13 hours** to buy the new suit.

36. Find the number of chocolate sweets.
$$2 \times 8 = 16$$
Find the number of the mint sweets.
$$3 \times 12 = 36$$
Find the difference.
$$36 - 16 = 20$$
Mila bought **20 more mint sweets than chocolate sweets.**

Video Explanations at argoprep.com/shsat

37. First, use the distributive property to get rid of the parentheses:
$$3(x + 2) - y(x - 6) + 4xy - 2(2y + xy)$$
$$= 3x + 6 - yx + 6y + 4xy - 4y - 2xy$$
Then, rewrite the expression and combine like terms:
$$3x + 6 - yx + 6y + 4xy - 4y - 2xy$$
$$= 3x + 6y - 4y - yx + 4xy - 2xy + 6$$
$$= \mathbf{3x + 2y + xy + 6}$$

38. Let x = cost of one hat.

Let y = cost of one scarf.

Therefore, we can write two equations:
$$3x + 4y = 56.5$$
$$4x + 2y = 67$$
Rewrite the first equation for x and substitute the result into the second equation. Then solve for y.
$$x = \frac{56.5 - 4y}{3}$$
$$4\left(\frac{56.5 - 4y}{3}\right) + 2y = 67$$
Use the distributive property:
$$\frac{226 - 16y}{3} + 2y = 67$$
Multiply each term by 3 to get rid of the denominator:
$$226 - 16y + 6y = 201$$
$$-10y = -25$$
$$y = 2.5$$
Substitute the result into the equation for y and find x:
$$x = \frac{56.5 - 4 \cdot 2.5}{3} = 15.5$$
Therefore, the price of one hat is **$15.50**.

39. First we need to find the value of a:
$$4^2 - 4^4 + 2a = 0$$
$$2a = 256 - 16 = 240$$
$$a = 120$$
Now we can find the value of $f(-1)$:
$$f(-1) = (-1)^2 - (-1)^4 + 2 \times 120 = \mathbf{240}$$

40. The average speed is the ratio of the total distance to the total time.

Total distance = $80 \times 4 + 75 \times 5 = 695$ miles.

We have:
$$\frac{695}{4 + 5} = 77.2$$
The average speed was **77.2 miles per hour**.

Video Explanations
at argoprep.com/shsat

Geometry

ARGOPREP
ARGOPREP.COM/SHSAT

1. In a right triangle, one of the angles is 30°. Find the measure of the other two angles.

A. 90°, 30°   C. 90°, 60°

B. 90°, 40°   D. 60°, 30°

Difficulty: Easy

2. Find the measure of y.

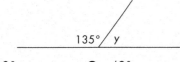

E. 60°   G. 40°

F. 45°   H. 30°

Difficulty: Easy

3. *ABCD* is a parallelogram. If the measure of angle *A* is 52°, what is the measure of angle *B*?

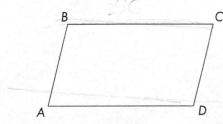

A. 160°   C. 70°

B. 128°   D. 48°

Difficulty: Medium

4. What is the measure of x, y and z respectively?

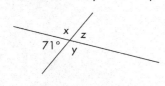

E. 109°, 109°, 71°

F. 98°, 50°, 90°

G. 109°, 60°, 50°

H. 60°, 60°, 80°

Difficulty: Medium

5. Find the measure of angle x.

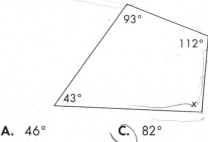

A. 46°   C. 82°

B. 68°   D. 112°

Difficulty: Easy

6. Find the measure of x.

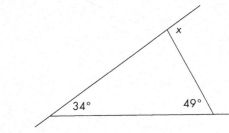

E. 125°   G. 83°

F. 109°   H. 54°

Difficulty: Medium

7. Find the measure of x, if ∠A = 38° and ∠B = 67°.

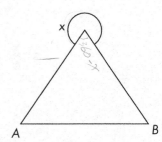

A. 285°   C. 164°

B. 198°   D. 125°

Difficulty: Medium

Video Explanations
at argoprep.com/shsat

6   90

8. What is the value of x?

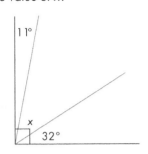

11°

x

32°

E. 100°   G. 51°
F. 87°   H. 47°

Difficulty: Easy

9. ABCD is a parallelogram. If $\angle A = (3x - 14)°$ and $\angle C = (2x - 5)°$, find the measure of angle C.

$x = 9$

A. 22°   C. 13°
B. 18°   D. 9°

Difficulty: Hard

$5x + 12 = 180$
$5x = 168$

10. Find the value of x.

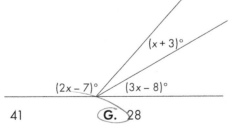

$(x + 3)°$

$(2x - 7)°$ $(3x - 8)°$

E. 41   G. 28
F. 32   H. 25

Difficulty: Medium

11. In a regular hexagon, the measure of one angle is x. Find the sum of the three angles of this hexagon.

A. 415°   B. 360°   C. 324°   D. 280°

Difficulty: Hard

12. Find the measures of angles x, y, and z.

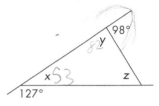

98°
y 82
x 53
z
127°

E. 53°, 45°, 91°   G. 86°, 34°, 29°
F. 92°, 45°, 67°   H. 53°, 82°, 45°

Difficulty: Hard

13. ABCD is a parallelogram. Find $\angle ABD$, if $\angle C = 54°$ and $\angle BDC = 24°$.

25
$6) 168$
-12
48

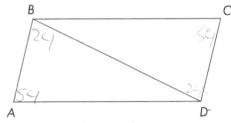

A. 56°   B. 42°   C. 24°   D. 18°

Difficulty: Hard

14. What is the value of x and y respectively?

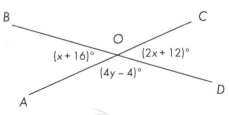

$(x + 16)°$ $(2x + 12)°$
$(4y - 4)°$

E. 15.5, 18   G. 4, 41
F. 12, 4   H. 2, 32.5

Difficulty: Hard

15. What is the value of y?

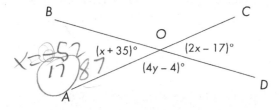

A. 24.25   **C.** 52
B. 33   **D.** 68

Difficulty: Hard

16. Determine the values of x and y.

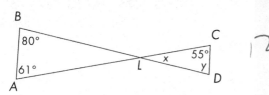

E. 39°, 86°   **G.** 72°, 31°
F. 34°, 58°   **H.** 43°, 56°

Difficulty: Medium

17. What is the value of x?

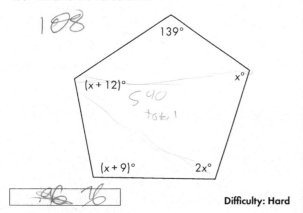

Difficulty: Hard

18. What is the measure of angle y?

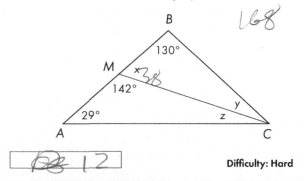

Difficulty: Hard

19. What is y?

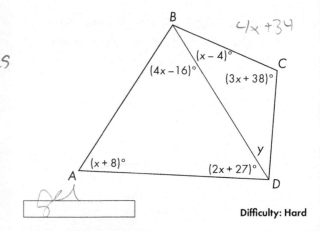

Difficulty: Hard

20. What is the measure of angle y?

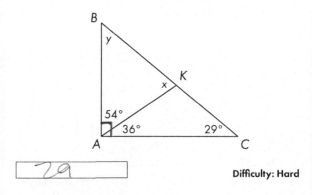

Difficulty: Hard

Video Explanations
at argoprep.com/shsat

1. In a right triangle, one of the angles must be 90°. The sum of all angles of a triangle is 180°.

   Let x represent the missing angle.

   Write the equation to find the last missing angle.
   $$90 + 30 + x = 180$$
   $$x = 180 - 90 - 30 = 60°$$

   The correct answer is C.

2. The angle measure 135° and angle y are supplementary (they both add up to 180 degrees since they are on a straight line).

   Write an equation:
   $$135 + y = 180$$

   Solve for y:
   $$y = 180 - 135 = 45°$$

   The correct answer is F.

3. You must remember that opposite angles on a parallelogram are congruent and that consecutive angles are supplementary.

   Therefore, we have:

   $52° + B = 180°$

   $B = 180° - 52° = 128°$

   The correct answer is B.

4. The measure of angle z is equal to the angle of measure 71°, since both angles are vertical.

   Angle z and angle x are supplementary. Therefore, we have:
   $$71° + x = 180°$$
   $$x = 180° - 71° = 109°$$

   The measure of angle y is equal to the measure of angle x, since both x and y are vertical angles. The measure of angle y is 109°.

   The correct answer is E.

5. The sum of the angles of a quadrilateral is 360°.

   Therefore, we have:
   $$43 + 93 + 112 + x = 360$$

   Solve for x:
   $$x = 360 - 112 - 93 - 43$$
   $$x = 112$$

   The correct answer is D.

6. First, find the measure of the third angle in the triangle given.
   The sum of the angles of a triangle is 180°.
   Let y be the measure of the third angle.

   Therefore, we have:
   $$34° + 49° + y = 180°$$
   $$y = 180° - 49° - 34 = 97°$$
   Angles y and x are supplementary.
   $$97° + x = 180°$$
   $$x = 180° - 97° = 83°$$

   The correct answer is G.

7. First, find the measure of the third angle in the triangle given.
   The sum of the angles of a triangle is 180°.
   Let y = the measure of the third angle.
   Therefore, we have:
   $$38° + 67° + y = 180°$$
   $$y = 180° - 67° - 38° = 75°$$
   Therefore, we have:
   $$x + 75° = 360°$$
   $$x = 360° - 75° = 285°$$

   The correct answer is A.

8. There is a right angle shown on the picture given. The sum of all three angles must be equal to 90°.

   Therefore, we have:
   $$11° + x + 32° = 90°$$
   $$x = 90° - 32° - 11° = 47°$$

   The correct answer is H.

9. You must remember that opposite angles on a parallelogram are congruent.
   Therefore, we have:
   $$3x - 14 = 2x - 5$$
   Solve for x:
   $$3x - 2x = 14 - 5$$
   $$x = 9$$
   We can find the measure of angle C.
   $$\angle C = 2x - 5 = 2 \times 9 - 5 = 13°$$

   The correct answer is C.

10. These angles are supplementary and they add up to 180°. We have:
    $$(2x - 7) + (x + 3) + (3x - 8) = 180$$
    $$6x = 192$$
    $$x = 32°$$

    The correct answer is F.

11. In a regular hexagon all angles are equal and the sum of the angles is 720°. Write an equation:
$$6x = 720°$$
Divide both sides of the equation by 6:
$$x = 120°$$
The sum of the three angles is $3 \times 120 = 360°$.
The correct answer is B.

12. Angle x and an angle that measures 127° are supplementary. Therefore, we have:
$$x = 180° - 127° = 53°$$
Angle y and an angle that measures 98° are supplementary. Therefore, we have:
$$y = 180° - 98° = 82°$$
The sum of all angles of a triangle is equal to 180°. We have:
$$z = 180° - 53° - 82° = 45°$$
The correct answer is H.

13. Let $\angle ABD = x$.
The sum of all angles of a triangle is equal to 180°. Therefore, we have:
$$x = 180 - \angle A - \angle ADB$$
You must remember that opposite angles on a parallelogram are congruent and that consecutive angles are supplementary. So, $\angle A = \angle C = 54°$.
$$\angle ADB = 180 - 54 - 24 = 102.$$
Therefore, we have:
$$x = 180 - 54 - 102 = 24°$$
The correct answer is C.

14. Angles AOB and DOC are vertical. Therefore, they are equal. We can use the following equation:
$$x + 16 = 2x + 12$$
$$-x = -4$$
$$x = 4$$
We know that AOD and angle COD are supplementary. We can use the following equation:
$$4y - 4 + 2x + 12 = 180$$
$$4y - 4 + 2(4) + 12 = 180$$
$$4y - 4 + 8 + 12 = 180$$
$$4y + 16 = 180$$
$$4y = 164$$
$$y = 41$$
The correct answer is G.

15. Angles AOB and DOC are vertical. Therefore, they are equal. We can use the following equation:
$$x + 35 = 2x - 17, \quad 52 = x$$
We know that AOD and angle COD are supplementary. Set up the following equation:
$$4y - 4 + 2x - 17 = 180, \quad 4y - 4 + 2(52) - 17 = 180$$
$$4y - 4 + 104 - 17 = 180, \quad 4y + 83 = 180, \quad 4y = 97$$
$$y = 24.25$$
The correct answer is E.

16. First, find the measure of angle ALB. Note that the sum of all angles of a triangle is 180°. Therefore we have:
$$\angle ALB = 180° - 80° - 61° = 39°$$
Angle $x = \angle ALB = 39°$ because they are vertical. So we can find y:
$$y = 180° - 55° - 39° = 86°$$
The correct answer is E.

17. In a pentagon, the sum of the angles is 540°. Therefore, we have:
$$x + 12 + x + 9 + 2x + x + 139 = 540°, \quad 5x = 380°$$
$$x = \mathbf{76°}$$

18. Angle x and an angle that measures 142° are supplementary. Therefore, we have:
$$x = 180° - 142° = 38°$$
We can now solve for y since we know the other 2 angles.
$$y = 180° - 130° - 38° = \mathbf{12°}$$

19. The sum of all angles of a triangle is equal to 180°. Use this information to find x:
$$x + 8 + 4x - 16 + 2x + 27 = 180°, \quad 7x = 161$$
$$x = 23$$
From $\triangle BCD$, we have: $(x - 4) + (3x + 38) + y = 180°$
Plug in the value of 23 where you see x.
$$(23 - 4) + (3(23) + 38) + y = 180, \quad 19 + 107 + y = 180$$
$$126 + y = 180$$
$$y = \mathbf{54}$$

20. First, find the measure of $\angle AKC$. Note that the sum of all angles of a triangle is equal to 180°. Therefore, we have:
$$\angle AKC = 180° - 36° - 29° = 115°$$
$\angle AKC$ and angle x are supplementary. Therefore, we have:
$$x = 180° - 115° = 65°$$
Finally, find y:
$$y = 180° - 54° - 65° = \mathbf{61°}$$

Video Explanations
at argoprep.com/shsat

1. Find the coordinates of the midpoint of the line segment $\overline{AB}$ if point A has the coordinates $(-2, 4)$ and point B has the coordinates $(2, 0)$.

   A. $(0, -2)$ **C.** $(-2, 0)$
   B. $(-2, 0)$ **D.** $(0, 2)$

   Difficulty: Medium

2. On the coordinate graph, point B is between the points A and C. The ratio of AB to BC is 2:3. If A is at $(-3, 2)$ and B is at $(3, -2)$, what are the coordinates of point C?

   E. $(-12, -8)$ **G.** $(12, -8)$
   F. $(3, -9)$ **H.** $(3, 6)$

   Difficulty: Hard⁺

3. What is the distance between the points $(3, -4)$ and $(3, -1)$?

   A. 3   **C.** 11
   B. 7   **D.** 15

   Difficulty: Medium

4. What is the midpoint of a line segment that begins at $(1, -8)$ and ends at $(5, -6)$?

   E. $(3, -7)$ **G.** $(-3, 2)$
   F. $(-8, 7)$ **H.** $(0, 1)$

   Difficulty: Medium

5. If $\overline{AB} = 24$, and $\overline{BC} = \frac{3}{8}\overline{AB}$, what is the length of $\overline{BC}$?

   A. 22   **C.** 12
   B. 16   **D.** 9

   Difficulty: Medium

6. What is the midpoint of a line segment that begins at $(-6, 12)$ and ends at $(-4, 0)$?

   E. $(1, -4)$ **G.** $(7, -3)$
   F. $(-5, 6)$ **H.** $(2, 1)$

   Difficulty: Medium

7. In rectangle $ABCD$, point B has coordinates $(7, -1)$ and point C has coordinates $(9, -3)$. What is the length of $\overline{BC}$?

   A. 8   **C.** $2\sqrt{2}$
   B. 2   **D.** $\sqrt{6}$

   Difficulty: Hard⁺

8. On the number line XZ, the position of point X is $7\frac{3}{8}$. If $XZ = \frac{5}{16}$, what is the position of point Z, if it is located to the left of point X?

   E. 9   **G.** $-\frac{1}{16}$
   F. $7\frac{1}{16}$ **H.** $-2\frac{1}{8}$

   Difficulty: Medium

9. On the number line $MN = 3\frac{8}{9}$. Point K is located between point N and M. The position of point N is 2. Which value below is a possible position for point K?

   A. 7   **B.** 5.98   **C.** 3.8   **D.** 1.6

   Difficulty: Medium

10. Find the center of the circle with a diameter having endpoints at $(-3, 2)$ and $(1, 6)$.

    E. $(-1, 4)$ **G.** $(7, 4)$
    F. $(2, -3)$ **H.** $(9, 2)$

    Difficulty: Medium

Video Explanations
at argoprep.com/shsat

11. On the number line AB, the position of point B is $4\frac{5}{9}$. If $AB = 18$, what is the position of point A?

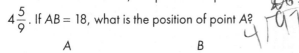

A. $3\frac{1}{9}$ B. $1\frac{7}{9}$ C. $-7\frac{2}{9}$ D. $-13\frac{4}{9}$

Difficulty: Medium

12. Point L $(0, 2)$ is the midpoint of the line AB. A has the coordinates $(-6, 4)$. Find the coordinates of B.

E. $(1, -1)$ G. $(6, 0)$
F. $(2, -1)$ H. $(0, 3)$

Difficulty: Medium

13. Find y so that the distance between the points $(-5, -9)$ and $(1, y)$ is equal to 8.

A. $y = 2$ or $y = -4$
B. $y = -9 + 2\sqrt{7}$ or $y = -9 - 2\sqrt{7}$
C. $y = 3$ or $y = -9$
D. $y = 8$

Difficulty: Hard⁺

14. Find x and y if $(6, -3)$ is the midpoint of points (x, y) and $(1, 3)$.

E. $(7, -2)$ G. $(5, -4)$
F. $(1, 3)$ H. $(11, -9)$

Difficulty: Medium

15. Find the distance between point $(8, 1)$ and the midpoint of the line segment with the endpoints $(-4, 1)$ and $(-8, 7)$.

A. 15
B. $\sqrt{205}$
C. $2\sqrt{13}$
D. 8

Difficulty: Hard

16. On the number line, point M is between the points L and N. The ratio of LM to MN is 4:7. If L is at $(-1, 5)$ and M is at $(3, -4)$, what are the coordinates of point N?

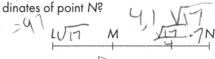

E. $(-1, 5)$ G. $(1, -1)$
F. $(4, -7)$ H. $(10, -19.75)$

Difficulty: Hard

17. Find the value of k if $(-1, 2)$ is the midpoint of $(k, 8)$ and $(-2, -4)$.

Difficulty: Medium

18. Point W has coordinates $(-1, 7)$ and point V has coordinates $(5, -1)$. What are the coordinates of point K that divides WV in the ratio 1:3?

Difficulty: Hard⁺

19. Is $y = 3x + 1$ a bisector of the line segment with endpoints at $(-2, 4)$ and $(4, 6)$?

Difficulty: Hard⁺

20. Points A, B, C, D are on a straight line. $\overline{AB} = 3\frac{3}{4}$, $\overline{AD} = 6\frac{1}{4}$ and $\overline{CD} = 1\frac{1}{8}$. The position of B is $2\frac{2}{3}$.

What is the position of point C?

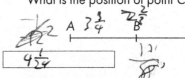

Difficulty: Hard

 Video Explanations
at argoprep.com/shsat

1. Use the following formula to find the midpoint:

    Midpoint $= \left(\dfrac{x_1 + x_2}{2}, \dfrac{y_1 + y_2}{2}\right)$. Therefore, we have:

    $$\left(\dfrac{-2+2}{2}, \dfrac{4+0}{2}\right) = \left(\dfrac{0}{2}, \dfrac{4}{2}\right) = (0, 2)$$

    The coordinates of the midpoint of the line segment $\overline{AB}$ is (0, 2).

    The correct answer is D.

2. First, find the shift in x-coordinates for points A and B.

    $$3 - (-3) = 3 + 3 = 6$$

    Now you can find the x-coordinate for the point C. Set up the proportion to find the shift in x from point A to point C:

    $$\dfrac{6}{x} = \dfrac{2}{3}$$

    Find x:

    $$x = \dfrac{6 \times 3}{2} = 9$$

    Therefore, the x-coordinate of point C is $3 + 9 = 12$. Now find the shift in y-coordinates for points A and B:

    $$-2 - 2 = -4$$

    Set up the proportion to find the shift in y-coordinate from point A to point C:

    $$\dfrac{-4}{y} = \dfrac{2}{3}$$

    Find y:

    $$y = \dfrac{3(-4)}{2} = \dfrac{-12}{2} = -6$$

    Therefore, the y-coordinate for point C is $-2 + (-6) = -8$. The coordinates of point C are $(12, -8)$.

    The correct answer is G.

3. Use the distance formula:

    $$D = \sqrt{(x_2 - x_1)^2 + (y_2 - y_1)^2}$$

    Fill in the values:

    $$D = \sqrt{(3-3)^2 + (-1-(-4))^2} = \sqrt{0+9} = 3$$

    The correct answer is A.

4. Use the following formula to find the midpoint:

    $$M = \left(\dfrac{x_1 + x_2}{2}, \dfrac{y_1 + y_2}{2}\right)$$

    Therefore, we have:

    $$M = \left(\dfrac{1+5}{2}, \dfrac{-6-8}{2}\right) = \left(\dfrac{6}{2}, \dfrac{-14}{2}\right) = (3, -7)$$

    The coordinates of the midpoint of the line segment are $(3, -7)$.

The correct answer is E.

5. Substitute the value of $\overline{AB}$ into the equation for $\overline{BC}$ and calculate the length of $\overline{BC}$:

    $$\overline{BC} = \dfrac{3}{8}\overline{AB} = \dfrac{3}{8} \times 24 = 9$$

    The correct answer is D.

6. Use the following formula to find the midpoint:

    $$M = \left(\dfrac{x_1 + x_2}{2}, \dfrac{y_1 + y_2}{2}\right)$$

    Therefore, we have:

    $$M = \left(\dfrac{-6-4}{2}, \dfrac{12+0}{2}\right) = \left(\dfrac{-10}{2}, \dfrac{12}{2}\right) = (-5, 6)$$

    The coordinates of the midpoint of the line segment are $(-5, 6)$.

    The correct answer is F.

7. Use the distance formula:

    $$D = \sqrt{(x_2 - x_1)^2 + (y_2 - y_1)^2}$$

    Therefore, we have:

    $$BC = \sqrt{(9-7)^2 + (-3-(-1))^2} = \sqrt{4+4} = 2\sqrt{2}$$

    The correct answer is C.

8. Use the following equation to find the position of point Z:

    $$Z = 7\dfrac{3}{8} - \dfrac{5}{16}$$

    $$Z = \left(\dfrac{2}{2}\right)\dfrac{59}{8} - \dfrac{5}{16}$$

    $$Z = \dfrac{118}{16} - \dfrac{5}{16}$$

    $$Z = \dfrac{113}{16}$$

    Convert to mixed number:

    $$= 7\dfrac{1}{16}$$

    The correct answer is F.

9. Since $MN = 3\dfrac{8}{9}$, point M is located at $2 + 3\dfrac{8}{9} = \dfrac{18}{9} + \dfrac{35}{9}$

    $\dfrac{53}{9} = 5\dfrac{8}{9}$. K must be between point 2 and $5\dfrac{8}{9}$. Point M can be written as 5.89.

    The only option given that lies between those two points is 3.8.

    The correct answer is C.

Video Explanations
at argoprep.com/shsat

10. The center of the circle is at the midpoint of a diameter. Use the following formula to find the midpoint:

$$\text{Midpoint} = \left(\frac{x_1 + x_2}{2}, \frac{y_1 + y_2}{2}\right)$$

Therefore, we have:

$$\left(\frac{-3+1}{2}, \frac{2+6}{2}\right) = \left(\frac{-2}{2}, \frac{8}{2}\right) = (-1, 4)$$

The center of the circle is (– 1, 4).

The correct answer is E.

---

11. To find A, subtract B – A and set it equal to the length:

$$4\frac{5}{9} - A = 18$$

$$A = 4\frac{5}{9} - 18$$

$$A = \frac{41 - 18(9)}{9} = -\frac{121}{9} = -13\frac{4}{9}$$

The correct answer is D.

---

12. Let the coordinates of B be (x_2, y_2).
You can use the midpoint formula to find the coordinates of B.

$$\text{Midpoint} = \left(\frac{x_1 + x_2}{2}, \frac{y_1 + y_2}{2}\right)$$

First, find the x-coordinate of point B:

$$0 = \frac{-6 + x_2}{2}$$

$$x_2 - 6 = 0$$

$$x_2 = 6$$

Then, find the y-coordinate of point B:

$$2 = \frac{4 + y_2}{2}$$

$$y_2 + 4 = 4$$

$$y_2 = 0$$

Point B has the coordinates (6, 0).

The correct answer is G.

---

13. Use the distance formula:

$$D = \sqrt{(x_2 - x_1)^2 + (y_2 - y_1)^2}$$

Fill in the values:

$$D = \sqrt{(1 - (-5))^2 + (y - (-9))^2} = \sqrt{36 + (y+9)^2} = 8$$

Square both sides:

$$36 + (y+9)^2 = 64$$
$$(y+9)^2 = 28$$

Then take the square root of both sides to find x:

$$y + 9 = \sqrt{28} = 2\sqrt{7}$$

Or

$$y + 9 = -2\sqrt{7}$$

We have:

$$y = -9 + 2\sqrt{7}$$

Or

$$y = -9 - 2\sqrt{7}$$

This is a challenging question, so we encourage you to watch our video explanation on your computer where we break this down in detail.

The correct answer is B.

---

14. We can use the midpoint formula to solve this problem. Simply plug in your known numbers.

$$\text{Midpoint} = \left(\frac{x_1 + x_2}{2}, \frac{y_1 + y_2}{2}\right)$$

Therefore, we have:

$$(6, -3) = \left(\frac{x+1}{2}, \frac{y+3}{2}\right)$$

Equate the x-coordinates to find x:

$$6 = \frac{x+1}{2}$$

$$x + 1 = 12$$

$$x = 11$$

Then equate the y-coordinates to find y:

$$-3 = \frac{y+3}{2}$$

$$y + 3 = -6$$

$$y = -6 - 3 = -9$$

The correct answer is H.

---

15. First find the coordinates of the midpoint of the line segment: (– 4, 1) and (– 8, 7).
Use the following formula to find the midpoint:

$$\text{Midpoint} = \left(\frac{x_1 + x_2}{2}, \frac{y_1 + y_2}{2}\right)$$

Therefore, we have:

$$M = \left(\frac{-4 - 8}{2}, \frac{1+7}{2}\right) = (-6, 4)$$

Then use the distance formula:

$$D = \sqrt{(x_2 - x_1)^2 + (y_2 - y_1)^2}$$

Fill in the values:

$$D = \sqrt{(-6 - 8)^2 + (4 - 1)^2} = \sqrt{196 + 9} = \sqrt{205}$$

The correct answer is B.

▶ **Video Explanations**
at argoprep.com/shsat

16. First, find the shift in x-coordinates for points L and M.

$$3 - (-1) = 3 + 1 = 4$$

Now you can find the x-coordinate for point N. Set up the proportion to find the shift in x from point L to point N:

$$\frac{4}{x} = \frac{4}{7}$$

Find x:

$$x = \frac{4 \times 7}{4} = 7$$

Therefore, the x-coordinate of point N is $3 + 7 = 10$.

Now find the shift in y-coordinates for points L and M:

$$-4 - 5 = -9$$

Set up the proportion to find the shift in y-coordinate from the point L to point N:

$$\frac{-9}{y} = \frac{4}{7}$$

Find y:

$$y = \frac{(-9) \times 7}{4} = -15.75$$

Therefore, the y-coordinate of point N is $-4 - 15.75 = -19.75$.

The coordinates of point C are $(10, -19.75)$.

The correct answer is H.

---

17. Use the midpoint formula and plug in your known information.

$$\text{Midpoint} = \left(\frac{x_1 + x_2}{2}, \frac{y_1 + y_2}{2} \right)$$

Therefore, we have:

$$(-1, 2) = \left(\frac{k-2}{2}, \frac{8-4}{2} \right)$$

We have:

$$-1 = \frac{k-2}{2}$$

$$k - 2 = -2$$

$$k = -2 + 2 = \mathbf{0}$$

---

18. First, find the midpoint, M, of WV. Use the following formula to find the midpoint:

$$M = \left(\frac{x_1 + x_2}{2}, \frac{y_1 + y_2}{2} \right)$$

Therefore, we have:

$$\left(\frac{-1+5}{2}, \frac{7-1}{2} \right) = \left(\frac{4}{2}, \frac{6}{2} \right) = (2, 3)$$

Then, find the midpoint K of WM:

$$K = \left(\frac{-1+2}{2}, \frac{7+3}{2} \right) = \left(\frac{1}{2}, \frac{10}{2} \right) = (0.5, 5)$$

The coordinates of the point K are **(0.5, 5)**.

19. Find the midpoint to see if the midpoint is actually a point on the given line.

Use the following formula to find the midpoint:

$$\text{Midpoint} = \left(\frac{x_1 + x_2}{2}, \frac{y_1 + y_2}{2} \right)$$

Therefore, we have:

$$\left(\frac{-2+4}{2}, \frac{4+6}{2} \right) = \left(\frac{2}{2}, \frac{10}{2} \right) = (1, 5)$$

Then check if this point is on the line:

$$y = (3 \times 1) + 1 = 4 \neq 5$$

This is not a bisector.

---

20. First, use $\overline{AB} = 3\frac{3}{4}$ to find the location of A:

$$A = 2\frac{2}{3} - 3\frac{3}{4}$$

$$A = \frac{8}{3} - \frac{15}{4} = \boxed{\frac{-13}{12}}$$

Then use $\overline{AD} = 6\frac{1}{4}$ to find the location of D:

$$D = \frac{-13}{12} + 6\frac{1}{4}$$

$$D = \frac{-13}{12} + \frac{25}{4} = \boxed{\frac{31}{4}}$$

Finally, use $\overline{CD} = 1\frac{1}{8}$ to find the location of C:

$$C = \frac{31}{6} - 1\frac{1}{8}$$

$$C = \frac{31}{6} - \frac{9}{8} = \boxed{\frac{97}{24}}$$

The position of point C is $\frac{\mathbf{97}}{\mathbf{24}}$.

1. Triangle ABC is an isosceles triangle. ∠A = 50°. Find ∠B.

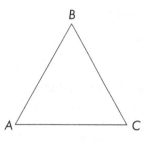

  A. 90°   **C.** 65°
  B. 80°   **D.** 40°

Difficulty: Easy

2. Find the length of the hypotenuse of the right triangle shown below.

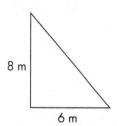

  E. 14 m   **G.** 8 m
  F. 10 m   **H.** 5 m

Difficulty: Easy

3. The perimeter of an equilateral triangle is 360 mm. What is the length of one of the sides of the triangle?

  A. 50 mm   **C.** 100 mm
  B. 78 mm   **D.** 120 mm

Difficulty: Easy

4. The area of a triangle is 56 cm². If the length of the base is 8 cm, what is the height of the triangle?

  E. 14 cm   **G.** 23 cm
  F. 18 cm   **H.** 27 cm

Difficulty: Medium

5. If ABC is an isosceles triangle and its perimeter is 45 cm, what is the length of AC?

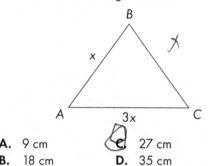

  A. 9 cm   **C.** 27 cm
  B. 18 cm   **D.** 35 cm

Difficulty: Medium

6. Find the length of the hypotenuse of the larger triangle if the triangles shown below are similar.

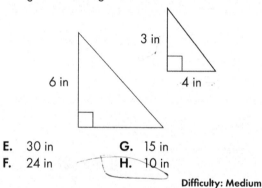

  E. 30 in   **G.** 15 in
  F. 24 in   **H.** 10 in

Difficulty: Medium

7. In triangle ABC, AC = 8 mm and BH is 3 more than AC. Find the area of the triangle.

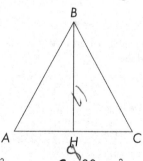

  A. 51 mm²   **C.** 38 mm²
  B. 44 mm²   **D.** 22 mm²

Difficulty: Medium

Video Explanations
at argoprep.com/shsat

154

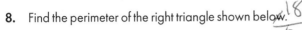
8. Find the perimeter of the right triangle shown below.

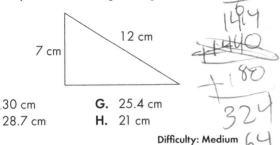

7 cm
12 cm

E. 30 cm
G. 25.4 cm
F. 28.7 cm
H. 21 cm

Difficulty: Medium

9. Find the value of x if the triangle shown below is a right triangle. Round the answer to the nearest tenth.

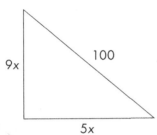

9x
100
5x

A. 2.2   **B.** 9.7   **C.** 14.8   **D.** 24.6

Difficulty: Hard⁺

10. In the triangle ABC shown below, MN is parallel to AC. Find the perimeter of triangle ABC.

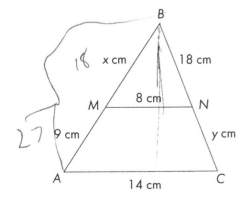

B
x cm   18 cm
M   8 cm   N
9 cm   y cm
A   14 cm   C

E. 72 cm
G. 60 cm
F. 66.5 cm
H. 54 cm

Difficulty: Hard

11. If the area of triangle ABC is 96 m², and the length of AC = 12 m, find the length of AB.

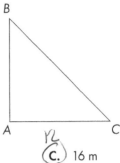

B
A   C

A. 25 m
C. 16 m
B. 20 m
D. 12 m

Difficulty: Hard

12. Find the values of x and y from the triangle shown below.

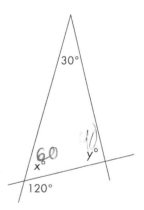

30°
x°   y°
120°

E. 30, 45
G. 85, 20
F. 60, 90
H. 50, 40

Difficulty: Hard

13. In triangle ABC, AB : BC : AC = 2 : 3 : 5. Find the difference of lengths AB and BC, if the perimeter of triangle ABC is 120 cm.

A. 36 cm
C. 24 cm
B. 28 cm
D. 12 cm

Difficulty: Hard

14. Find the measure of angle A from the triangle shown below.

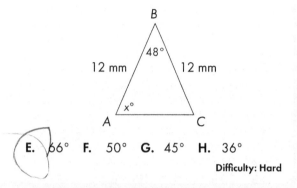

E. 66° **F.** 50° **G.** 45° **H.** 36°

Difficulty: Hard

15. In an isosceles triangle the base is x cm and one of the sides is 5 more than the base. What is the measure of the base if the perimeter of this triangle is equal to 46 cm?

A. 22 cm   **C.** 15 cm
B. 18 cm   **D.** 12 cm

Difficulty: Hard

16. If ABC is a right triangle, $\angle B = (x + 5)°$ and $\angle C$ is two less than $\angle B$, find the measure of $\angle B$.

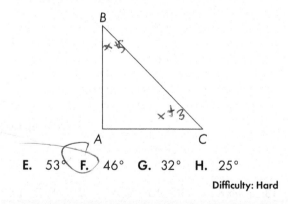

E. 53° **F.** 46° **G.** 32° **H.** 25°

Difficulty: Hard

17. Triangles ABC and LMK are similar. Find the ratio of the perimeter of $\angle ABC$ to the perimeter of $\angle LMK$.

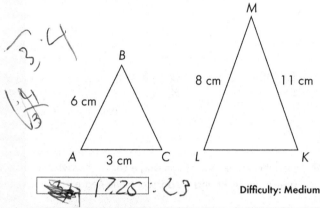

Difficulty: Medium

18. In triangle ABC, AB is 2 cm more than BC and AC is 3 cm less than AB. If BC = 8 cm, what is the perimeter of triangle ABC?

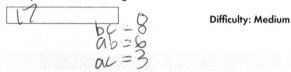

Difficulty: Medium

19. The ratio of the area of triangle ABC to the area of triangle EFG is 2:3. Find the ratio of the heights, if the length of the base of triangle ABC is 4 cm and the length of the base of triangle EFG is 8 cm.

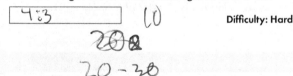

Difficulty: Hard

20. Find the height of a triangle if the length of the base is 6 m and the area of this triangle is 144 m².

Difficulty: Hard

Video Explanations
at argoprep.com/shsat

1. Since ABC is an isosceles triangle, $\angle C = \angle A = 50°$.
   The sum of all angles is $180°$.
   Therefore, we have:
   $$\angle B = 180 - 50 - 50 = 80°$$
   The correct answer is B.

2. Let x be the length of the hypotenuse.
   Use the Pythagorean theorem to find x:
   $$x^2 = 8^2 + 6^2$$
   $$x^2 = 100$$
   $$x = 10$$
   The correct answer is F.

3. In an equilateral triangle, all sides are equal. Let x be the length of a side.
   Therefore, we have:
   $$x + x + x = 360$$
   $$3x = 360$$
   $$x = 120 \text{ mm}$$
   The correct answer is D.

4. The area formula for a triangle is $\frac{1}{2}bh$, where b is the length of the base and h is the height.
   Plug in the known values and solve for h.
   $$56 = \frac{1}{2} \times 8 \times h$$
   $$h = 14 \text{ cm}$$
   The correct answer is E.

5. First we need to find the value of x.
   Since ABC is an isosceles triangle, $BC = AB = x$. The perimeter is the sum of all sides.
   Therefore, we have:
   $$45 = x + x + 3x$$
   $$5x = 45$$
   $$x = 9$$
   $$AC = 3 \times 9 = 27 \text{ cm}$$
   The correct answer is C.

6. In similar triangles, the corresponding sides have lengths in the same proportion.
   Let h be the hypotenuse of the smaller triangle, and H the hypotenuse of the larger triangle.
   Therefore, we have:
   $$\frac{6}{3} = \frac{H}{h}$$
   Find the length of h using the Pythagorean theorem:
   $$h^2 = 3^2 + 4^2 = 9 + 16 = 25$$
   $$h = \sqrt{25} = 5 \text{ inches}$$
   We have:
   $$\frac{6}{3} = \frac{H}{5}$$
   Cross multiply:
   $$30 = 3H$$
   $$H = 10 \text{ inches}$$
   The correct answer is H.

7. The area of a triangle is half the product of the height and base.
   In this case we have:
   $$A = \frac{1}{2} \times AC \times BH$$
   BH is 3 more than AC, so $BH = 8 + 3 = 11$ mm.
   Substitute the appropriate values and find the area:
   $$A = \frac{1}{2} \times 8 \times 11 = 44 \text{ mm}^2$$
   The correct answer is B.

8. Perimeter is the sum of all sides.
   Let x be an unknown side of the triangle given.
   Use the Pythagorean theorem to find x:
   $$12^2 = 7^2 + x^2$$
   $$x^2 = 144 - 49 = 95$$
   $$x = \sqrt{95} \approx 9.7$$
   The perimeter is
   $$P = 7 + 12 + 9.7 = 28.7 \text{ cm}$$
   The correct answer is F.

9. Use the Pythagorean theorem to find x:
   $$(9x)^2 + (5x)^2 = 100^2$$
   $$106x^2 = 100,000$$
   Don't let this question trick you. You do not have to do actual calculations in order to solve this question. Use the estimation strategy. $106x^2$ is close to $100x^2$. So $\frac{100,000}{100} = 100$.

Video Explanations
at argoprep.com/shsat

$$x^2 = 100$$
$$x = 10$$

The actual answer is close to the number 10, and if you analyze the answer choices, only answer choice B, 9.7 fits appropriately. The other answer choices are either too small or too large to consider as answers.

The correct answer is B.

---

10. Perimeter is the sum of all sides.

First, find the length of x and y.

Angle BMN and angle BAC are congruent. Angle BNM and BCA are congruent. Therefore, triangle ABC and triangle MBN are similar and the lengths of their sides are proportional.

Therefore, we have:

$$\frac{AB}{MB} = \frac{AC}{MN} = \frac{BC}{BN}$$

Substitute the appropriate values:

$$\frac{x+9}{x} = \frac{14}{8} = \frac{y+18}{18}$$

For x we have:

$$\frac{x+9}{x} = \frac{14}{8}$$

Cross multiply and solve for x:

$$8(x+9) = 14x$$
$$8x + 72 = 14x$$
$$6x = 72$$
$$x = 12$$

For y we have:

$$\frac{14}{8} = \frac{y+18}{18}$$

Cross multiply and solve for y:

$$252 = 8(y+18)$$
$$252 = 8y + 144$$
$$8y = 108$$
$$y = 13.5$$

Perimeter of triangle ABC is :

$$P = AB + BC + AC = 9 + 12 + 18 + 13.5 + 14 = 66.5 \, \text{cm} \,.$$

The correct answer is F.

---

11. The area of the right triangle is $\frac{1}{2} \cdot b \cdot h$, where h corresponds to AB and b corresponds to the base AC.

Substitute the appropriate values:

$$96 = \frac{1}{2} \cdot 12 \cdot AB$$

Solve for AB:

$$AB = \frac{96 \cdot 2}{12} = 16 \, \text{m}$$

The correct answer is C.

---

12. Angle x and an angle that measures 120° are supplementary. Therefore, we have:

$$x = 180 - 120 = 60°$$

The sum of all angles in a triangle is equal to 180°. Therefore, we have:

$$y = 180 - 30 - 60 = 90°$$

The correct answer is F.

---

13. Let $AB = 2x$, $BC = 3x$ and $AC = 5x$.

Perimeter is the sum of all sides.

Therefore, we have:

$$2x + 3x + 5x = 120$$
$$10x = 120$$
$$x = 12$$

$AB = 2 \times 12 = 24 \, \text{cm}$ and $BC = 3 \times 12 = 36 \, \text{cm}$.

Then find the difference:

$$BC - AB = 36 - 24 = 12 \, \text{cm}$$

The correct answer is D.

---

14. In triangle ABC, two sides are equal, so this triangle is an isosceles triangle. Angle C is equal to angle A with a measure of $x°$.

The sum of all angles in a triangle is equal to 180°.

Therefore, we have:

$$x + x + 48 = 180$$
$$2x = 180 - 48 = 132$$
$$x = 66$$

The correct answer is E.

---

15. The base is x cm. The second and third side are $(x + 5)$ cm each because in an isosceles triagle, 2 sides are equal.

Perimeter is the sum of all sides.

Therefore, we have:

$$x + 2(x + 5) = 46$$
$$3x = 46 - 10$$
$$3x = 36$$
$$x = 12$$

The length of the base is 12 cm.

The correct answer is D.

Video Explanations
at argoprep.com/shsat

16. If $\angle B = (x+5)^\circ$, then $\angle C = (x+5-2)^\circ = (x+3)^\circ$.
ABC is a right triangle, so $\angle A = 90^\circ$ and $\angle B + \angle C = 90^\circ$.
Therefore, we have:

$$x + 5 + x + 3 = 90$$
$$2x = 82$$
$$x = 41$$

$\angle B = 46^\circ$.

The correct answer is F.

---

17. Perimeter is the sum of all sides. Hence, we need to find the length of side BC of the smaller triangle and the length of side LK for the larger triangle.

In similar triangles, the corresponding sides have lengths in the same proportion.

First, find the length of side BC. Use a proportion:

$$\frac{8}{6} = \frac{11}{BC}$$

Cross multiply:

$$8BC = 66$$
$$BC = 8.25 \, cm$$

Then, find the length of side LK using a proportion:

$$\frac{8}{6} = \frac{LK}{3}$$

Cross multiply:

$$6LK = 24$$
$$LK = 4 \, cm$$

Now, find the perimeter of $\triangle ABC$ and the perimeter of $\triangle LMK$.

Perimeter of $\triangle ABC$ is $6 + 3 + 8.25 = 17.25 \, cm$

Perimeter of $\triangle LMK$ is $8 + 11 + 4 = 23 \, cm$

The ratio of the perimeter of $\triangle ABC$ to perimeter of $\triangle LMK$ is **17.25:23.**

---

18. Perimeter is the sum of all sides.

$$P = AB + BC + AC$$

Find the length of AB: $AB = 2 + BC = 2 + 8 = 10 \, cm$.

Then find the length of AC: $AC = AB - 3 = 10 - 3 = 7 \, cm$.

Therefore, perimeter of triangle ABC is $10 + 7 + 8 = 25 \, cm$.

19. The area of a triangle is $\frac{1}{2} \cdot b \cdot h$, where b is the length of the base and h is the height.

Let h_1 represent the height of triangle ABC and h_2 represent the height of triangle EFG.

Substitute the appropriate values to find the ratio of the heights:

$$\frac{\frac{1}{2} \times 4 \times h_1}{\frac{1}{2} \times 8 \times h_2} = \frac{2}{3}$$

$$\frac{h_1}{2h_2} = \frac{2}{3}$$

$$\frac{h_1}{h_2} = \frac{4}{3}$$

The ratio of the height of triangle ABC to the height of triangle EFG is 4:3.

---

20. The area of the triangle is $\frac{1}{2}bh$, where b is the length of the base and h is the height.

Substitute the appropriate values into the formula below to find h:

$$144 = \frac{1}{2} \cdot 6 \cdot h$$
$$6h = 288$$
$$h = 48 \, m$$

Video Explanations
at argoprep.com/shsat

1. What is the circumference of a circle, whose radius is 12 cm? Use π = 3.14 and round your answer to the nearest tenth.

   A. 75.4 cm
   B. 70.8 cm
   C. 64.9 cm
   D. 51.3 cm

   Difficulty: Easy

2. What is the area of a circle whose radius is 4 m? Use π = 3.14.

   E. 60.81 m²
   F. 50.24 m²
   G. 46 m²
   H. 35 m²

   Difficulty: Easy

3. Find the radius of a circle whose circumference is 36π cm.

   A. 36 cm
   B. 27 cm
   C. 18 cm
   D. 10 cm

   Difficulty: Medium

4. Find the measure of ∠OAB if ∠OBA = 60° and arc AB = 68°.

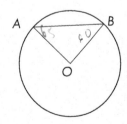

   E. 67°   G. 43°
   F. 52°   H. 36°

   Difficulty: Hard⁺

5. Triangle ABC is a right triangle. AB = 12 inches and BC = 16 inches. What is the radius of the circle?

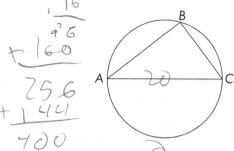

   A. 4 in   B. 6 in   C. 10 in   D. 13 in

   Difficulty: Medium

6. The area of a semicircle is 25.12 m². What is the diameter of the semicircle?

   E. 14 m   F. 11 m   G. 8 m   H. 5 m

   Difficulty: Medium

7. Find the radius of a circle if its circumference is 16 ft. Use π = 3.14. Round the answer to the nearest tenth.

   A. 9.3 cm   C. 2.5 cm
   B. 5.4 cm   D. 1.7 cm

   Difficulty: Medium

8. Find the area of a sector if ∠AOB = 60° and the radius of a circle is 5 cm. Round your answer to the nearest whole number.

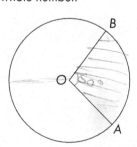

   E. 25 cm²   G. 15 cm²
   F. 18 cm²   H. 13 cm²

   Difficulty: Medium

Video Explanations
at argoprep.com/shsat

9. The ratio of the radius of the first circle to the radius of the second circle is 3:4. If the radius of the first circle is 6 mm, find the sum of the diameters of the two circles.

A. 34 mm C. 22 mm
B. 28 mm D. 15 mm

Difficulty: Hard

10. A circular cake costs $12.75. What is the cost of 1 cm² of the cake, if the diameter of the cake is 25 cm? Round your answer to the nearest thousandth.

E. $1.150 G. $0.026
F. $0.898 H. $0.001

Difficulty: Hard

11. A circular cake costs $15.7. What is the cost of 1 cm² of the cake, if the diameter of the cake is 4 cm?

A. $1.25 C. $0.5
B. $0.9   D. $0.02

Difficulty: Hard

12. Find the length of CE if CE = x + 5 cm, BE = x, AE = 2 cm and DE = 7 cm.

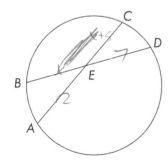

E. 12 cm
F. 7 cm
G. 4 cm
H. 2 cm

Difficulty: Hard

13. The ratio of circumferences of a larger circle to a smaller circle is 32:28. If the radius of the larger circle is 8 feet, find the radius of the smaller circle.

A. 24 feet
B. 12 feet
C. 7 feet
D. 3 feet

Difficulty: Hard

14. Find the area of a semicircle whose diameter is 12 mm. Use π = 3.14.

E. 62.40 mm² G. 45.48 mm²
F. 56.52 mm² H. 41.15 mm²

Difficulty: Hard

15. If the area of a sector is 49 cm² and the radius of a circle is 4 cm, find the measure of the central angle in degrees.

A. 156° C. 305°
B. 255° D. 351°

Difficulty: Hard

16. If point O represents the center of the circle below, AO = (2x + 4) cm and OB = (3x − 1) cm. Find the radius of the circle.

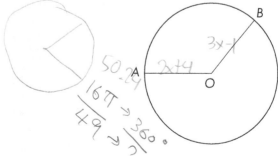

E. 11 cm   G. 21 cm
F. 14 cm   H. 24 cm

Difficulty: Hard

Video Explanations
at argoprep.com/shsat

17. The radius of the outer circle is 6 cm and the radius of the inner circle is 3 cm. Find the area of the shaded region in terms of π.

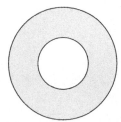

Difficulty: Medium

18. The ratio of the diameter of a smaller circle to the diameter of a larger circle is 5:7. If the diameter of a larger circle is 4 cm more than the diameter of a smaller circle, what is the diameter of the larger circle?

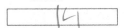

Difficulty: Medium

19. If point O is the center of the circle below, $BD = (5x - 2)$ cm and $AC = (8x - 5)$ cm. Find the radius of the circle.

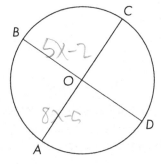

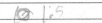

Difficulty: Hard

20. The ratio of the area of the first circle to the second circle is 4:9. Find the ratio of the radii of those circles.

Difficulty: Hard

Answer Explanation

1. Use the formula for circumference $C = 2\pi r$, where r is the radius. Substitute the appropriate values into this formula:
$$C = 2 \times 3.14 \times 12 = 75.36 \text{ cm}$$
Round to the nearest tenths place. $C = 75.4$ cm
The correct answer is A.

2. The area of a circle is $A = \pi r^2$, where r is the radius. Therefore, we have:
$$A = 3.14 \times 16 = 50.24 \text{ m}^2$$
The correct answer is F.

3. Use the formula for circumference $C = 2\pi r$, where r is the radius. Substitute the appropriate values into the formula:
$$36 \times \pi = 2 \times \pi \times r$$
$$36 = 2 \times r$$
$$r = \frac{36}{2} = 18 \text{ cm}$$
The correct answer is C.

4. This is not a concept tested on the SHSAT and therefore labeled as a challenging question.

Check our video explanation for a detailed overview for this question. $\angle AOB$ is the central angle and is equal to the angle measure of arc AB.

The sum of all sides of a triangle is 180°. Therefore, we have:
$$180 = \angle AOB + \angle OBA + \angle OAB$$
Substitute the appropriate values:
$$180 = 60 + 68 + \angle OAB$$
$$\angle OAB = 180 - 60 - 68 = 52°$$
The correct answer is B.

5. If $\angle ABC$ is a right triangle then AC, the hypotenuse of the right triangle, is a diameter of the circle.

Find the hypotenuse using Pythagorean theorem.
$$AC^2 = AB^2 + BC^2$$
Substitute the appropriate values:
$$AC^2 = 144 + 256 = 400$$
$$AC = \sqrt{400} = 20 \text{ in.}$$

Video Explanations
at argoprep.com/shsat

Diameter $d = 20$ in. Then, radius is $\frac{20}{2} = 10$ inches.

The correct answer is C.

6. The area of a circle is $A = \pi r^2$, where r is the radius of a circle.

    Then, the area of a semicircle is $A = \frac{1}{2}\pi r^2$.

    The diameter is $2r$ so $r = \frac{d}{2}$ and $r^2 = \frac{d^2}{4}$. Therefore, we have:

    $$25.12 = \frac{1}{2} \times 3.14 \times \frac{d^2}{4}$$
    $$3.14 \times d^2 = 25.12 \times 2 \times 4 = 200.96$$
    $$d^2 = 64$$
    $$d = 8 \text{ m}$$

    The correct answer is G.

7. The circumference formula is $C = 2\pi r$, where r is the radius.

    Substitute the appropriate values into this formula to find r:

    $16 = 2 \times 3.14 \times r$

    $$r = \frac{16}{2 \times 3.14} \approx 2.547 \approx 2.5 \text{ cm}$$

    Remember, you do not have a calculator on the exam.

    Estimation is a great strategy for this question. We have $8 = 3.14r$. Please do not divide 8 by 3.14. Instead think of 3.14 as just the number 3 and 8 divided by 3 is ~2.6. Answer choice G is the only answer choice with the number 2, so it has to be answer choice G.

    Watch the video explanation for this question where we explain in detail about the estimation strategy!

    The correct answer is C.

8. The area of a sector is $\frac{\pi R^2 n^\circ}{360^\circ}$, where n° is the measure of the central angle.

    Substitute the appropriate values :

    $$A = \frac{3.14 \times 25 \times 60}{360} = 13.083 \approx 13 \text{ (cm}^2)$$

    The correct answer is H.

9. First, find the radius of the second circle.

    Let r_1 represent the radius of the first circle and r_2 represent the radius of the second circle.

    Therefore, we have:

    $$\frac{r_1}{r_2} = \frac{3}{4}$$
    $$\frac{6}{r_2} = \frac{3}{4}$$

Cross multiply:

$$3r_2 = 24$$
$$r_2 = 8$$

The diameter of a circle is twice the radius.

Then $d_1 = 2 \times r_1 = 12$ mm and $d_2 = 2 \times r_2 = 16$ mm .

The sum of the diameters is $12 + 16 = 28$ mm .

The correct answer is B.

10. To solve this problem, find the area of a circular cake and then divide the cost of the cake by the result. The area of a circle is $A = \pi \times r^2$, where r is a radius.

    Note that radius is half of the diameter. Substitute the appropriate values.

    $$A = 3.14 \times 12.5^2 = 490.625 \text{ cm}^2$$

    The cost of 1 cm^2 is $\frac{12.75}{490.625} \approx \$0.026$.

    The correct answer is G.

11. To solve this problem, find the area of a circular cake and then divide the cost of the cake by the result.

    The area of a circle is $A = \pi \times r^2$, where r is a radius. Note that a radius is half of the diameter.

    Substitute the appropriate values :

    $$A = 3.14 \times 2^2 = 12.56 \text{ cm}^2$$

    The cost of 1 cm^2 is $\frac{15.7}{12.56} = \$1.25$.

    The correct answer is A.

12. When the two lines are secants of the circle and intersect inside the circle we have:

    $$CE \cdot AE = DE \cdot BE$$

    Substitute the appropriate values :

    $$2(x + 5) = 7x$$
    $$2x + 10 = 7x$$
    $$5x = 10$$
    $$x = 2$$

    The length of CE is $x + 5 = 2 + 5 = 7$ cm

    The correct answer is F.

▶ **Video Explanations**
at argoprep.com/shsat

13. Use the formula for circumference $C = 2\pi r$, where r is the radius. The ratio of circumferences of the larger circle to smaller circle is 36:28. Let r be the radius of smaller circle.

Therefore, we have:
$$\frac{2 \times \pi \times 8}{2 \times \pi \times r} = \frac{32}{28}$$
$$\frac{8}{r} = \frac{32}{28}$$

Cross multiply:
$$32\,r = 224$$
$$r = 7 \text{ feet}$$

The correct answer is C.

14. The area of a circle is $A = \pi \times r^2$, where r is the radius. Therefore the area of semicircle is $\frac{1}{2}\pi r^2$.

First, find the radius of the circle:
$$r = \frac{d}{2} = \frac{12}{2} = 6\,mm$$

Then, substitute the appropriate values into the formula for the area of semicircle.
$$A = \frac{1}{2} \times \pi \times 36 = 56.52\,mm^2$$

The correct answer is F.

15. The area of a sector is $\frac{\pi R^2 n^\circ}{360^\circ}$, where n°. Substitute the appropriate values.
$$49 = \frac{3.14 \times 16 \times n}{360}$$
$$17640 = 50.24n$$
$$n \approx 351^\circ$$

The correct answer is D.

16. Both lines, AO and OB are the radii of the circle. First equate the expressions for AO and OB to find x:
$$2x + 4 = 3x - 1$$
$$x = 5$$

Then substitute the value of x into the expression for AO:
$$AO = 2 \times 5 + 4 = 14 \text{ cm}$$

The correct answer is F.

17. To find the area of the shaded region subtract the area of the inner circle from the area of the outer circle. Use the formula for the area of a circle: $A = \pi \times r^2$, where r is the radius. For the outer circle, we have:
$$A = \pi \times 6^2 = 36\pi \text{ cm}^2$$
For the inner circle, we have:
$$A = \pi \times 3^2 = 9\pi \text{ cm}^2$$
The area of the shaded region is $36\pi - 9\pi = \mathbf{27\pi}$ **cm²**.

18. Let x represent the diameter of the smaller circle. Then $x + 4$ is the diameter of the larger circle.
$$\frac{x}{x+4} = \frac{5}{7}$$
Cross multiply and solve for x:
$$7x = 5(x+4) = 5x + 20$$
$$2x = 20$$
$$x = 10$$
The diameter of the larger circle is $10 + 4 = \mathbf{14}$ **cm**.

19. AC and BD are the diameters of the circle. The radius of the circle is half of AC or BD. Find x:
$$5x - 2 = 8x - 5$$
$$3x = 3$$
$$x = 1$$
The diameter is $5 \bullet 1 - 2 = 3 \text{ cm}$

Then the radius is $\frac{3}{2} = 1.5 \text{ cm}$.

20. The area of a circle is $A = \pi r^2$. Let r be the radius of the first circle and R is the radius of the second circle.

Therefore, we have:
$$\frac{\pi r^2}{\pi R^2} = \frac{4}{9}$$
$$\left(\frac{r}{R}\right)^2 = \frac{4}{9}$$

Take the square root of both sides:
$$\frac{r}{R} = \frac{2}{3}$$

The ratio of the radii is **2:3**.

Video Explanations
at argoprep.com/shsat

Fti 7/16

1. Maria drinks 2 liters of water every day. How much water, in milliliters, does she drink every day?

   A. 2000 mL
   B. 200 mL
   C. 2 mL
   D. 0.2 mL

   Difficulty: Easy

2. A rectangular house has the dimensions 9 feet by 15 feet. Find the perimeter of the house in meters. Note: 1 foot = 0.305 meters

   E. 20.43 m   G. 14.64 m
   F. 17.82 m   H. 10.83 m

   Difficulty: Easy

3. Wardrobes *M* and *N* have the same area. Wardrobe *M* is 9 m by 14 m and the length of wardrobe *N* is 10 m. Find the width of wardrobe *N*, in millimeters.

   A. 14,000 mm   C. 12,000 mm
   B. 12,600 mm   D. 9,400 mm

   Difficulty: Easy

4. A side of a square decreased by 30%. What percent did the area decrease by?

   E. 60%   G. 49%
   F. 51%   H. 37%

   Difficulty: Medium

5. Jack drove 5 miles to the west. What is the distance that he drove in feet? Note: 1 mile = 5,280 feet.

   A. 46,300 feet
   B. 35,500 feet
   C. 26,400 feet
   D. 18,800 feet

   Difficulty: Easy

6. Mark is 189 cm tall and Mia is 171 cm tall. Find the difference between Mark's and Mia's height in meters.

   E. 2 m
   F. 1.1 m
   G. 0.4 m
   H. 0.18 m

   Difficulty: Medium

7. Natalie has 11 dollars. She wants to exchange the dollars for dalts. If 1 dollar = 0.5 dalts, how many dalts will she get?

   A. 22 dalts
   B. 11 dalts
   C. 5.5 dalts
   D. 1.1 dalts

   Difficulty: Easy

8. If a cloth has the dimensions 7 cm by 10 cm, find the perimeter of this cloth in inches. Use the conversion 2.54 centimeters = 1 inch and round your answer to the nearest tenth.

   E. 15 in.   G. 9 in.
   F. 13.4 in.   H. 7.7 in.

   Difficulty: Medium

9. How many millimeters are in 5 meters and 90 cm?

   A. 5900 mm   C. 59 mm
   B. 590 mm   D. 5.9 mm

   Difficulty: Medium

10. A bottle contains 350 milliliters of orange juice. How many liters of juice are in the bottle?

    E. 0.7 L   G. 0.035 L
    F. 0.35 L   H. 0.0035 L

    Difficulty: Medium

Video Explanations
at argoprep.com/shsat

11. The movie theatre is 30 km away from Emma's home. She traveled 27 km by train and has to walk the remaining distance. How many miles does Emma have to walk to get to the theatre? Note: 1 mile = 1.6 km

A. 2 miles   **C.** 1.6 mile
B. 1.875 miles   **D.** 1 mile

Difficulty: Medium

12. Karina bought 2 kg of candy. She ate 75 g of candies and divided the rest between her 8 friends. How many grams of candy did each of her friends get?

E. 500 g   **G.** 240.625 g
F. 250 g   **H.** 230 g

Difficulty: Hard

13. A cuboid has the dimensions 2 × 4 × 8 in. Find the volume of this cuboid in cubic yards. Use the approximation 1 cubic inch = 0.0000214 cubic yards.

A. 0.15 yd.³   **C.** 0.002 yd.³
B. 0.01 yd.³   **D.** 0.0014 yd.³

Difficulty: Hard

14. Find the distance between two houses in feet, if the distance in meters is 74 meters. Use the conversion 1 meter = 3.28 feet.

E. 328 feet   **G.** 180.34 feet
F. 242.72 feet   **H.** 135 feet

Difficulty: Easy

15. A book has the dimensions 34 cm by 17 cm. Find the area of the book in square inches. Use the approximation 1 meter = 39.37 inches.

A. 89.6 in.²   **C.** 68.3 in.²
B. 76.5 in.²   **D.** 54.4 in.²

Difficulty: Hard

16.

1 mile = 63360 inches
1 mile = 5280 feet

Using the conversions above, how many feet are in 1 inch?

E. 12 feet   **G.** 0.1 feet
F. 0.7 feet   **H.** 0.083 feet

Difficulty: Hard

17. There are 1000 grams in 1 kilogram, and 1000 milligrams in 1 gram.

How many milligrams are there in 1000 grams?

1,000,000

Difficulty: Medium

18. Sophia wants to hike 231 miles in 7 days. How many kilometers will she walk every day if Sophia divides the distance evenly? Use the conversion 1 mile = 1.6 km.

52.8 km

Difficulty: Medium

19. There are three books on Michael's table. The first book weighs 4 kg, the second book weighs 3 kg and the third book weighs 8 kg. Michael states that adding the weight of these 3 books together results in 33 pounds. Is Michael correct? Note: 1 kg = 2.2 pounds.

yesh

Difficulty: Medium

20. The distance from Alec's house to school is 5 miles and the distance from Bella's house to school is 4 kilometers. Who is closer to the school: Alec or Bella?

Bella

Difficulty: Medium

Video Explanations
at argoprep.com/shsat

1. Note that $1\,L = 1000\,mL$.
   Therefore, we have:
   $$2\,L = 2 \times 1000 = 2000\,mL$$
   The correct answer is A.

2. Perimeter is the sum of all sides.
   We have:
   $$P = 2 \times 9 + 2 \times 15 = 18 + 30 = 48\,ft.$$
   Then, convert to meters. The question gives you the conversion 1 foot = 0.305 meters.
   Therefore, we have:
   $$P = 48 \times 0.305\,m = 14.64\,m$$
   The correct answer is G.

3. Let x be the width of the wardrobe N.
   If the two wardrobes have the same area, we have:
   $$9 \times 14 = 10 \times x$$
   $$x = \frac{9 \times 14}{10} = 12.6\,m$$
   Convert your answer to millimeters. 1m = 1,000 mm.
   We have:
   $$W = 12.6 \times 1000\,mm = 12,600\,mm$$
   The correct answer is B.

4. The square has an area $a \times a$, where a is the side of a square.
   After decreasing, the area is $0.7a \times 0.7\,a = 0.49a^2$
   We have:
   $$1 - 0.49 = 0.51$$
   $$0.51 \times 100\% = 51\%$$
   An easier way to solve this problem is using a hypothetical value. Use the number 10 for the side length. The area of a square whose side measures 10 is $(10 \times 10) = 100$. If we decrease the side by 30%, the side now measures 7. The area of a square whose side measures 7 is $(7 \times 7) = 49$. Take the difference to get 51 which represents the percent decrease in the area.
   The correct answer is F.

5. Note: 1 mile = 5,280 feet.
   Therefore, we have:
   $$5\,miles = 5 \times 5280 = 26,400\,feet$$
   The correct answer is C.

6. You should already know that 1m = 100 cm.
   Therefore:
   $$189\,cm = 1.89\,m$$
   $$171\,cm = 1.71\,m$$
   Take the difference of the two numbers. $1.89 - 1.71 = 0.18\,m$.
   The correct answer is H.

7. If 1 dollar = 0.5 dalts, then 11 dollars = 11×0.5 dalts = 5.5 dalts.
   The correct answer is C.

8. First, find the perimeter of the cloth.
   The perimeter is $(2 \times 7) + (2 \times 10) = 34$ cm.
   Use proportions to make the conversions:
   $$\frac{2.54}{34} = \frac{1}{x}$$
   $$x = \frac{34}{2.54} = 13.38\,in.$$
   After rounding $x = 13.4$ inches.
   Watch our video explanation where we show you the best way to approach this problem. You should not be solving for $\frac{34}{2.54}$. Instead you should be using the estimation or plug & check strategy.
   The correct answer is F.

9. Note that 1 meter = 100 cm and 1 cm = 10 mm.
   Therefore, we have:
   $$5\,m\ 90\,cm = 5 \times 100 + 90 = 590\,cm$$
   Then convert to millimeters:
   $$590\,cm = 590 \times 10\,mm = 5900\,mm.$$
   The correct answer is A.

10. Note that $1\,L = 1000\,mL$.
    Convert 350 milliliters to liters by diving by 1000:
    $$\frac{350}{1000} = 0.35$$
    The bottle contains 0.35 L of orange juice.
    The correct answer is F.

Video Explanations
at argoprep.com/shsat

11. First find out how far Emma has to walk.

Emma has to walk $(30 - 27)$ km = 3 km.

Convert 3 kilometers to miles by dividing by 1.6:

$$3\,km = \frac{3}{1.6} = 1.875\,miles$$

Emma has to walk 1.875 miles.

The correct answer is B.

---

12. Note that 1 kg = 1000g.

First convert 2 kg to g. We have: 2 kg = 2 × 1000 g = 2000 g.

She ate 75 g, so 2000 − 75 = 1925 g left.

To find how many grams of candy each of Karina's friends got, divide 1925g by 8:

$$\frac{1925}{8} = 240.625\,g$$

The correct answer is G.

---

13. The volume of the cuboid is $2 \times 4 \times 8 = 64$ in^3.

Calculate 64 in^3 in cubic yards using the conversion provided in the question.

$$64\text{ in.}^3 \times 0.0000214 = 0.0014\text{ yd.}^3$$

The correct answer is D.

---

14. We are given the conversion 1 meter = 3.28 feet. The distance is 74 meters and in order to convert that into feet, we need to multiply 74 by 3.28.

$$74 \times 3.28 = 242.72 \text{ feet}$$

The correct answer is F.

---

15. First find the area in centimeters.

We have:

$$A = 34 \times 17 = 578 \text{ cm}^2$$

Then convert the area to square meters. Note that 1 cm = 0.01 m.

$$A = 578 \text{ cm}^2 = 578 \times 0.01^2 \text{ m}^2 = 0.0578 \text{ m}^2$$

Use the conversion 1 meter = 39.37 inches to convert square meters to square inches.

$$A = 0.0578 \times 39.37^2 \text{ in}^2 \approx 89.6 \text{ in}^2$$

The correct answer is A.

16. This is a "trick" question. Notice the question is asking how many feet are in one inch. You can set up a proportion using the conversion of miles to inches and feet but that is unnecessary and a waste of time since you are dealing with big numbers.

We know that 12 inches = 1 foot and in order to solve for how many feet are in one inch, we can simply divide both sides of the equation by 12.

$$1 \text{ inch} = \frac{1}{12} \text{ feet}$$

The fraction $\frac{1}{12}$ is approximately 0.083.

The correct answer is H.

---

17. Let x represent the amount of milligrams in 1000 grams.

Set up a proportion:

$$\frac{1000\,mg}{1g} = \frac{x\,mg}{1000\,g}$$

Solve for x: **1,000,000** milligrams are in 1000 grams.

---

18. First divide the distance in miles by 7: $\frac{231}{7} = 33$.

If 1 mile = 1.6 km, 33 miles = 33 × 1.6 km = 52.8 km.

Sophia will walk **52.8 km** every day.

---

19. First find out the total weight in kg: 4 + 3 + 8 = 15 kg.

If 1 kg = 2.2 pounds, 15 kg = 15 × 2.2 pounds = 33 pounds.

Therefore, Michael is correct.

---

20. Remember the conversion 1 mile = 1.6 kilometers.

Then 5 miles = 5 × 1.6 kilometers = 8 kilometers.

8 km > 4 km, so **Bella** is closer to school than Alec.

 **Video Explanations**
at argoprep.com/shsat

Fri 7/16

1. Find the perimeter of a square with side $a = 4$ cm.

A. 16 cm   **C.** 24 cm
B. 20 cm   **D.** 29 cm

Difficulty: Easy

2. Find the area of this triangle, if $a = 12$ cm, and $h = 8$ cm.

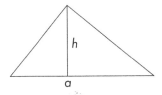

E. 67 cm²   **G.** 48 cm²
F. 56 cm²   **H.** 36 cm²

Difficulty: Easy

3. What is the perimeter of a rectangle that has a length of 7 cm and a width of 5 cm?

A. 35 cm   **C.** 24 cm
B. 30 cm   **D.** 15 cm

Difficulty: Easy

4. Find the area of a parallelogram if the length of the base, a, is 14 cm and the height, h, is 10 cm.

E. 80 cm²
F. 100 cm²
G. 140 cm²
H. 180 cm²

Difficulty: Medium

5. What is the perimeter of a triangle whose sides measure 4 cm, 7 cm, and 9 cm?

A. 20 cm   **C.** 12 cm
B. 15 cm   **D.** 8 cm

Difficulty: Easy

6. Find the area of figure *ABCDEF* below.

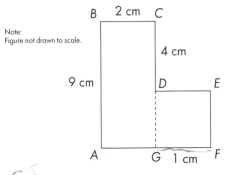

Note:
Figure not drawn to scale.

E. 23 cm²   **G.** 36 cm²
F. 30 cm²   **H.** 44 cm²

Difficulty: Hard

7. In the right triangle *ABC*, $AB = 4$ cm, $BC = 3$ cm. Find the perimeter of *ABC*.

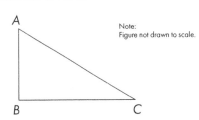

Note:
Figure not drawn to scale.

A. 36 cm   **C.** 18 cm
B. 28 cm   **D.** 12 cm

Difficulty: Medium

8. Find the area of the trapezoid below.

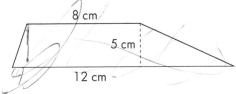

E. 60 cm²
F. 50 cm²
G. 45 cm²
H. 40 cm²

Difficulty: Medium

Video Explanations
at argoprep.com/shsat

9. Find the perimeter of the figure below.

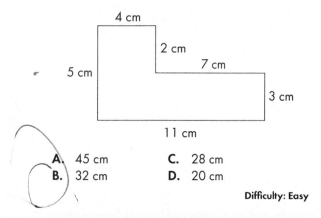

A. 45 cm   C. 28 cm
B. 32 cm   D. 20 cm

Difficulty: Easy

10. Find the area of *ABCD*.

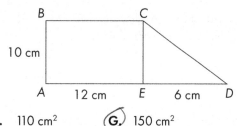

E. 110 cm²   G. 150 cm²
F. 135 cm²   H. 180 cm²

Difficulty: Medium

11. The figure below is an isosceles trapezoid. *BC* = 6 mm, *AD* = 8 mm, *BH* = 4 mm and *AH* = 1cm. Find the perimeter of *ABCD*.

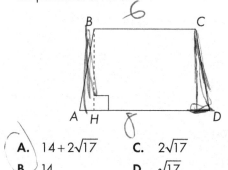

A. $14 + 2\sqrt{17}$ C. $2\sqrt{17}$
B. 14   D. $\sqrt{17}$

Difficulty: Hard

12. Find the surface area of the cube whose edge is 9 cm.

E. 110 cm² F. 486 cm² G. 560 cm² H. 600 cm²

Difficulty: Hard

13. Find the perimeter of the circle whose diameter is 9.5 cm. Do not round the final answer.

A. 30 cm B. 29.83 cm C. 25 cm D. 21.5 cm

Difficulty: Hard

14. Find the surface area of a cylinder in terms of π, whose height, *H* = 16 mm, and radius, *R* = 7 mm.

E. 322 πmm²   G. 780 πmm²
F. 546 πmm²   H. 857 πmm²

Difficulty: Hard

15. Find the perimeter of the shaded area.

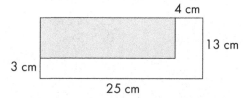

A. 75 cm B. 62 cm C. 40 cm D. 35 cm

Difficulty: Hard

16. Find the area of the shaded region, if *AB* = 6 cm, *AC* = 8 cm, and the radius of the circle is 2 cm.

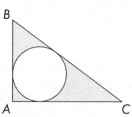

E. 15 cm²   G. 11.44 cm²
F. 12.33 cm²   H. 9.86 cm²

Difficulty: Hard

Video Explanations
at argoprep.com/shsat

17. If ABCD is a rectangle, DC = 12 cm and BC = 16 cm, find the perimeter of triangle ABD.

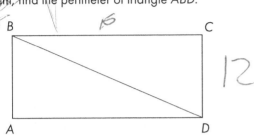

48

Difficulty: Hard

19. Find the area of the shaded portion of the figure if the radius of the circle is 2 cm.

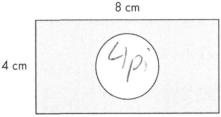

32-4pi

Difficulty: Hard

18. Find the perimeter of this figure.

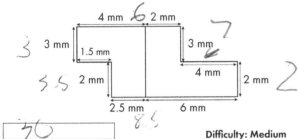

Difficulty: Medium

20. If the area of the trapezoid below is 176 mm², find the height of this trapezoid.

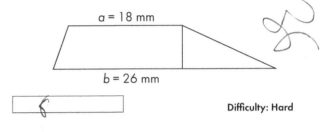

Difficulty: Hard

Answer Explanation

1. The perimeter is the sum of all sides. In a square, all sides are equal so the perimeter is $P = 4 \times 4 = 16$ cm.
The correct answer is A.

2. Area formula for a triangle is $A = \frac{1}{2}bh$.
Substitute the values of b and h into the formula:
$$A = \frac{1}{2} \times 12 \times 8 = 6 \times 8 = 48 \text{ cm}^2$$
The correct answer is G.

3. The perimeter is the sum of all sides. In a rectangle, two opposite sides are equal. We have:
$$P = 2 \times 7 + 2 \times 5 = 24 \text{ cm}.$$
The correct answer is C.

4. Note that the area of a parallelogram is $A = b \times h$. Substitute the appropriate values into this formula. Therefore, we have:
$$A = 14 \times 10 = 140 \text{ cm}^2$$
The correct answer is G.

5. The perimeter is the sum of all sides. Therefore, we have:
$$P = 4 + 7 + 9 = 20 \text{ cm}$$
The correct answer is A.

6. This is labeled as a hard question because the diagram is clearly not drawn to scale which can trick many students. Additionally, the diagram looks like it contains a square but it is actually a rectangle.
In order to calculate the area of the figure, divide the figure into 2 smaller figures.
The area of ABCDEF is the sum of areas of ABCG and GDEF.

 **Video Explanations** at argoprep.com/shsat

ABCG and GDEF are rectangles.

The area of a rectangle is the product of the width and length.

Therefore, for ABCG we have:

$$A_1 = 9 \times 2 = 18 \text{ cm}^2$$

In order to find the area of GDEF, first find the length of EF:

$$EF = 9 - 4 = 5 \text{ cm}$$

Then find the area of GDEF:

$$A_2 = 1 \times 5 = 5 \text{ cm}^2$$

Finally, find the area of ABCDEF:

$$A = 18 + 5 = 23 \text{ cm}^2$$

The correct answer is E.

---

7. The perimeter is the sum of all sides.

To find the perimeter, find the length of AC first.

Use the Pythagorean theorem:

$$AC^2 = AB^2 + BC^2 = 16 + 9 = 25$$

$$AC = \sqrt{25} = 5 \text{ cm}$$

Then find the perimeter:

$$P = AB + BC + AC = 3 + 4 + 5 = 12 \text{ cm}$$

The correct answer is D.

---

8. The area of a trapezoid can be found by using the formula

$$A = \frac{1}{2}(a+b)h$$

Substitute the appropriate values:

$$A = \frac{1}{2} \times (8+12) \times 5 = 50 \text{ cm}^2$$

The correct answer is F.

---

9. The perimeter is the sum of all sides.

Therefore, we have:

$$P = 4 + 2 + 7 + 3 + 11 + 5 = 32 \text{ cm}$$

The correct answer is B.

---

10. The area of ABCD can be presented as the sum of areas ABCE and ECD.

ABCE is a rectangle and the area can be determined by the product of the width and length.

For ABCE we have:

$$A_{ABCE} = 10 \times 12 = 120 \text{ cm}^2$$

ECD is a right triangle.

The area of a triangle is $\frac{1}{2}ab$.

Therefore, for ECD we have:

$$A_{ECD} = \frac{1}{2} \times 6 \times 10 = 30 \text{ cm}^2$$

Add the area of the rectangle and triangle to get the area of ABCD:

$$A = 120 + 30 = 150 \text{ cm}^2$$

The correct answer is G.

---

11. The perimeter is the sum of all sides.

Use the Pythagorean theorem to find the length of AB. Since this is an isosceles trapezoid, the length of AB is also equal to the length of CD.

$$AB^2 = AH^2 + BH^2 = 1 + 16 = 17$$

$$AB = \sqrt{17}$$

Therefore, we have:

$$P = AB + BC + CD + AD = 6 + 8 + 2\sqrt{17} = 14 + 2\sqrt{17}$$

The correct answer is A.

---

12. We are asked for the surface area of the cube. Notice that a cube has the same length and width since any face of the cube is a square. The cube also consists of 6 faces.

The area of one face is $9 \times 9 = 81 \text{ cm}^2$. The surface area is the area of all six faces of the cube so we can multiply $81 \times 6 = 486 \text{ cm}^2$.

The correct answer is F.

---

13. The perimeter of a circle is the circumference of a circle. Don't let the word perimeter confuse you. The formula for the circumference of a circle is πd.

Therefore, we have:

$$P = \pi d = 3.14 \times 9.5 = 29.83 \text{ cm}$$

The correct answer is B.

---

14. The surface area is the sum of the lateral area and twice the area of the base.

The base of the cylinder is a circle, so the lateral area is equal to $2\pi RH$.

The area of the base is $2\pi R^2$.

Therefore, we have:

$$A = 2\pi RH + 2\pi R^2 = 2\pi R(H + R) = 2 \times \pi \times 7 (16 + 7)$$
$$= 322\pi \text{ mm}^2$$

The correct answer is E.

 **Video Explanations**
at argoprep.com/shsat

15. The perimeter of a rectangle is equal to the sum of all the sides. However, since a rectangle's opposite sides are the same, we only need to know the length and width of the shaded area.

Length is equal to $25 - 4 = 21$ cm.

Width is equal to $13 - 3 = 10$ cm.

Therefore, we have:
$$P = 2 \times 21 + 2 \times 10 = 42 + 20 = 62 \text{ cm}$$

The correct answer is B.

16. To find the area of the shaded region, find the area of a right triangle and subtract the area of a circle that is inscribed into the triangle.

Area of a triangle is
$$A = \frac{1}{2} \times AB \times AC = \frac{1}{2} \times 6 \times 8 = 24 \text{ cm}^2$$

Formula for the area of a circle is $A = \pi r^2$.

Therefore, for area of circle we have:
$$A = 3.14 \times 2^2 = 12.56 \text{ cm}^2$$

Then find the area of the shaded figure:
$$A = 24 - 12.56 = 11.44 \text{ cm}^2$$

The correct answer is G.

17. The perimeter is the sum of all sides.

If $ABCD$ is a rectangle, then $AB = DC = 12$ cm, $AD = BC = 16$ cm and $\angle A = 90°$.

Use the Pythagorean theorem to find the third side of triangle ABD:
$$BD = \sqrt{AB^2 + AD^2} = \sqrt{144 + 256} = 20$$

Then find the perimeter of ABD.
$$P_{ABD} = 12 + 16 + 20 = \textbf{48 cm.}$$

18. The perimeter is the sum of all sides.

Therefore, we have:
$$P = 2.5 + 2 + 1.5 + 3 + 4 + 2 + 3 + 4 + 2 + 6 = \textbf{30 mm.}$$

19. To find the area of the shaded portion, we can find the area of the rectangle followed by the area of the circle and subtract the two areas.

Area of a rectangle is length × width.
$$A = 4 \times 8 = 32 \text{ cm}^2$$

Area of a circle is $A = \pi r^2$.
$$A = 3.14 \times 2^2 = 12.56 \text{ cm}^2$$

Subtract the two areas to find the area of the shaded portion.
$$A = 32 - 12.56 = \textbf{19.44 cm}^2$$

20. The area of a trapezoid can be found by using the formula $A = \frac{1}{2}(a+b)h$, where h is the height.

Substitute the appropriate values:
$$176 = \frac{1}{2} \times (18 + 26) \times h$$
$$352 = 44 \times h$$
$$h = \textbf{8 mm}$$

1. What is the volume of a cube whose side measures 4 cm?

A. 90 cm³ **B.** 64 cm³ **C.** 56 cm³ **D.** 45 cm³

Difficulty: Easy

2. What is the volume of a sphere whose radius is 3 cm? Note: Use the formula $V = \frac{4}{3}\pi r^3$.

E. 70.35 cm³ **G.** 113.04 cm³
F. 108.12 cm³ **H.** 120.67 cm³

Difficulty: Medium

3. What is the volume of a cone that has a height of 21 cm and a radius of 10 cm? Note: Use the formula $V = \frac{1}{3}\pi r^2 h$.

A. 3086.6 cm³ **C.** 1560.78 cm³
B. 2198 cm³ **D.** 1000 cm³

Difficulty: Medium

4. What is the volume of a cylinder whose height is 8 mm and has a radius of 2 mm? Note: Use the formula $V = \pi r^2 h$.

E. 100.48 mm³ **G.** 49 mm³
F. 72.9 mm³ **H.** 27.03 mm³

Difficulty: Medium

5. What is the volume of a cuboid whose length is 12 cm, width is 5 cm and height is 4 cm?

A. 115 cm³ **C.** 200 cm³
B. 160 cm³ **D.** 240 cm³

Difficulty: Medium

6. Find the volume of the sphere, in terms of π, whose radius is 3 m.

A. 36 π m³ **C.** 80 π m³
B. 58 π m³ **D.** 110 π m³

Difficulty: Medium

7. Find the volume of the rectangular prism below.

14 yd

2 yd

6 yd

A. 168 yd³ **C.** 100 yd³
B. 147 yd³ **D.** 87 yd³

Difficulty: Easy

8. Find the volume of a hemisphere, whose radius is 5 in. Round the answer to the nearest tenth. Note: The volume formula for a sphere is $V = \frac{4}{3}\pi r^3$.

E. 360.8 in³ **G.** 261.7 in³
F. 312.4 in³ **H.** 138.9 in³

Difficulty: Hard+

9. Find the volume of the figure below.

18 cm

7 cm

A. 980.45 cm³
B. 1015.30 cm³
C. 1335.68 cm³
D. 1780.38 cm³

Difficulty: Hard

 **Video Explanations** at argoprep.com/shsat

10. Find the length of an edge of a cube that has a volume of 64 mm³.

    E.   10 mm   G.   4 mm
    F.   6 mm   H.   2 mm

    Difficulty: Hard

11. A rectangular prism has a volume of 540 cm³. The rectangular base has a length of 15 cm and a width of 9 cm. What is the height of the rectangular prism?

    A.   12 cm   B.   9 cm   C.   5 cm   D.   4 cm

    Difficulty: Medium

12. What is the volume of a cuboid whose length is 10 cm, width is 6 cm and height is 2.5 cm?

    E.   100 cm³   G.   163 cm³
    F.   150 cm³   H.   172 cm³

    Difficulty: Hard

13. Find the volume of the cube, if the area of one square face of a cube is equal to 81 ft². `81` `89` `79` `72`

    A.   890 ft.³   C.   729 ft.³
    B.   830 ft.³   D.   625 ft.³

    Difficulty: Medium

14. The volume of the cylinder is 226.08 mm³ and the height is 18 mm. Find the radius of a cylinder, if $\pi = 3.14$.

    E.   15 mm   G.   6 mm
    F.   10 mm   H.   2 mm

    Difficulty: Hard

15. The volume of the sphere is 288π in³. Find the volume of the sphere, in terms of π, if the radius of the sphere increased by 3 in.

    A.   1240 π in³   C.   895 π in³
    B.   972 π in³   D.   678 π in³

    Difficulty: Hard

16. What is the height of a cylinder, if the radius is 2 cm and volume is 56 cm³? Round your answer to the tenths place. Note: Use the formula $V = \pi r^2 h$.

    E.   8.4 cm   G.   4.5 cm
    F.   5.2 cm   H.   3.2 cm

    Difficulty: Hard

17. Find the volume of the rectangular prism whose height is 12 cm and base is a square with sides of 9 cm.

    `972`

    Difficulty: Hard

18. Find the volume of the shaded figure if the radius of the larger sphere is 6 cm and the radius of the smaller sphere is 3 cm. Note: The volume of a sphere formula is $V = \frac{4}{3}\pi r^3$.

    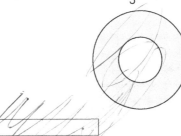

    Difficulty: Hard⁺

19. The rectangular prism below has a volume of 1120 cm³. What is the height? `16`

    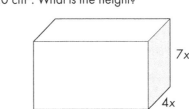

    `16x=1120` `x=70`
    `140x=1120` `x=8`

    Difficulty: Hard

20. The ratio of the volumes of two cubes is 1:8. If the side of the first cube is 4 in., find the side of the second cube.

    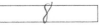 `8`

    Difficulty: Hard⁺

ARGOPREP SHSAT   – Geometry – Volume – Answer Explanation

1. The formula for the volume of a cube is: $V = s^3$, where s is a side length.
   Therefore, we have:
   $$V = 4^3 = 64 \text{ cm}^3$$
   The correct answer is B.

---

2. The volume of a sphere $= \frac{4}{3} \times \pi \times r^3$, where r is the radius.
   Substitute the appropriate values:
   $$V = \frac{4}{3} \times 3.14 \times 3^3 = 113.04 \text{ cm}^3$$
   The correct answer is G.

---

3. The volume of a cone $= \frac{1}{3} \times \pi \times r^2 \times h$, where h is the height and r is the radius.
   Substitute the appropriate values:
   $$V = \frac{1}{3} \times 3.14 \times 10^2 \times 21 = 2198 \, cm^3$$
   The correct answer is B.

---

4. Use the formula for the volume of a cylinder: $V = \pi r^2 h$, where r is the radius and h is the height.
   Substitute the appropriate values:
   $$V = 3.14 \times 4 \times 8 = 100.48 \text{ mm}^3$$
   The correct answer is E.

---

5. Use the formula for the volume of a cuboid: $V = a \times b \times c$, where a is the side length, b is the width and c is the height.
   Substitute the appropriate values:
   $$V = 12 \times 5 \times 4 = 240 \text{ cm}^3$$
   The correct answer is D.

---

6. The volume of a sphere $= \frac{4}{3} \pi r^3$, where r is the radius.
   Substitute the appropriate values:
   $$V = \frac{4}{3} \times \pi \times (3)^3 = 36\pi \text{ m}^3$$
   The correct answer is A.

---

7. The volume of a prism is the product of the area of the base and the height of the prism.
   The base is a rectangle so the area of the base is
   $$A = 6 \times 2 = 12 \text{ yd}^2$$
   Multiply the area of the base by the height.

$$V = 12 \times 14 = 168 \text{ yd}^3$$
The correct answer is A.

---

8. You will not be tested on hemispheres on the exam and therefore this question is rated as a Hard⁺.
   Realize a hemisphere is simply "half" of a sphere, so you can find the volume of the sphere and then divide by 2 to get your answer.
   The volume of a sphere $= \frac{4}{3} \times \pi \times r^3$, where r is the radius.
   Therefore, we have:
   $$V = \frac{4}{3} \times 3.14 \times 5^3 = 523.3 \text{ in}^3$$
   Then divide by 2:
   $$V = \frac{523.3}{2} = 261.65 \text{ in}^3$$
   After rounding to the nearest tenth, the answer is 261.7 in³.
   The correct answer is G.

---

9. This question is rated hard because you need to realize you are working with a cylinder. Although we did not provide you the volume formula in the question directly, you can find the volume formula for a cylinder on Question #4. Use the formula of the volume of a cylinder: $V = \pi r^2 h$, where r is the radius and h is the height.
   In the diagram, you are given the diameter. We want the radius so we can divide the diameter in half.
   $$r = \frac{d}{2} = \frac{18}{2} = 9 \text{ cm}$$
   Substitute the appropriate values:
   $$V = 3.14 \times 9^2 \times 7 = 1780.38 \text{ cm}^3$$
   The correct answer is D.

---

10. Use the formula for the volume of a cube: $V = s^3$, where s represents the edge.
    Substitute appropriate values to find a:
    $$64 = s^3$$
    $$s = \sqrt[3]{64} = 4 mm$$
    The correct answer is G.

---

11. Substitute appropriate values:
    $$540 = 15 \times 9 \times h$$
    $$540 = 135h$$
    $$h = 4 \text{ cm}$$
    The correct answer is D.

Video Explanations
at argoprep.com/shsat

12. Use the formula for the volume of a cuboid:

$V = a \times b \times c$, where a is the side length, b is the width and c is the height.

Substitute the appropriate values:

$$V = 10 \times 6 \times 2.5 = 150 \text{ cm}^3$$

The correct answer is F.

---

13. The volume of cube is $V = s^3$.

Area of the square $= s^2$.

Substitute the appropriate values to find a:

$$s^2 = 81$$
$$s = \sqrt{81} = 9 \text{ ft.}$$

Now we can find the volume:

$$V = 9^3 = 729 \text{ ft.}^3$$

The correct answer is C.

---

14. The volume of the cylinder with height h and radius r is $\pi r^2 h$.

Substitute the appropriate values and find r.

$$226.08 = 3.14 \times 18 \times r^2$$
$$r^2 = 4$$
$$r = 2 \text{ mm}$$

The correct answer is H.

---

15. First, find the initial radius.

The volume of a sphere $= \frac{4}{3}\pi r^3$, where r is the radius.

Substitute the appropriate values:

$$288\pi = \frac{4}{3} \times \pi \times r^3$$
$$r^3 = 216$$
$$r = 6 \text{ in.}$$

Then find the volume:

$$V = \frac{4}{3} \times \pi \times (6+3)^3 = 972\pi \text{ in.}^3$$

The correct answer is B.

---

16. The volume of a cylinder is $\pi r^2 h$, where r is the radius and h is the height.

Substitute the appropriate values and calculate the value of h:

$$56 = 3.14 \times 4 \times h$$
$$h = 4.458 \text{ cm}$$

After rounding, the answer is 4.5 cm.

The correct answer is G.

17. The volume of a prism is the area of the base times the height of prism.

The base of the prism is a square. The area of square is s^2, where s is the side of a square.

The area of square is

$$A = 9^2 = 81 \text{ cm}^2$$

Hence the volume of the prism is

$$V = 81 \times 12 = \textbf{972 cm}^3$$

---

18. To find the volume of the shaded figure, find the volume of the larger and smaller spheres and subtract them.

The volume of a sphere is $\frac{4}{3}\pi r^3$.

Therefore, the volume of the larger sphere is

$$\frac{4}{3} \times 3.14 \times 6^3 = 904.32 \text{ cm}^3$$

The volume of the smaller sphere is

$$\frac{4}{3} \times 3.14 \times 3^3 = 113.04 \text{ cm}^3$$

The volume of the shaded figure is $904.32 - 113.04 =$ **791.28 cm³**

---

19. The volume of a prism is the product of the area of the base and its height. The base is a rectangle so the area of the base is $5x \cdot 4x = 20x^2 \text{ cm}^2$

We have:

$$1120 = 20x^2 \times 7x = 140x^3$$
$$x^3 = 8$$
$$x = 2$$

The height $= 7x = 7 \times 2 = \textbf{14 cm.}$

---

20. The volume of a cube is s^3, where s is the side . The ratio of volumes is 1:8.

Let x represent a measure of the side of the second cube.

Use a proportion to find x:

$$\frac{4^3}{x^3} = \frac{1}{8}$$
$$x^3 = \frac{8 \times 4^3}{1} = 512$$
$$x = \sqrt[3]{512} = \textbf{8 inches}$$

▶ **Video Explanations**
at argoprep.com/shsat

1. Find the distance between points $A(2, -1)$ and $B(6, -4)$.

   A. 5   **C.** 9
   B. 7   **D.** 12

   Difficulty: Easy

2. If $AB = 8$ cm, point A has the coordinates $(4, 0)$, and point B has the coordinates $(6, y)$, what is the value of y?

   E. 0   **G.** $\sqrt{60}$
   F. 6.6   **H.** $\sqrt{62}$

   Difficulty: Medium

3. Find the length of FS if point F is located on $(7, -2)$ and point S is located on $(9, 2)$.

   A. 1   **C.** 4
   B. $2\sqrt{5}$ **D.** 7

   Difficulty: Medium

4. Point C has an x-coordinate that is 2 more than the x-coordinate of point A, and the y-coordinate of point C is 5 less than the y-coordinate of point B. If point A has the coordinates $(4, -3)$ and B has the coordinates $(6, -5)$, find the coordinates of point C.

   E. $(4, 3)$ **G.** $(6, -4)$
   F. $(-10, -1)$ **H.** $(6, -10)$

   Difficulty: Easy

5. If the length of $\overline{AB} = 14$ cm and length of $\overline{BC} = \frac{4}{7}\overline{AB}$, what is the length of $\overline{BC}$?

   A. 16   **C.** 5
   B. 8   **D.** 3

   Difficulty: Medium

6. On the number line NH, the position of point N is $2\frac{3}{4}$ and point H is located to the right of point N. If $NH = \frac{5}{7}$, what is the position of point H?

   E. $2\frac{1}{28}$ **G.** $-2\frac{45}{67}$
   F. $1\frac{5}{7}$ **H.** $3\frac{13}{28}$

   Difficulty: Medium

   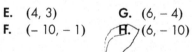

7. In triangle LSM, point L has the coordinates $(4, -2)$ and point M has the coordinates $(2, -1)$. What is the length of LM?

   A. $\sqrt{5}$ **C.** 7
   B. 6   **D.** $3\sqrt{5}$

   Difficulty: Medium

8. In parallelogram $ABCD$, point A has the coordinates $(0, 0)$, point B has the coordinates $(3, 4)$, point C has the coordinates $(8, 4)$, and point D has the coordinates (x, y). What are the coordinates of point D?

   E. $(0, 5)$ **G.** $(5, 0)$
   F. $(8, 0)$ **H.** $(4, 0)$

   Difficulty: Hard⁺

9. On the number line WV, the position of point V is $\frac{3}{4}$. If point W is located to the right from point V and $WV = 5\frac{1}{3}$, what is the position of point W?

   A. $\frac{3}{4}$ **C.** $4\frac{1}{12}$
   B. -1 **D.** $6\frac{1}{12}$

   Difficulty: Medium

▶ **Video Explanations**
at argoprep.com/shsat

10. In parallelogram $ABCD$, point A has the coordinates $(4, 6)$ and point C has the coordinates $(-2, -4)$. What is the value of the diagonal AC?

   E. 15
   F. $\sqrt{34}$

   G. 17
   H. $2\sqrt{34}$

   Difficulty: Medium

11. On the number line AB, the position of point B is $-\frac{2}{5}$. If point A is to the right of point B and $AB = 3$, what is the position of point A?

   A. $2\frac{3}{5}$
   B. $-\frac{3}{2}$

   C. $-3\frac{2}{5}$
   D. -4

   Difficulty: Medium

12. Points A, B, and C are on a straight line, and B is between A and C. $\overline{AB} = 6\,\text{cm}$, $\overline{BC} = \frac{2}{3}\overline{AB}$. What is the length of $\overline{AC}$?

   E. 4
   F. 8

   G. 10
   H. 12

   Difficulty: Hard

13. Points L, N, M, and K are on a number line, and points N and M are between L and K. $\overline{LN} = 1\frac{1}{2}$, $\overline{LK} = 4\frac{3}{4}$ and $\overline{MK} = 2\frac{1}{3}$. The position of point N is $\frac{4}{5}$. What is the position of point M?

   A. $1\frac{56}{100}$
   B. $2\frac{3}{8}$

   C. $-3\frac{4}{5}$
   D. $1\frac{43}{60}$

   Difficulty: Hard

14. Points A, B, C, and D are on the number line. Points B and C are between A and D and A, B, C, and D are integers. $AB{:}BC{:}CD = 5{:}3{:}1$. The position of point A is -2 and the position of point D is 7. What is the value of $\overline{AC}$?

   E. 13
   F. 11

   G. 8
   H. 5

   Difficulty: Hard

15. On a number line, XY has a length of $1\frac{2}{3}$. Point Z is located between point X and Y. The position of Point X is 4. What is a possible value for point Z?

   A. 7
   B. 6

   C. 5.8
   D. 4.1

   Difficulty: Hard

16. In triangle ABC, $AB = 4$, $BC = 5$, $AC = 6$. Point A has the coordinates $(-1, 0)$ and point B has the coordinates $(0, 0)$. Determine the third point of triangle.

   E. $(-1, -3)$
   F. $(5, 0)$

   G. $(0, 0)$
   H. $(-3, -2)$

   Difficulty: Hard

17. Points J, L, and K are on a straight line, and L is between J and K. $\overline{JK} = 10\,\text{cm}$, and $\overline{JL} = \frac{4}{5}\overline{JK} - 5$. What is the length of $\overline{LK}$?

   _____

   Difficulty: Hard

18. On the number line NM, the position of point N is $7\frac{3}{4}$. If point N is to the left of point M and $NM = 9$, what is the position of point M?

   _____

   Difficulty: Medium

▶ **Video Explanations**
at argoprep.com/shsat

19. Points A, B, C, D are on a straight line, and points B and C are between A and D. $\overline{AB} = 1\frac{1}{6}$, $\overline{AD} = 2\frac{5}{6}$ and $\overline{CD} = 1\frac{2}{3}$. The position of B is $\frac{5}{6}$. What is the position of point C?

Difficulty: Hard

20. Points Q, W, E, and R are on the number line. Points W and E are between Q and R and Q, W, E, and R are integers. $QW{:}WE{:}ER = 3{:}4{:}5$. The position of Q is 1 and the position of R is 13. What is the value of $\overline{QE}$?

Difficulty: Hard

Answer Explanation

1. Use the distance formula:
$$D = \sqrt{(x_2 - x_1)^2 + (y_2 - y_1)^2}$$
Substitute the values and find the distance:
$$D = \sqrt{(6-2)^2 + (-4+1)^2} = \sqrt{16+9} = 5$$
The correct answer is A.

2. Use the distance formula to solve this problem:
$$D = \sqrt{(x_2 - x_1)^2 + (y_2 - y_1)^2}$$
Substitute the values into the distance formula for AB:
$$8 = \sqrt{(6-4)^2 + (y-0)^2} = \sqrt{4+y^2}$$
Take the square root of both sides:
$$64 = 4 + y^2$$
$$y^2 = 64 - 4 = 60$$
$$y = \sqrt{60}$$
The correct answer is G.

3. Use the distance formula:
$$D = \sqrt{(x_2 - x_1)^2 + (y_2 - y_1)^2}$$
Fill in the values and calculate the length of FS:
$$D = \sqrt{(9-7)^2 + (2+2)^2} = \sqrt{4+16} = 2\sqrt{5}$$
The correct answer is B.

4. First find the x-coordinate of point C. If it is 2 more than the x-coordinate of point A, the x-coordinate of point C is $4 + 2 = 6$.

Next find the y-coordinate of point C. If it is 5 less than the y-coordinate of point B, then the y-coordinate of point C is $-5 - 5 = -10$.

The correct answer is H.

5. Substitute the value of $\overline{AB}$ into the expression of $\overline{BC}$:
$$\overline{BC} = \frac{4}{7}\overline{AB} = \frac{4}{7} \times 14 = 8$$
The correct answer is B.

6. Find H by setting up the following equation:
$$2\frac{3}{4} + \frac{5}{7} = H$$
$$H = 2\frac{3}{4} + \frac{5}{7} = \frac{11}{4} + \frac{5}{7} = \frac{77}{28} + \frac{20}{28} = \frac{97}{28} = 3\frac{13}{28}$$
The correct answer is H.

7. Use the distance formula:
$$D = \sqrt{(x_2 - x_1)^2 + (y_2 - y_1)^2}$$
Therefore, we have:
$$LM = \sqrt{(2-4)^2 + (-1-(-2))^2} = \sqrt{4+1} = \sqrt{5}$$
The correct answer is A.

8. $ABCD$ is a parallelogram, so $BC = AD$.

Draw a quick sketch of the coordinate graph to help you visually see where point D belongs.

We know $AB = CD$ since the figure is a parallelogram and we can easily calculate the distance of BC without using the distance formula. The distance of BC is 5 and therefore, AD must also have a distance of 5. Since the coordinate of point A is at $(0, 0)$ point D must be at $(0, 5)$.

The correct answer is G.

Video Explanations
at argoprep.com/shsat

9. Find the position of point W by solving the following equation:

$$W - \frac{3}{4} = 5\frac{1}{3}$$

$$W = \frac{3}{4} + 5\frac{1}{3} = \frac{3}{4} + \frac{16}{3} = \frac{9+64}{12} = \frac{73}{12} = 6\frac{1}{12}$$

The correct answer is D.

---

10. To find the value of the AC, use the distance formula:

$$D = \sqrt{(x_2 - x_1)^2 + (y_2 - y_1)^2}$$

Fill in the values of the coordinates A and C and find the value of AC.

$$AC = \sqrt{(-2-4)^2 + (-4-6)^2} = \sqrt{36+100} = 2\sqrt{34}$$

The correct answer is H.

---

11. Find the position of point A by solving the following equation:

$$-\frac{2}{5} + 3 = A$$

$$A = 3 - \frac{2}{5}$$

$$A = \frac{15-2}{5} = \frac{13}{5} = 2\frac{3}{5}$$

The correct answer is A.

---

12. Since $\overline{AB} = 6$ cm, we can use the following equation to find $\overline{BC}$:

$$\overline{BC} = \frac{2}{3}\overline{AB} = \frac{2}{3} \times 6 = 4 \text{ cm}$$

$$\overline{AC} = \overline{AB} + \overline{BC} = 6 + 4 = 10 \text{ cm}$$

The correct answer is G.

---

13. First, use $\overline{LN} = 1\frac{1}{2}$ to find the location of point L:

$$\frac{4}{5} - L = 1\frac{1}{2}$$

$$L = \frac{4}{5} - 1\frac{1}{2}$$

$$L = -\frac{7}{10}$$

Then use $\overline{LK} = 4\frac{3}{4}$ to find the location of point K:

$$K - \left(-\frac{7}{10}\right) = 4\frac{3}{4}$$

$$K - \left(-\frac{7}{10}\right) = 4\frac{3}{4}$$

$$K + \frac{7}{10} = 4\frac{3}{4}$$

$$K = 4\frac{3}{4} - \frac{7}{10} = \frac{81}{20}$$

Finally, use $\overline{MK} = 2\frac{1}{3}$ to find the location of point M:

$$\frac{81}{20} - M = 2\frac{1}{3}$$

$$M = \frac{81}{20} - 2\frac{1}{3} = \frac{103}{60} = 1\frac{43}{60}$$

The correct answer is D.

---

14. Convert the ratios into fractions of AD. Use the sum of the ratios for the denominator.

$$AB = \frac{5}{5+3+1} = \frac{5}{9}$$

$$BC = \frac{3}{9} = \frac{1}{3}$$

The part of AD that is AC is the sum of those fractions:

$$AC = \frac{5}{9} + \frac{3}{9} = \frac{8}{9}$$

Find the length of AD:

$$AD = 7 - (-2) = 9$$

We have:

$$AC = \frac{8}{9} \times 9 = 8$$

The correct answer is G.

---

15. Since $\overline{XY} = 1\frac{2}{3}$, point Y is located at $4 + 1\frac{2}{3} = 5\frac{2}{3}$. Z must be between 4 and $5\frac{2}{3}$. Point Y can be written as 5.67.

Then only option given that lies between those two points is 4.1.
The correct answer is D.

---

16. Use the distance formula:

$$D = \sqrt{(x_2 - x_1)^2 + (y_2 - y_1)^2}$$

Let's consider the coordinates of point C is (x, y).

Therefore, the distance between from C to A and from C to B will be:

$$AC = \sqrt{(x+1)^2 + (y-0)^2} = 6$$

$$BC = \sqrt{(x-0)^2 + (y-0)^2} = 5$$

Therefore, we have:

$$(x+1)^2 + y^2 = 36$$

$$x^2 + y^2 = 25$$

From the first equation:

$$(x+1)^2 + y^2 = x^2 + 2x + 1 + y^2 = x^2 + y^2 + 2x + 1$$

Since $x^2 + y^2 = 25$, then substitute the second equation into the first one and solve for x:

$$25 + 2x + 1 = 36$$
$$2x = 10$$
$$x = 5$$

Now, find the y-coordinate:

$$25 + y^2 = 25$$
$$y^2 = 0$$
$$y = 0$$

Point C has the coordinates (5, 0).

The correct answer is F.

---

17. Since $\overline{JK} = 10$ cm, use that to find $\overline{JL}$:

$$\overline{JL} = \frac{4}{5}\overline{JK} - 5 = \frac{4}{5} \times 10 - 5 = 8 - 5 = 3 \text{ cm}$$

$$\overline{LK} = \overline{JK} - \overline{JL} = 10 - 3 = \textbf{7 cm}$$

---

18. Find the position of point M by solving the following equation:

$$M - 7\frac{3}{4} = 9$$

$$M = 9 + 7\frac{3}{4}$$

$$M = 9 + \frac{31}{4}$$

$$\boldsymbol{M = 16\frac{3}{4}}$$

19. First, use $\overline{AB} = 1\frac{1}{6}$ to find the location of A:

$$\frac{5}{6} - A = 1\frac{1}{6}$$

$$A = \frac{5}{6} - 1\frac{1}{6} = -\frac{2}{6}$$

Then use $\overline{AD} = 2\frac{5}{6}$ to find the location of D:

$$D - \left(-\frac{2}{6}\right) = 2\frac{5}{6}$$

$$D + \frac{2}{6} = \frac{17}{6}$$

$$D = \frac{7}{6} - \frac{2}{6} = \frac{15}{6} = 2\frac{1}{2}$$

Finally, use $\overline{CD} = 1\frac{2}{3}$ to find the location of C:

$$2\frac{1}{2} - C = 1\frac{2}{3}$$

$$C = 2\frac{1}{2} - 1\frac{2}{3} = \frac{5}{6}$$

---

20. Convert the ratios into fractions of QR. Use the sum of the ratios for the denominator.

$$QW = \frac{3}{3+4+5} = \frac{3}{12} = \frac{1}{4}$$

$$WE = \frac{4}{3+4+5} = \frac{4}{12} = \frac{1}{3}$$

The part of QR that is QE is the sum of those fractions:

$$QE = \frac{1}{4} + \frac{1}{3} = \frac{7}{12}$$

Find the length of QR:

$$QR = 13 - 1 = 12$$

We have:

$$QE = \frac{7}{12} \times 12 = \textbf{7}$$

Video Explanations
at argoprep.com/shsat

1. Find the slope of the line that passes through the points (4, 3) and (– 1, 1).

   A. 4

   B. 2

   C. $\frac{2}{5}$

   D. – 1

   Difficulty: Easy

2. What is the slope of the line $5y - x = 15$?

   E. 5

   F. 3

   G. $\frac{1}{5}$

   H. – 1

   Difficulty: Medium

3. Find the slope of the line that passes through the points (– 5, 2) and (3, – 6).

   A. – 1   B. 2   C. 4   D. 7

   Difficulty: Medium

4. What is the slope of the line $x = 9$?

   E. 9

   F. 0

   G. – 9

   H. undefined

   Difficulty: Hard

5. What is the slope of the line $y = -4$?

   A. 4

   B. 1

   C. 0

   D. – 4

   Difficulty: Medium

6. Find an equation of the line that has slope $\frac{2}{3}$ and passes through the point (3, – 2).

   E. $y = \frac{2}{3}x + 2$

   F. $y = \frac{2}{3}x - 1$

   G. $y = \frac{2}{3}x - 4$

   H. $y = \frac{2}{3}x + \frac{2}{3}$

   Difficulty: Medium

7. If the equation of the line is $\frac{3y}{x} = 12$, then what is the slope of the line?

   A. 1

   B. 4

   C. 7

   D. 8

   Difficulty: Medium

8. Find the slope of the line that passes through the points (– 1, – 3) and (5, 2).

   E. $\frac{5}{6}$

   F. $\frac{2}{3}$

   G. 1

   H. $\frac{5}{7}$

   Difficulty: Easy

9. What is the slope of the line parallel to the line whose equation is $-6y = -2x + 12$?

   A. 3

   B. $\frac{2}{5}$

   C. $\frac{3}{7}$

   D. $\frac{1}{3}$

   Difficulty: Hard

10. Find an equation of the line that has the slope – 1 and passes through the point (1, 1).

    E. $y = -x - 7$

    F. $y = -x + 2$

    G. $y = 2x - 10$

    H. $y = -x$

    Difficulty: Hard

11. What is the slope of the line parallel to the line whose equation is $-3y = 12x - 6$?

    A. 8

    B. 4

    C. – 4

    D. – 8

    Difficulty: Hard

Video Explanations
at argoprep.com/shsat

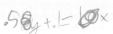

12. What is the slope of the line perpendicular to the line whose equation is $-2y = -9x + 3$?

  E. $-\dfrac{2}{9}$ G. 2

  F. $\dfrac{1}{9}$ H. $2\dfrac{1}{9}$

  Difficulty: Hard

13. If the equation of the line is $\dfrac{5y+1}{10} = x$, then what is the slope of the line?

  A. 10   C. 2
  B. 5   D. -1

  Difficulty: Hard

14. Given the line $y = mx - 4$, which passes through the point $(2, -6)$, what is the slope of that line?

  E. -1 G. 6
  F. 3   H. 8

  Difficulty: Hard

15. Find an equation of the straight line in slope-intercept form that passes through the points $(4, -3)$ and $(1, 0)$.

  A. $y = -x + 1$ C. $y = 5x - 7$
  B. $y = -3x + 1$ D. $y = x - 1$

  Difficulty: Hard

16. Find the equation of the line that is parallel to $12x - 4y = 28$ and passes through the point $(6, -3)$.

  E. $y = x - 21$ G. $y = x - 2$
  F. $y = 3x + 21$ H. $y = 3x - 21$

  Difficulty: Hard⁺

17. Find an equation of the straight line that is perpendicular to $x - y = 5$ and passes through the point $(8, -1)$.

  Difficulty: Hard

18. Find the equation of the line in slope-intercept form that passes through the points $(12, 4)$ and $(4, 6)$.

  Difficulty: Hard

19. Triangle ABC has the following points: $A(1, 2)$, $B(2, 3)$ and $C(2, 1)$. Is triangle ABC a right triangle?

  Difficulty: Hard⁺

20. Are the points $A(1, 2)$, $B(3, -1)$ and $C(2, 4)$ collinear?

  Difficulty: Hard⁺

Answer Explanation

1. Use the slope formula to solve the equation.

$$m = \frac{y_2 - y_1}{x_2 - x_1}$$

Substitute appropriate values into the formula and calculate the value of the slope.
Therefore, we have:

$$m = \frac{1-3}{-1-4} = \frac{2}{5}$$

The correct answer is C.

2. Rewrite the equation in slope-intercept form:

$$5y = x + 15, \quad y = \frac{x}{5} + 3$$

The slope of the given line is $\dfrac{1}{5}$.
The correct answer is G.

3. To solve the problem, use the slope formula:

$$m = \frac{y_2 - y_1}{x_2 - x_1}$$

Video Explanations
at argoprep.com/shsat

Substitute appropriate values into the formula and calculate the slope. Therefore, we have:

$$m = \frac{-6-2}{3-(-5)} = \frac{-8}{8} = -1$$

The correct answer is A.

4. The given equation is perpendicular to the x-axis. Therefore, its slope is undefined. Check out our video explanation where we go into detail about undefined slopes and when a slope is equal to 0.
The correct answer is H.

5. The given equation is a line parallel to the x-axis. Therefore, its slope is equal to 0.
The correct answer is C.

6. An equation of a line in slope-intercept form is
$$y = mx + b$$
We know that the slope is $\frac{2}{3}$ so the equation is
$$y = \frac{2}{3}x + b$$
Then use the point $(3, -2)$ to find b:
$$-2 = \frac{2}{3} \times 3 + b, \; b = -2 - 2 = -4$$
The equation of the line is $y = \frac{2}{3}x - 4$.

The correct answer is G.

7. First, rewrite the equation in slope-intercept form. Cross multiply to get rid of the denominator:
$$3y = 12x$$
Divide both sides by 3:
$$y = 4x$$
The slope is 4.
The correct answer is B.

8. To solve the problem above, use the following formula to calculate the slope:
$$m = \frac{y_2 - y_1}{x_2 - x_1}$$
Substitute appropriate values into the formula and calculate the slope value. Therefore, we have
$$m = \frac{2-(-3)}{5-(-1)} = \frac{5}{6}$$
The correct answer is E.

9. Rewrite the equation of the line in slope-intercept form by diving both sides by − 6. Therefore, we have:
$$-6y = -2x + 12$$
$$y = \frac{1}{3}x - 2$$
The slope of the given line is $\frac{1}{3}$. Two parallel lines have equal slopes. Therefore, the slope of the line parallel to the given line is also equal to $\frac{1}{3}$.

The correct answer is D.

10. An equation of a line in the slope-intercept form is $y = mx + b$. Since we know that the slope is − 1, the equation is $y = -x + b$. Then use the point $(1, 1)$ to find b:
$$1 = -1 \times 1 + b$$
$$b = 1 + 1 = 2$$
The equation of the line is $y = -x + 2$.
The correct answer is F.

11. Rewrite in slope-intercept form by dividing both sides of the equation by 3. Therefore, we have:
$$-y = 4x - 2$$
$$y = -4x + 2$$
The slope of the given line is − 4. Two parallel lines have equal slopes. Therefore, the slope of the line parallel to the given line is also equal to − 4.
The correct answer is C.

12. Divide both sides of the equation by − 2 to get the equation of the line in slope-intercept form:
$$y = \frac{9}{2}x - \frac{3}{2}$$
The slope of the given line is $\frac{9}{2}$. Two perpendicular lines have slopes m_1 and m_2 related as follows:
$$m_1 \times m_2 = -1$$
If we set $m_1 = \frac{9}{2}$ then m_2, the slope of the line perpendicular to the given line, is equal to $-\frac{2}{9}$.

In other words, the slope of the line perpendicular to the given line must be a negative reciprocal. If we know the slope of the given line, simply flip the numerator and denominator and change the sign.

The correct answer is E.

Video Explanations
at argoprep.com/shsat

13. First, rewrite this equation in the slope-intercept form. Cross multiply to get rid of the denominator:

$$5y+1=10x \text{ , } 5y=10x-1, \text{ } y=2x-\frac{1}{5}$$

The slope is 2.

The correct answer is C.

---

14. Substitute $x=2$ and $y=-6$ into the equation of a line. Therefore, we have:

$$-6=m \times 2-4, \text{ } 2m=-2$$

Divide both sides by 2:

$$m=-1$$

The correct answer is E.

---

15. The equation of the line in slope-intercept form is $y=mx+b$. Use the slope formula to find m:

$$m=\frac{y_2-y_1}{x_2-x_1}=\frac{0-(-3)}{1-4}=\frac{3}{-3}=-1$$

Since the slope is -1, the equation of the line is $y=-x+b$. Then use the point $(1, 0)$ to find b:

$$0=-1+b$$
$$b=1$$

The equation of the line is $y=-x+1$.

The correct answer is A.

---

16. Rewrite the equation in slope-intercept form. The equation of a line in slope-intercept form is $y=mx+b$. Therefore, we have:

$$-4y=-12x+28, \text{ } y=3x-7$$

The slope of the given line is 3. Two parallel lines have equal slopes. Therefore, the slope of the line parallel to the given line is also equal to 3. Using the point-slope form, we have:

$$y-(-3)=3(x-6), \text{ } y+3=3x-18$$
$$y=3x-21$$

The correct answer is H.

---

17. Rewrite the equation in slope-intercept form. The equation of a line in slope-intercept form is $y=mx+b$. Therefore, we have:

$$y=x-5$$

The slope of the given line is 1. Two perpendicular lines have slopes m_1 and m_2 related as follows:

$$m_1 \times m_2=-1$$

In other words, the slope of the line perpendicular to the given line must be a negative reciprocal. If we know the slope of the given line, simply flip the numerator and denominator and change the sign!

If we set $m_1=1$ then m_2, the slope of the line perpendicular to the given line, is equal to -1.

Using the point-slope form, we have:

$$y-(-1)=-(x-8), \text{ } y+1=-x+8$$
$$y=-x+7$$

---

18. The equation of the line in slope-intercept form is $y=mx+b$. Use the slope formula to find m:

$$m=\frac{y_2-y_1}{x_2-x_1}=\frac{6-4}{4-12}=\frac{2}{-8}=-\frac{1}{4}$$

Since the slope is $-\frac{1}{4}$, the equation of the line is $y=-\frac{1}{4}x+b$.

Then use the point $(4, 6)$ to find b:

$$6=-\frac{1}{4} \times 4+b \text{ , } b=6+1=7$$

The equation of the line is $y=-\frac{1}{4}x+7$.

---

19. Use the slope formula:

$$m=\frac{y_2-y_1}{x_2-x_1}$$

First, find the slope defined by points $A(1, 2)$ and $B(2, 3)$.

$$m(AB)=\frac{3-2}{2-1}=1$$

Then find the slope defined by points $A(1, 2)$ and $C(2, 1)$.

$$m(AC)=\frac{1-2}{2-1}=-1$$

The product of the slopes is equal to -1. What does that tell us? It means that lines AB and AC are perpendicular and the triangle whose vertices are points A, B, and C **is a right triangle**.

---

20. In order to answer this question, we need to know what the term collinear means! Points lying in the same straight line are said to be collinear. To determine if these points are lying on the same straight line, we can use the slope formula.

$$m=\frac{y_2-y_1}{x_2-x_1}$$

First, find the slope defined by points $A(1, 2)$ and $B(3, -1)$.

$$m(AB)=\frac{-1-2}{3-1}=-\frac{3}{2}$$

Then find the slope defined by points $B(3, -1)$ and $C(2, 4)$.

$$m(BC)=\frac{4-(-1)}{2-3}=-5$$

The two slopes are not equal. Therefore the points are not collinear.

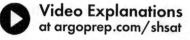

Video Explanations
at argoprep.com/shsat

1. Find the measure of x.

   A. 40°   C. 23°
   B. 32°   D. 17°

   Difficulty: Easy

2. The equation of the line is $\dfrac{2y-1}{x} = 6$. What is the slope of the line?

   E. 10   F. 6   G. 4   H. 3

   Difficulty: Medium

3. What is the circumference of a circle, whose radius is 4 cm? Use π = 3.14 and round your answer to the nearest hundredth.

   A. 25.12 cm   C. 15.60 cm
   B. 20.14 cm   D. 10.45 cm

   Difficulty: Medium

4. Find the area of the trapezoid shown below.

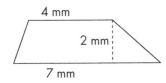

   E. 20 mm²   G. 8 mm²
   F. 11 mm²   H. 5 mm²

   Difficulty: Medium

5. If $\overline{AB} = 26$ cm and $\overline{BC} = \dfrac{1}{2}\overline{AB}$. What is the length of $\overline{BC}$?

   A. 18 cm   C. 13 cm
   B. 15 cm   D. 9 cm

   Difficulty: Medium

6. Find the distance between points A(6, 0) and B(0, − 1).

   E. $\sqrt{37}$ G. $\sqrt{17}$
   F. 5   H. 3

   Difficulty: Medium

7. The area of a triangle is 72 cm². If the length of the base is 12 cm, find the corresponding height.

   A. 19 cm   C. 12 cm
   B. 17 cm   D. 10 cm

   Difficulty: Medium

8. What is the measure of x?

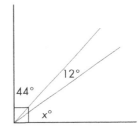

   E. 68°   F. 45°   G. 34°   H. 27°

   Difficulty: Medium

9. What is the perimeter of a rectangle that measures 19 cm in length and 14 cm in width?

   A. 75 cm   C. 47 cm
   B. 66 cm   D. 34 cm

   Difficulty: Easy

10. In triangle ABC, point A has the coordinates (7, − 1), point B has the coordinates (− 4, 3) and point C has the coordinates (− 3, − 2). What is the length of AC, in cm?

   E. $\sqrt{101}$ cm   G. 6 cm
   F. 8 cm   H. 2 cm

   Difficulty: Medium

Video Explanations
at argoprep.com/shsat

11. Find the perimeter of the right triangle shown below.

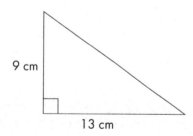

9 cm

13 cm

   A. 37.8 cm   **C.** 24.9 cm
   B. 31 cm   **D.** 19.3 cm

Difficulty: Medium

12. Find the volume of a cuboid that has a length of 8 cm, width of 16 cm, and height of 6 cm.

   E. 900 cm³   **G.** 768 cm³
   F. 835 cm³   **H.** 670 cm³

Difficulty: Easy

13. Find the slope of the line that passes through the points (8, − 4) and (2, − 2).

   A. 2   **C.** $-\dfrac{1}{3}$

   B. − 1   **D.** $-\dfrac{2}{3}$

Difficulty: Easy

14. Find the equation of the straight line that has slope $\dfrac{1}{4}$ and passes through the point (1, 0).

   E. $y = \dfrac{1}{4}x - 5$ **G.** $y = \dfrac{1}{4}x - 2$

   F. $y = \dfrac{1}{4}x + 7$ **H.** $y = \dfrac{1}{4}x - \dfrac{1}{4}$

Difficulty: Hard

15. A rectangular house has the dimensions 3 m by 7 m. Find the perimeter of the house in inches. Use the approximation 1 meter = 39.37 inches.

   A. 784.4 inches   **C.** 544.2 inches
   B. 658 inches   **D.** 480 inches

Difficulty: Medium

16. On the number line *RS*, the position of point *S* is $\dfrac{4}{7}$. If $RS = 3\dfrac{2}{7}$, what is the position of point *R*?

   E. $\dfrac{5}{7}$ **G.** $-4\dfrac{5}{7}$

   F. 1   **H.** $-2\dfrac{5}{7}$

Difficulty: Medium

17. The length and width of a rectangular box is increased by 10%. What percent has the area increased by?

   A. 40% **B.** 32% **C.** 21% **D.** 10%

Difficulty: Hard

18. Find the volume of a sphere, whose radius is 5 cm. Note: The volume formula for a sphere is $V = \dfrac{4}{3}\pi r^3$.

   E. 608.48 cm³   **G.** 450.18 cm³
   F. 523.33 cm³   **H.** 379.96 cm³

Difficulty: Medium

19. The ratio of the radius of the first circle to the radius of the second circle is 4:5. If the radius of the first circle is 12 cm, find the difference in the diameters.

   A. 24 cm   **C.** 6 cm
   B. 15 cm   **D.** 2 cm

Difficulty: Hard

Video Explanations
at argoprep.com/shsat

20. In triangle *ABC*, *AC* = 10 m and *BH* is 5 more than *AC*. Find the area of the triangle.

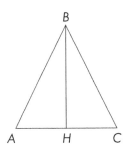

E. 75 m² **G.** 40 m²
F. 55 m² **H.** 35 m²

Difficulty: Medium

21. What is the midpoint of the straight line segment joining the points (1, − 6) and (7, 2)?

A. (4, − 2) **C.** (3, − 3)
B. (9, − 1) **D.** (2, − 1)

Difficulty: Medium

22. How many grams are in 4 kilograms and 500 grams?

E. 45,000 g **G.** 450 g
F. 4500 g **H.** 45 g

Difficulty: Medium

23. What is the value of *x* and *y* respectively?

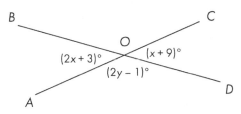

A. 6, 83 **C.** 17, 56
B. 9, 15 **D.** 12, 69

Difficulty: Medium

24. What is the midpoint of the straight line segment joining the points (− 8, − 12) and (− 4, − 4)?

E. (5, − 5) **G.** (− 6, − 8)
F. (3, 1) **H.** (− 9, − 1)

Difficulty: Medium

25. The volume of a cone is 449 cm³ and the height is 9 cm. Find the radius of this cone.

A. 14 cm **C.** 7 cm
B. 10 cm **D.** 5 cm

Difficulty: Hard

26. Find the measure of angle *A* from the triangle shown below, if *AB* = *BC*.

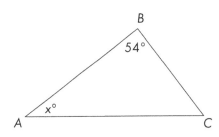

E. 80° **F.** 63° **G.** 30° **H.** 15°

Difficulty: Hard

27. Find the length of the hypotenuse of the larger triangle. The triangles shown below are similar.

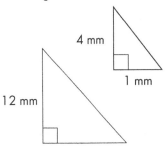

A. 3√17 mm **C.** 7 mm
B. 5 mm **D.** 9 mm

Difficulty: Hard

28. Point A has coordinates (6, − 3). What are the coordinates of point B, if the midpoint of the segment AB is (2, − 4)?

    E. (5, 7)
    F. (0, − 3)
    G. (− 2, − 5)
    H. (− 2, − 1)

    Difficulty: Hard

29. The rectangular prism depicted below has a volume of 432 in³. Find its height. Round the final answer to the nearest tenth as needed.

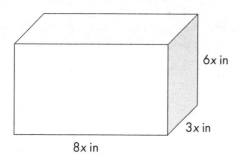

    6x in

    3x in

    8x in

    A. 16 in.
    B. 11 in.
    C. 9.3 in.
    D. 8.4 in.

    Difficulty: Hard

30. Find an equation of the line that is parallel to $3x − y = 15$ and passes through the point (1, − 1).

    E. $y = 3x + 15$
    F. $y = 3x − 4$
    G. $y = 3x + 3$
    H. $y = 3x − 15$

    Difficulty: Hard

31. Points A, B, C, and D are on the number line. Points B and C are between A and D and A, B, C, and D are integers. AB:BC:CD = 4:5:3. The position of A is − 12 and the position of D is 9. What is the value of $\overline{AC}$?

    A. 38   **C.** 26
    B. 31.5   **D.** 15.75

    Difficulty: Hard

32. Points A, B, and C are on a straight line, and B is between A and C. The length of $\overline{AC} = 32$ cm and the length of $\overline{AB} = \frac{3}{8}\overline{AC} − 1$. What is the length of $\overline{BC}$?

    E. 33 cm   **G.** 21 cm
    F. 27 cm   **H.** 15 cm

    Difficulty: Hard

33. Find the volume of the quadrangular prism whose height is 20 cm and base is a square with sides of 6 cm.

    Difficulty: Medium

34. Find an equation of the straight line in slope-intercept form that passes through the points (− 2, 6) and (0, 2).

    Difficulty: Hard

35. Find the surface area of a cylinder, whose height, $h = 8$ mm, and radius, $r = 3$ mm. Round the final answer to the nearest hundredth. Use 3.14 as the value of π.

    Difficulty: Hard

36. What is the area of a circle, whose diameter is 14 m? Write the answer in terms of π.

    Difficulty: Medium

Video Explanations
at argoprep.com/shsat

37. Find the measures of angles x, y, and z.

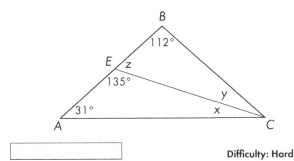

Difficulty: Hard

38. Are the points A(3, 4), B(– 2, 1) and C(6, – 4) collinear?

Difficulty: Hard

39. Find the area of the shaded region if AB = 12 cm, AC = 16 cm, and the radius of the circle is 4 cm.

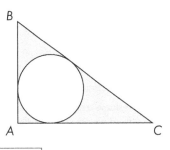

Difficulty: Hard

40. The ratio of the diameter of a smaller circle to the diameter of a larger circle is 9:11. If the diameter of the larger circle is 6 m more than the diameter of the smaller circle, what is the diameter of the larger circle?

Difficulty: Hard

Answer Explanation

1. Angle x and an angle that measures 135° are supplementary angles. Write an equation and find x:
$$148 + x = 180$$
$$x = 180 - 148 = 32°$$
The correct answer is B.

2. First, rewrite the equation in slope-intercept form. Cross multiply to get rid of the denominator:
$$2y - 1 = 6x$$
$$y = 3x + \frac{1}{2}$$
The slope is 3.
The correct answer is H.

3. Use the formula for circumference, $C = 2\pi r$, where r is the radius. Substitute the appropriate values into the formula:
$C = 2 \times 3.14 \times 4 = 25.12$ cm
After rounding, $C = 25.12$ cm.
The correct answer is A.

4. Area of a trapezoid is $A = \frac{1}{2}(a+b)h$
Substitute the appropriate values:
$$A = \frac{1}{2} \times (4+7) \times 2 = 11 \ mm^2$$
The correct answer is F.

5. Substitute the value of $\overline{AB}$ in the equation for $\overline{BC}$:
$$\overline{BC} = \frac{1}{2}\overline{AB} = \frac{1}{2} \times 26 = 13 \ cm$$
The correct answer is C.

6. Use the distance formula:
$$D = \sqrt{(x_2 - x_1)^2 + (y_2 - y_1)^2}$$
Fill in the values:
$$D = \sqrt{(0-6)^2 + (-1-0)^2} = \sqrt{37}$$
The correct answer is E.

Video Explanations
at argoprep.com/shsat

7. The area of a triangle is $A = \frac{1}{2} bh$, where b = the side of the triangle and h = the height.

Substitute the appropriate values and find h:

$$72 = \frac{1}{2} \times 12 \times h$$

$$h = 12 \text{ cm}$$

The correct answer is C.

---

8. The picture given shows a right angle. The sum of all angles that comprise the right angle are equal to 90°.

Therefore, we have:

$$44 + 12 + x = 90°$$

$$x = 90° - 44° - 12° = 34°$$

The correct answer is G.

---

9. The perimeter is the sum of all sides. In a rectangle the two opposite sides are equal.

We have:

$$P = 2 \times 19 + 2 \times 14 = 66 \text{ cm.}$$

The correct answer is B.

---

10. Use the distance formula:

$$D = \sqrt{(x_2 - x_1)^2 + (y_2 - y_1)^2}$$

Therefore, we have:

$$AC = \sqrt{(-3-7)^2 + (-2-(-1))^2} = \sqrt{100+1} = \sqrt{101} \text{ cm}$$

The correct answer is E.

---

11. Perimeter is the sum of all sides.

Let x represent an unknown side of the triangle.

Use the Pythagorean theorem to find x:

$$x^2 = 13^2 + 9^2$$

$$x^2 = 169 + 81 = 250$$

$$x = \sqrt{250} \approx 15.8$$

The perimeter is

$P = 13 + 9 + 15.8 = 37.8 \text{ cm}$

The correct answer is A.

---

12. Use the formula of the volume of a cuboid: $V = a \times b \times c$, where a is the length, b is the width and c is the height.

Substitute the appropriate values:

$$V = 8 \times 16 \times 6 = 768 \text{ cm}^3$$

The correct answer is G.

---

13. To solve the problem use the slope formula:

$$m = \frac{y_2 - y_1}{x_2 - x_1}$$

Substitute appropriate values into the formula. Therefore, we have:

$$m = \frac{-2 - (-4)}{2 - 8} = -\frac{2}{6} = -\frac{1}{3}$$

The correct answer is C.

---

14. The equation of a line in slope-intercept form is

$$y = mx + b$$

The slope is $\frac{1}{4}$ so the equation is

$$y = \frac{1}{4} x + b$$

Then use the point $(1, 0)$ to find the value of b:

$$0 = \frac{1}{4} \times 1 + b$$

$$b = -\frac{1}{4}$$

The equation of the line is $y = \frac{1}{4} x - \frac{1}{4}$.

The correct answer is H.

---

15. Perimeter is the sum of all sides. We have:

$$P = 2 \times 3 + 2 \times 7 = 6 + 14 = 20 \text{ m}$$

Then, convert to inches.

Therefore, we have:

$$20 \text{ m} = 20 \times 39.37 \text{ in.} = 787.4 \text{ inches}$$

The correct answer is A.

---

16. To find R, subtract $S - R$ and set it equal the length:

$$\frac{4}{7} - R = 3\frac{2}{7}$$

$$R = \frac{4}{7} - 3\frac{2}{7}$$

$$R = -\frac{19}{7} = -2\frac{5}{7}$$

The correct answer is H.

---

17. The rectangular box has area $l \times w$, where l is length and w is width. After the increase, the area is $1.1 l \times 1.1 w = 1.21 l \times w$

We have:

$$1.21 - 1 = 0.21$$

$$0.21 \times 100\% = 21\%$$

The correct answer is C.

Video Explanations
at argoprep.com/shsat

ARGOPREP **– Geometry – Challenge questions – Answer Explanation**
SHSAT

18. The volume of a sphere $=\frac{4}{3}\times\pi\times r^3$, where r is a radius.
Substitute the appropriate values:
$$V=\frac{4}{3}\times3.14\times5^3=523.33\,cm^3$$
The correct answer is F.

19. Let r_1 represent the radius of the first circle and r_2 the radius of the second circle.
Therefore, we have:
$$\frac{r_1}{r_2}=\frac{4}{5}\,,\,\frac{12}{r_2}=\frac{4}{5}$$
Cross multiply:
$$4r_2=60$$
$$r_2=15$$
The diameter of a circle is twice its radius.
Then $d_1=2\times r_1=12\times2=24\,cm$ and $d_2=2\times r_2=2\times15=30\,cm$.
The difference of the diameters is $30-24=6$ cm.
The correct answer is C.

20. The area of a triangle is half the product of the base and the height.
In this case, we have:
$$S=\frac{1}{2}\times AC\times BH$$
BH is 5 more than AC, so $BH=10+5=15$ m.
Substitute the appropriate values and find the area:
$$A=\frac{1}{2}\times10\times15=75\text{ m}^2$$
The correct answer is E.

21. Use $M=\left(\frac{x_1+x_2}{2};\frac{y_1+y_2}{2}\right)$.
In this case: $x_1=1,y_1=-6,x_2=7,y_2=2$
Therefore, we have:
$$M=\left(\frac{1+7}{2},\frac{-6+2}{2}\right)=(4,-2)$$
The correct answer is A.

22. Note that 1 kg = 1000 g.
Therefore, we have:
4 kg 500 g = 4 × 1000 g + 500 g = 4500 g
The correct answer is F.

23. Angles AOB and DOC are equal as verticals angles.
Therefore, we have:
$$2x+3=x+9$$
$$x=6$$
Angle AOD and angle COD are supplementary.
We have:
$$2y-1=180-x-9=180-6-9=$$
$$2y=166$$
$$y=83$$
The correct answer is A.

24. Use $M=\left(\frac{x_1+x_2}{2};\frac{y_1+y_2}{2}\right)$.
In this case: $x_1=-8,y_1=-12,x_2=-4,y_2=-4$
Therefore, we have:
$$M=\left(\frac{-8-4}{2},\frac{-12-4}{2}\right)=(-6,-8)$$
The correct answer is G.

25. The volume of a cone with height h and radius r is $V=\frac{1}{3}\pi r^2h$.
Substitute the appropriate values and find r.
$$449=\frac{1}{3}\times3.14\times9\times r^2$$
$$r^2\approx47.7$$
$$r\approx7$$
The correct answer is C.

26. In triangle ABC, two sides are equal, so this triangle is isosceles and angle C is equal to angle A with a measure of $x°$.
The sum of all angles in a triangle is equal to $180°$.
Therefore, we have:
$$x+x+54=180$$
$$2x=180-54=126$$
$$x=63$$
The correct answer is F.

27. In similar triangles, the corresponding sides have lengths in the same proportion.
Let h be the hypotenuse of the smaller triangle, and H the hypotenuse of the larger triangle.
Therefore, we have:
$$\frac{12}{4}=\frac{H}{h}$$

Video Explanations
at argoprep.com/shsat

Find the length of h using the Pythagorean theorem:

$$h^2 = 4^2 + 1^2 = 16 + 1 = 17$$
$$h = \sqrt{17} \text{ mm}$$

We have:

$$\frac{12}{4} = \frac{H}{\sqrt{17}}$$

Cross multiply:

$$12\sqrt{17} = 4H$$
$$H = 3\sqrt{17} \text{ mm}$$

The correct answer is A.

28. Use $M = \left(\dfrac{x_1 + x_2}{2}; \dfrac{y_1 + y_2}{2}\right)$. In this case: $x_1 = 6, y_1 = -3$. Point B has coordinates (x_2, y_2).

Substitute the appropriate values to find the x-coordinate of point B:

$$2 = \frac{6 + x_2}{2}$$
$$x_2 + 6 = 4$$
$$x_2 = 4 - 6 = -2$$

Then find the y-coordinate:

$$-4 = \frac{-3 + y_2}{2}$$
$$y_2 - 3 = -8$$
$$y_2 = -8 + 3 = -5$$

Point B has coordinates $(-2, -5)$.

The correct answer is G.

29. The volume of a prism is a product of the area of the base and the height of prism.

The base is a rectangle, so the area of the base is $8x \cdot 3x = 24x^2$

We have:

$$432 = 24x^2 \times 6x = 144x^3$$
$$x^3 = 3$$
$$x \approx 1.4$$

The height = $6 \times 1.4 = 8.4$ in.

The correct answer is D.

30. Rewrite the equation in slope-intercept form.

The general equation of a line in slope-intercept form is

$$y = mx + b$$

Therefore, we have:

$$-y = -3x + 15$$
$$y = 3x - 15$$

The slope of the given line is 3. Two parallel lines have equal slopes. Therefore, the slope of the line parallel to the given line is also equal to 3.

Using the point-slope form, we have:

$$y - (-1) = 3(x - 1)$$
$$y + 1 = 3x - 3$$
$$y = 3x - 4$$

The correct answer is F.

31. Convert the ratios into fractions of AD. Use the sum of the ratios in the denominator.

$$AB = \frac{4}{4 + 5 + 3} = \frac{4}{12} = \frac{1}{3}$$
$$BC = \frac{5}{12}$$

The part of AD that is AC is the sum of those fractions:

$$AC = \frac{4}{12} + \frac{5}{12} = \frac{9}{12} = \frac{3}{4}$$

Find the length of AD:

$$AD = 9 - (-12) = 21$$

We have:

$$AC = \frac{3}{4} \times 21 = 15.75$$

The correct answer is D.

32. Since $\overline{AC} = 32$ cm, use that to find $\overline{AB}$:

$$\overline{AB} = \frac{3}{8}\overline{AC} - 1 = \frac{3}{8} \times 32 - 1 = 12 - 1 = 11 \text{ cm}$$
$$\overline{BC} = \overline{AC} - \overline{AB} = 32 - 11 = 21 \text{ cm}$$

The correct answer is G.

33. The volume of a prism is product of the area of the base by the height of prism. The base of this prism is square. The area of a square is s^2, where s is the side of square. The area of the square is:

$$A = 6^2 = 36 \text{ cm}^2$$

Hence the volume of the prism is:

$$V = 20 \times 36 = \textbf{720 cm}^3$$

34. The equation of the line in slope-intercept form is

$$y = mx + b$$

Use the slope formula to find m:

$$m = \frac{y_2 - y_1}{x_2 - x_1} = \frac{2 - 6}{0 - (-2)} = \frac{-4}{2} = -2$$

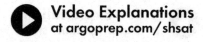

Video Explanations
at argoprep.com/shsat

The equation is as follows:

$$y = -2x + b$$

Then use the point (0, 2) to calculate the value of b:

$$2 = 0 + b$$
$$b = 2$$

The equation of the line is **$y = -2x + 2$**.

---

35. The surface area is the sum of the lateral area and twice the area of the base.

The base of the cylinder is a circle so the area of the base is πr^2.

Lateral surface area is equal to $2\pi rh$.

Therefore, we have:

$A = 2 \cdot \pi \cdot r \cdot h + 2 \cdot \pi \cdot r^2 = (2 \cdot 3.14 \cdot 3 \cdot 8) + (2 \cdot 3.14 \cdot 9) =$
$150.72 + 56.52 = $ **207.24 mm²**.

---

36. The area of a circle is $A = \pi r^2$, where r is the radius of a circle.

The diameter is twice the radius, so the radius is $\frac{14}{2} = 7$ m.

Therefore, we have:

$$A = \pi \times 7^2 = \mathbf{49\pi m^2}$$

---

37. First, find the measure of x. Note the sum of all angles of triangle is equal to 180°.

$$x = 180 - 135 - 31 = 14°$$

Angle z and an angle that measures 135° are supplementary.

Therefore, we have:

$$z = 180 - 135 = 45°$$

Finally, find y:

$$y = 180 - 112 - 45 = \mathbf{23°}$$

---

38. Use the slope formula.

$$m = \frac{y_2 - y_1}{x_2 - x_1}$$

First, find the slope defined by the points $A(3, 4)$ and $B(-2, 1)$.

$$m(AB) = \frac{1 - 4}{-2 - 3} = \frac{3}{5}$$

Then find the slope defined by the points $B(-2, 1)$ and $C(6, -4)$.

$$m(BC) = \frac{-4 - 1}{6 - (-2)} = -\frac{5}{8}$$

The two slopes are not equal. Therefore, the points are not collinear.

Therefore, the answer is no.

39. To find the area of the shaded region, find the area of a right triangle and subtract the area of the circle.

Area of triangle is

$$S = \frac{1}{2} \times AB \times AC = \frac{1}{2} \times 12 \times 16 = 96 \, cm^2.$$

The formula for area of a circle is $S = \pi r^2$.

Find the area of the circle:

$$S = 3.14 \times 4^2 = 50.24 \, cm^2$$

Then find the area of the shaded region:

$$S = 96 - 50.24 = \mathbf{45.76 \, cm^2}$$

---

40. Let x represent the diameter of the smaller circle. Then $x + 6$ is the diameter of the larger circle.

$$\frac{x}{x+6} = \frac{9}{11}$$

Cross multiply and solve for x:

$$11x = 9(x + 6) = 9x + 54$$
$$2x = 54$$
$$x = 27$$

The diameter of the larger circle is $27 + 6 = $ **33 m**.

Video Explanations
at argoprep.com/shsat

Probability and Statistics

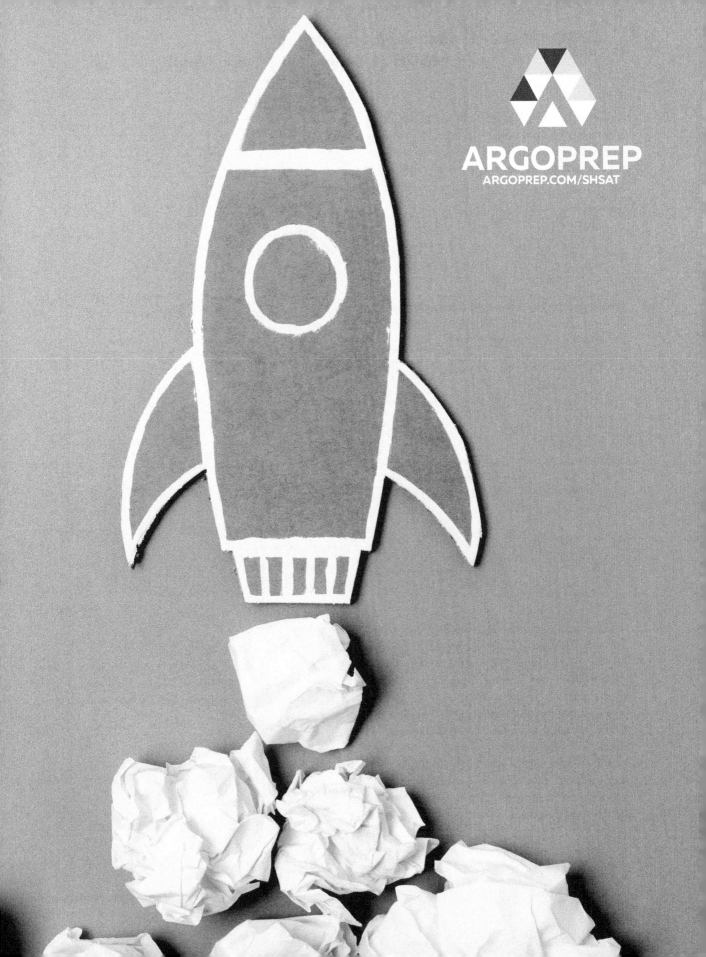

1. There are 8 green marbles, 4 black marbles and 3 white marbles in a bag. If you draw two marbles without replacement, what is the probability that the first marble is white and the second marble is green?

   A. $\frac{4}{35}$ B. $\frac{5}{12}$ C. $\frac{8}{75}$ D. $\frac{11}{15}$

   Difficulty: Hard

	Improved	Not improved
Medication	95	55
Sugar pill	40	110

   E. $\frac{19}{27}$ F. $\frac{19}{60}$ G. $\frac{7}{15}$ H. $\frac{11}{20}$

   Difficulty: Hard

2. There are 5 yellow marbles, 3 black marbles and 7 blue marbles in a bag. What is the probability of drawing a marble that is not blue?

   E. $\frac{3}{15}$ F. $\frac{5}{15}$ G. $\frac{7}{15}$ H. $\frac{8}{15}$

   Difficulty: Medium

5. A die was rolled 50 times and the outcomes are summarized in the table below:

Outcome	Frequency
1	12
2	7
3	9
4	11
5	8
6	3
Total	50

   What is the probability of rolling a number less than 3?

   A. $\frac{19}{50}$ B. $\frac{14}{25}$ C. $\frac{6}{25}$ D. $\frac{31}{50}$

   Difficulty: Easy

3. Suppose you have a bag of discs numbered from 1 to 9. A disc is drawn, then replaced, and a second disc is drawn. What is the probability that both discs were odd?

   A. $\frac{5}{18}$ B. $\frac{5}{81}$ C. $\frac{16}{81}$ D. $\frac{25}{81}$

   Difficulty: Medium

4. A pharmaceutical company is testing new medication which they claim is effective against chronic cough. To test the hypothesis, they chose 300 patients with chronic cough and divided them into two equal groups. The first group received the new medication, while the second group received a sugar pill. After 3 weeks of treatment, they reported whether or not their condition was improved. Using the table that follows, what is the probability that patients who reported an improvement of their condition had actually received the new medication?

6. Mia draws a ball from a box that contains 5 green balls, 3 yellow balls, 7 blue balls and 2 black balls. What is the probability that Mia will select a yellow ball?

   E. $\frac{1}{17}$ F. $\frac{3}{17}$ G. $\frac{9}{17}$ H. $\frac{14}{17}$

   Difficulty: Medium

Video Explanations
at argoprep.com/shsat

7. An ace and a spade were drawn from a standard deck of cards and replaced. Calculate the probability of both events occurring together.

A. $\frac{17}{52}$ B. $\frac{4}{13}$ C. $\frac{1}{52}$ D. $\frac{1}{169}$

Difficulty: Hard

8. Joey draws two cards from a standard deck of cards without replacement. What is the probability of Joey drawing an ace and then a king?

E. $\frac{1}{663}$ F. $\frac{4}{663}$ G. $\frac{1}{52}$ H. $\frac{1}{13}$

Difficulty: Hard

9. Timothy selects one card from a standard deck. What is the probability he will NOT select a heart?

A. $\frac{1}{4}$ B. $\frac{1}{2}$ C. $\frac{3}{4}$ D. $\frac{12}{13}$

Difficulty: Medium

10. A coin is tossed and a six-sided die is rolled. What is the probability of getting a tail on the coin and a number less than or equal to 3 on the die?

E. $\frac{1}{2}$ F. $\frac{1}{4}$ G. $\frac{1}{6}$ H. $\frac{1}{12}$

Difficulty: Hard

11. Maria has 2 children. What is the probability that her third child will be a girl?

A. $\frac{2}{3}$ B. $\frac{1}{2}$ C. $\frac{1}{3}$ D. $\frac{1}{6}$

Difficulty: Medium

12. Olivia bought a pack of balloons. There are 4 green balloons, 5 yellow balloons, 3 blue balloons and 6 red balloons. What is the probability of drawing a green balloon, replacing it, drawing a red balloon, replacing it, and then drawing a blue balloon?

E. $\frac{1}{81}$ F. $\frac{1}{54}$ G. $\frac{1}{27}$ H. $\frac{2}{9}$

Difficulty: Hard

13. In a pack of 20 candies, 8 are fruit candies and 12 are chocolate candies. If 3 candies are selected at random from the pack, one at a time without replacement, what is the probability that the first two candies are NOT fruit candies and the third candy is NOT a chocolate candy?

A. $\frac{44}{285}$ C. $\frac{12}{125}$

B. $\frac{18}{125}$ D. $\frac{14}{285}$

Difficulty: Hard

14. A spinner is divided into 8 equal sections as shown below. Tom spins the spinner 1 time. What is the probability that the spinner will land on Purple?

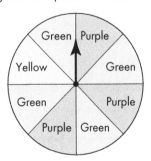

E. $\frac{1}{8}$ F. $\frac{1}{4}$ G. $\frac{3}{8}$ H. $\frac{1}{2}$

Difficulty: Medium

15. In a group of 20 students, there are 12 boys and 5 of them can speak Spanish. Three of the 8 girls can speak Spanish. If a student is selected randomly from the group, find the probability that the selected student **cannot** speak Spanish.

A. $\frac{1}{5}$ B. $\frac{2}{5}$ C. $\frac{3}{5}$ D. $\frac{1}{2}$

Difficulty: Hard

16. In a bag of 50 marbles, 20% of the marbles are green. What is the probability of randomly drawing a marble that is NOT green?

E. $\frac{1}{5}$ F. $\frac{2}{5}$ G. $\frac{4}{5}$ H. $\frac{1}{2}$

Difficulty: Medium

17. A box contains 30 books: 10 of them are non-fiction books and 4 of them are poetry. If Matthew picked one book at random, what is the probability that he picked a book that is NOT non-fiction or poetry?

Difficulty: Medium

18. A math test was given to a group of 35 students. Their results are summarized in the table below.

Range of scores	Number of students
81 – 85	9
86 – 89	12
90 – 95	11
96 – 100	3

What is the probability that a randomly picked student scored less than 90 on the math test?

Difficulty: Medium

19. Virginia rolled a die 5 times. What is the probability of the die landing on the number three all 5 times?

Difficulty: Medium

20. Calculate the probability of picking an even number from the list of numbers below:

54, 65, 32, 18, 19, 47, 84, 105

Difficulty: Medium

Answer Explanation

1. There are $8 + 4 + 3 = 15$ marbles in a bag.

The probability of drawing the white marble first is $\frac{3}{15}$ or $\frac{1}{5}$.

After drawing one marble, there are 14 marbles left. The probability of drawing a green marble is $\frac{8}{14}$ or $\frac{4}{7}$.

Multiply both probabilities to get the final result: $\frac{1}{5} \times \frac{4}{7} = \frac{4}{35}$.
The correct answer is A.

2. There are a total of $5 + 3 + 7 = 15$ marbles in a bag. Seven marbles are blue, therefore, $15 - 7 = 8$ marbles are not blue.

The probability of drawing the marble that is not blue is $\frac{8}{15}$.
The correct answer is H.

3. First, count the number of odd discs from 1 to 9: 1, 3, 5, 7, 9. Therefore, there are 5 odd discs. The probability of drawing an odd disc is $\frac{5}{9}$.

The disc is being replaced so the probability of selecting another odd disc will also be $\frac{5}{9}$.

The probability that both discs are odd is $\frac{5}{9} \times \frac{5}{9} = \frac{25}{81}$.

The correct answer is D.

4. First, find the number of patients whose condition was improved: $95 + 40 = 135$.

Now, we can find the probability that the patient who reported an improvement received a new medication: $\frac{95}{135} = \frac{19}{27}$.
The correct answer is E.

Video Explanations
at argoprep.com/shsat

5. The numbers that are less than 3 are 1 and 2. The frequency of rolling a 1 is 12 and the frequency of rolling a 2 is 7. The sum is $12 + 7 = 19$. The total number of outcomes is 50.

Therefore, the probability of rolling a number less than 3 is $\frac{19}{50}$.

The correct answer is A.

---

6. The total number of balls in the box is $5 + 3 + 7 + 2 = 17$. There are 3 yellow balls in the box so the probability of drawing a yellow ball is $\frac{3}{17}$.

The correct answer is F.

---

7. A standard deck of cards has 52 cards and there are 4 aces and 13 spades in it.

The probability of drawing an ace first is $\frac{4}{52}$.

Since the cards were drawn and then replaced, the events are independent and there are 52 possible outcomes in total for the second event.

Therefore, the probability of drawing a spade is $\frac{13}{52}$.

The probability of both events occurring together is $\frac{4}{52} \times \frac{13}{52} = \frac{1}{13} \times \frac{1}{4} = \frac{1}{52}$.

The correct answer is C.

---

8. The standard deck of cards has 52 cards and there are 4 aces and 4 kings.

The probability of drawing an ace first is $\frac{4}{52}$.

Since the cards were drawn without replacement, the events are dependent and there are 51 possible outcomes in total for the second event.

Therefore, the probability of drawing a king is $\frac{4}{51}$.

We can calculate the probability of these two events by multiplying: $\frac{4}{52} \times \frac{4}{51} = \frac{1}{13} \times \frac{4}{51} = \frac{4}{663}$.

The correct answer is F.

---

9. There are 13 hearts in a standard deck of cards. Therefore, there are $52 - 13 = 39$ cards, which are not hearts.

The probability of not selecting a heart is $\frac{39}{52} = \frac{3}{4}$.

The correct answer is C.

---

10. If a coin is tossed, there are only two possible outcomes – head or tail. Therefore, the probability of the coin landing on a tail is $\frac{1}{2}$.

When a six-sided die is rolled, there are 6 outcomes – 1, 2, 3, 4, 5, or 6.

Therefore, the probability of getting a number less than or equal to 3 is $\frac{3}{6}$ or $\frac{1}{2}$.

Multiply both probabilities to get the final result: $\frac{1}{2} \times \frac{1}{2} = \frac{1}{4}$.

The correct answer is F.

---

11. Don't get tricked by this question! The gender of a child is an independent event where you have only two possible outcomes - a boy or a girl. Therefore, the probability of having a third child that is a girl will be $\frac{1}{2}$.

The correct answer is B.

---

12. The total number of balloons in a pack is $4 + 5 + 3 + 6 = 18$.

The probability of drawing a green balloon is $\frac{4}{18} = \frac{2}{9}$.

When dealing with probability questions, you always want to be aware of replacement vs. no replacement. Since we are replacing, the events are independent and there will be 18 possible outcomes for the next drawing.

The probability of drawing a red balloon is $\frac{6}{18} = \frac{1}{3}$.

The probability of drawing a blue balloon is $\frac{3}{18} = \frac{1}{6}$.

Multiply to calculate the probability: $\frac{2}{9} \times \frac{1}{3} \times \frac{1}{6} = \frac{1}{81}$.

The correct answer is E.

---

13. The probability of selecting a candy that is not a fruit candy is the same as the probability of selecting a chocolate candy and it equals $\frac{12}{20} = \frac{3}{5}$.

The probability that a second candy is not a fruit candy (note that selection is made without replacement) is $\frac{11}{19}$.

Since the third selection is made without replacement, the probability of selecting a candy that is not a chocolate candy is the same as the probability of selecting a fruit candy and it equals $\frac{8}{18} = \frac{4}{9}$.

Multiply the three probabilities to get the final answer:

$$\frac{3}{5} \times \frac{11}{19} \times \frac{4}{9} = \frac{1}{5} \times \frac{11}{19} \times \frac{4}{3} = \frac{44}{285}$$

The correct answer is A.

14. First, count the number of purple sections, which is equal to 3. There are 8 sections in total, therefore, the probability of landing on a purple section is $\frac{3}{8}$.

The correct answer is G.

15. 5 of the 12 boys speak Spanish, therefore, $12 - 5 = 7$ boys cannot speak Spanish. 3 of the 8 girls can speak Spanish, therefore, $8 - 3 = 5$ girls cannot speak Spanish.

The number of the students who cannot speak Spanish is $7 + 5 = 12$.

There are 20 students in total, therefore the probability that the selected student cannot speak Spanish is $\frac{12}{20} = \frac{3}{5}$.

The correct answer is C.

16. First, find the number of marbles that are green: $50 \times 0.2 = 10$ marbles.

Then the number of marbles that are not green is $50 - 40 = 10$.

Find the probability of drawing a marble that is not green: $\frac{40}{50} = \frac{4}{5}$.

The correct answer is G.

17. First, find the number of books in the box other than non-fiction and poetry books: $30 - 10 - 4 = 16$.

Then the probability of drawing a book that is neither non-fiction nor poetry book is $\frac{16}{30} = \frac{8}{15}$.

18. Find the number of students that scored less than 90: $9 + 12 = 21$. The total number of students is 35 so the probability that a randomly picked student scored less than 90 is $\frac{21}{35} = \frac{3}{5}$.

19. The probability of landing on a 3 after a single die is rolled is $\frac{1}{6}$.

Rolling a die five times and landing on the number 3 is an independent event for each roll of the die.

Therefore, the probability of her landing on a three all five dice rolls is:

$$\frac{1}{6} \times \frac{1}{6} \times \frac{1}{6} \times \frac{1}{6} \times \frac{1}{6} = \frac{1}{7776}$$

20. There are eight numbers on the list.

There are four numbers that are even.

Therefore, the probability of picking a number that is even is $\frac{4}{8} = \frac{1}{2}$.

Video Explanations
at argoprep.com/shsat

1. James received the following scores on the last 5 math tests: 85, 87, 84, 82, 88. What score does James need on his sixth test to have an average of 86 on his math exams?

   A. 86   **B.** 87   **C.** 90   **D.** 93

   Difficulty: Medium

2. Michael has 5 candies, Steven has 3 candies, and Matt has 7 candies. If they want to divide the amount of candies evenly so everyone gets the same number of candies, how many candies would each of the three friends get?

   E. 3   **F.** 4   **G.** 5   **H.** 6

   Difficulty: Easy

3. Lucy has 5 cats, which weigh 4, 9, 7, 5 and 3 pounds respectively. What is the median weight?

   A. 4 lbs.   **B.** 5 lbs.   **C.** 6.5 lbs.   **D.** 8 lbs.

   Difficulty: Easy

4. The following table shows the scores on a biology quiz for a college class. Calculate the mean quiz score for the class. Round your answer to the nearest tenth.

Score	Number of students
85	6
89	4
87	5
91	3

   E. 85.5   **F.** 87.4   **G.** 88.2   **H.** 89.7

   Difficulty: Hard

5. The following table shows the scores on a math quiz for a college class. Calculate the median quiz score of the class.

Score	Number of students
82	3
84	3
87	2
90	4

   A. 83   **B.** 85.5   **C.** 86.5   **D.** 87.2

   Difficulty: Easy

6. The following table shows the scores of a college placement exam for a group of students. What is the mode?

Score	Number of students
84	3
86	4
89	6
92	4

   E. 85   **F.** 86.5   **G.** 89   **H.** 90

   Difficulty: Easy

7. John can run two miles in 15 minutes, Mark in 14, Jessica in 16, Julia in 13, Tommy in 12. What is the average run time for the five individuals?

   A. 12   **B.** 13.5   **C.** 14   **D.** 15.5

   Difficulty: Medium

8. Hilary sells ice cream and the following list shows the number of ice creams she sold last week.

   64, 75, 54, 86, 36, 49, 90

   What is the median number of ice creams Hilary sold last week?

   E. 86   **F.** 75.5   **G.** 64   **H.** 53

   Difficulty: Medium

Video Explanations
at argoprep.com/shsat

9. Daniel runs in the local park every morning. On Monday he ran 4 laps, on Tuesday 5 laps, on Wednesday 5 laps, on Thursday 7 laps, and on Friday 6 laps. If 1 lap is equal to 1.4 km, what is the average distance, in km, Daniel ran each day during the last 5 days?

A. 7.56 km   C. 7 km
B. 7.28 km   D. 5.4 km

Difficulty: Hard

10. The scores for a chemistry quiz are as follows: 15, 17, 16, 14, 19, 17, 18, 14, 13. What is the mean? Round your answer to the nearest tenth.

E. 17.6   G. 15.9
F. 16.5   H. 14.8

Difficulty: Medium

11. The scores for a math quiz are as followed: 15, 17, 16, 14, 19, 17, 18, 14, 15, 13. What is the median?

A. 14.5   B. 15   C. 15.5   D. 17

Difficulty: Easy

12. The daytime temperatures recorded over 5 consecutive days in January were −4.3°C, −5.5°C, 0.5°C, −2.7°C, and 1.5°C. What was the average temperature for the 5 days?

E. 0°C   G. −2.1°C
F. −1.5°C   H. −2.7°C

Difficulty: Medium

13. The following list of values shows the number of hours students spent working on their homework last week: 7, 6, 4, 6, 7, 8, 6, 5, 4, 6, 6, 10, and 7. What is the mode?

A. 5.4   B. 6   C. 6.3   D. 7

Difficulty: Easy

14. Julia has two sisters and one brother. The first sister is three years older than Julia. The second sister is two years younger than Julia. Julia's brother is five years older than Julia. Julia is 9 years old. What is the average of the ages of Julia and her siblings?

E. 11.5   F. 10.5   G. 10   H. 9

Difficulty: Hard

15. Carla kept track of the number of hours she slept each night for the past week. She organized the data in a table as shown below:

Day	Number of hours Carla slept
Monday	7
Tuesday	6
Wednesday	7
Thursday	8
Friday	6
Saturday	9
Sunday	9

What is the average number of hours Carla slept each night for the past week? Round your answer to the nearest tenth.

A. 8.3   B. 8   C. 7.4   D. 6

Difficulty: Medium

16. Robert's scores on the algebra tests were 78, 85, 87, 83, and 90 and his scores on the biology tests were 85, 89, 81, 93, and 90. What is the sum of the mean of algebra tests and the median of the biology tests?

E. 165.6   G. 170.5
F. 169   H. 173.6

Difficulty: Hard

Video Explanations
at argoprep.com/shsat

17. Eight people in a group weigh 65 kg, 75 kg, 59 kg, 80 kg, 68 kg, 77 kg, 63 kg, and 72 kg. What is the median?

Difficulty: Medium

18. Mia bought a pack of candies and decided to share with her friends. Two of her friends received three candies each, three of her friends received two candies each and five of her friends received one candy each. What is the average number of candies each friend received? Round your answer to the nearest tenth.

Difficulty: Hard

19. A local restaurant sold 34, 56, 45, and 29 pizzas over the last 4 days. How many pizzas should the restaurant sell on the fifth day, if they would like to have an average of 45 pizzas sold over the past 5 days?.

Difficulty: Hard

20. A group of friends went running in the city park. Two friends ran two miles, four friends ran 2.5 miles, three friends ran three miles, two friends ran 4.2 miles and the last two friends ran five miles. What is the median distance run (in miles)?

Difficulty: Medium

Answer Explanation

1. Let x be the score for the sixth test:

Use the average formula and plug in your known numbers to solve the problem.

$$\frac{85+87+84+82+88+x}{6} = 86$$

Cross multiply:

$$85+87+84+82+88+x = 516$$
$$426 + x = 516$$
$$x = 516 - 426 = 90$$

James needs to score a 90 on the sixth test in order to get an average math score of 86.

The correct answer is C.

2. Add the number of candies the three friends have and divide by the number of friends.

$$\frac{5+3+7}{3} = \frac{15}{3} = 5$$

Each of the three friends would get 5 candies.

The correct answer is G.

3. Arrange the weights of cats in ascending order.

We have: 3, 4, 5, 7, 9. The median is the middle value. Since we have 5 numbers, the median is the third number, which is 5.

The correct answer is B.

4. To calculate the mean quiz score, multiply each score by the corresponding number of students, add the results together, and divide by the total number of students in the class.

$$\frac{(85\times6)+(89\times4)+(87\times5)+(91\times3)}{18} = \frac{510+356+435+273}{18} \approx 87.4$$

The correct answer is F.

5. Write down all the scores: 82, 82, 82, 84, 84, 84, 87, 87, 90, 90, 90, 90. Our list is already in ascending order so we can find the median. There are two numbers in the middle (84 and 87) so we will need to find the average of these two numbers to find the median. $\frac{84+87}{2} = 85.5$. The median is 85.5.

The correct answer is B.

6. The mode is the number that is repeated more often than any other number. The right hand column of the table shows the frequency of students, so the largest number in that column will represent the mode. We have 6 students who scored an 89, so the mode is 89.

The correct answer is G.

7. Use the average formula.

$$\frac{15+14+16+13+12}{5} = \frac{70}{5} = 14$$

The correct answer is C.

▶ **Video Explanations**
at argoprep.com/shsat

8. Arrange the numbers in ascending order: 36, 49, 54, 64, 75, 86, 90. We have 7 data values so the middle number is $\frac{7+1}{2} = 4$. The 4th number is 64. Therefore, the median is 64.

The correct answer is G.

9. Convert the distances to kilometers for each day:

Monday = 4 × 1.4 = 5.6 km

Tuesday = 5 × 1.4 = 7 km

Wednesday = 5 × 1.4 = 7 km

Thursday = 7 × 1.4 = 9.8 km

Friday = 6 × 1.4 = 8.4 km

To find the mean, add all the distances together and divide by the number of days.

$$\frac{5.6+7+7+9.8+8.4}{5} = 7.56 \text{ km}$$

The correct answer is A.

10. To find the mean of the scores, add all the scores together and divide the result by the total number of scores.

$$\frac{15+17+16+14+19+17+18+14+13}{9} \approx 15.9$$

The correct answer is G.

11. Arrange the numbers in ascending order: 13, 14, 14, 15, 15, 16, 17, 17, 18, 19. There are two middle numbers and in order to find the median, we need to find the average of the 5th and 6th term. $\frac{15+16}{2} = 15.5$.

Therefore, the median is 15.5.

The correct answer is C.

12. Add all the temperatures together and divide by the number of days:

$$\frac{-4.3+(-5.5)+0.5+(-2.7)+1.5}{5} = \frac{-4.3-5.5+0.5-2.7+1.5}{5}$$

$$= \frac{-10.5}{5} = -2.1°C$$

The correct answer is G.

13. Examine the list of data values and count which number is repeated more often than any other number. The number 6 is repeated five times and is repeated more than any of the other numbers.

Therefore, the mode is 6.

The correct answer is B.

14. The question tells us that Julia is 9 years old. We can find the ages of her siblings. Her first sister is three years older, so 9 + 3 = 12. Her second sister is two years younger, so 9 − 2 = 7. Her brother is five years older, so 9 + 5 = 14.

Add the ages of Julia and her siblings to find the sum and divide by 4.

$$\frac{9+12+7+14}{4} = 10.5$$

The average is 10.5.

The correct answer is F.

15. Add the numbers together and divide by 7, which is the number of days.

$$\frac{7+6+7+8+6+9+9}{7} = \frac{52}{7} \approx 7.4$$

The mean number of hours Carla slept is 7.4 hours.

The correct answer is C.

16. Calculate the mean of the algebra tests. To find the mean, add all scores together and divide by the number of algebra tests Robert took.

$$\frac{78+85+87+83+90}{5} = 84.6$$

Then, find the median of the biology tests that Robert took. Put the numbers in ascending order: 81, 85, 89, 90, 93.

The middle value is $\frac{5+1}{2} = 3$rd value, which equals to 89.

Therefore, the sum of the mean of the algebra tests and the median of biology tests is $84.6+89 = 173.6$.

The correct answer is H.

17. Put the numbers in ascending order: 59, 63, 65, 68, 72, 75, 77, 80.

The middle value is $\frac{8+1}{2} = 4.5$, which equals to $\frac{68+72}{2} = 70$.

Therefore, the median is **70 kg**.

18. The total number of friends is: 2 + 3 + 5 = 10.

Calculate the total number of candies each friend received.

$$(2\times3)+(3\times2)+(5\times1) = 6+6+5 = 17$$

Divide the total number of candies by the total number of friends to find the average.

$$\frac{17}{10} = \textbf{1.7 candies}$$

Video Explanations
at argoprep.com/shsat

19. Let x represent the number of pizzas sold on the fifth day.

Use the average formula and plug in the values.

$$\frac{34+56+45+29+x}{5} = 45$$

Cross multiply and find the value of x :

$$34+56+45+29+x = 225$$
$$164+x = 225$$
$$x = 225-164 = 61$$

The restaurant should sell 61 pizzas on the fifth day.

---

20. Write down all the data values and pay attention to the number of individuals that correspond to each distance.

Therefore, we have: 2, 2, 2.5, 2.5, 2.5, 2.5, 3, 3, 3, 4.2, 4.2, 5, 5. We have 13 data values. Therefore, the middle value is $\frac{13+1}{2} = 7$, which equals 3.

Therefore, the median is 3.

1. What is the number of possible rearrangements of the letters in the word WORLD?

   A. 5   **B.** 24   **C.** 60   **D.** 120

   Difficulty: Medium

2. Jenny has 5 jackets and 6 pairs of shoes. How many different combinations of jackets and shoes can she make?

   E. 5   **F.** 11   **G.** 30   **H.** 45

   Difficulty: Medium

3. A restaurant allows the selection of one salad, one soup, one main course and one dessert. Steven has the option to choose from five salads, four soups, six main courses and four desserts. What is the possible number of combinations Steven could have for lunch?

   A. 480   **B.** 120   **C.** 80   **D.** 19

   Difficulty: Medium

4. There are 3 spaces to fill and 6 choices for each. How many combinations are there to fill the spaces?

   E. 2   **F.** 9   **G.** 18   **H.** 216

   Difficulty: Medium

5. Tommy flipped a coin and rolled a die. What is the total number of possible outcomes?

   A. 12   **B.** 8   **C.** 4   **D.** 3

   Difficulty: Hard

6. Natalie is going for an interview and she has to choose what to wear. She has 6 shirts, 4 pairs of pants, and 5 pairs of shoes. How many possible outfit combinations does she have?

   E. 15   **F.** 29   **G.** 34   **H.** 120

   Difficulty: Medium

7. Joanna has a list of her seven favorite movies and she wants to watch them in a specific order. In how many different ways can she choose to watch the movies?

   A. 5040   **C.** 49
   B. 120   **D.** 7

   Difficulty: Hard

8. Michael is creating a password which must have 4 letters without repetition followed by 3 digits that may be repeated. How many different passwords can be formed?

   E. 12   **G.** 362
   F. 260   **H.** 358,800,000

   Difficulty: Hard

9. A coin is tossed 8 times. What is the total number of possible outcomes?

   A. 8   **C.** 256
   B. 16   **D.** 16,777,216

   Difficulty: Hard

10. Four dies are rolled. What is the total number of possible outcomes?

    E. 10   **G.** 1296
    F. 24   **H.** 4096

    Difficulty: Medium

11. Tania is going from city A to city D passing through cities B and C. There are 3 different roads between cities A and B, 4 different roads between cities B and C, and 2 different roads between cities C and D. How many routes can Tania take to go from city A to city D passing through cities B and C?

    A. 3   **B.** 9   **C.** 14   **D.** 24

    Difficulty: Medium

Video Explanations
at argoprep.com/shsat

12. Jaleen can select one of 3 non-fiction books, one of 4 fiction books and one of 5 poetry books to check out from the library. How many possible combinations are there for Jaleen to select one non-fiction, one fiction and one poetry book?

E. 60   **F.** 23   **G.** 12   **H.** 3

Difficulty: Medium

13. A pizza restaurant offers 7 meat toppings, 6 vegetable toppings, and 5 cheese toppings. How many different kinds of pizzas can be ordered with 1 meat topping, 1 vegetable topping and 1 cheese topping?

A. 3   **B.** 13   **C.** 18   **D.** 210

Difficulty: Medium

14. Laura went to dinner at her local restaurant. She can choose from 3 appetizers, 3 soups, 5 salads, 4 main courses, 8 beverages and 3 desserts. Laura must select: one appetizer, soup, salad, main course, beverage and dessert.

How many possible combinations are there?

E. 4320   **G.** 256
F. 1250   **H.** 26

Difficulty: Medium

15. How many six-character codes are possible if the first three characters are numerical and the last three characters are letters? Repetition of letters and numbers is allowed.

A. 11,232,000   **C.** 15,600,000
B. 12,654,720   **D.** 17,576,000

Difficulty: Hard

16. Mark plans to buy a computer system. He can choose from 3 computers, 5 monitors, 3 keyboards, and 4 printers. How many possible system combinations are there?

E. 4   **F.** 15   **G.** 180   **H.** 240

Difficulty: Medium

17. At a local blood bank, each blood sample is labeled according to the blood type and Rh factor. If there are four blood types and two Rh factors possible, what is the total number of ways the blood samples can be labeled?

Difficulty: Medium

18. Maria wants to buy an ice cream and a frozen juice. An ice cream shop offers 7 different fruit ice creams and 6 kinds of frozen juices. In addition, you can choose a small, medium or large waffle cone for the ice cream.

What are the possible combinations Maria could have if she chooses 1 ice cream and 1 fruit juice?

Difficulty: Hard

19. John and Marta are looking to purchase a furniture set for their new house. They are choosing from 5 couches, 7 tables, 4 book shelves, and 5 double beds. How many different combinations are possible?

Difficulty: Medium

20. On each of the five weekdays, Monica can take a quiz in either math, biology, chemistry, history, or literature. Repetition is not allowed and she can complete only one quiz per day. How many combinations are there in which Monica can arrange her quizzes to be completed in 5 days?

Difficulty: Hard

Video Explanations
at argoprep.com/shsat

1. Since there are 5 letters in the word WORLD and all of them are distinct, simply calculate the value of 5!

   Having trouble with the Counting Principle? Check out our video lectures at www.argoprep.com/shsat

   We have:
   $$5! = 5 \times 4 \times 3 \times 2 \times 1 = 120$$
   The correct answer is D.

2. The first event is choosing a jacket and it has 5 options, while the second event is choosing a pair of shoes and it has 6 different options. Therefore, the total number of possible combinations is $5 \times 6 = 30$.

   The correct answer is G.

3. Multiply the numbers together to find the number of possible combinations Steven can use to choose the lunch.

   We have:
   $$5 \times 4 \times 6 \times 4 = 480$$
   The correct answer is A.

4. Since 6 choices are available for each of 3 spaces, then using the fundamental counting principle, we can calculate the number of ways we can fill the spaces:
   $$6 \times 6 \times 6 = 216$$
   The correct answer is H.

5. Flipping a coin gives us two outcomes, while rolling a die has 6 outcomes.

   According to the fundamental counting principle, when each of two events has a certain number of outcomes, then the number of ways the two events can occur is calculated by multiplying their number of outcomes.

   Therefore, we have:
   $$2 \times 6 = 12$$
   Tommy can get 12 outcomes when flipping a coin and rolling a die together.

   The correct answer is A.

6. According to the fundamental counting principle, if there are m ways to make a first selection and n ways to make a second selection, then there are $m \times n$ ways to make selections.

   Therefore, we have:
   $$6 \times 4 \times 5 = 120$$
   Natalie can choose her outfit for an interview in 120 ways.

   The correct answer is H.

7. There are 7 movies to choose from for the first movie Joanna will select. The second movie Joanna will select has only 6 options since Joanna already selected one movie for the first one. The third movie Joanna will select has only 5 options and so on. Notice each time we decrease by one.

   Therefore, we have:
   $$7 \times 6 \times 5 \times 4 \times 3 \times 2 \times 1 = 5040$$
   Joanna can arrange 7 movies in 5040 ways.

   The correct answer is A.

8. Since repetition is not allowed for letters, 26 letters (the number of letters in the alphabet) are possible for the first letter, 25 for the second letter, 24 for the third letter, and 23 for the fourth letter. On the other hand, 10 choices of digits are available: 0, 1, 2, 3, 4, 5, 6, 7, 8, 9. Since repetition is allowed for digits, each of 3 digits has 10 choices.

   Therefore, the number of possible passwords is:
   $$26 \times 25 \times 24 \times 23 \times 10 \times 10 \times 10 = 358,800,000$$
   You are not required to do the actual calculations for this problem. Notice answers E, F, G all have small answer choices. It would be extremely time consuming to do the actual calculation for this question and the SHSAT exam will not give you a question that requires lengthy and time-consuming calculations. Always analyze the answer choices and see how to use that to your advantage.

   The correct answer is H.

9. Each time the coin is tossed, there will be only two outcomes – heads or tails. Therefore, if the coin is tossed 8 times, we have the following:
   $$2 \times 2 \times 2 \times 2 \times 2 \times 2 \times 2 \times 2 = 256$$
   If the coin is tossed 8 times, the number of possible outcomes is 256.

   The correct answer is C.

10. When a single die is rolled, the number of possible outcomes is 6. Since rolling four dice is an independent event, the total number of possible outcomes equals $6 \times 6 \times 6 \times 6 = 1296$.

    The correct answer is G.

11. According to the fundamental counting principle, you need to multiply the number of roads between each pair of cities to get the number of ways Tania can go from city A to city D passing through cities B and C.

    Therefore, we have:
    $$3 \times 4 \times 2 = 24$$
    The correct answer is D.

Video Explanations at argoprep.com/shsat

12. According to the fundamental counting principle, if there are m ways to make a first selection and n ways to make a second selection, then there are $m \times n$ ways to make selections.

Therefore, we have:
$$3 \times 4 \times 5 = 60$$

Jaleen can select a non-fiction, fiction and poetry book a total of 60 ways.

The correct answer is E.

---

13. According to the fundamental counting principle, if there are m ways to make a first selection and n ways to make a second selection, then there are $m \times n$ ways to make selections.

Therefore, we have:
$$7 \times 6 \times 5 = 210$$

210 different kinds of pizza can be ordered.

The correct answer is D.

---

14. According to the fundamental counting principle, if there are m ways to make a first selection and n ways to make a second selection, then there are $m \times n$ ways to make selections.

Therefore, we have:
$$3 \times 3 \times 5 \times 4 \times 8 \times 3 = 4320$$

Therefore, they can choose their menu 4320 ways.

The correct answer is E.

---

15. Since the repetition of letters and numbers is allowed, there are 26 letters for each of the first three characters and 10 numerical options (0, 1, 2, 3, 4, 5, 6, 7, 8, 9) for each of the last three characters.

Therefore, we have:
$$26 \times 26 \times 26 \times 10 \times 10 \times 10 = 17,576,000$$

Although this question looks like it has lengthy calculations, you are working with easy numbers. You can calculate 26 × 26 × 26 = 17,576. We also have 10 × 10 × 10 which is just adding three more zeros to the number 17,576 to get 17,576,000.

The correct answer is D.

---

16. According to the fundamental counting principle, if there are m ways to make a first selection and n ways to make a second selection, then there are $m \times n$ ways to make selections.

Therefore, we have:
$$3 \times 5 \times 3 \times 4 = 180$$

Mark can choose from 180 computer systems.

The correct answer is G.

17. According to the fundamental counting principle, if there are m ways to make a first selection and n ways to make a second selection, then there are $m \times n$ ways to make selections.

Therefore, we have:
$$4 \times 2 = 8$$

The correct answer is 8.

---

18. According to the fundamental counting principle, if there are m ways to make a first selection and n ways to make a second selection, then there are $m \times n$ ways to make selections. Maria can choose from 7 kinds of ice creams, 3 sizes of waffle cone for the ice cream, and from 6 kinds of frozen juice.

Therefore, we have:
$$7 \times 3 \times 6 = 126$$

The answer is **126**.

---

19. According to the fundamental counting principle, if there are m ways to make a first selection and n ways to make a second selection, then there are $m \times n$ ways to make selections.

Therefore, we have:
$$5 \times 7 \times 4 \times 5 = 700$$

700 different combinations are possible.

---

20. There are 5 subjects to choose from for the first day, 4 subjects for the second day, 3 subjects for the third day, 2 subjects for the fourth day, and 1 subject for the fifth day. Therefore, the number of ways she can arrange the quizzes is equal to $5 \times 4 \times 3 \times 2 \times 1 =$ **120 ways**.

Video Explanations
at argoprep.com/shsat

1. If James chooses a number at random from the list below, what is the probability that he will pick an odd number?

   3, 7, 18, 4, 75, 53, 97, 86, 115, 43

   A. $\frac{1}{5}$ B. $\frac{3}{10}$ C. $\frac{7}{10}$ D. $\frac{4}{5}$

   Difficulty: Easy

2. What is the number of possible rearrangements of the letters in the word MOTHER?

   E. 6   G. 720
   F. 120   H. 46656

   Difficulty: Medium

3. Nina is going for a walk and she is choosing her outfit. She can choose from 5 skirts, 7 shirts, and 4 pairs of shoes. What is the number of possible outfits?

   A. 185 B. 140 C. 16 D. 3

   Difficulty: Medium

4. Michael has a list of his 9 favorite books and he wants to read them in a specific order. In how many ways can he choose to read these books?

   E. 91   G. 362,800
   F. 81   H. 387,420,489

   Difficulty: Hard

5. A bank account password must be composed of 5 numeric digits without repetition. What is the possible number of passwords that can be generated?

   A. 5   C. 30,240
   B. 10   D. 100,000

   Difficulty: Hard

6. Ronald tossed a coin 3 times and rolled a die 2 times. What is the probability of getting 3 heads and 2 fours?

   E. $\frac{1}{5}$ F. $\frac{1}{92}$ G. $\frac{1}{240}$ H. $\frac{1}{288}$

   Difficulty: Hard

7. At a student buffet, George can choose lunch from 3 salads, 2 soups, 4 main courses, and 5 drinks. How many combinations are there in which George can choose his lunch if he can select one salad, one soup, one main course and one drink?

   A. 120 B. 60 C. 14 D. 4

   Difficulty: Medium

8. Tina worked out at a gym four days during the week. She spent 50 minutes at the gym on Monday, 45 minutes on Wednesday, 70 minutes on Friday, and 55 minutes on Sunday. What is the average time she spent at the gym?

   E. 48 minutes   G. 55 minutes
   F. 53 minutes   H. 60 minutes

   Difficulty: Medium

9. The temperature for five different cities around the world in the month of March were as follows:

City	Temperature
New York	11°C
Hong Kong	28°C
Vancouver	10°C
Auckland	18°C
London	7°C

   What is the average temperature of these 5 cities?

   A. 11.2°C   C. 16.5°C
   B. 14.8°C   D. 18.3°C

   Difficulty: Medium

 **Video Explanations**
at argoprep.com/shsat

10. Mike sells notebooks at a local computer store. On the first week of January, he sold 5 notebooks, on the second week – 7 notebooks, on the third week – 4 notebooks, and on the fourth week – 8 notebooks. What is the median number of notebooks sold?

E. 4.5 **F.** 5 **G.** 6 **H.** 6.5

Difficulty: Medium

11. A die is rolled 100 times and the results are shown in the table below:

Outcome	Frequency
1	14
2	18
3	23
4	21
5	15
6	9

What is the probability of getting a number greater than or equal to 4?

A. 0.24 **C.** 0.45
B. 0.36 **D.** 0.58

Difficulty: Medium

12. John and Marta have 3 sons and 4 daughters. What is the probability that their next child will be a boy?

E. $\frac{2}{3}$ **F.** $\frac{1}{2}$ **G.** $\frac{1}{3}$ **H.** $\frac{1}{4}$

Difficulty: Medium

13. Alex is drawing two cards from a standard deck, one at a time, without replacement. What is the probability of getting two spades?

A. $\frac{1}{17}$ **B.** $\frac{2}{17}$ **C.** $\frac{4}{17}$ **D.** $\frac{1}{4}$

Difficulty: Hard

14. Jessica is choosing a running outfit. She chooses one each from 5 pairs of running shoes, 8 pairs of running pants, and 5 running T-shirts. How many running outfit combinations does Jessica have?

E. 3 **F.** 18 **G.** 120 **H.** 200

Difficulty: Medium

15. What is the number of possible rearrangements of the letters in the word CHEMISTRY?

A. 9 **C.** 2,564
B. 81 **D.** 362,880

Difficulty: Hard

16. What is the probability of randomly choosing the letter O in LOCATION?

E. $\frac{3}{4}$ **F.** $\frac{2}{3}$ **G.** $\frac{1}{4}$ **H.** $\frac{1}{8}$

Difficulty: Medium

17. The following list of numbers shows the scores that the students got on a math entrance exam:

525, 580, 545, 598, 525, 495,
587, 482, 547, 574

What is the median of the scores?

A. 525 **C.** 546
B. 545.8 **D.** 569.5

Difficulty: Medium

18. Three cards are chosen at random, one at a time, from a standard deck of cards, without replacement. What is the probability that the first card is an ace, the second card is a queen, and the third card is a king?

E. $\frac{3}{52}$ **G.** $\frac{1}{2197}$

F. $\frac{1}{13}$ **H.** $\frac{8}{16575}$

Difficulty: Hard

Video Explanations
at argoprep.com/shsat

19. There are 8 white marbles, 8 yellow marbles, and 8 green marbles in a bag. If three marbles are drawn at random, one at a time and without replacement, what is the probability that the first marble is white, the second marble is yellow and the third marble is green?

A. $\frac{1}{512}$ B. $\frac{32}{759}$ C. $\frac{1}{8}$ D. $\frac{3}{8}$

Difficulty: Hard

20. A spinner is divided into 8 equal sections. Maria spins a spinner one time. What is the probability of the spinner landing on Purple or Yellow?

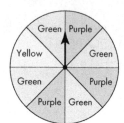

E. $\frac{1}{8}$ F. $\frac{3}{8}$ G. $\frac{1}{2}$ H. $\frac{2}{3}$

Difficulty: Hard

21. Mia picked a card from a standard deck, replaced it, and picked a new card. What is the probability that the first card was red and the second card was black?

A. $\frac{1}{2}$ B. $\frac{1}{4}$ C. $\frac{1}{5}$ D. $\frac{1}{13}$

Difficulty: Hard

22. A restaurant offers a special dinner package that allows diners to select one salad, one soup, one main course, one dessert and one beverage. Diners can select from two salads, four soups, five main courses, three desserts and seven beverages. How many possible meal combinations are there?

E. 5 F. 21 G. 840 H. 1120

Difficulty: Medium

23. On a chemistry final exam, twelve students scored 85, five students scored 89, seven students scored 93 and fifteen students scored 83. What is the mode of the scores?

A. 83 B. 85 C. 86.2 D. 88.4

Difficulty: Easy

24. On a chemistry final exam, twelve students scored 85, five students scored 89, seven students scored 93 and fifteen students scored 83. What is the median of the scores? Round your answer to the nearest tenth.

E. 87.5 G. 85
F. 86.2 H. 83

Difficulty: Medium

25. On a chemistry final exam, twelve students scored 85, five students scored 89, seven students scored 93 and fifteen students scored 83. What is the average of the scores? Round your answer to the nearest tenth.

A. 83 C. 86.2
B. 85 D. 87.3

Difficulty: Medium

26. How many four-character codes are possible if the first two characters are letters and the last two characters are numbers? Repetition of letters and numbers is not allowed.

E. 4 G. 58,500
F. 24 H. 67,600

Difficulty: Hard

27. Kevin is traveling to a new country and he is planning to see five different places in five days. In how many ways can he arrange his itinerary?

A. 5 B. 25 C. 65 D. 120

Difficulty: Medium

Video Explanations
at argoprep.com/shsat

28. In a group of 35 students, 20% are Spanish, 40% are Caucasian and the rest are American. What is the probability that a student chosen at random is neither Spanish nor American?

E. $\frac{2}{5}$ **F.** $\frac{4}{35}$ **G.** $\frac{1}{5}$ **H.** $\frac{3}{5}$

Difficulty: Hard

29. There are 30 students in a class and 13 of them are boys. If 2 boys and 3 girls are absent, what is the probability that a randomly selected student is not a boy?

A. $\frac{11}{25}$ **B.** $\frac{14}{25}$ **C.** $\frac{11}{30}$ **D.** $\frac{7}{15}$

Difficulty: Hard

30. Julia bought a pack of balloons. There are 5 yellow balloons, 7 violet balloons, 6 green balloons and 8 red balloons. If she randomly picks a balloon, replaces it, picks a second balloon, and then picks a third balloon without replacement of the second balloon, what is the probability that all three balloons are not red?

E. $\frac{128}{4,225}$ **G.** $\frac{112}{4,225}$

F. $\frac{1,377}{4,225}$ **H.** $\frac{1,377}{4,394}$

Difficulty: Hard

31. A pair of dice is rolled. What is the probability of getting a number less than 3 on the first die and a number greater than or equal to 4 on the second die?

A. $\frac{1}{6}$ **B.** $\frac{1}{3}$ **C.** $\frac{2}{3}$ **D.** $\frac{5}{6}$

Difficulty: Hard

32. If a fair coin is flipped 20 times, what is the probability of landing on heads the first 10 times and landing it on tails the last 10 times?

E. $\frac{1}{2}$ **G.** $\frac{1}{100}$

F. $\frac{1}{20}$ **H.** $\frac{1}{1,048,576}$

Difficulty: Hard+

33. A card is selected at random from a standard deck, then replaced, and the second card is selected. Let's call the first selection of the card Event A, which results in the drawing of a red card. The selection of the second card, Event B, results in an ace. Are events A and B dependent?

Difficulty: Medium

34. John spins a spinner and rolls a die. What is the probability of getting A on the spinner and 5 on the die?

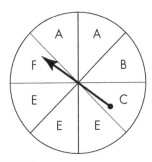

Difficulty: Hard

35. Mike spins a spinner and flips a coin. What is the probability of getting E on the spinner and the coin landing on heads?

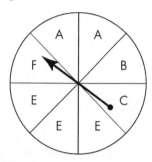

Difficulty: Hard

36. Jimmy runs every morning. His running speeds on 5 different days were 6 miles/hour, 7 miles/hour, 4 miles/hour, 5 miles/hour, and 6 miles/hour. What is the average speed for these five days?

Difficulty: Medium

37. What is the median for the list below?

153, 81, 64, 89, 63, 78, 36, 73, 95, 34

Difficulty: Medium

38. Michael needs to take a chemistry, biology, history and math exam in the next four days. He can only take one exam per day and he can choose the order in which he wants to take the exam. In how many different combinations can Michael choose to take the exams?

Difficulty: Medium

39. Virginia bought 3 apples, 4 mangos, 5 bananas, 6 pears and 10 lemons and put them in one bag. What is the probability that she randomly selects a fruit that is not a lemon or a pear?

Difficulty: Hard

40. The heights of twelve toddlers were recorded at a local health center. The unit of measurement was centimeters.

67, 68, 71, 69, 65, 75, 63, 71, 65, 62, 61, 70

What is the average height of the twelve toddlers?

Difficulty: Medium

Answer Explanation

1. The number is odd when it is not a multiple of two. Therefore, there are 7 odd numbers. There are 10 numbers in the list. The probability that James picked an odd number is $\frac{7}{10}$.
The correct answer is C.

2. Since there are 6 letters in the word MOTHER and all of them are distinct, calculate the value of 6! to find the number of possible rearrangements:
$$6! = 6 \times 5 \times 4 \times 3 \times 2 \times 1 = 720$$
The correct answer is G.

3. According to the fundamental counting principle, if there are m ways to make a first selection and n ways to make a second selection, then there are $m \times n$ ways to make selections.
Therefore, we have:
$$5 \times 7 \times 4 = 140$$
The correct answer is B.

4. Michael can place 9 books in the first place, 8 books in the second place, 7 books in the third place, and so on.
Therefore, we have:
$$9 \times 8 \times 7 \times 6 \times 5 \times 4 \times 3 \times 2 \times 1 = 362,880$$
The correct answer is G.

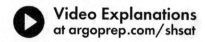
Video Explanations
at argoprep.com/shsat

5. There are 10 digits in total: 0, 1, 2, 3, 4, 5, 6, 7, 8, 9.

Since repetition is not allowed, the first position can be chosen from 10 digits, the second position from 9 digits, and so on.

Therefore, we have:

$$10 \times 9 \times 8 \times 7 \times 6 = 30,240$$

The SHSAT is unlikely to give you a problem like this due to the lengthy calculations. However, these are some great probability questions which you should know!

The correct answer is C.

6. There are two possible outcomes when tossing a coin: heads or tails. The probability of getting a head is $\frac{1}{2}$. There are 6 possible outcomes when rolling a die: 1, 2, 3, 4, 5, 6. The probability of getting a four is $\frac{1}{6}$.

All events are independent of each other so we have:

$$\frac{1}{2} \times \frac{1}{2} \times \frac{1}{2} \times \frac{1}{6} \times \frac{1}{6} = \frac{1}{288}$$

The correct answer is H.

7. According to the fundamental counting principle, if there are m ways to make a first selection and n ways to make a second selection, then there are $m \times n$ ways to make selections.

Therefore, we have:

$$3 \times 2 \times 4 \times 5 = 120$$

The correct answer is A.

8. To find the average time she spent at the gym, add the numbers together and divide by the number of days Tina worked out at the gym.

Therefore, we have:

$$\frac{50+45+70+55}{4} = 55$$

The average time Tina spent at the gym is 55 minutes.

The correct answer is G.

9. To find the average temperature, calculate the temperature together and divide by the number of cities.

$$\frac{11+28+10+18+7}{5} = 14.8°C$$

The correct answer is B.

10. The list of the number of notebooks sold during 4 weeks in January is 5, 7, 4, 8.

Order the numbers in ascending order: 4, 5, 7, 8.

The median value is $\frac{(4+1)}{2} = 2.5$, which is equal to $\frac{5+7}{2} = 6$.

The median is 6.

The correct answer is G.

11. The probability of getting a number greater than or equal to 4 means getting 4, 5, or 6 as an outcome. Therefore, add the frequencies of getting 4, 5, and 6 and divide by 100.

$$\frac{21+15+9}{100} = \frac{45}{100} = 0.45$$

The correct answer is C.

12. Having a son or daughter is independent of the gender of other children. There are only two possible outcomes: son or daughter. Therefore, the probability that John's and Marta's next child will be a boy is $\frac{1}{2}$.

The correct answer is F.

13. The two events are dependent because the drawing of the cards was made without replacement. There are 13 spades in a standard deck of cards so the probability of getting a spade is $\frac{13}{52} = \frac{1}{4}$. The probability of getting a second spade is $\frac{12}{51} = \frac{4}{17}$.

The probability of getting two spades is $\frac{1}{4} \times \frac{4}{17} = \frac{1}{17}$.

Confused with these dependent vs. independent events? Check out our video lectures at www.argoprep.com/shsat

The correct answer is A.

14. According to the fundamental counting principle, if there are m ways to make a first selection and n ways to make a second selection, then there are $m \times n$ ways to make selections.

Therefore, we have:

$$5 \times 8 \times 5 = 200$$

Jessica can choose 200 different running outfits.

The correct answer is H.

15. There are 9 letters in the word CHEMISTRY and all of them are distinct. Therefore, 9 letters can be placed in the first position, 8 letters in the second position, and so on.

We have:

$$9\times8\times7\times6\times5\times4\times3\times2\times1=362{,}880$$

Therefore, the number of possible rearrangements of letters in the word CHEMISTRY is 362,880.

The SHSAT is unlikely to give you a problem like this due to the lengthy calculations. However, these are some great probability questions which you should know!

The correct answer is D.

16. The number of letters in the word LOCATION is 8 and the number of O's is 2.

Find the probability of getting the letter O:

$$\frac{2}{8}=\frac{1}{4}$$

The correct answer is G.

17. Before finding the median value, arrange the numbers in ascending order:

482, 495, 525, 525, 545, 547, 574, 580, 587, 598

There are 10 values in the list so the median value is between the 5th and 6th value.

$$\frac{545+547}{2}=546$$

The median is 546.

The correct answer is C.

18. There are 52 cards in a standard deck: 4 aces, 4 queens, and 4 kings.

Note that cards were chosen without replacement.

The probability that the first card is an ace is $\frac{4}{52}=\frac{1}{13}$.

The probability that the second card is a queen is $\frac{4}{51}$.

The probability that the third card is a king is $\frac{4}{50}=\frac{2}{25}$.

Multiply the probabilities to get the final result:

$\frac{1}{13}\times\frac{4}{51}\times\frac{2}{25}=\frac{8}{16575}$.

The correct answer is H.

19. The number of marbles in the bag is 8 + 8 + 8 = 24.

The probability that the first marble is white is $\frac{8}{24}=\frac{1}{3}$.

The probability that the second marble is yellow is $\frac{8}{23}$.

The probability that the third marble is green is $\frac{8}{22}=\frac{4}{11}$.

Therefore, the probability that the first marble is white, the second marble is yellow, and the third marble is green is

$\frac{1}{3}\times\frac{8}{23}\times\frac{4}{11}=\frac{32}{759}$.

The correct answer is B.

20. There are 3 Purple sections and 1 Yellow section. Landing either on Purple or on Yellow equals 3 + 1 = 4.

The probability of landing either on Purple or on Yellow is $\frac{4}{8}=\frac{1}{2}$.

The correct answer is G.

21. There are 26 black cards and 26 red cards in a standard deck.

The probability of picking a red card is $\frac{26}{52}=\frac{1}{2}$. Since the selection was made with replacement, then the probability of drawing a black card is the same.

Multiply both probabilities to find the probability that the first card was red and the second card was black: $\frac{1}{2}\times\frac{1}{2}=\frac{1}{4}$.

The correct answer is A.

22. According to the fundamental counting principle, if there are m ways to make a first selection and n ways to make a second selection, then there are $m \times n$ ways to make selections.

Therefore, we have:

$$2\times4\times5\times3\times7=840$$

There are 840 ways to choose the dinner from the available options.

The correct answer is G.

23. Mode is a value that repeats more often than the other values.

As seen from the problem statement above, 83 has the highest number of repeats because the highest number of students (15) scored 83 on the chemistry exam.

Therefore, the mode is 83.

The correct answer is A.

24. Arrange the scores in ascending order. The lowest score is 83 and the largest score is 93.

The total number of students is 12 + 5 + 7 + 15 = 39.

The median value is $\frac{39+1}{2}=20$.

▶ **Video Explanations** at argoprep.com/shsat

We have 15 students that scored 83 and 12 students that scored 85, therefore the 20th value is 85.

Therefore, the median is 85.

The correct answer is G.

---

25. The total number of students is $12 + 5 + 7 + 15 = 39$.

Multiply each score by the corresponding number of students, add the results together, and divide by the total number of students.

We have:

$$\frac{12(85) + 5(89) + 7(93) + 15(83)}{39} = 86.2$$

The mean is 86.2.

The correct answer is C.

---

26. Since the repetition of letters and numbers is not allowed, the selection can be made from 26 letters for the first position and from 25 letters for the second position. For the third digit, 1 out of 10 numerical options (0, 1, 2, 3, 4, 5, 6, 7, 8, 9) is possible, and for the fourth position, 1 out of 9 numerical options is possible.

We have:

$$26 \times 25 \times 10 \times 9 = 58,500$$

Therefore, 58,500 codes are possible.

The correct answer is G.

---

27. Kevin can choose 1 out of 5 places to see on the first day, 1 out of 4 places to see on the second day, and so on.

The number of combinations can be found in the following way:

$$5 \times 4 \times 3 \times 2 \times 1 = 120$$

Kevin has 120 ways to plan his itinerary.

The correct answer is D.

---

28. The probability of randomly selecting a student that is neither Spanish nor American is the same as the probability that a randomly chosen student is Caucasian.

40% of 35 students is equal to 14. The number of Caucasian students in the group is 14.

Find the probability of choosing the Caucasian student:

$$\frac{14}{35} = \frac{2}{5}$$

The correct answer is E.

---

29. If 2 boys and 3 girls are absent, then there are $30 - 2 - 3 = 25$ students in the class.

The probability that a randomly chosen student is not a boy is the same as the probability that a randomly chosen student is a girl.

From 30 students, there are $30 - 13 = 17$ girls in the class. Since 3 girls are absent, then the actual number of girls is $17 - 3 = 14$.

Therefore, the probability is $\frac{14}{25}$.

The correct answer is B.

---

30. Find the total number of balloons: $5 + 7 + 6 + 8 = 26$.

There are 8 red balloons. Calculate the probability of choosing a red balloon: $\frac{8}{26} = \frac{4}{13}$.

Therefore, the probability of picking a balloon that is not red is $1 - \frac{4}{13} = \frac{13}{13} - \frac{4}{13} = \frac{9}{13}$.

The probability of the first and second selection are the same and equal to $\frac{9}{13}$. After the second selection, replacement was not made, therefore the probability of choosing the balloon that is not red is $\frac{17}{25}$.

Multiply all three probabilities to find the final result:

$$\frac{9}{13} \times \frac{9}{13} \times \frac{17}{25} = \frac{1,377}{4,225}$$

The correct answer is F.

---

31. The possible outcomes that are less than 3 are 1 and 2.

The probability of getting a number less than 3 is $\frac{2}{6} = \frac{1}{3}$.

The possible outcomes that are greater than or equal to 4 are 4, 5, and 6.

The probability of getting a number that is greater than or equal to 4 is $\frac{3}{6} = \frac{1}{2}$.

Multiply the probabilities to find the final result:

$$\frac{1}{3} \times \frac{1}{2} = \frac{1}{6}$$

The correct answer is A.

Video Explanations
at argoprep.com/shsat

32. When a coin is flipped, the probability of landing on heads is the same as the probability of landing on tails and equals $\frac{1}{2}$. Each coin flip is independent of the others.

The probability of the coin landing on heads in the first 10 times and tails in the last 10 times is:

$$\left(\frac{1}{2}\right)^{20} = \frac{1}{1,048,576}$$

Once again, you should not be doing the actual calculations. You can see the denominator is raised to the 20th power. This number is clearly going to be very big and answer choice H has a significantly larger denominator compared to the other choices.

The correct answer is H.

---

33. Since the selection of cards was made with replacement, both events are independent.

Events A and B are NOT dependent.

---

34. There are 8 sections on the spinner and the number of A sections is 2.

The probability of landing on A is $\frac{2}{8}$ or $\frac{1}{4}$.

The probability of landing on 5 on a die roll is $\frac{1}{6}$.

The probability of landing on E on the spinner and landing on heads on a coin clip is $\frac{1}{4} \times \frac{1}{6} = \frac{1}{24}$.

---

35. There are 8 sections on the spinner and the number of E sections is 4.

The probability of landing on E is $\frac{4}{8}$ or $\frac{1}{2}$.

The probability of landing on heads when flipping a coin is $\frac{1}{2}$.

The probability of landing on E on a spinner and head is $\frac{1}{2} \times \frac{1}{2} = \frac{1}{4}$.

---

36. To find the average, add all the values together and divide by the number of days.

We have:

$$\frac{6+7+4+5+6}{5} = \frac{28}{5} = \textbf{5.6 miles/hour}$$

37. Put the numbers in ascending order: 34, 36, 63, 64, 73, 78, 81, 89, 95, 153.

The median is the $\frac{10+1}{2} = 5.5$, which equals $\frac{73+78}{2} = $ **75.5**

---

38. Michael can choose 1 out of 4 exams to complete on the first day, 1 out of 3 exams to complete on the second day, and so on.

We have:

$$4 \times 3 \times 2 \times 1 = 24$$

Michael has **24** ways he can order the exams.

---

39. Find the total number of fruits: $3 + 4 + 5 + 6 + 10 = 28$.

The probability of not selecting a lemon or pear is the same as selecting an apple, a mango or a banana. There are $3 + 4 + 5 = 12$ favorable outcomes. There are a total of 28 fruits so the probability of selecting a fruit that is not a lemon or pear is $\frac{12}{28}$.

Simplify the fraction to get $\frac{3}{7}$.

---

40. To find the average height, add the heights together and divide the result by the number of toddlers.

We have:

$$\frac{67+68+71+69+65+75+63+71+65+62+61+70}{12} = 67.25$$

The average height of 12 toddlers is **67.25 cm**.

Video Explanations
at argoprep.com/shsat

Get into your dream
Specialized High School
with **ArgoPrep**

Practice Test

- This exam covers only the math portion of the SHSAT Exam. Recommended time for this test is 90 minutes.
- Try to take this full exam in one sitting to simulate real test conditions.
- While taking this exam, refrain from hearing music or watching T.V.
- Please note, calculators are not permitted! Allocate your test time accordingly.

Concentrate and GOOD LUCK!

ARGOPREP
ARGOPREP.COM/SHSAT

MATHEMATICS
INSTRUCTIONS

90 MINUTES • 57 QUESTIONS

Select the best answer from the choices given by carefully solving each problem. Bubble the letter of your answer on the answer sheet. Please refrain from making any stray marks on the answer sheet. If you need to erase an answer, please erase thoroughly.

Important Notes:

1. There are no formulas or definitions in the math section that will be provided.
2. Diagrams may or may not be drawn to scale. Do not make assumptions based on the diagram unless it is specifically stated in the diagram or question.
3. Diagrams are not in more than one plane, unless stated otherwise.
4. Graphs are drawn to scale, therefore, you can assume relationships according to the graph. If lines appear parallel, then you can assume the lines to be parallel. This is also true for right angles and so forth.
5. Simplify fractions completely.

Practice Test 1 (Questions 1-57)

GRID IN

Directions: The following five questions are grid-in problems. On the answer sheet, please be sure to write your answer in the boxes at the top of the grid. Start on the left side of each grid.

1. What is the sum of angle *x* and *y*?

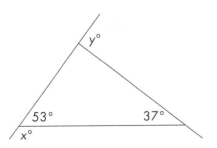

CONTINUE ON TO THE NEXT PAGE ➡

2. There are 18 yoga mats in a gym. The ratio of white yoga mats to black yoga mats is 4:5. How many black yoga mats are in the gym?

4. In a shop, the number of jackets is 8 more than three times the number of coats. If there are a total of 56 jackets and coats, how many jackets are in the shop?

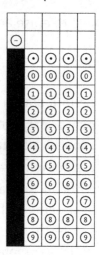

3. In the equation below, what is the value of x?

$$\frac{x+12}{4} = 8$$

5. If the sum of two consecutive integers is 33, find their sum after adding 4 to each integer.

CONTINUE ON TO THE NEXT PAGE →

6. In the equation below, what is the value of x?

$$4(x-3) = 24$$

    A. 12
    B. 9
    C. 6
    D. 2

7. Bella has 800 grams of candies. What is the weight in kilograms?

    E. 800 kg
    F. 80 kg
    G. 8 kg
    H. 0.8 kg

8. There are eight cars present in a parking lot on Monday, 14 cars on Tuesday, and 18 cars on Wednesday and Thursday. What is the average number of cars in the parking lot for the four days?

    A. 18
    B. 14.5
    C. 10
    D. 4.5

9. There are x rooms in Luna's house, 2 more rooms in Cora's house than in Luna's house and 1 less room in Noah's house than in Cora's house. How many rooms are in Noah's house, if there are 12 rooms in total?

    E. 8
    F. 6
    G. 4
    H. 3

10. The height of a tree is 2 meters and 30 centimeters. How tall is the tree in inches? Use the approximation 1 meter = 39.37 inches.

    A. 100 in.
    B. 90.551 in.
    C. 81.83 in.
    D. 54.335.

11. Oliver wants to run at least 24 km. If he runs 4 km each day, what is the minimum number of days he needs to reach his goal?

    E. 10
    F. 6
    G. 4
    H. 2

12. What is the surface area of a cylinder, whose height $h = 10$ cm and radius $r = 3$ cm? (Use the approximation 3.14 for π).

    A. 244.92 cm^2
    B. 216.66 cm^2
    C. 205.62 cm^2
    D. 189.15 cm^2

13. In a triangle, the largest side is 5 more than the smallest side. The last side is 2 less than the largest side. If the perimeter of the triangle is 44 cm, what is the length of the largest side of the triangle?

    E. 17 cm
    F. 12 cm
    G. 8 cm
    H. 5 cm

CONTINUE ON TO THE NEXT PAGE →

14. What is the value of x in the inequality below?

$$14x - 10 \leq 6(x + 5)$$

A. $x \leq 12$
B. $x \leq 8$
C. $x \leq 5$
D. $x \leq -3$

15. The sides of a triangle measure 20 mm, 16 mm and 7 mm. What is the perimeter of the triangle in centimeters?

E. 430 cm
F. 43 cm
G. 4.3 cm
H. 0.43 cm

16. There are 38 people in a volleyball team. Twelve of them are women, 14 are men and 12 are children. If the captain randomly chooses one person to serve the ball, what is the probability that the captain chose a child?

A. 1

B. $\dfrac{6}{7}$

C. $\dfrac{7}{19}$

D. $\dfrac{6}{19}$

17. In a pencil case, the ratio of pens to pencils is 3:4. If there are 14 pens and pencils in total, how many pens are in the pencil case?

E. 18
F. 12
G. 6
H. 4

18. Find the area of a rectangle that has a width of 6 m and length of 12 m.

A. 84 m^2
B. 72 m^2
C. 57 m^2
D. 43 m^2

19. From a group of 40 people, 25% like classical music, 65% like pop music and the rest like rock music. How many people like rock music?

E. 2
F. 4
G. 8
H. 12

20. Charlotte purchased five books, each with the same price tag, on a website. Shipping costs for the entire order was $2.80. If Charlotte spent $25.70 in total, what was the price of one book?

A. $8.25
B. $6.70
C. $4.58
D. $3.75

CONTINUE ON TO THE NEXT PAGE ➡

21. There are eight bananas, twelve apples and six oranges in a box. If Maria chooses a fruit randomly, what is the probability of her selecting a banana?

    E. $\dfrac{4}{13}$

    F. $\dfrac{1}{3}$

    G. $\dfrac{1}{2}$

    H. $\dfrac{2}{3}$

22. Sophia walks 5 miles every day. Tania walks 1.5 kilometers less than Sophia. How many miles does Tania walk every day? (Use the approximation 1 kilometer = 0.62 miles.)

    A. 5 miles
    B. 4.07 miles
    C. 3.5 miles
    D. 2 miles

23. Lucas spent $33 on the first day and $45 on the second day while on vacation. How much money did Lucas spend on the third day, if the average money spent during the three days was $38?

    E. $42
    F. $38
    G. $36
    H. $32

24. Abigail earns $940 each month. If her salary increases by 40%, how much will she receive each month?

    A. $1,000
    B. $1,200
    C. $1,316
    D. $1,450

25. What is the product of the two smallest prime factors of 210?

    E. 18
    F. 14
    G. 6
    H. 2

26. The ratio of croissants to cakes in a bakery is 3:8. If the bakery has 12 croissants, how many cakes are there?

    A. 44
    B. 32
    C. 26
    D. 18

27. The ratio of boys to girls in Class A is 3:2. The ratio of boys to girls in Class B is 4:5. If there are eight girls in Class A and 12 boys in Class B, how many total students are there in Class A and B?

    E. 54
    F. 47
    G. 38
    H. 20

CONTINUE ON TO THE NEXT PAGE →

28. Simplify the expression below:

$$\frac{1}{4}+\frac{1}{3}\left(4\frac{3}{8}-1\frac{1}{2}\right)\times\frac{3}{4}$$

A. $\frac{31}{32}$

B. $\frac{23}{32}$

C. $\frac{1}{8}$

D. $\frac{1}{32}$

29. Zoe joined a fitness class for the last two weeks and lost a total of 5 pounds. If Zoe's starting weight was 67 kilograms, how much does she weigh now? (Use the approximation 1 pound = 0.45 kilogram.)

E. 66 kg
F. 64.75 kg
G. 62 kg
H. 58.8 kg

30. At the farmers market, customer A purchased three times as many oranges than customer B. If customer A and B have a total of 20 oranges, how many oranges did customer A purchase?

A. 3
B. 9
C. 12
D. 15

31. Find all the distinct odd prime factors of 126.

E. 3, 7   G. 7, 9
F. 5, 9   H. 9, 11

32. Find the four consecutive integers whose sum is equal to 66.

A. 2, 4, 6, 8
B. 9, 12, 13, 15
C. 11, 12, 13, 14
D. 15, 16, 17, 18

33. Violet and Nora own a home bakery business. Violet bakes five cakes on a daily basis. Nora bakes three more cakes than Violet. If each of their cakes sell for $2.30 and they sell all their cakes on a daily basis, how much will they have earned in the period of two days?

E. $59.8   G. $36.8
F. $42.3   H. $24

34. There are three kinds of flowers in a vase: 9 tulips, 15 roses and 6 lilies. Aurora selected one flower at random from the vase. What is the probability that the flower is NOT a lily or a tulip?

A. $\frac{1}{6}$

B. $\frac{2}{3}$

C. $\frac{1}{2}$

D. 1

CONTINUE ON TO THE NEXT PAGE ➡

35. Lucas and Jacob can paint a house in 1 hour working together. If Jacob works alone, he can paint the house in 1.5 hours. How long would it take Lucas to complete the job on his own?

   E. 1 hour   **G.** 2 hours
   F. 1.5 hours   **H.** 3 hours

36. On the number line above, $AB = 18$ and $BC = \frac{1}{3} AB$. Find the position of point C, if the position of point A is $-2\frac{4}{5}$.

   A. 24

   B. $21\frac{1}{5}$

   C. $12\frac{3}{5}$

   D. $9\frac{1}{3}$

37. What is the sum of the number of distinct prime factors in 210 and 378?

   E. 3   **G.** 7
   F. 5   **H.** 9

38. Lily spent one-fifth of her salary on a pair of new shoes and then received $90 as a birthday present from her mom. If Lily now has $340, how much money did she begin with?

   A. $360   **C.** $312.5
   B. $340   **D.** $280

39. What is the value of the expression below, if $a = 4$ and $b = 1$?

$$\frac{b(a-b)}{(a+b)(3a-1)} \div \frac{a-b}{3a-1}$$

   E. $\frac{1}{5}$

   F. $\frac{1}{2}$

   G. 1

   H. $1\frac{1}{2}$

40. The number 789 is divisible by which of the following number?

   A. 3
   B. 5
   C. 9
   D. 10

41.

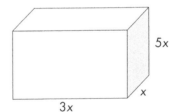

The rectangular prism above has a volume of 960 in³. What is the measure of the height?

   E. 20 in
   F. 25 in
   G. 33 in
   H. 40 in

CONTINUE ON TO THE NEXT PAGE ➡

42.

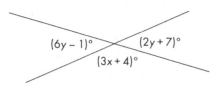

$(6y - 1)°$ $(2y + 7)°$
$(3x + 4)°$

What are the values of x and y respectively?

A. 55, 2
B. 30, 12
C. 15, 25
D. 6, 20

43. In the equation below, what is the value of n, if n is a positive number?

$$\frac{9}{n} = \frac{3}{16}$$

E. 18
F. 28
G. 36
H. 48

44.

On the number line above $LK = 35$, MN is two more than LM and NK is half the measure of MN. Find NK.

A. 25.6
B. 12.8
C. 7.4
D. 4.6

45.

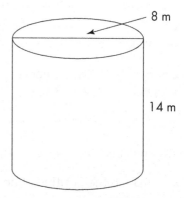

8 m

14 m

Find the volume of the cylinder above in terms of π.

E. 180 πm³
F. 210 πm³
G. 224 πm³
H. 260 πm³

46. There are 40 animals in a zoo. The number of elephants is $\frac{1}{5}$ of the total number of animals, the number of tigers is half the number of elephants and the number of giraffes is 5 less than the sum of tigers and elephants. What is the ratio of tigers to giraffes?

A. 3:2
B. 3:4
C. 4:7
D. 2:5

CONTINUE ON TO THE NEXT PAGE ➡

47.

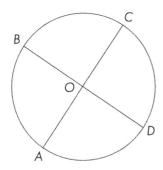

If point *O* is the center of the circle above, *BD* = (11*x* – 9) mm and *AC* = (5*x* + 3) mm, what is the radius of the circle?

E. 3 mm
F. 6.5 mm
G. 12 mm
H. 13 mm

48. If $\frac{3}{8}$ of a number is 24, what is the number?

A. 64
B. 58
C. 46
D. 35

49. One side of a triangle measures three more than the smallest side of the triangle. If the third side is 11 cm and the perimeter of the triangle is 32 cm, what is the measure of the smallest side of the triangle?

E. 3 cm
F. 6 cm
G. 9 cm
H. 12 cm

50. What is the value of the expression below?

$$15+(0.03+8)30-(0.7+0.3)^{3}$$

A. 254.9
B. 187.7
C. 143.5
D. 112

51. There are 8 red pens, 7 black pens, 14 green pens and *x* blue pens in a shop. Anna randomly chooses one pen. If the probability of selecting a green pen is $\frac{1}{3}$, how many blue pens are in the stationary shop?

E. 25
F. 16
G. 13
H. 7

52.

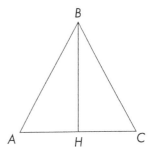

In triangle *ABC*, *BH* = 16 cm and *AC* is 2 less than *BH*. What is the area of the triangle?

A. 64 cm²
B. 112 cm²
C. 133 cm²
D. 224 cm²

CONTINUE ON TO THE NEXT PAGE ➡

53. The height of a building is 40 feet and 30 centimeters. What is the height of the building in meters? Use the approximation 1 feet = 30.48 cm.

   E. 12,492 m
   F. 1,249.2 m
   G. 124.92 m
   H. 12.492 m

54. On the number line above, $AB = 4$ and $BC = 5$. What is the position of point A, if the position of point C is $1\frac{2}{3}$.

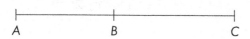

   A. $3\frac{5}{7}$

   B. $1\frac{2}{3}$

   C. $-4\frac{3}{5}$

   D. $-7\frac{1}{3}$

55. Find the value of x, if $y = 12$ and $z = -1$.

$$\frac{x + 2z}{4} = \frac{y}{2}$$

   E. 32
   F. 26
   G. 12
   H. 6

56.

Number of purchases	Number of customers
0	8
1	48
2	31
3	23
4	15
5	10
6	3

The table above shows the number of customers that made a purchase. What is the average number of purchases per customer?

   A. $\frac{31}{138}$

   B. $1\frac{31}{138}$

   C. $2\frac{1}{2}$

   D. $2\frac{31}{138}$

57. There are three kinds of fishes in an aquarium: red fishes, yellow fishes and blue fishes. The ratio of red fishes to yellow fishes to blue fishes is 2:3:5. If there are 6 yellow fishes, what is the sum of the number of red and blue fishes in the aquarium?

   E. 4
   F. 7
   G. 10
   H. 14

THIS IS THE END OF THE TEST.

MATHEMATICS

Practice Test 1 (Answers and Explanations)

1. **217**

Find the measure of x. Angle x and angle of measure 53° are supplementary.

Therefore, we have:

$x = 180 - 53 = 127°$

Then find the measure of the third angle of a triangle. The sum of interior angles of a triangle is 180°.

The measure of the third angle is

$180 - 53 - 37 = 90°$

Angle y and angle of measure 90° are supplementary.

Therefore, we have:

$y = 180 - 90 = 90°$

$x = 127$ and $y = 90$. The sum is $127 + 90 = 217°$

2. **10** yoga mats

Let x represent the number of white yoga mats and y represent the number of black yoga mats.

If there are 18 yoga mats in total, we can represent the given information as system of equations.

We have:

$x + y = 18$

$\dfrac{x}{y} = \dfrac{4}{5}$

Solve the second equation for x and substitute the result into the first equation. Then solve for y.

$x = \dfrac{4y}{5}$

$\dfrac{4y}{5} + y = 18$

Multiply both sides by 5 to get rid of the denominator:

$4y + 5y = 18 \times 5$

$9y = 90$

$y = 10$

There are 10 black yoga mats in the gym.

3. **20**

Multiply both sides by 4 to get rid of the denominator:

$x + 12 = 8 \times 4 = 32$

Subtract 12 from each side:

$x + 12 - 12 = 32 - 12$

$x = 20$

4. **44**

Let x represent the number of jackets and y represent the number of coats.

We can create the following two equations. :

$x + y = 56$

$x = 3y + 8$

Substitute the second equation into the first one and solve for y.

$3y + 8 + y = 56$

$4y = 48$

$y = 12$

There are 12 coats in the shop.

Find the number of jackets:

$x = 3 \times 12 + 8 = 36 + 8 = 44$

There are 44 jackets in the shop.

5.   **41**

Let x represent the smaller consecutive integer and $x + 1$ represent the larger consecutive integer.

Write an equation:

$x + x + 1 = 33$

$2x = 32$

$x = 16$

Adding 4 to the smaller consecutive integer results in 20 and the larger consecutive integer is 21. The sum of $20 + 21 = 41$.

6.   **B**   Solve the equation by isolating the variable. Divide both sides by 4.

$\dfrac{4(x-3)}{4} = \dfrac{24}{4}$

$x - 3 = 6$

Add 3 to each side to solve for x.

Therefore, we have:

$x - 3 + 3 = 6 + 3$

$x = 9$

The correct answer is B.

7.   **H**   You need to know the conversion 1 kg = 1000 g.

To convert grams to kilograms, divide 800 grams by 1000:

$\dfrac{800 \text{ g}}{1000} = 0.8 \text{ kg}$

The correct answer is H.

8.   **B**   To find the average number of cars, add the number of cars on each day and then divide by the number of days.

Therefore, we have:

$\dfrac{8 + 14 + 18 + 18}{4} = 14.5$

The correct answer is B.

9.   **G**   There are x rooms in Luna's house, then in Cora's house: $x + 2$ rooms, and in Noah's house: $x + 2 - 1 = x + 1$ rooms.

We have the equation:

$x + x + 2 + x + 1 = 12$

$3x = 9$

$x = 3$

So, there are $3 + 1 = 4$ rooms in Noah's house.

The correct answer is G.

10.   **B**   Convert 2 meters and 30 centimeters to meters.

Note that 1 m = 100 cm.

2 m 30 cm = 2 m + 0.3 m = 2.3 m

Then, convert to inches using the approximation 1 m = 39.37 in.

Therefore, we have:

2.3 m = 2.3 × 39.37 in. = 90.551 in.

The correct answer is B.

11. F Let x represent the number of days Oliver needs to reach his goal.

Write an equation:

$4x \geq 24$

$x \geq 6$

The correct answer is F.

12. A The surface area is the sum of the lateral area and twice the area of the base.

The base of the cylinder is a circle and the lateral area is equal to $2\pi rh$.

The area of the base is πr^2.

Therefore, we have:

$A = 2\pi rh + 2\pi r^2 = \pi r(h + r)$

$= 2 \times 3.14 \times 3(10 + 3) = 244.92$ cm^2

The correct answer is A.

13. E Let x represent the length of the smallest side. Then the length of the largest side is $x + 5$ and the length of the third side is $x + 5 - 2 = x + 3$.

Since the perimeter is the sum of all sides, we have:

$x + x + 5 + x + 3 = 44$

$3x = 44 - 8 = 36$

$x = 12$

The length of the largest side is $12 + 5 = 17$ cm.

The correct answer is E.

14. C Eliminate the parentheses and simplify the inequality:

$14x - 10 \leq 6x + 30$

$14x - 6x \leq 30 + 10$

$8x \leq 40$

$x \leq 5$

The correct answer is C.

15. G Find the perimeter of the triangle.

The perimeter is the sum of all sides.

Therefore, we have:

$P = 20 + 16 + 7 = 43$ mm

Then, convert millimeters to centimeters. Note that 1 cm = 10 mm.

Convert:

43 mm $= \dfrac{43}{10}$ cm $= 4.3$ cm

The perimeter of the triangle is 4.3 cm.

The correct answer is G.

16. D The probability of an event happening is the ratio of the number of favorable outcomes to the total number of outcomes.

The favorable outcomes in this question is 12.

The total number of outcomes is 38.

Therefore, the probability that the captain chose a child is $\dfrac{12}{38} = \dfrac{6}{19}$.

The correct answer is D.

17. G Let x represent the number of pens and y represent the number of pencils. If there are 14 pens and pencils in total and the ratio of pens to pencils is 3:4, we can write a system of equations.

Therefore, we have:

$x + y = 14$

$\dfrac{x}{y} = \dfrac{3}{4}$

Solve the second equation for x and substitute the result into the first equation. Then solve for y.

$x = \dfrac{3y}{4}$

$\dfrac{3y}{4} + y = 14$

Multiply both sides by 4 to get rid of the denominator :

$3y + 4y = 14 \times 4 = 56$

$7y = 56$

$y = 8$

The number of pens is $x = \dfrac{3 \times 8}{4} = 6$.

The correct answer is G.

18. **A**   The area of a rectangle is the product of the width and length.

We have:

$A = 6 \times 12 = 72 \ m^2$

The correct answer is B.

19. **F**   Calculate what percent of the group likes rock music.

$100\% - 25\% - 65\% = 10\%$

Since there are 40 people in the group, we can calculate the number of people who like rock music by finding out 10% of 40.

$40 \times 0.1 = 4$

The correct answer is F.

20. **C**   Let x represent the price of 1 book.

Write an equation :

$5x + 2.80 = 25.70$

$5x = 25.70 - 2.80 = 22.90$

$x = 4.58$

One book costs \$4.58.

The correct answer is C.

21. **E**   The probability of an event happening is the ratio of the number of favorable outcomes to the total number of outcomes.

The number of favorable outcomes is 8.

The total number of outcomes is $8 + 12 + 6 = 26$.

Therefore, the probability of Maria selecting a banana is $\dfrac{8}{26} = \dfrac{4}{13}$.

The correct answer is E.

22. **B**   Convert 1.5 kilometers to miles using the approximation:

$1.5 \ km = 1.5 \times 0.62 \ miles = 0.93 \ miles$

Tania walks 0.93 miles less than Sophia, which equals to 4.07 miles.

The correct answer is B.

23. **G**   Let Lucas spend x amount of money on the third day. If, on average, he spent \$38, we have:

$\dfrac{33 + 45 + x}{3} = 38$

Multiply both sides by 3 and solve for x:

$33 + 45 + x = 114$

$x = 114 - 33 - 45 = 36$

Lucas spent $36 on the third day.

The correct answer is G.

24. C If Abigail's salary increased by 40%, we can multiply $640 \times 0.4 = 376$ dollars.

Abigail is earning $376 more so we need to add that amount with her salary.

$940 + $376 = $1,316.

The correct answer is C.

25. G List the prime factors of 210: 2, 3, 5, 7.

The two smallest prime factors are 2 and 3.

Their product is 6.

The correct answer is G.

26. B Let x represent the number of cakes.

Set up a proportion:

$$\frac{12}{x} = \frac{3}{8}$$

Cross multiply:

$$x = \frac{12 \times 8}{3} = 32$$

There are 32 cakes in the bakery.

The correct answer is B.

27. F Let x represent the number of boys for Class A.

We have:

$$\frac{x}{8} = \frac{3}{2}$$

$$x = \frac{8 \times 3}{2} = 12$$

There are $12 + 8 = 20$ children in class A.

Let x represent the number of girls for Class B.

We have:

$$\frac{12}{x} = \frac{4}{5}$$

$$x = \frac{12 \times 5}{4} = 15$$

There are $15 + 12 = 27$ children in class B.

In total, there are $20 + 27 = 47$ children in class A and B.

The correct answer is F.

28. A Convert each mixed fraction to an improper fraction.

$$4\frac{3}{8} = \frac{35}{8}$$

$$1\frac{1}{2} = \frac{3}{2}$$

Then perform the calculations according to PEMDAS.

$$\frac{1}{4} + \frac{1}{3}\left(4\frac{3}{8} - 1\frac{1}{2}\right) \times \frac{3}{4} = \frac{1}{4} + \frac{1}{3}\left(\frac{35}{8} - \frac{3}{2}\right) \times \frac{3}{4}$$

$$= \frac{1}{4} + \frac{1}{3}\left(\frac{35 - 3(4)}{8}\right) \times \frac{3}{4} = \frac{1}{4} + \frac{1}{3} \times \frac{23}{8} \times \frac{3}{4}$$

$$= \frac{1}{4} + \frac{23}{32} = \frac{1(8) + 23(1)}{32} = \frac{31}{32}$$

The correct answer is A.

29. **F** Convert pounds to kilograms with the given conversion.

5 pounds = 5×0.45 kilograms = 2.25 kilograms

Then subtract it from the initial weight.

67 kg – 2.25 kg = 64.75 kg

The correct answer is F.

30. **D** We can use variables to represent the number of oranges bought by Customer A and B. Let x represent the number of oranges bought by Customer A. Let y represent the number of oranges bought by Customer B.

We can set up a system of equations from the information provided in the question.

$x = 3y$

$x + y = 20$

Substitute the value of x into the second equation and solve for y.

$3y + y = 20$

$4y = 20$

$y = 5$

Customer A has $3 \times 5 = 15$ plums.

The correct answer is D.

31. **E** List the factors of 126: 2, 3, 3, 7.

There are two distinct odd factors: 3 and 7.

The correct answer is E.

32. **D** Represent the four numbers with variables $x, x + 1, x + 2$ and $x + 3$.

If their sum is 66, we have:

$x + x + 1 + x + 2 + x + 3 = 66$

$4x = 60$

$x = 15$

So, the first integer is 15, second is 16, third is 17 and fourth is 18.

The correct answer is D.

33. **E** Violet bakes 5 cakes and Nora bakes $5 + 3 = 8$ cakes.

Together they bake $5 + 8 = 13$ cakes on a daily basis.

We want the amount earned for a period of two days, so Violet and Nora baked $13 \times 2 = 26$ cakes.

If one cake costs $2.30, they earned $26 \times 2.30 = \$59.8$

The correct answer is E.

34. **C** The probability that the flower is not a lily or a tulip is the same as the probability that the flowers is a rose.

The probability of an event happening is the number of favorable outcomes to the total number of outcomes.

The number of favorable outcomes is 15.

The total number of outcomes is $9 + 15 + 6 = 30$.

Therefore, the probability that the flower is not a lily or tulip is $\frac{15}{30} = \frac{1}{2}$.

The correct answer is C.

35. **H** Let t represent the time required for Lucas to do the job alone.

Let the completed job = 1.

Then:

$$\frac{1}{1.5}+\frac{1}{t}=1$$

Multiply the equation by $1.5t$ to get rid of the denominators:

$$t+1.5=1.5t$$

$$0.5t=1.5$$

$$t=3$$

This is a tricky question and we recommend watching our video explanation on our website at www.argoprep.com/shsat

The correct answer is H.

36. **B** Find the length of BC.

$$BC=\frac{1}{3}AB=\frac{1}{3}\times18=6$$

Then, find AC:

$$AC=AB+BC=18+6=24$$

To find C, subtract $C-A$ and set it equal to the length:

$$C-\left(-2\frac{4}{5}\right)=24$$

$$C=24-2\frac{4}{5}$$

$$C=\frac{106}{5}=21\frac{1}{5}$$

The correct answer is B.

37. **G** List the distinct prime factors of 210: 2, 3, 5, 7. There are four distinct prime factors.

Then, list the distinct prime factors of 378: 2, 3, 7.

There are three distinct prime factors.

The sum is $4+3=7$.

The correct answer is G.

38. **C** Let x represent the number of money Lily began with.

Write an equation:

$$x-\frac{1}{5}x+90=340$$

Multiply by 5 to get rid of the denominator:

$$5x-x+450=1700$$

$$4x=1250$$

$$x=312.5$$

The correct answer is C.

39. **E** Simplify the expression.

Rewrite the expression as

$$\frac{b(a-b)}{(a+b)(3a-1)}\cdot\frac{3a-1}{a-b}$$

$$\frac{b(a-b)}{(a+b)(3a-1)}\cdot\frac{3a-1}{a-b}=\frac{b}{a+b}$$

Then substitute the appropriate values:

$$\frac{b}{a+b}=\frac{1}{4+1}=\frac{1}{5}$$

The correct answer is E.

40. **A** There are two ways to solve this problem! Of course, you can try to divide 789 by each of the answer choices, but there is a better way.

Knowing your divisibility rules will help you answer this question faster.

For a full detailed overview of the divisibility rules, you can watch our video lecture on our website under the Mathematics Introduction titled "Divisibility Rules".

Scan your answer choices. If a number ends in 0, the number is divisible by 10. If the last digit of a number is 0 or 5, the number is divisible by 5. We are working with the number 789, and automatically we can rule out that this number is not divisible by 5 or 10. Answer choices B and D are eliminated.

The divisibility rule by 3 is if the sum of the digits of the number is divisible by 3, that number is also divisible by 3.

Take the sum of the digits for 789. $7 + 8 + 9 = 24$. 24 IS divisible by 3 and therefore 789 must be divisible by 3.

The correct answer is A.

41. E   The volume of a prism is the area (length × width) multiplied by the height.

The area is $x \times 3x = 3x^2$ in^2

Set up an equation.

$960 = 3x^2 \times 5x = 15x^3$

$x^3 = 64$

$x = 4$

The height $= 5x = 5 \times 4 = 20$ in

The correct answer is E.

42. A   Angle of measure $(6y - 1)°$ and angle

of measure $(2y + 7)°$ are equal as verticals angles.

Therefore, we have:

$6y - 1 = 2y + 7$

$4y = 8$

$y = 2$

Angle of measure $(3x + 4)°$ and angle of measure $(2y + 7)°$ are supplementary.

Therefore, we have:

$3x + 4 = 180 - 2y - 7 = 180 - 2 \times 2 = 7$

$3x = 165$

$x = 55$

The correct answer is A.

43. H   Perform cross multiplication to get rid of the fractions:

$3n = 16 \cdot 9$

Divide both sides by 3:

$n = 16 \cdot 3 = 48$

The correct answer is H.

44. C   Let $LM = x$, then $MN = x + 2$ and $NK = \dfrac{x+2}{2}$.

If $LK = 35$, then we can set up the following equation:

$35 = x + x + 2 + \dfrac{x+2}{2}$

Multiply both sides by 2:

$70 = 2x + 2x + 4 + x + 2$

$5x = 64$

$x = 12.8$

Substitute the value of x into the

expression for *NK*:

$$NK = \frac{12.8+2}{2} = 7.4$$

The correct answer is C.

45. G Use the formula of the volume of a cylinder: $V = \pi r^2 h$, where r is the radius and h is the height .

We are given the diameter in the figure. You can easily calculate the radius by taking half of the diameter.

$$r = \frac{d}{2} = \frac{8}{2} = 4 \text{ m}$$

Substitute the appropriate values:

$$V = \pi \times 4^2 \times 14 = 224 \ \pi m^3$$

The correct answer is G.

46. C Find out the number of elephants:

$$\frac{1}{5} \times 40 = 8.$$

Next let's find the number of tigers:

$$\frac{8}{2} = 4$$

The number of giraffes is 5 less than the sum of tigers and elephants, so, the number of giraffes is $4 + 8 - 5 = 7$.

Thus, the ratio of tigers to giraffes is 4:7.

The correct answer is C.

47. F *AC* and *BD* are the diameters of the circle and therefore equal to each other. The radius of the circle is half of *AC* or *BD*.

Set the expressions for *AC* and *BD* equal to each other to find *x*.

$$11x - 9 = 5x + 3$$

$$6x = 12$$

$$x = 2$$

The diameter is $11 \times 2 - 9 = 13$ mm

Then the radius is $\frac{13}{2} = 6.5$ mm

The correct answer is F.

48. A Let *x* represent the number.

$$\frac{3}{8}x = 24$$

Isolate *x* :

$$x = 24 \div \frac{3}{8} = 24 \times \frac{8}{3} = 64$$

The correct answer is A.

49. G Let *x* represent the smallest side of the triangle. The other side can be noted as $x + 3$.

The perimeter is the sum of all sides so we can set up the following equation.

$$x + x + 3 + 11 = 32$$

$$2x = 18$$

$$x = 9$$

The smallest side of the triangle is 9 cm.

The correct answer is G.

50. A Solve the expression above by following the PEMDAS rule.

$15 + (0.03 + 8)30 - (0.7 + 0.3)^3$

$= 15 + 8.03 \times 30 - 1^3 = 15 + 240.9 - 1 = 254.9$

The correct answer is A.

51. G The probability of an event happening is the number of favorable outcomes to the total number of outcomes.

The number of favorable outcomes is 14.

The total number of outcomes is $8 + 7 + 14 = x$.

Set up a proportion:

$\dfrac{1}{3} = \dfrac{14}{8 + 7 + 14 + x}$

Cross multiply:

$42 = 29 + x$

$x = 42 - 29 = 13$

The correct answer is G.

52. B The area of a triangle is half the product of the height and base.

In this case we have:

$A = \dfrac{1}{2} \times AC \times BH$

AC is 2 less than BH, so $AC = 16 - 2 = 14$ cm.

Substitute the appropriate values and find the area:

$A = \dfrac{1}{2} \times 16 \times 14 = 112 \, cm^2$

53. H Convert 40 feet 30 centimeters to centimeters using the approximation:

$40 \, ft. \, 30 \, cm = (40 \times 30.48 + 30) \, cm = 1249.2 \, cm$

Then, convert centimeters to meters. Although this conversion is not given directly on the question, this is something you are required to already know. 1 m = 100 cm.

Therefore, we have:

$1249.2 \, cm = \dfrac{1249.2}{100} \, m = 12.492 \, m$

The correct answer is H.

54. D Find the length of AC:

$AC = AB + BC = 4 + 5 = 9$

Then, subtract $C - A$ and set it equal to the length:

$1\dfrac{2}{3} - A = 9$

$A = 1\dfrac{2}{3} - 9 = \dfrac{5}{3} - \dfrac{9(3)}{3}$

$A = -\dfrac{22}{3} = -7\dfrac{1}{3}$

The correct answer is D.

55. F Perform cross multiplication to get rid of the fractions:

$2(x + 2z) = 4y$

Then, substitute the value of y and z:

$2(x + 2 \times (-1)) = 4 \times 12$

$2(x - 2) = 48$

Divide both sides by 2 and then add 2 to both sides.

$x - 2 = 24$

$x - 2 + 2 = 24 + 2$

$x = 26$

The correct answer is F.

56. **D** Calculate the total number of purchases. Multiply the number of purchases by the number of customers and add all the results.

The total number of purchases is:

$(0 \times 8) + (1 \times 48) + (2 \times 31) + (3 \times 23) + (4 \times 15) + (5 \times 10) + (6 \times 3) = 307$

Then find the number of customers:

$8 + 48 + 31 + 23 + 15 + 10 + 3 = 138$

Finally, find the mean number of purchases per customer:

$$\frac{307}{138} = 2\frac{31}{138}$$

The correct answer is D.

57. **H**

Since the ratio of the red fishes, yellow fishes and blue fishes is 2:3:5 and we have 6 yellow fishes in the aquarium, we can see that the original ratio has doubled.

Multiply the ratio 2:3:5 by 2 to get 4:6:10. So we have 4 red fishes, 6 yellow fishes and 10 blue fishes in the aquarium. The question asks for the sum of the red and blue fishes which is $4 + 10 = 14$ fishes.

The correct answer is H.